NEXT GENERATION GRAMMAR 3

Pamela Vittorio

Jennifer Recio Lebedev

Series Editor
David Bohlke

Next Generation Grammar 3

Pearson Education, 10 Bank Street, White Plains, NY 10606

Staff credits: The people who made up the *Next Generation Grammar 3* team, representing editorial, production, design, and manufacturing—are Andrea Bryant, Aerin Csigay, Dave Dickey, Nancy Flaggman, Gosia Jaros-White, Mike Kemper, Maria Pia Marrella, Amy McCormick, Liza Pleva, Massimo Rubini, Robert Ruvo, Ruth Voetmann, and Adina Zoltan.

Cover art: Diane Fenster
Text composition: ElectraGraphics, Inc.
Text font: Minion Pro

Library of Congress Cataloging-in-Publication Data
Cavage, Christina.
Next generation grammar 1 / Christina Cavage, Stephen T. Jones.
p. cm.
ISBN 978-0-13-256063-4 — ISBN 978-0-13-276054-6 — ISBN 978-0-13-276055-3 — ISBN 978-0-13-276057-7
1. English language—Grammar—Study and teaching. 2. English language—Study and teaching—Foreign speakers. I. Jones, Stephen T. II. Title. III. Title: Next generation grammar one.
PE1065.C528 2013
428.2'4—dc23

2012024734

For photo and illustration credits, see page xx.

Printed in the United States of America

ISBN 10: 0-13-276055-X (with MyEnglishLab)
ISBN 13: 978-0-13-276055-3 (with MyEnglishLab)

1 2 3 4 5 6 7 8 9 10—V082—18 17 16 15 14 13

Welcome to *Next Generation Grammar*

When do we use one of the present forms for future, as opposed to using *will* or *be going to*? Which modal verbs do we tend to use to make requests, from least formal to most formal? In what types of writing might we find more instances of passive forms than active forms? And how and why do we reduce certain adverbial clauses? These and many other questions are all answered in *Next Generation Grammar,* a groundbreaking new series designed to truly meet the needs of today's students. In addition to learning through the textbook, learners engage with innovative digital content, including interactive learning software, video, and continuous online assessment.

At its heart, *Next Generation Grammar* is a comprehensive grammar course that prepares students to communicate accurately in both writing and speaking. The grammar points are presented naturally, through a variety of high-interest reading texts followed by extensive practice and application. Each new grammar point is practiced using all four skills, with extra emphasis on grammar for writing. This task-centered approach allows immediate feedback on learning outcomes so students can track their own progress.

The series is truly for a new generation—one that is busy, mobile, and demanding. It respects that learners are comfortable with technology and use it as part of their daily lives. The series provides a traditional textbook (in either print or eText format) along with dynamic online material that is an integral, not a supplementary, part of the series. This seamless integration of text and digital offers a streamlined, 21st century learning experience that will engage and captivate learners.

Next Generation Grammar boasts a highly impressive author team. I would like to thank Sigrun Biesenbach-Lucas, Donette Brantner-Artenie, Christina Cavage, Arlen Gargagliano, Steve Jones, Jennifer Recio Lebedev, and Pamela Vittorio for their tireless dedication to this project. I would also like to thank Pietro Alongi, Andrea Bryant, Gosia Jaros-White, Amy McCormick, Massimo Rubini, and the entire Pearson editorial, production, and marketing team for their vision and guidance through the development of this series.

David Bohlke
Series Editior

About the Series Editor. David Bohlke has 25 years of experience as a teacher, trainer, program director, editor, and materials developer. He has taught in Japan, Korea, Saudi Arabia, and Morocco, and has conducted multiple teacher-training workshops around the world. David is the former publishing manager for adult courses for Cambridge University Press and the former editorial manager for Global ELT for Cengage Learning. He is the coauthor of *Listening Power 2* (Pearson Education), *Four Corners* (Cambridge University Press), and *Speak Now* (Oxford University Press), and is the series editor for *Interchange,* Fourth Edition (Cambridge University Press).

What's next in grammar?

Imagine a grammar course that gives you the freedom to devote class time to what you think is most important; a grammar course that keeps students engaged and on-track; a grammar course that extends learning beyond the classroom through compelling digital content.

Introducing *Next Generation Grammar*

Print or eText?

You make the choice. The course book content is presented in two formats, print or eText, offering maximum flexibility for different learning styles and needs.

Blended instruction

Optimize instruction through a blend of course book (in either print or eText format) and online content. This seamless integration will allow for spending more class time on meaningful, communicative work. Learners will practice and apply new language online and can also access our engaging video reviews if they have missed a lesson, or simply need additional help with a grammar point.

Rich online content

Explore the online component. It offers a wealth of interactive activities, grammar reference material, audio files, test material, and video reviews with our Grammar Coach, Jennifer Lebedev, YouTube's *JenniferESL.* The dynamic multimedia content will keep learners focused and engaged. You can also track class progress through an intuitive and comprehensive learner management system.

Ongoing assessment

Use the extensive assessment suite for targeted instruction. The interactive nature of the assessments (including timely feedback, goal tracking, and progress reports) allows you to track progress, and also allows learners to see for themselves which areas have been mastered and which require more effort. In the course book, assessment occurs at the end of each unit. The online component offers pre- and post-unit tests, as well as end-of-chapter tests.

The **next generation of grammar** courses is here. **Anytime, anywhere, anyplace.**

Teacher-directed

Student-centered

Print or eText

Practical tasks

Seamless integration of course book and digital

Grammar coach

Ongoing assessment

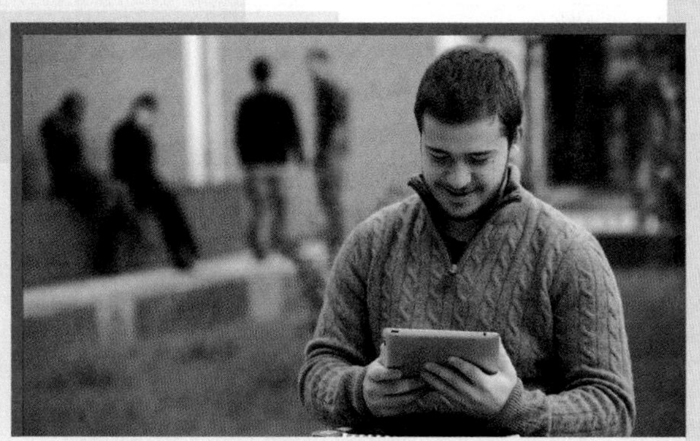

Anytime, anywhere, anyplace

CONTENTS

UNIT 1 THE ART DETECTIVES	Student Book Outcomes	MyEnglishLab
Chapter 1 page 2 **Deception and Detection** Simple present Present progressive	Getting Started Reading: *Art Deception and Detection: Real or Fake?* Grammar Focus 1 and 2 Listening, Speaking, and Writing	Vocabulary Check + Reading Comprehension Grammar Plus 1 and 2 Listen for it, Sounding Natural Linking Grammar to Writing Diagnostic Test
Chapter 2 page 10 **Inspection and Restoration** Future: *Will* and *be going to* Future progressive Present forms with future meaning	Getting Started Reading: *Great Forgeries and Restorations in Upcoming Exhibits* Grammar Focus 1, 2, and 3 Listening, Speaking, and Writing	Vocabulary Check + Reading Comprehension Grammar Plus 1 and 2 Listen for it, Sounding Natural Linking Grammar to Writing Diagnostic Test
Unit Assessments page 20	Grammar Summary Self-Assessment Unit Project	Grammar Summary Unit Test Search it!

UNIT 2 LIFE IN PICTURES	Student Book Outcomes	MyEnglishLab
Chapter 3 page 24 **Get the Picture!** Simple past and past progressive *Used to*	Getting Started Reading: Interview with a photographer Grammar Focus 1 and 2 Listening, Speaking, and Writing	Vocabulary Check + Reading Comprehension Grammar Plus 1 and 2 Listen for it, Sounding Natural Linking Grammar to Writing Diagnostic Test
Chapter 4 page 32 **Pictures—in Motion and Still** Nouns: Proper, common, count, and noncount Subject–verb agreement	Getting Started Reading: *Great Events in the History of Motion Pictures and Television: What's Next?* Grammar Focus 1 and 2 Listening, Speaking, and Writing	Vocabulary Check + Reading Comprehension Grammar Plus 1 and 2 Listen for it, Sounding Natural Linking Grammar to Writing Diagnostic Test
Unit Assessments page 40	Grammar Summary Self-Assessment Unit Project	Grammar Summary Unit Test Search it!

UNIT 3 WE NEED A HERO	Student Book Outcomes	MyEnglishLab
Chapter 5 page 44 **The Bold and the Brave** Articles Quantifiers Adjectives	Getting Started Reading: *The Bold and the Brave: The Formula for a Superhero* Grammar Focus 1, 2, and 3 Listening, Speaking, and Writing	Vocabulary Check + Reading Comprehension Grammar Plus 1, 2, and 3 Listen for it, Sounding Natural Linking Grammar to Writing Diagnostic Test
Chapter 6 page 54 **Myths, Folklore, Fairy Tales, and Legends** Adjective clauses Relative pronouns in adjective clauses	Getting Started Reading: *Tell Me a Story about the Princess who . . . .* Grammar Focus 1 and 2 Listening, Speaking, and Writing	Vocabulary Check + Reading Comprehension Grammar Plus 1 and 2 Listen for it, Sounding Natural Linking Grammar to Writing Diagnostic Test
Unit Assessments page 62	Grammar Summary Self-Assessment Unit Project	Grammar Summary Unit Test Search it!

UNIT 4 ANIMAL INSTINCT / EXTINCT ANIMALS	**Student Book** Outcomes	MyEnglishLab
Chapter 7 page **66** **The *Real* Horse Whisperer** Present perfect Present perfect progressive Adjective clauses with *where* and *when*	Getting Started Reading: *Unusual Careers with Animals* Grammar Focus 1, 2, and 3 Listening, Speaking, and Writing	Vocabulary Check + Reading Comprehension Grammar Plus 1, 2, and 3 Listen for it, Sounding Natural Linking Grammar to Writing Diagnostic Test
Chapter 8 page **76** **On the Verge of Extinction** Past perfect Past perfect progressive	Getting Started Reading: *And then there was one . . .* Grammar Focus 1 and 2 Listening, Speaking, and Writing	Vocabulary Check + Reading Comprehension Grammar Plus 1 and 2 Listen for it, Sounding Natural Linking Grammar to Writing Diagnostic Test
Unit Assessments page **84**	Grammar Summary Self-Assessment Unit Project	Grammar Summary Unit Test Search it!

UNIT 5 TRENDING AND SPENDING	**Student Book** Outcomes	MyEnglishLab
Chapter 9 page **88** **What's in Your Closet?** Phrasal verbs: Overview and separable Multi-word phrasal verbs	Getting Started Reading: *When Fashion Trends Make a Comeback* Grammar Focus 1 and 2 Listening, Speaking, and Writing	Vocabulary Check + Reading Comprehension Grammar Plus 1 and 2 Listen for it, Sounding Natural Linking Grammar to Writing Diagnostic Test
Chapter 10 page **96** **Why We Buy What We Buy** Phrasal verbs: Inseparable Intransitive phrasal verbs	Getting Started Reading: *Why We Buy What We Buy* Grammar Focus 1 and 2 Listening, Speaking, and Writing	Vocabulary Check + Reading Comprehension Grammar Plus 1 and 2 Listen for it, Sounding Natural Linking Grammar to Writing Diagnostic Test
Unit Assessments page **104**	Grammar Summary Self-Assessment Unit Project	Grammar Summary Unit Test Search it!

UNIT 6 GET THE MESSAGE	**Student Book** Outcomes	MyEnglishLab
Chapter 11 page **108** **From Diaries to Blogs** Modals and semi-modals Modals and semi-modals: Necessity Modals and semi-modals: Certainty	Getting Started Reading: 19th-century Diaries and Letters Grammar Focus 1, 2, and 3 Listening, Speaking, and Writing	Vocabulary Check + Reading Comprehension Grammar Plus 1, 2, and 3 Listen for it, Sounding Natural Linking Grammar to Writing Diagnostic Test
Chapter 12 page **120** **Across the Wires** Modals and semi-modals: Necessity in the past Modals and semi-modals: Certainty in the past	Getting Started Reading: A Look Back at Early Communication Grammar Focus 1 and 2 Listening, Speaking, and Writing	Vocabulary Check + Reading Comprehension Grammar Plus 1 and 2 Listen for it, Sounding Natural Linking Grammar to Writing Diagnostic Test
Unit Assessments page **128**	Grammar Summary Self-Assessment Unit Project	Grammar Summary Unit Test Search it!

UNIT 7 ECHOING VOICES	**Student Book** Outcomes	MyEnglishLab
Chapter 13 page **132** **The Book that Has Never Been Read . . .** Simple present and past and use of the *by*-phrase Perfect forms and other uses of the passive	Getting Started Reading: *The book that wasn't judged by its cover* Grammar Focus 1 and 2 Listening, Speaking, and Writing	Vocabulary Check + Reading Comprehension Grammar Plus 1 and 2 Listen for it, Sounding Natural Linking Grammar to Writing Diagnostic Test
Chapter 14 page **140** **Enduring Voices** Stative passive Participial adjectives	Getting Started Reading: *Rescuing an Endangered Language* Grammar Focus 1 and 2 Listening, Speaking, and Writing	Vocabulary Check + Reading Comprehension Grammar Plus 1 and 2 Listen for it, Sounding Natural Linking Grammar to Writing Diagnostic Test
Unit Assessments Page **148**	Grammar Summary Self-Assessment Unit Project	Grammar Summary Unit Test Search it!

UNIT 8 BRAIN POWER	**Student Book** Outcomes	MyEnglishLab
Chapter 15 page **152** **Unlocking Your Brain's Potential** Gerunds as subjects Gerunds as objects and possessive gerunds Other uses of gerunds	Getting Started Reading: *Mapping the Brain and Unlocking Its Hidden Potential* Grammar Focus 1, 2, and 3 Listening, Speaking, and Writing	Vocabulary Check + Reading Comprehension Grammar Plus 1, 2, and 3 Listen for it, Sounding Natural Linking Grammar to Writing Diagnostic Test
Chapter 16 page **162** **How to Think Like a Genius** Infinitives as subjects and objects Infinitives of purpose Other uses of infinitives	Getting Started Reading: *Brainstorming: How to Think Like a Genius* Grammar Focus 1, 2, and 3 Listening, Speaking, and Writing	Vocabulary Check + Reading Comprehension Grammar Plus 1, 2, and 3 Listen for it, Sounding Natural Linking Grammar to Writing Diagnostic Test
Unit Assessments page **172**	Grammar Summary Self-Assessment Unit Project	Grammar Summary Unit Test Search it!

UNIT 9 ACROSS THE UNIVERSE	Student Book Outcomes	MyEnglishLab
Chapter 17 page **176** **Out of This World** Present and past factual (real) conditionals: Habitual events and facts Factual (real) conditionals: Inferences, predictions, and intentions	Getting Started Reading: *Voyager's Golden Mission: If someone answers our message, how will we reply?* Grammar Focus 1 and 2 Listening, Speaking, and Writing	Vocabulary Check + Reading Comprehension Grammar Plus 1 and 2 Listen for it, Sounding Natural Linking Grammar to Writing Diagnostic Test
Chapter 18 page **184** **Time and Space** Imaginative (unreal) conditionals: Present and future Imaginative (unreal) conditionals: Past and mixed time periods Omitting information in conditional sentences	Getting Started Reading: *What if we could travel through time? What scientists* really *think.* Grammar Focus 1, 2, and 3 Listening, Speaking, and Writing	Vocabulary Check + Reading Comprehension Grammar Plus 1, 2, and 3 Listen for it, Sounding Natural Linking Grammar to Writing Diagnostic Test
Unit Assessments page **194**	Grammar Summary Self-Assessment Unit Project	Grammar Summary Unit Test Search it!

UNIT 10 SIGNS OF THE TIMES	Student Book Outcomes	MyEnglishLab
Chapter 19 page **198** **It's a Sign** Direct speech Reported speech	Getting Started Reading: *Reading between the Signs* Grammar Focus 1 and 2 Listening, Speaking, and Writing	Vocabulary Check + Reading Comprehension Grammar Plus 1 and 2 Listen for it, Sounding Natural Linking Grammar to Writing Diagnostic Test
Chapter 20 page **208** **Signs of Life** Embedded questions Tag questions and negative questions	Getting Started Reading: *Signs of Life: From Paintings in Caves to Men on the Moon* Grammar Focus 1 and 2 Listening, Speaking, and Writing	Vocabulary Check + Reading Comprehension Grammar Plus 1 and 2 Listen for it, Sounding Natural Linking Grammar to Writing Diagnostic Test
Unit Assessments page **216**	Grammar Summary Self-Assessment Unit Project	Grammar Summary Unit Test Search it!

Appendices
- Stative verbs A-1
- Irregular verbs A-1
- Spelling rules for plural nouns A-4
- Irregular plural nouns A-4
- Categories of noncount (mass) nouns A-5
- Collective and aggregate nouns A-5
- Nationalities (Generic references) A-6
- Quantifiers for count and noncount nouns A-7
- Quantifying collective nouns A-7
- Unit nouns (Partitives) A-8
- Linking verbs that come before an adjective A-8
- Linking verbs that refer to a state of being / change in condition A-8
- Separable phrasal verbs A-9
- N Transitive separable multi-word phrasal verbs A-9
- O Intransitive multi-word phrasal verbs A-10
- P Intransitive phrasal verbs A-11
- Q Verbs followed by gerunds A-11
- R *Go* + gerund for recreational activities A-11
- S Verb + preposition + gerund; adjective + preposition + gerund A-12
- T Noun + preposition + gerund A-12
- U Verbs followed by infinitives A-12
- V Verb + noun object + infinitive A-13
- W Nouns commonly followed by infinitives A-13
- X Adjectives followed by infinitives A-13
- Y Reporting verbs A-14
- Z Reference words in reported speech A-14

Index .... page I-1

Tour of a Unit

Each unit in ***Next Generation Grammar*** begins with an engaging opener that provides a quick overview of the unit. A list of learning outcomes establishes each chapter's focus and helps students preview the grammar content. The outcomes can also be used as a way to review and assess progress as students master chapter content.

MyEnglishLab

Before they begin the unit, students go online and complete the ***What do you know?*** section to assess what they already know about the grammar featured in the unit. This directs students' focus to the grammar and also helps teachers target instruction to their learners' specific needs.

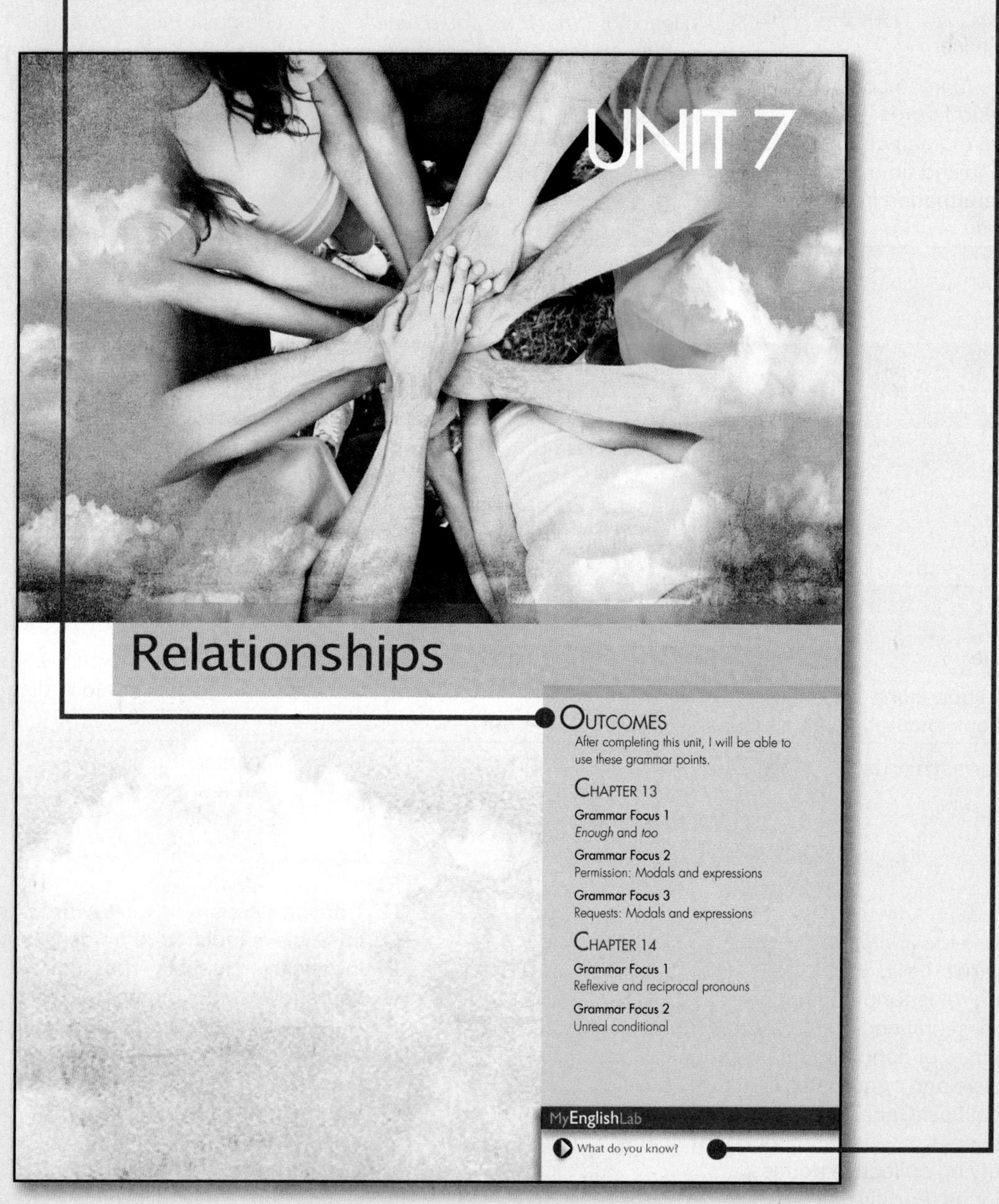

UNIT 7
Relationships
OUTCOMES
After completing this unit, I will be able to use these grammar points.
CHAPTER 13
Grammar Focus 1
Enough and too
Grammar Focus 2
Permission: Modals and expressions
Grammar Focus 3
Requests: Modals and expressions
CHAPTER 14
Grammar Focus 1
Reflexive and reciprocal pronouns
Grammar Focus 2
Unreal conditional
MyEnglishLab
What do you know?

The ***Getting Started*** section begins with the introduction of the chapter's themes. Students engage in lighthearted, motivating, and personal tasks that introduce and preview the chapter's grammar points.

In the ***Reading*** section students are further exposed to the chapter's grammar through high-interest, real-world texts that reflect the unit's theme. Beginning with a pre-reading warm-up, tasks progress from schema building to a detailed comprehension check.

MyEnglishLab

The ***Vocabulary Check*** activities on *MyEnglishLab* allow students to review and practice the vocabulary necessary for reading comprehension. Students are encouraged to complete these activities before they begin the ***Reading*** section.

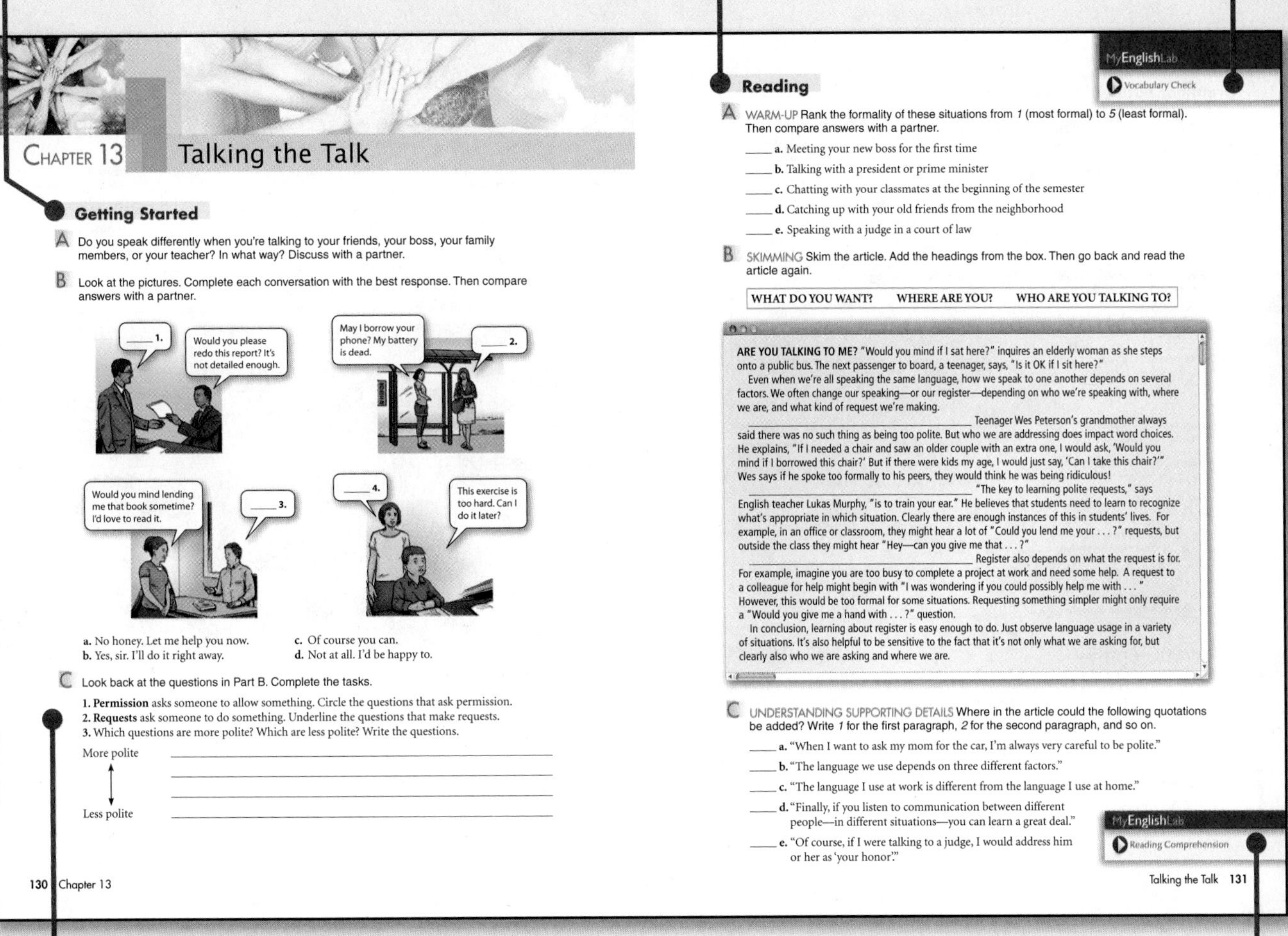

CHAPTER 13 Talking the Talk

Getting Started

A Do you speak differently when you're talking to your friends, your boss, your family members, or your teacher? In what way? Discuss with a partner.

B Look at the pictures. Complete each conversation with the best response. Then compare answers with a partner.

a. No honey. Let me help you now.
b. Yes, sir. I'll do it right away.
c. Of course you can.
d. Not at all. I'd be happy to.

C Look back at the questions in Part B. Complete the tasks.

1. **Permission** asks someone to allow something. Circle the questions that ask permission.
2. **Requests** ask someone to do something. Underline the questions that make requests.
3. Which questions are more polite? Which are less polite? Write the questions.

More polite ____

____

____

Less polite ____

130 Chapter 13

Reading

MyEnglishLab Vocabulary Check

A WARM-UP Rank the formality of these situations from *1* (most formal) to *5* (least formal). Then compare answers with a partner.

____ a. Meeting your new boss for the first time
____ b. Talking with a president or prime minister
____ c. Chatting with your classmates at the beginning of the semester
____ d. Catching up with your old friends from the neighborhood
____ e. Speaking with a judge in a court of law

B SKIMMING Skim the article. Add the headings from the box. Then go back and read the article again.

WHAT DO YOU WANT? WHERE ARE YOU? WHO ARE YOU TALKING TO?

ARE YOU TALKING TO ME? "Would you mind if I sat here?" inquires an elderly woman as she steps onto a public bus. The next passenger to board, a teenager, says, "Is it OK if I sit here?"

Even when we're all speaking the same language, how we speak to one another depends on several factors. We often change our speaking—or our register—depending on who we're speaking with, where we are, and what kind of request we're making.

____ Teenager Wes Peterson's grandmother always said there was no such thing as being too polite. But who we are addressing does impact word choices. He explains, "If I needed a chair and saw an older couple with an extra one, I would ask, 'Would you mind if I borrowed this chair?' But if there were kids my age, I would just say, 'Can I take this chair?'" Wes says if he spoke too formally to his peers, they would think he was being ridiculous!

____ "The key to learning polite requests," says English teacher Lukas Murphy, "is to train your ear." He believes that students need to learn to recognize what's appropriate in which situation. Clearly there are enough instances of this in students' lives. For example, in an office or classroom, they might hear a lot of "Could you lend me your . . . ?" requests, but outside the class they might hear "Hey—can you give me that . . . ?"

____ Register also depends on what the request is for. For example, imagine you are too busy to complete a project at work and need some help. A request to a colleague for help might begin with "I was wondering if you could possibly help me with . . ." However, this would be too formal for some situations. Requesting something simpler might only require a "Would you give me a hand with . . . ?" question.

In conclusion, learning about register is easy enough to do. Just observe language usage in a variety of situations. It's also helpful to be sensitive to the fact that it's not only what we are asking for, but clearly also who we are asking and where we are.

C UNDERSTANDING SUPPORTING DETAILS Where in the article could the following quotations be added? Write *1* for the first paragraph, *2* for the second paragraph, and so on.

____ a. "When I want to ask my mom for the car, I'm always very careful to be polite."
____ b. "The language we use depends on three different factors."
____ c. "The language I use at work is different from the language I use at home."
____ d. "Finally, if you listen to communication between different people—in different situations—you can learn a great deal."
____ e. "Of course, if I were talking to a judge, I would address him or her as 'your honor.'"

MyEnglishLab Reading Comprehension

Talking the Talk 131

This section culminates with an important inductive step that asks students to look back at the previous tasks and focus on form or function. By circling, underlining, charting, or answering questions, students focus on differences in meaning.

MyEnglishLab

Upon completion of the ***Reading*** section, students can further engage with the chapter's reading selection on *MyEnglishLab*. The ***Reading Comprehension*** activities provide students with an additional check of understanding.

The ***Grammar Focus*** sections present the chapter's target structures in clear, easy-to-read charts. Each chart presents example sentences taken from the chapter reading that illustrate the structure in context. The language notes give short and clear explanations of the form, meaning, and use of the target structure.

Grammar Focus 1 *Enough* and *too*

Examples	Language notes
(1) She was **smart enough**, but she didn't try. Did he finish **quickly enough**? I **did**n't **study enough**. I failed the test.	As we saw in Chapter 11, the word ***enough*** means "sufficient" or "the right amount." It has a positive meaning. In addition to modifying nouns, *enough* can also modify **adjectives**, **adverbs**, and **verbs**. Use: **adjective / adverb / verb +** ***enough***
(2) This report is **not detailed enough**. He did**n't** work **fast enough**. You are**n't** eating **enough**.	***Not enough*** means that something is insufficient or less than the right amount. Use: ***not*** **+ adjective +** ***enough*** ***not*** + verb + **adverb +** ***enough*** helping verb + ***not*** + verb + ***enough***
(3) He didn't move fast **enough to get** a seat. Do you think she has **enough to do**?	We often add an **infinitive**: ***enough*** **+ infinitive**
(4) Don't be **too friendly** with strangers. Does he speak **too formally** to his peers?	As we saw in Chapter 11, the word ***too*** means "more than is needed." The meaning is usually negative. In addition to modifying quantifiers, ***too*** can also modify **adjectives** and **adverbs**.
(5) My kids are**n't too interested** in history. Do**n't** work **too hard**!	We use ***not too*** to say that something is **lacking**. Use: ***not*** + ***too*** + adjective / adverb
(6) You are **too busy to complete** a project. Did he arrive **too late to get** into the movie?	We often add an **infinitive**: ***too*** **+ adjective / adverb + infinitive**
(7) There are **too many people** on the bus. There are **too few seats** on the bus. **Q:** Did the teacher present **too much information**? **A:** No, she presented **too little**. / She did**n't** present **enough**.	As we saw in Chapter 11, we can also use *(not)* ***enough*** and ***too*** with **count and noncount nouns**. • The opposite of ***too many*** is ***too few*** (for count nouns). • The opposite of ***too much*** is ***too little*** (for noncount nouns). We more commonly say "not enough."

Grammar Practice

MyEnglishLab
Grammar Plus 1
Activities 1 and 2

A Complete the sentences. Use *enough* or *too*.

1. I don't have ________________ money to pay my taxi fare. Could you lend me some?
2. You are speaking ________________ quickly. Would you mind slowing down?
3. Kevin hates to wait. He has ________________ little patience.
4. I had no trouble finding your house. Your directions were easy ________________.
5. Your instructions aren't clear ________________. Can you say it in a different way?
6. Hal is ________________ short to get the book off the shelf. He needs a ladder.
7. Nancy doesn't have a driver's license. She's not old ________________.
8. The movie is sold out. We arrived ________________ late.
9. My grandma says I'm too thin. She always says, "You don't eat ________________."

B Rewrite these sentences to say the opposite. Use *enough* or *too*. More than one correct answer may be possible.

1. She is walking too quickly. *She is not walking fast enough.*
2. He is old enough to enter the contest. ________________
3. We were too slow to get seats on the subway. ________________
4. There are too many people in our discussion group. ________________
5. She was strong enough to lift the box. ________________
6. There are too few grammar exercises in this book. ________________

C Look at the picture. Write sentences with *enough* or *too*.

1. ________________
2. ________________
3. ________________
4. ________________
5. ________________
6. ________________

132 Chapter 13

Talking the Talk 133

In the ***Grammar Practice*** sections, students are given the opportunity to apply the grammar structures in a variety of contextualized, controlled exercises that allow them to practice both the forms and the uses of the new structures.

MyEnglishLab

Grammar practice continues online in the ***Grammar Plus*** activities. Each ***Grammar Plus*** includes two additional practice activities to further reinforce new structures. Instant scoring and meaningful feedback show students their progress and highlight areas that may require more effort. Students also have the opportunity to see a video review featuring our expert grammar coach. The videos provide a quick, engaging review—perfect for allowing students to check their understanding before proceeding to further assessment.

In the ***Listening*** sections students have the opportunity to hear the target grammar in context and to practice their listening skills. Activities are developed to practice both top-down and bottom-up listening skills.

MyEnglishLab

Listening activities continue online with ***Listen for it***. These activities assess both grammar in context and listening comprehension, and include instant scoring and feedback.

MyEnglishLab

Before students do the ***Writing***, they go online to complete ***Linking Grammar to Writing***. Several guided writing tasks link the grammar to the skill of writing, enabling students to then move back to the textbook and complete the ***Writing*** section with full confidence.

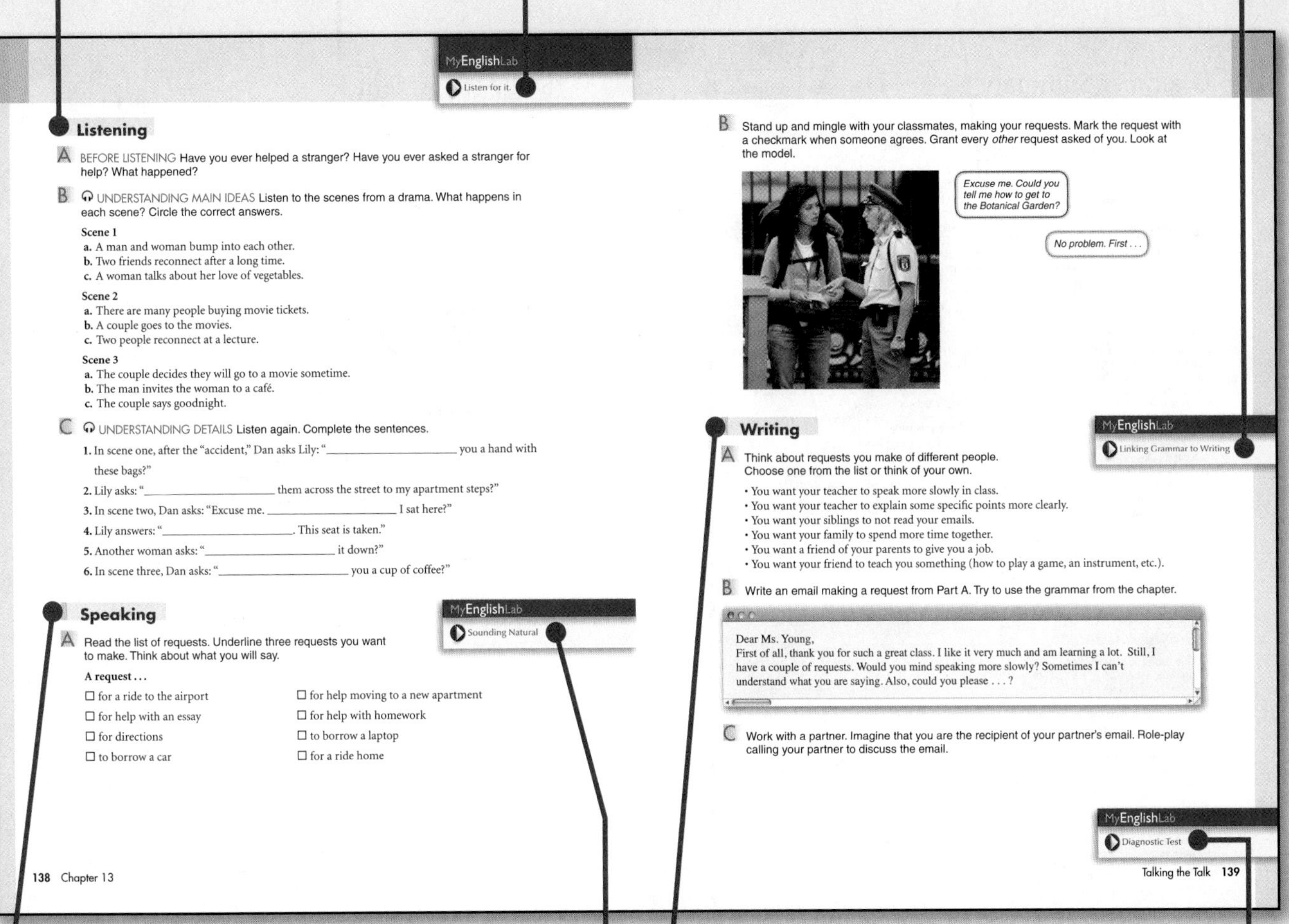

MyEnglishLab
Listen for it.

Listening

A BEFORE LISTENING Have you ever helped a stranger? Have you ever asked a stranger for help? What happened?

B UNDERSTANDING MAIN IDEAS Listen to the scenes from a drama. What happens in each scene? Circle the correct answers.

Scene 1
a. A man and woman bump into each other.
b. Two friends reconnect after a long time.
c. A woman talks about her love of vegetables.

Scene 2
a. There are many people buying movie tickets.
b. A couple goes to the movies.
c. Two people reconnect at a lecture.

Scene 3
a. The couple decides they will go to a movie sometime.
b. The man invites the woman to a café.
c. The couple says goodnight.

C UNDERSTANDING DETAILS Listen again. Complete the sentences.

1. In scene one, after the "accident," Dan asks Lily: "________ you a hand with these bags?"
2. Lily asks: "________ them across the street to my apartment steps?"
3. In scene two, Dan asks: "Excuse me. ________ I sat here?"
4. Lily answers: "________. This seat is taken."
5. Another woman asks: "________ it down?"
6. In scene three, Dan asks: "________ you a cup of coffee?"

Speaking

MyEnglishLab
Sounding Natural

A Read the list of requests. Underline three requests you want to make. Think about what you will say.

A request . . .

☐ for a ride to the airport
☐ for help with an essay
☐ for directions
☐ to borrow a car
☐ for help moving to a new apartment
☐ for help with homework
☐ to borrow a laptop
☐ for a ride home

138 Chapter 13

B Stand up and mingle with your classmates, making your requests. Mark the request with a checkmark when someone agrees. Grant every *other* request asked of you. Look at the model.

Excuse me. Could you tell me how to get to the Botanical Garden?

No problem. First . . .

Writing

MyEnglishLab
Linking Grammar to Writing

A Think about requests you make of different people. Choose one from the list or think of your own.

• You want your teacher to speak more slowly in class.
• You want your teacher to explain some specific points more clearly.
• You want your siblings to not read your emails.
• You want your family to spend more time together.
• You want a friend of your parents to give you a job.
• You want your friend to teach you something (how to play a game, an instrument, etc.).

B Write an email making a request from Part A. Try to use the grammar from the chapter.

Dear Ms. Young,
First of all, thank you for such a great class. I like it very much and am learning a lot. Still, I have a couple of requests. Would you mind speaking more slowly? Sometimes I can't understand what you are saying. Also, could you please . . . ?

C Work with a partner. Imagine that you are the recipient of your partner's email. Role-play calling your partner to discuss the email.

MyEnglishLab
Diagnostic Test

Talking the Talk 139

ne ***Speaking*** section provides students with the pportunity to use the chapter's grammar naturally d appropriately in a variety of engaging interactive eaking activities.

EnglishLab

e ***Sounding Natural*** activities are pronunciation tivities relating to the chapter's grammar and ernating between productive and receptive tasks. the receptive tasks, students listen to prompts and ect correct answers. In the productive tasks, students en to prompts, record themselves, and compare their omissions with a model.

The ***Writing*** section provides students with the opportunity to use the chapter's grammar naturally and appropriately in a variety of activities. Students are provided with a whole or partial model and a more open-ended writing task.

Each chapter culminates with an online ***Diagnostic Test*** that assesses students' comprehension and mastery of the chapter's grammar structures. The test tracks students' progress and allows teachers to focus on the specific student needs.

The ***Grammar Summary*** chart provides a concise, easy-to-read overview of all the grammar structures presented in the unit. It also serves as an excellent reference for review and study.

A quick 20- or 25-point ***Self-Assessment*** gives students an additional opportunity to check their understanding of the unit's target structures. This gives students one more chance to assess what they may still need to master before taking the online ***Unit Test***.

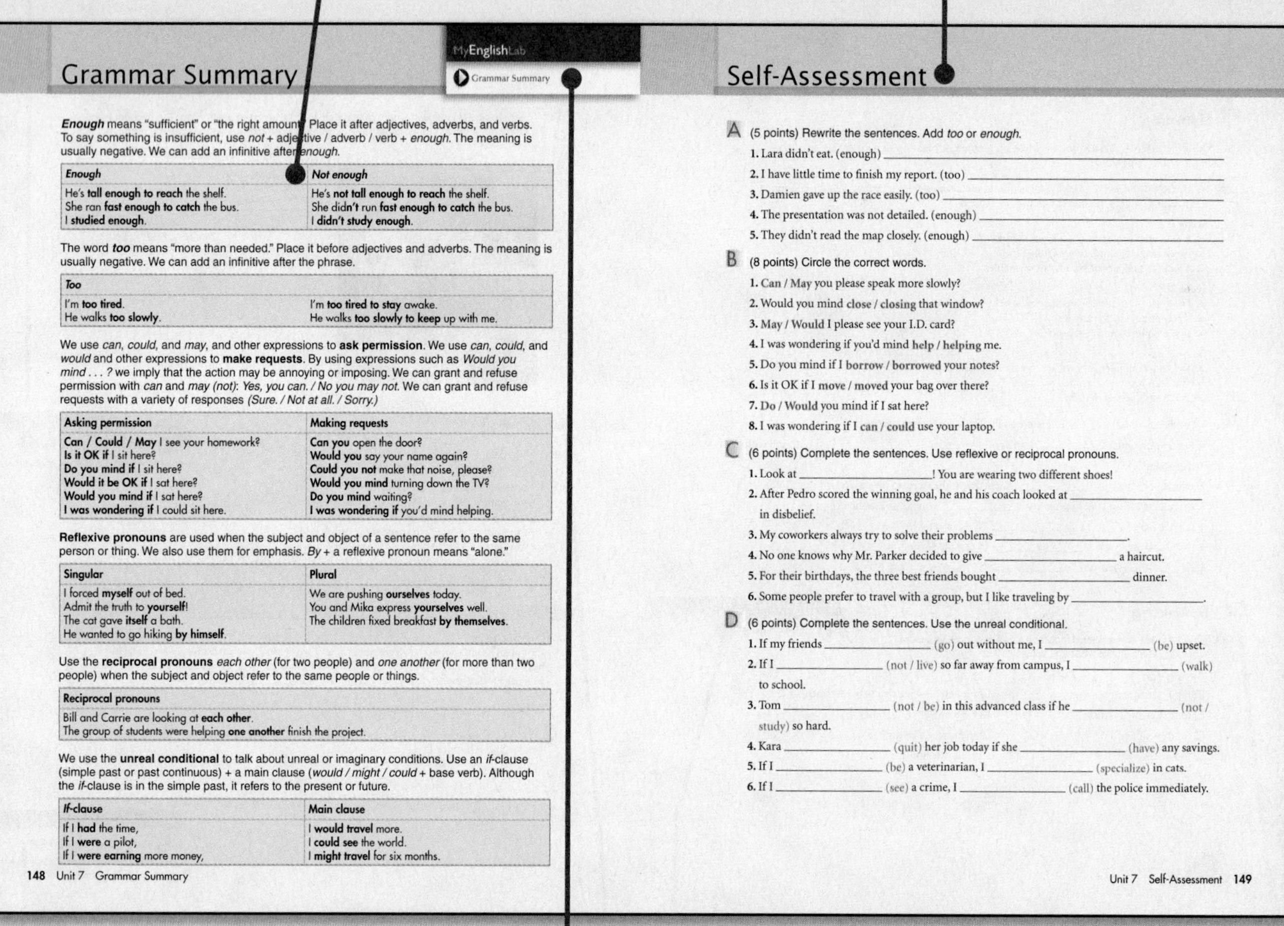

Grammar Summary

MyEnglishLab

Grammar Summary

Enough means "sufficient" or "the right amount." Place it after adjectives, adverbs, and verbs. To say something is insufficient, use *not* + adjective / adverb / verb + *enough*. The meaning is usually negative. We can add an infinitive after *enough*.

Enough	*Not enough*
He's **tall enough to reach** the shelf. She ran **fast enough to catch** the bus. I **studied enough**.	He's **not tall enough to reach** the shelf. She **didn't** run **fast enough to catch** the bus. I **didn't study enough**.

The word ***too*** means "more than needed." Place it before adjectives and adverbs. The meaning is usually negative. We can add an infinitive after the phrase.

Too	
I'm **too tired**. He walks **too slowly**.	I'm **too tired to stay** awake. He walks **too slowly to keep** up with me.

We use *can, could,* and *may,* and other expressions to **ask permission**. We use *can, could,* and *would* and other expressions to **make requests**. By using expressions such as *Would you mind . . . ?* we imply that the action may be annoying or imposing. We can grant and refuse permission with *can* and *may (not): Yes, you can. / No you may not.* We can grant and refuse requests with a variety of responses *(Sure. / Not at all. / Sorry.)*

Asking permission	Making requests
Can / Could / May I see your homework? **Is it OK if** I sit here? **Do you mind if** I sit here? **Would it be OK if** I sat here? **Would you mind if** I sat here? **I was wondering if** I could sit here.	**Can you** open the door? **Would you** say your name again? **Could you not** make that noise, please? **Would you mind** turning down the TV? **Do you mind** waiting? **I was wondering if** you'd mind helping.

Reflexive pronouns are used when the subject and object of a sentence refer to the same person or thing. We also use them for emphasis. *By* + a reflexive pronoun means "alone."

Singular	Plural
I forced **myself** out of bed. Admit the truth to **yourself**! The cat gave **itself** a bath. He wanted to go hiking **by himself**.	We are pushing **ourselves** today. You and Mika express **yourselves** well. The children fixed breakfast **by themselves**.

Use the **reciprocal pronouns** *each other* (for two people) and *one another* (for more than two people) when the subject and object refer to the same people or things.

Reciprocal pronouns
Bill and Carrie are looking at **each other**. The group of students were helping **one another** finish the project.

We use the **unreal conditional** to talk about unreal or imaginary conditions. Use an *if*-clause (simple past or past continuous) + a main clause (*would / might / could* + base verb). Although the *if*-clause is in the simple past, it refers to the present or future.

If-clause	Main clause
If I **had** the time, If I **were** a pilot, If I **were earning** more money,	I **would travel** more. I **could see** the world. I **might travel** for six months.

148 Unit 7 Grammar Summary

Self-Assessment

A (5 points) Rewrite the sentences. Add *too* or *enough*.

1. Lara didn't eat. (enough) ________
2. I have little time to finish my report. (too) ________
3. Damien gave up the race easily. (too) ________
4. The presentation was not detailed. (enough) ________
5. They didn't read the map closely. (enough) ________

B (8 points) Circle the correct words.

1. Can / May you please speak more slowly?
2. Would you mind close / closing that window?
3. May / Would I please see your I.D. card?
4. I was wondering if you'd mind help / helping me.
5. Do you mind if I borrow / borrowed your notes?
6. Is it OK if I move / moved your bag over there?
7. Do / Would you mind if I sat here?
8. I was wondering if I can / could use your laptop.

C (6 points) Complete the sentences. Use reflexive or reciprocal pronouns.

1. Look at ________! You are wearing two different shoes!
2. After Pedro scored the winning goal, he and his coach looked at ________ in disbelief.
3. My coworkers always try to solve their problems ________.
4. No one knows why Mr. Parker decided to give ________ a haircut.
5. For their birthdays, the three best friends bought ________ dinner.
6. Some people prefer to travel with a group, but I like traveling by ________.

D (6 points) Complete the sentences. Use the unreal conditional.

1. If my friends ________ (go) out without me, I ________ (be) upset.
2. If I ________ (not / live) so far away from campus, I ________ (walk) to school.
3. Tom ________ (not / be) in this advanced class if he ________ (not / study) so hard.
4. Kara ________ (quit) her job today if she ________ (have) any savings.
5. If I ________ (be) a veterinarian, I ________ (specialize) in cats.
6. If I ________ (see) a crime, I ________ (call) the police immediately.

Unit 7 Self-Assessment 149

MyEnglishLab

Students can go to *MyEnglishLab* for a ***Grammar Summary*** review, which includes activities and a video to help students prepare for the ***Self-Assessment*** and ***Unit Test***.

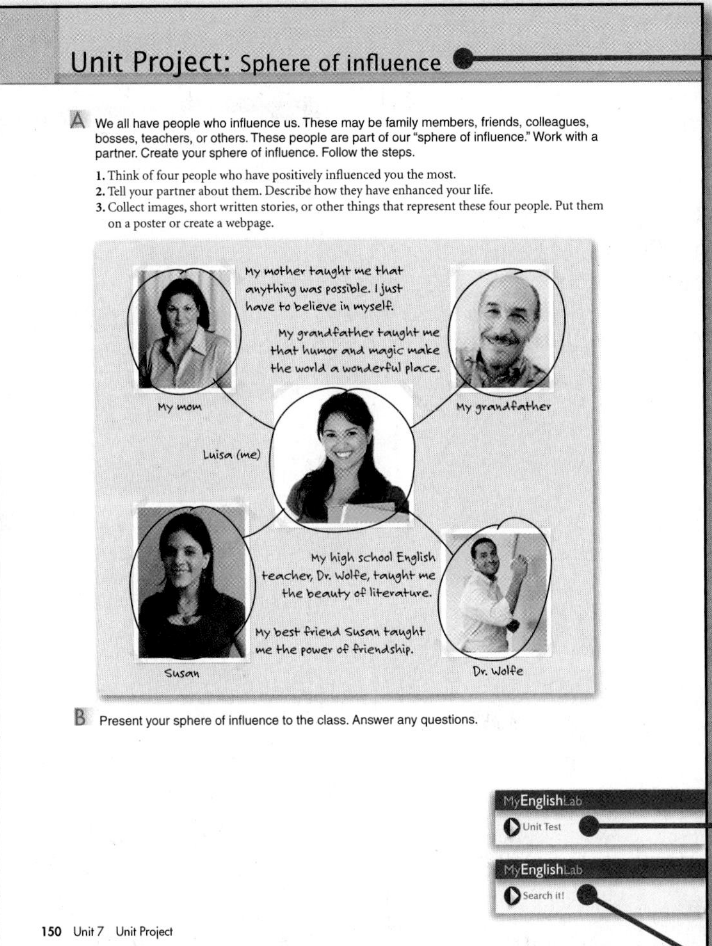

Unit Project: Sphere of influence
A We all have people who influence us. These may be family members, friends, colleagues, bosses, teachers, or others. These people are part of our "sphere of influence." Work with a partner. Create your sphere of influence. Follow the steps.
1. Think of four people who have positively influenced you the most.
2. Tell your partner about them. Describe how they have enhanced your life.
3. Collect images, short written stories, or other things that represent these four people. Put them on a poster or create a webpage.
My mother taught me that anything was possible. I just have to believe in myself.
My grandfather taught me that humor and magic make the world a wonderful place.
My mom
My grandfather
Luisa (me)
My high school English teacher, Dr. Wolfe, taught me the beauty of literature.
My best friend Susan taught me the power of friendship.
Susan
Dr. Wolfe
B Present your sphere of influence to the class. Answer any questions.
MyEnglishLab
Unit Test
MyEnglishLab
Search it!
150 Unit 7 Unit Project

Each unit ends with an interesting and engaging group ***Unit Project*** that encourages students to synthesize the new grammar structures and to integrate the unit's theme and skills. The project promotes collaboration, creativity, and fluency and exposes students to a variety of real-world situations.

MyEnglishLab

The unit's final, cumulative assessment is a comprehensive online ***Unit Test***. This test allows students to check their mastery of the unit's grammar structures, see their progress, and identify areas that may need improvement. The test allows teachers to track students' progress and to focus on areas that might benefit from more attention.

MyEnglishLab

The ***Search it!*** activity allows students to do a fun online search for content that relates to the chapter's theme. Teachers may choose to have students complete these real-world tasks individually, in pairs, or in small groups.

Next Generation Grammar Digital

MyEnglishLab

A dynamic, easy-to-use online learning and assessment program, integral to the *Next Generation Grammar* program

- **Original activities** focusing on grammar, vocabulary, and skills that extend the *Next Generation Grammar* program
- **Multiple** reading, writing, listening, and speaking activities that practice grammar in context, including *Linking Grammar to Writing*, which guides students in the practical use of the chapter's grammar
- **Video** instruction from a dynamic grammar coach that provides an engaging and comprehensive grammar review
- **Extensive** and ongoing assessment that provides evidence of student learning and progress on both the chapter and unit level
- **Individualized** instruction, instant feedback, and study plans that provide personalized learning
- A **flexible gradebook** that helps instructors monitor student progress

And remember, *Next Generation Grammar* is available both in print and as an eText.

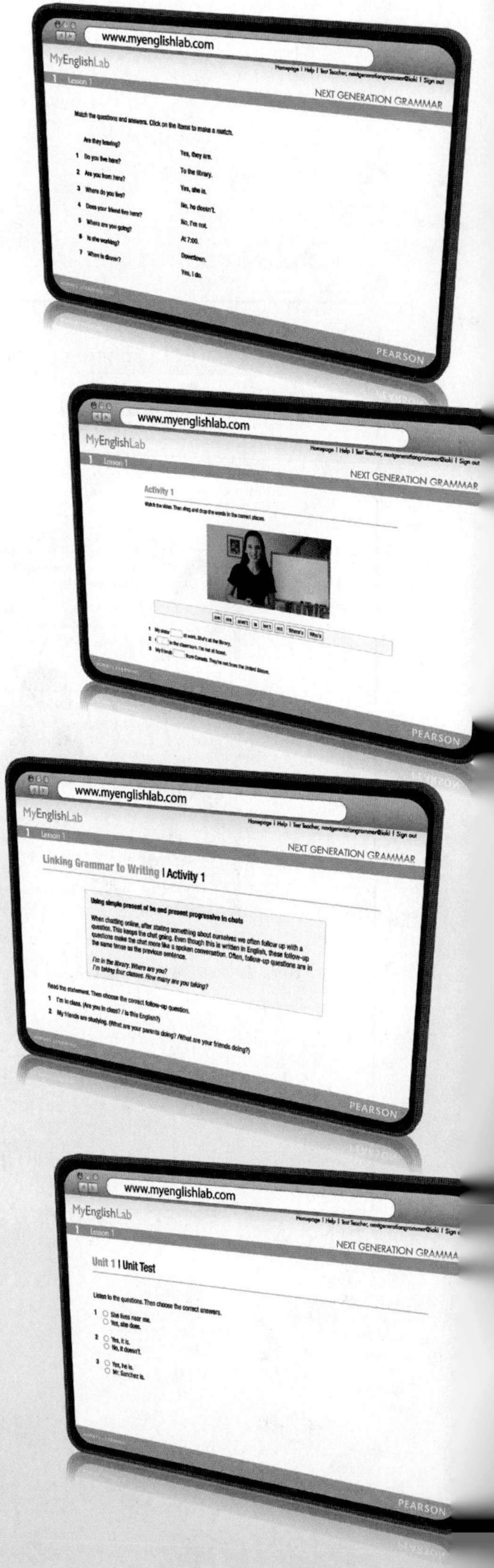

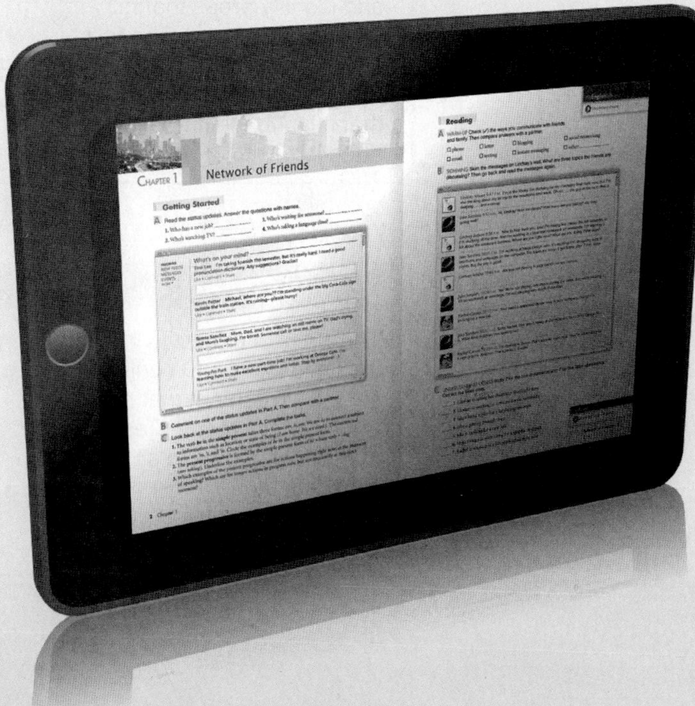

ActiveTeach

A powerful digital resource that provides the perfect solution for seamless lesson planning and exciting whole-class teaching

- A **Digital Student Book** with interactive whiteboard (IWB) software
- **Useful notes** that present teaching suggestions, corpus-informed grammar tips, troublesome grammar points, and culture notes
- Instant one-stop **audio** and **video grammar coach**
- **Printable** audio scripts, video scripts, and answer keys
- **Capability** for teachers to:
  - Write, highlight, erase, and create notes
  - Add and save newly-created classroom work
  - Enlarge any section of a page

Teacher's Note

Teacher's Note p3
Unit 1, Chapter 1
B Reading Skills
When you **skim** a text, you look it over quickly to get a general idea of what it is about. Do not read every word and do not use a dictionary. Instead, look at the title, pictures, bold, or italicized words, and the first line of each paragraph to get a sense of the general idea.

About the Authors

Pamela Vittorio has worked in many aspects of ELT publishing and ESL/ESOL education since the 1990s: as author, editor, instructor, program manager, teacher trainer, and assessment test developer. She is currently a P-T assistant professor at the New School University, NY, where she was a nominee for the Distinguished University Teaching award. Pamela is the author of *Testbuilder for TOEFL iBT* (Macmillan) and co-author of *Excellent English: 4* (McGraw-Hill/Cambridge) and has contributed to several ESL textbooks and video series. She has been a presenter at both local and international TESOL conferences since 1998.

Jennifer Recio Lebedev has taught English as a foreign and second language since 1996. She has been working online as an instructor and content creator since 2007. Her Pearson-sponsored blog won the 2010 EDDIE Award in the category ESL Website Blog. As *JenniferESL* on YouTube, she has gained thousands of subscribers worldwide, and in 2011 her channel was recognized in YouTube's "On the Rise" contest. Jennifer has presented at TESOL independently and by invitation. She is a co-author of the *Vocabulary Power* series and contributed support materials to *New Password.*

Acknowledgments

As with any major publication, these materials are the result of an amazing group effort. We are thankful we could benefit from the support and expertise of the people at Pearson, especially Massimo Rubini, Andrea Bryant, Amy McCormick, Gosia Jaros-White, and David Bohlke.—*PV & JL*

I sincerely thank Jennifer Lebedev for being an exceptional writing partner, for making this process enjoyable and engaging, and for bringing her knowledge, energy, and wonderful personality to the creation of this book. My heartfelt appreciation to Massimo Rubini, whose love of grammar and language magnetically drew together an incredible team of writers. Thanks to Andrea Bryant for her support, humor, and upbeat attitude. To my many students—both past and present—who have inspired and always challenged me to find new ways to help them learn and be a better educator. I would also like to express deep love and gratitude to my family for their endless patience and unwavering support.—*PV*

I would like to express my appreciation of the entire writing team, and in particular give my heartfelt thanks to my co-author, Pamela Vittorio, for testing and developing my knowledge of grammar, for leading the way while still allowing me the freedom to create, and for holding me to a standard of which we can both be proud. I also wish to say thank you to Massimo for encouraging me and to Amy for always believing in me. I cannot forget to acknowledge the hundreds of students and teachers who have written to me over the years and by doing so challenged and supported me in my professional growth. Finally, I express my love and thanks to my husband, Kostya, and our children. Without their support and understanding, none of this would be possible.—*JL*

Reviewers

We are grateful to the following reviewers for their many helpful comments:

Yukiko Arita, Ibaraki University, Mito, Japan; **Asmaa Awad,** University of Sharjah, Sharjah, United Arab Emirates; **Kim Bayer,** Hunter College CUNY, New York, NY; **Michelle Bell,** University of South Florida, Tampa, FL; **Jeff Bette,** Westchester Community College SUNY, Valhalla, NY; **Leslie Biaggi,** Miami Dade College, Miami, FL; **Celina Costa,** George Brown College, Toronto, Ontario, Canada; **Eric Dury,** University of Sharjah, Sharjah, United Arab Emirates; **Katie Entigar,** Kaplan's English Scool, Boston, MA; **Margaret Eomurian,** Houston Community College, Central College, Houston, TX; **Liz Flynn,** San Diego Community College, San Diego, CA: **Ruth French,** Hunter College CUNY, New York, NY; **Jas Gill,** University of British Columbia, Vancouver, British Columbia, Canada; **Joanne Glaski,** Suffolk County Community College, Selden, NY; **Sandra Hartmann,** University of Houston, Houston, TX; **Cora Higgins,** Boston Academy of English, Boston, MA; **Carolyn Ho,** Lone Star College-Cyfair, Cypress, TX; **Gretchen Irwin-Arada,** Hunter College CUNY, New York, NY; **Bob Jester,** Hunter College CUNY, New York, NY; **Patricia Juza,** Baruch College CUNY, New York, NY; **Liz Kara,** Alberta College, Alberta, Canada; **Jessica March,** American University of Sharjah, Sharjah, United Arab Emirates; **Alison McAdams,** Approach International Student Center, Boston, MA; **Kathy Mehdi,** University of Sharjah, Sharjah, United Arab Emirates; **April Muchmore-Vokoun,** Hillsborough Community College, Dale Mabry Campus, Tampa, FL; **Forest Nelson,** Tokai University, Toyko, Japan; **Dina Paglia,** Hunter College CUNY, New York, NY; **DyAnne Philips,** Houston Community College, Southwest College, Gulfton Center, Houston, TX; **Russell Pickett,** Sam Houston State University, Huntsville, TX; **Peggy Porter,** Houston Community College, Northwest College, Houston, TX; **Tahani Qadri,** American University of Sharjah, Sharjah, United Arab Emirates; **Alison Rice,** Hunter College CUNY, New York, NY; **Kevin Ryan,** Showa Women's University, Tokyo, Japan; **Yasser Salem,** University of Sharjah, Sharjah, United Arab Emirates; **Janet Selitto,** Seminole State College of Florida, Sanford, FL; **Laura Sheehan,** Houston Community College, Southwest College, Stafford Campus, Houston, TX; **Barbara Smith-Palinkas,** Hillsborough Cummunity College, Dale Mabry Campus, Tampa, FL; **Maria Spelleri,** State College of Florida Manatee-Sarasota, Venice, FL; **Marjorie Stamberg,** Hunter College CUNY, New York, NY; **Gregory Strong,** Aoyama Gakuin University, Tokyo, Japan; **Fausto G. Vergara,** Houston Community College, Southeast College, Houston, TX; **Khristie Wills,** American University of Sharjah, Sharjah, United Arab Emirates; **Nancy Ramirez Wright,** Santa Ana College, Santa Ana, CA.

Credits

Photo credits: Page iv Pearson; v Pearson, (coach) Courtesy of Jennifer Lebedev; p. 1 (left) olly/Shutterstock, (painting) dred2010/Fotolia, (frame) Michal Adamczyk/Fotolia, (glass) PhotoDisc, (bottom) Getideaka/Shutterstock; p. 2 (left) IMAGE ASSET MANAGEMEN/age fotostock, (right) INTERFOTO/age fotostock; p. 3 PhotoDisc; p. 8 (top right) Fine Art Photographic/Getty Images, (left) SuperStock/SuperStock, (right) Mondadori Portfolio/UIG/Getty Images; p. 9 (left) The Art Gallery Collection/Alamy, (right) Artved/Getty Images; p. 10 Bernd Tschakert/Alamy; p. 22 (left) IMAGE ASSET MANAGEMEN/age fotostock, (right) INTERFOTO/age fotostock; p. 23 (top row) tiero/Fotolia, Roman Samokhin/Fotolia, olly/Fotolia, Vladislav Lebedinski/Fotolia, Lou Oates/Shutterstock, (middle row) tiptoee/Fotolia, tuja66/Fotolia, NinaMalyna/Fotolia, fergregory/Fotolia, (bottom) piai/Fotolia; p. 24 (top right) Science & Society Picture Library/SSPL/Getty Images, (A) Eve Arnold/Magnum Photos, (B) Image copyright © The Metropolitan Museum of Art. Image source: Art Resource, NY, (C) Shoosmith Photographer Collection/Alamy, (D) Margaret Bourke-White/Time & Life Pictures/Getty Images, (E) NASA/Splash News/Newscom; p. 30 (top right) Everett Collection Inc/Alamy, (left) Old Paper Studios/Alamy, (right) ClassicStock/Alamy; p. 31 sonya etchison/Shutterstock; p. 32 (top right) Everett Collection Inc/Alamy, (A) Science and Society/SuperStock, (B) Science and Society/SuperStock, (C) Science & Society Picture Library/Getty Images, (D) Dorling Kindersley; p. 38 (top row) Scott Griessel/Fotolia, fStop/Alamy, Gemenacom/Shutterstock, Gemenacom/Shutterstock, (bottom) Idealink Photography/Alamy; p. 39 WARNER BROS. PICTURES/Album/Newscom; p. 42 Courtesy Everett Collection; p. 43 (left) IMAGEMORE/age fotostock, (middle) WARNER BROS TV/Album/Newscom, (right) akg-images/Newscom; p. 44 Everett Collection/Everett Collection; p. 49 Columbia Pictures/courtesy Everett Collection; p. 52 (left) WARNER BROS TV/Album/Newscom, (middle left) 20TH CENTURY FOX / HAYES, KERRY / Album/Newscom, (middle right) Photo ITAR-TASS Itar-Tass Photos/Newscom, (right) Courtesy Everett Collection; p. 54 (left) IMAGEMORE/age fotostock, (right) Darla Hallmark/Shutterstock; p. 59 akg-images/Newscom; p. 61 akg-images/Newscom; p. 65 (top left) Dmytro Smaglov/Fotolia, (top middle) UryadnikovS/Fotolia, (top right) Hunta/Fotolia, (bottom left) Popova Olga/Fotolia, (bottom middle) Natalia Pavlova/Fotolia, (bottom right) UryadnikovS/Fotolia; p. 66 PaulShlykov/Fotolia; p. 74 CANDACE BARBOT KRT/Newscom; p. 75 (top) Everett Collection Inc/Alamy, (bottom) Byron Purvis/AdMedia/Newscom; p. 76 (A) Dale Wilson/Alamy, (B) jack thomas/Alamy, (C) North Wind Picture Archives/Alamy, (D) Richard Ellis/Photo Researchers, Inc.; p. 77 (left) AFP/Getty Images/Newscom, (top right) blickwinkel/Alamy, (bottom right) martin1985/Fotolia; p. 86 (right) Globe Turner/Shutterstock; p. 87 (background) Losevsky Photo and Video/Shutterstock, (left) shamtor/Fotolia, (top middle) thawats/Fotolia, (bottom middle) antiksu/Fotolia, (right) soup studio/Fotolia; p. 88 (left) Trinity Mirror/Mirrorpix/Alamy, (middle left) ClassicStock.com/SuperStock, (middle right) PhotoAlto/Alamy, (right) Red Images, LLC/Alamy; p. 92 (A) Allstar Picture Library / Alamy, (B) Keystone Pictures USA / Alamy, (C) Fitzgerald/CandidatePhotos/Newscom, (D) WARNER BROTHERS/Album/Newscom, (E) Allstar Picture Library/Alamy, (F) Trinity Mirror/Mirrorpix/Alamy; p. 94 (left to right) PARAMOUNT PICTURES/Album/Newscom, Al Dunlop/Toronto Star/ZUMA Press/Newscom, Kristin Callahan/Everett Collection/Alamy, Everett Collection Inc/Alamy, ZUMA Wire Service/Alamy; p. 96 pedrosala/Fotolia; p. 97 (left) Maksim Toome/Fotolia, (middle) gerardfritz/Fotolia, (right) BeTa-Artworks/Fotolia; p. 106 pressmaster/Fotolia; p. 107 (iphone) Courtesy of Diane Fenster, (laptop) Courtesy of Diane Fenster, (man) igor/Fotolia, (letter) Niday Picture Library/Alamy, (bird) Klaus Rose/Fotolia, (pole) Mary Lane/Fotolia, (phone) Kirill Smirnov/Fotolia; p. 111 epantha/Fotolia; p. 120 (top left) Stockbyte/Getty Images, (top middle) Presselect/Alamy, (bottom left) INTERFOTO/Alamy, (bottom middle) INTERFOTO/Alamy, (bottom right) Peter Zijlstra/Shutterstock; p. 126 (1) Keystone-France/Getty Images, (2) GoSeeFoto/Alamy, (3) stoonn/Fotolia, (4) DIZ Muenchen GmbH, Sueddeutsche Zeitung Photo/Alamy; p. 130 (top) by-studio/Fotolia, (middle) baffineri/Fotolia, (bottom) INTERFOTO/Alamy; p. 131 (background) pixcub/Shutterstock, (totem) Terry Alexander/Fotolia, (face) Laurin Rinder/Fotolia, (book) franco bissoni/Fotolia, (sign) Pierre-Jean Durieu/Shutterstock, (stone) Ozgur Guvenc/Fotolia; p. 132 (a) Daily Mail/Rex/Alamy, (b) World History Archive/Alamy, (c) Classic Image/Alamy, (d) INTERFOTO /Alamy; p. 135 SuperStock/Alamy; p. 151 (cheek) Svetlana Fedoseeva/Fotolia, (bite) stockyimages/Fotolia, (eyes) Yuri Arcurs/Fotolia, (mouth) sakura/Fotolia, (nose) Yuri Arcurs/Fotolia, (ear) Piotr Marcinski/Fotolia, (brain) storm/Fotolia, (head) Image Source IS2/Fotolia; p. 152 Scott Camazine/Alamy; p. 158 uwimages/Fotolia; p. 163 Foto Flare/Fotolia; p. 166 (left) David Coleman/Alamy, (right) TRIPPETT/SIPA/Newscom; p. 175 (stars) PhotoDisc, (planets) PhotoDisc, (clock) Courtesy of Diane Fenster; p. 179 Warner Bros/Courtesy Everett Collection; p. 181 COLUMBIA PICTURES/Album/Newscom; p. 184 PARAMOUNT PICTURES/Album/Newscom; p. 188 Universal/Courtesy Everett Collection; p. 197 (woman) auremar/Fotolia, (petroglyphs) pedrosala/Fotolia, (man) Santhosh Kumar/Fotolia, (sign) Terry Morris/Fotolia, (graffiti) David Acosta Allely/Fotolia, (emotion heads) Tommaso Lizzul/Fotolia; p. 201 20thCentFox/Courtesy Everett Collection; p. 204 (top) goodluz/Fotolia, (bottom) Adam Pretty/Getty Images; p. 205 (top) iofoto/Shutterstock, (bottom) Yuri Arcurs/Fotolia; p. 206 (left) Fancy/Alamy, (middle left) Beyond Fotomedia GmbH/Alamy, (middle right) PhotoAlto/SuperStock, (right) Devi/Shutterstock; p. 208 (A) Ben Chams/Fotolia, (B) jbk-editorial/Alamy, (C) Gary Bass/Alamy; p. 209 AP Images/Jean Clottes; p. 211 (top) imagebroker/Alamy, (bottom) Yurumi/Shutterstock; p. 214 (left) sardinelly/Fotolia, (middle) Nikreates/Alamy, (right) Eyebyte/Alamy.

Illustration credits: Diane Fenster pages 1, 23, 43, 65, 87, 107, 151; Josee Morin pp. 86, 89; Rob Schuster pp. 64 (top and bottom left), 79, 82, 83, 103, 126, 140, 145, 146, 150, 196; Ralph Voltz pp. 25, 64 (middle left, middle right, bottom right), 102, 127, 152, 198.

UNIT 1

The Art Detectives

OUTCOMES

After completing this unit, I will be able to use these grammar points.

CHAPTER 1

Grammar Focus 1
Simple present

Grammar Focus 2
Present progressive

CHAPTER 2

Grammar Focus 1
Future: *Will* and *be going to*

Grammar Focus 2
Future progressive

Grammar Focus 3
Present forms with future meaning

MyEnglishLab

 What do you know?

CHAPTER 1 Deception and Detection

Getting Started

A Work with a partner. Look closely at the paintings. They are not exactly the same. Use the phrases below to discuss the differences you see.

I notice that . . .
In one painting there is . . .
I spot a difference in the paintings . . .
The . . . look different.
The painting on the left has . . , but the painting on the right has . . . .

B Read the list of actions about people in the art world. Which groups do which actions? Write *1* for *painters*, *2* for *art experts*, and *3* for *criminals*.

_____ **1.** They use brushes and different paint colors in their work.
_____ **2.** They sometimes try to sell fake paintings but claim the paintings are real.
_____ **3.** They place a value on a piece of art after they form an opinion on its quality.
_____ **4.** They are always looking for new subjects to paint.
_____ **5.** They are always improving their knowledge about art and their ability to judge it.
_____ **6.** They are creative, and they know how to make everyday life into beautiful art.
_____ **7.** They sometimes steal art from museums.
_____ **8.** They are able to distinguish a real painting from a fake because they use scientific methods.

C Look back at Part B. Complete the tasks.

1. Do the sentences refer to the past, present, or future? ____________________
2. Underline the **present form verbs** that describe an **existing state.**
3. Put parentheses around the present form verbs that express a **general truth.**
4. Circle the present form verbs that express **actions that occur frequently or regularly.**
5. Complete the chart. Then compare your work with a partner's.

Existing state	General truth	Actions that occur frequently or regularly

MyEnglishLab

Vocabulary Check

Reading

A WARM-UP What do you know about detectives and their work? What kinds of crimes do they try to solve and how do they do it? Now think about art detectives. How is their work similar to or different from other detective work?

B PREDICTING What kinds of evidence do you think art detectives look for when they investigate? Check (✓) all that you think are true. Then read the article and check your answers.

☐ fingerprints	☐ signatures	☐ smudges	☐ grease
☐ layers of paint	☐ chalk marks	☐ special brushstrokes	☐ hair

Art Deception and Detection: Real or Fake?

Paul Peter Biro is an art detective. Biro can tell if a painting is real or fake. He can also determine the artist of the painting. How does he do this? He looks carefully at the brushstrokes to see if the painting is a forgery. Biro is also an expert at art restoration and restores damaged paintings.

When Biro authenticates or restores a work of art, he spends a lot of time cleaning it. He also uses high-tech instruments to help see beneath the layers of dirt or paint. When he is cleaning a painting or a drawing, he often finds the artist's fingerprint.

The year is 1998. A collector buys a chalk and ink drawing called *Young Girl in Profile in Renaissance Dress*. The collector takes it to many experts to determine its real value. When Biro examines it, he discovers a thumbprint on the drawing. Biro believes the thumbprint belongs to Leonardo da Vinci.

After this discovery, Paul Peter Biro learns more about fingerprinting and understands how fingerprints should look. He compares the thumbprint on this drawing to a fingerprint he finds on one of Leonardo's earlier paintings. They match! The art world now believes this is one of the greatest discoveries of the century: Leonardo da Vinci's drawing of *La Bella Principessa*. The headlines in the newspapers read: "Art Expert Cracks da Vinci Code." But the question remains for many experts: is it real? Did Paul Peter Biro really discover a previously unknown work of Leonardo? Or, is Biro deceiving the art world?

Flash forward to the year 2009: David Grann, a reporter from the *New Yorker* magazine, interviews Biro at his home. During the interview, Biro shows Grann a close-up of Leonardo's thumbprint on his computer. In Grann's opinion, it just looks like a smudge. It is hard to believe it is a thumbprint. Grann grows suspicious. Biro demonstrates his scientific methods and process for Grann. But in Grann's mind, the evidence just doesn't add up. In different interviews, Grann asks Biro questions and begins to catch him in lies. The lies raise doubts about the authenticity of Paul Peter Biro's work. As Grann investigates Biro's past experience in art detection, he proves that Biro is a fraud. Biro tried to lead everyone to believe that *La Bella Principessa* and other works of art are authentic. Biro's art detection is really art deception.

C UNDERSTANDING FACTS AND DETAILS Write *T* for the true statements and *F* for the false statements.

_____ **1.** Brushstrokes help Biro to authenticate a painting.

_____ **2.** Biro uses simple tools to restore damaged paintings.

_____ **3.** By comparing fingerprints, some art experts can determine the artist of a painting.

_____ **4.** Biro wants to prove that *La Bella Principessa* is a forgery.

_____ **5.** Grann believes Biro did not want to deceive others, but that Biro just made a mistake.

MyEnglishLab

Reading Comprehension

Grammar Focus 1 Simple present

Examples	Language notes
(1) He **spends** a lot of time cleaning it.	Use the **simple present** for habitual actions, common events, and usual states or conditions.
(2) Paul Peter Biro **is** an art detective. He **restores** damaged artwork.	Use the simple present for facts and general truths.
(3) Biro often **finds** the artist's fingerprint. He **is** always careful in his work.	We use **adverbs of frequency** to express how often something happens. Adverbs of frequency usually go before the verb in the simple present. However, adverbs of frequency always go after the verb *be* in the simple present. Some examples of adverbs of frequency include: *always, often, usually, occasionally, sometimes, rarely, seldom, never.*
(4) After this discovery, Paul Peter Biro **studies** fingerprinting and **learns** how fingerprints should look.	We can also use the simple present to describe the plot of a movie or a book, or to tell a story.

Negative statements	*Wh-* questions
Grann **isn't** certain. Things just **don't make** sense.	How **does** he **do** this? What **does** Grann **believe**?
***Yes / No* questions**	**Short answers**
Is it real? **Does** he **spend** a lot of time cleaning it?	Yes, it **is**. / No, it **isn't**. Yes, he **does**. / No, he **doesn't**.

Grammar Practice

A Change the verbs in the simple past to the simple present to retell the story. Follow the example.

The Art of Crime

The painter carefully ~~**moved**~~ *moves* his brush on the canvas. One stroke. Two strokes. There! He **painted** the signature in the corner of the painting. He **stepped** back to view his work and **compared** it to the original, which **was** right beside it. Amazing! They **looked** the same. Which **was** the original and which **was** the forgery? "No one will know!" he **thought.** The painter **was** proud. His skill with brushes often **deceived** art lovers.

[*Knock, knock.*] Someone **was** at the door. The painter **knew** who it **was.** When the door **opened**, the guest **did not say** hello. She only **asked** if the painting **was** ready. The painter **nodded** and **pointed**.

"Good work, Ivan," the woman **commented.** "This work **proved** that you have great talent." Only a few experts in the world **were** able to determine that Ivan's works **were** fake. She **was** eager for the paint on the forgery to dry. She **wanted** to sell it as quickly as possible. She **took** out her cell phone and . . .

What do you think happens next? Who does the woman sell the painting to? What happens when the new owner asks an art expert to authenticate Ivan's painting?

B Change the false statements into true statements. Use the facts below. Begin each sentence with *That's not true. . . .* Include one negative verb in the simple present in each set of sentences.

1. With 35,000 works of art, the Louvre in Paris, France, has the largest art collection in the world.
   [Fact: The Hermitage in St. Petersburg, Russia, has over three million works of art.]
   That's not true. *The Louvre doesn't have the largest collection. The Hermitage has more works of art.*

2. Canadian artist Eric Waugh holds the record for creating the largest painting. *Hero* measures 41,400 square feet.
   [Fact: Swedish artist David Aberg's painting *Mother Earth* measures 86,000 square feet.]
   That's not true. ______________________________

3. Nineteenth-century painter Edgar Degas is famous for his many artworks of opera singers.
   [Fact: Degas's favorite subject was the ballet dancer. There are hundreds of paintings of dancers by Degas.]
   That's not true. ______________________________

4. The famous portrait of *Mona Lisa* is around 300 years old.
   [Fact: Leonardo da Vinci lived in the 16th century. Historians say he painted *Mona Lisa* in 1503.]
   That's not true. ______________________________

Grammar Focus 2 Present progressive

Examples	Language notes
(1) Biro **is restoring** a painting. Grann and others **are investigating** Biro's past work.	Use the **present progressive** to describe actions or events occurring now, which could mean at this exact moment or at the present time (today, this week, this month, etc.)
(2) The art world now **believes** this is one of the greatest discoveries of the century. ***Incorrect:*** The art world ~~**is now believing**~~ this is one of the greatest discoveries of the century.	We don't usually use **stative verbs** (non-action verbs) in the present progressive.
Biro **wants** Grann to believe him. ***Incorrect:*** Biro ~~**is wanting**~~ Grann to believe him.	Some examples of stative verbs include: *appear, believe, feel, look, love, seem, want.*
To David Grann, Biro **seems** to be lying. ***Incorrect:*** To David Grann, Biro ~~**is seeming**~~ to be lying.	To express states or conditions in the present, use the **simple present**.
(3) When he **is cleaning** a painting or drawing, he often finds the artist's fingerprint.	We can also use the present progressive for a habitual action in progress. It has the meaning of "during a specific process."

See Appendix A on page A-1 for stative verbs rarely used in progressive forms.

Negative statements	*Wh-* questions
Biro **isn't telling** the truth.	What **is** Biro **trying** to prove?
They **aren't listening** to Biro's lies.	Why **are** the art detectives **asking** questions?
***Yes / No* questions**	**Short answers**
Is he **trying** to deceive us?	Yes, he **is**. / No, he **isn't**.
Are they **listening** to his lies?	Yes, they **are**. / No, they **aren't**.

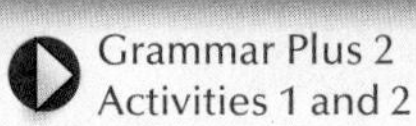

Grammar Plus 2
Activities 1 and 2

Grammar Practice

A Read about each person. Complete the descriptions of their present activities. Use the verbs given. Remember that we do not usually use stative verbs in the present progressive.

1. Tina is an expert in the restoration of damaged paintings. Right now, she *is restoring* (restore) a rare painting for a private client. She *needs* (need) to finish the project this month.
2. Steve is an art collector. He sometimes buys works of unknown artists. This week Steve __________ (look) at several pieces by a young artist. He determined their value this morning and he __________ (call) the artist to make an offer for the entire collection.
3. Yolanda is an expert at forgery. She makes money selling her fake works. Today she __________ (discuss) the sale of one painting with a buyer. The buyer __________ (not know) that Yolanda __________ (try) to deceive him with a forged painting.
4. Eric and Dana are students in the art history department. They __________ (attend) a lecture right now. They __________ (listen) to their professor explain how experts use scientific methods to authenticate paintings.
5. Mark dreams of being an artist, but his parents want him to go to law school. These days he __________ (not think) of school at all. He __________ (spend) all his free time painting. He __________ (believe) that he has to prove his skills to his parents in order to gain their support.

B Read the story and correct the present form errors. Look at the example. There are 12 more errors.

Artists work in different places. Some ~~are painting~~ *paint* in studios. Others, like Jean-Paul, create their art outside. Jean-Paul is a street artist. He is doing portraits for a living. Often he is sitting on the sidewalks of busy streets where tourists pass by. Today he sits in the park. He doesn't draw at the moment. It is still early in the morning, and Jean-Paul is simply enjoying the sights and sounds. The park is appearing to be almost empty.

Jean-Paul is seeing a woman enter the park. A young boy is with her. They hold hands, but the boy is wishing to run free. The mother lets him go, and he chases after some birds. Jean-Paul smiles when he is hearing the boy's laughter.

The boy soon stops and waits for his mother. She takes his hand, and they are beginning to walk together once again. Jean-Paul is wanting to draw their portrait. "Good morning," he calls to the pair. The mother sees the artist and smiles. "My son is like a bird. He can fly away at any moment," she explains.

"Ah," Jean-Paul is saying, "I'm an *expert* on birds." He welcomes them to sit down in front of him.

MyEnglishLab

Sounding Natural

Speaking

A Write questions about the painting. Then work with a partner, and ask and answer each other's questions. Use the present progressive in your questions and answers.

1. What? *What is the woman doing?*
2. What? ______
3. Why? ______
4. Where? ______
5. How? Or *Yes / No* question ______

B Work with a partner. Choose one of the paintings below. Look at it for one minute and close your book. Then describe the painting to your partner. What do the people look like? What are they doing? Try to remember as much as you can. When you are finished, switch roles.

In the first painting, a woman and her child are sitting next to a garden.
In the second painting, many men are riding horses.

Listening

MyEnglishLab

Listen for it.

A BEFORE LISTENING Talk to a partner. Would you buy an expensive piece of art? Imagine that you find a painting that looks like a famous artist's work. What would you do?

B UNDERSTANDING MAIN IDEAS Listen to a conversation between an art detective and an art collector. Talk to a partner. Write a few sentences describing the main points in the conversation.

C UNDERSTANDING FACTS AND DETAILS Listen again. Check (✓) the statements that are facts.

☐ **1.** The detective thinks the painting is from the 19th century.

☐ **2.** It is a scene of the countryside.

☐ **3.** The art collector believes the painting is by a famous painter.

☐ **4.** The detective is not going to determine the value of the painting.

☐ **5.** The art collector is examining the painting through special glasses.

☐ **6.** There is no signature on the painting.

☐ **7.** The detective tells the woman to come back tomorrow.

MyEnglishLab

Linking Grammar to Writing

Writing

A Talk with a partner. Imagine you are going to buy a work of art to hang in your home. What style do you like? What colors do you prefer?

B Choose one of the images. You are planning to buy it. In one or two paragraphs, describe the painting in an email to your friend. Make sure you answer the questions below.

- How old is the painting?
- Is the painting by your favorite artist?
- What colors do you see in the painting?
- What do you like about the painting?
- Are the brushstrokes unusual?
- What are the people in the painting [on the left] doing?
- Why will your friend like the painting?
- How are you going to get the painting home?
- Where will the painting hang in your home?

Today I bought a painting by Claude Monet. Monet is my favorite painter because he paints both people and nature. . . .
I am going to hang the painting in my living room so everyone can see it. It will look great because the colors will match with the furniture.

C Exchange descriptions with a classmate. Compare your descriptions and talk about their similarities and differences.

MyEnglishLab

Diagnostic Test

CHAPTER 2 Inspection and Restoration

Getting Started

A What do you think the art students are about to do? What will they do next?

B Work with a partner. Student A is a reporter for the university newspaper. Student B is the head of the art department. The art department is organizing an art show of students' works. Role-play an interview. Use the questions below as a guide.

1. What kinds of artwork will visitors see at the art show?
2. Are the artists going to be at the show to answer questions?
3. Where is the show taking place?
4. When does the show begin?
5. How will the art show help senior art students who are about to graduate?

C Look back at Part B. Then read the information in the box and choose the best answers to complete the statements below.

> We sometimes use the **simple present** and ***be*** + **present participle** to talk about **events scheduled in the future.**
> We use ***will*** + **base verb** to talk about a **future plan** or **make a prediction.**
> We use ***be going to*** + **base verb** to state an **intention in the future** or **make a promise.**
> We use ***about to*** + **base verb** to **introduce something** that will happen within a very short timeframe.

1. In question 1, *will see* refers to
   a. the past. **b.** the present. **c.** the future.
2. In question 2, *are going to be at* expresses
   a. a prediction. **b.** a plan. **c.** a promise.
3. In question 3, *is taking place* refers to
   a. an event planned for the future. **b.** an event occurring now. **c.** an event that occurred in the past.
4. In question 4, *does begin* refers to
   a. a predicted event. **b.** a promised event. **c.** a scheduled event.
5. In question 5, *are about to* refers to what the students
   a. want to do. **b.** promise to do. **c.** are ready to do.

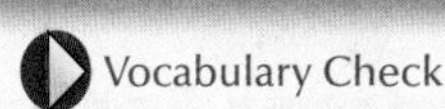

Reading

A WARM-UP Imagine that your school or university is holding an art event. Who are they going to invite? What are they going to display in the exhibits? What themes could the exhibits have?

B PREDICTING Read the title of the story from a university art department's website. What do you think the story will be about? Then read the whole story and check your answer.

University Announcements: Great Forgeries and Restorations in Upcoming Exhibits

For the first time in its history, the City Museum is about to exhibit the world's greatest forgeries and restorations. The exhibition will run from March 10 through November 15. Visitors will be able to play detective while viewing a unique show that will combine science and art. The show includes about 60 "fake" paintings, drawings, and sculptures by forgers of famous masters, such as van Gogh, Botticelli, Leonardo da Vinci, and Vermeer.

The museum will also display discoveries by one of the world's most famous art detectives. These paintings will raise awareness about fraud. The police's Art Crime Investigation Unit is going to display some of their investigative tools and techniques for detecting art forgeries. Art Detective Mike LaMonte will be at the museum this Saturday to give a free gallery talk. Mr. LaMonte is currently working on the restoration of a painting for the university's Art Department.

Jack Ames, an art crimes detective from the local unit says: "Museum visitors are about to see the best forgeries in the world. We're going to use this exhibit to warn collectors of the fakes and forgeries in the art world. The paintings are going to be both surprising and shocking to the viewers."

According to the exhibition's curator, Mary Johnson, "This is a great opportunity. Visitors will view forgeries that are usually impossible to distinguish with the naked eye—you will get to play detective with the actual tools experts use for inspection and detection."

"I'm working at the exhibit on opening day," says art restoration intern, Jenny Bloom. "This is going to be a chance for me to show visitors the kind of artwork I'll encounter some day. I'll be learning a lot about my future profession, as well as forgery and its detection. I'm about to graduate this spring, so this is really exciting for me. I'm restoring a painting as part of my senior project. I'm going to be presenting my work to different art experts as soon as it's finished."

In addition to the exhibit, a panel of leading detectives and art restoration experts will discuss the world of art forgery this Friday in the museum's lecture hall. The lecture begins at 7:00 P.M. Admission for students is $10 with a valid university ID.

C UNDERSTANDING FACTS AND DETAILS Write *T* for the true statements and *F* for the false statements.

_____ **1.** Some of the works at the exhibit are fakes.
_____ **2.** For safety reasons, visitors will not be allowed to inspect works closely.
_____ **3.** The exhibition combines artwork and detective work.
_____ **4.** Some forgeries will require the use of special instruments to distinguish them from the originals.
_____ **5.** Jenny Bloom encountered forgeries in the past.

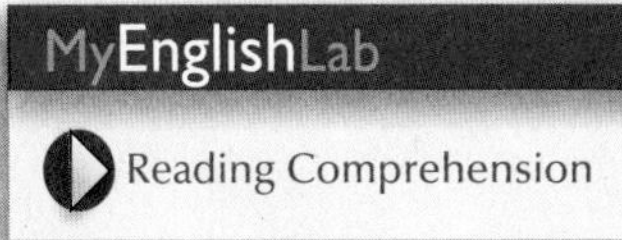

Grammar Focus 1 Future: *Will* and *be going to*

Examples	Language notes
(1) The exhibition **will run** from March until November. The local police's Art Crime Investigation Unit **is going to display** some of their investigative tools and techniques.	Use ***will*** or ***be going to*** for **future** events, states, or actions. To form the future, we use: *will* + base form of the verb *be going to* + base form of the verb Contractions with subject pronouns and *will* or *be going to* are common, especially in spoken English.
(2) This **is going to** be a chance for me to show visitors the kind of artwork I'**ll encounter** some day. This **will be** a chance for me to show visitors the kind of artwork I'**m going to** encounter some day.	Use *will* or *be going to* to make predictions.
(3) Everyone on campus is talking about the exhibit. We'**re going to** have many visitors.	Use *be going to* (not *will*) when a present situation leads us to make a prediction.
(4) The museum **will also display** discoveries by one of the world's most famous art detectives. The museum **is going to welcome** a panel of experts to speak about forgeries. The detective said, "We **will solve** this crime. That's a promise!"	Use *will* or *be going to* to make promises or plans or to state intentions.
(5) Is the lecture on Friday? I think I'**ll attend**.	Use *will* (not *be going to*) when we decide on an action while we are speaking.
(6) The lecture is on Friday at 7:00 P.M. **Will** you **go** with me?	Use *will* for invitations.
(7) Visitors **will not be able to distinguish** the forgeries with the naked eye. I **won't be** at the exhibition.	In **negative statements**, *will not* often contracts to *won't*, especially in spoken English.
(8) The museum **isn't going to** display original works by van Gogh.	Forms of *be* + *not* often contract, especially in spoken English.

Negative statements	*Wh-* questions
The museum **is not going to display** original works by van Gogh. [intention] Could we invite the artist to speak at the exhibit? —He **won't attend** because he doesn't like to be the center of attention. [refusal]	What **will** you **do** after graduation? How **are** you **going to find** a job?
***Yes / No* questions**	**Short answers**
Will we **meet** at the entrance? **Are** we **going to meet** at the entrance?	Yes, we **will**. / No, we **won't**. Yes, we **are**. / No, we **aren't**.

Grammar Practice

A Mary Johnson, the exhibition's curator and event organizer, is speaking to Nick Rossi, an art expert. Complete the statements with the letter of the correct statement.

a. "I'm going to list your name in the brochure as our special guest."
b. "I won't tell anyone."
c. "The audience will find your past and present work fascinating."
d. "Will you join the panel?"
e. "Maybe the audience won't like seeing a former criminal sitting on a panel."

1. [invitation] Mary Johnson wants Nick Rossi to speak at the lecture on Friday. She asks, ______.
2. [prediction] Mr. Rossi doesn't accept the invitation immediately. He is unsure. He has worked hard in order to gain respect and trust as an art expert, but it wasn't easy because he spent a number of years as a forger. In the past, he made good money selling his fake paintings. He comments, ______.
3. [prediction] Ms. Johnson wants to erase his doubts and says, ______.
4. [promise] Mr. Rossi is ready to accept Ms. Johnson's invitation, but he has one more worry. He explains that he gets nervous in front of large crowds. "I'm okay when I speak, but right before I go on stage, I get a bad case of the hiccups. I need a minute or two to calm myself." Ms. Johnson laughs and says, ______.
5. [plan] Mr. Rossi finally agrees to speak on Friday, and Ms. Johnson is very happy to include him. She says, ______.

B Complete the conversation between Jenny Bloom, the art restoration intern, and her roommate, Pauline. Use the verbs in parentheses.

JENNY: I'm so excited about the exhibit. Tomorrow is the opening day. I **1.** ______________ (be going to / arrive) early to help Ms. Johnson finish setting up the displays.

PAULINE: **2.** ______________ you ______________ (be going to / work) the whole evening or **3.** ______________ you ______________ (will / get) some time to enjoy the exhibit? I hope you **4.** ______________ (will not / stand) at the door handing out brochures all night.

JENNY: I **5.** ______________ (be going to / be) busy most of the evening, but I think Ms. Johnson **6.** ______________ (will / let) me attend part of the lecture. Actually, it's really wonderful that I **7.** ______________ (will / be able to) combine work and pleasure. Because I'm one of the workers, I **8.** ______________ (will / probably encounter) people who normally wouldn't notice me!

PAULINE: Who do you hope to meet?

JENNY: Maybe some of the art restoration experts. At the lecture, they **9.** ______________ (will / talk) about different works they restore and artwork they're asked to inspect. And there's Mike LaMonte. He's an art detective and an expert in distinguishing forgeries. He **10.** ______________ (be going to / give) a talk at the gallery on Saturday. . . . Hey! I don't have to work on Saturday. **11.** ______________ you ______________ (will / go) to the detective's talk with me?

PAULINE: Sure. I'd love to.

Grammar Focus 2 Future progressive

Examples	Language notes
(1) The tour guide said, "We'**ll be walking** through the gallery to view the forgeries." After graduation, I'**m going to be working** under the museum director.	To form the **future progressive**, use: *will* + *be* + present participle *be going to* + *be* + present participle Contractions with subject pronouns and *will* or *be* are common, especially in spoken English.
(2) I'**m going to be attending** a lecture tonight, so my cell phone won't be on. I'**ll be attending** a lecture tonight, so my cell phone won't be on.	We use the **future progressive** to talk about actions or events that will be in progress at a specific time in the future. Often, there is little difference in meaning between *will be* + present participle and *be going to* + present participle.
(3) Nick Rossi **will be joining** the panel.	We use *will be* + present participle in more formal statements to describe a course of action that will most likely occur in the future.
(4) Three panelists **are going to be speaking** at the event.	We usually use *be going to* + *be* + present participle to express future plans.
(5) We **will be serving** refreshments in the lobby while the discussion is in session. "They'**re going to be serving** some food and drinks later," I told my friend.	We usually use *will be* + present participle to describe an action that will be in progress at a future point in time. However, in spoken English this form is interchangeable with *be going to* + *be* + present participle.
(6) I'**m going to be presenting** my work to different art experts as soon as **it's** finished.	We do not use the future and future progressive tenses in time clauses beginning with words such as *as soon as, while, when, after,* and *before.* When we have a future tense in the main clause, use the simple present or present progressive in the time clause.
(7) The panel **won't be taking** any questions during the lecture.	In **negative statements**, *will not* often contracts to *won't*, especially in spoken English.
(8) Detective LaMonte **isn't going to be joining** the panel on Friday.	Forms of *be* + *not* often contract, especially in spoken English.
(9) **Will** you **be taking** questions after the lecture?	We use future progressive **questions** with *will* for polite inquiries and requests.

Negative statements	*Wh-* questions
I'**m not going to be working** at the museum that night. I **won't be working** when the exhibition takes place.	**Where will** the panel **be meeting** before the lecture? **What** time are they **going to be meeting**?
***Yes / No* questions**	**Short answers**
Are you **going to be working** with Mary Johnson at the museum?	Yes, we **will**. / No, we **won't**. Yes, I **am**. / No, I'**m not**.

Grammar Practice

A Write polite questions in the future progressive. Use the subjects and verbs in parentheses with *be going to* or *will be.*

1. Excuse me, Professor. When *will you be holding* (you / hold) office hours this week?
2. ________________ (we / discuss) our reports on art restoration this week?
3. Is it true? ________________ (Nick Rossi / join) the panel at Friday's lecture?
4. ________________ (you / attend) the exhibit on Saturday, too, Professor?
5. ________________ (who / speak) on Saturday? Another art detective?

6. Do we have to attend the exhibit Friday? ________________ (we / write) a report about the exhibit?
7. ________________ (you / combine) the grades from our tests and papers for a final grade?
8. I'm sorry. Just one more question, please. ________________ (you / give) us another oral exam?

B Look at Mary Johnson's schedule for Friday, the opening day of the art exhibition. Answer the questions about her schedule in complete sentences.

9:00 A.M.	Call university's food services to confirm food and drinks for the exhibit
9:30 A.M.	Call Mike LaMonte to confirm Saturday's talk at gallery
10:00 A.M.	Meet with tech team to inspect equipment for the lecture
11:00 A.M.	Talk with campus security

12:00 P.M.	Lunch with Jack Ames, Tic-Toc Café
2:00 P.M.	Meet student helpers at exhibit, check all the displays
5:00 P.M.	Dinner with Nick Rossi
6:00 P.M.	Open exhibit
6:30 P.M.	Make welcome speech
7:00 P.M.	Lecture with panelists
9:00 P.M.	Meet with campus security to close exhibit

1. Will Ms. Johnson be speaking to Mike LaMonte at 9:15 A.M.?
   No, she won't be speaking to Mike LaMonte at 9:15. She'll be speaking with the university's food services to confirm food and drinks for the exhibit.
2. Who will be inspecting the equipment on Friday morning?
   ____
3. What will Ms. Johnson be doing at 11:20 A.M.?
   ____
4. Where will Ms. Johnson be meeting Jack Ames for lunch?
   ____
5. After Ms. Johnson has lunch with Jack Ames, who is she going to be meeting?
   ____
6. What will the student helpers be doing at 2:30 P.M.?
   ____
7. What will Ms. Johnson be doing before she opens the exhibit?
   ____
8. When will the doors to the exhibit be opening?
   ____
9. What will Ms. Johnson be doing at 6:35 P.M.?
   ____
10. Why will Ms. Johnson be meeting campus security at 9:00 P.M.?
   ____

Grammar Focus 3 Present forms with future meaning

Examples	Language notes
(1) I'**m working at** the exhibit on opening day.	Use the **present progressive** to talk about future plans and intentions. ***Note***: Remember that we use *will* when we decide on an action while we are speaking.
(2) I'**m going to leave** right after the lecture.	Use the present progressive or *be going to* for decisions already made.
(3) The speakers **aren't taking** any questions during the lecture.	We often contract forms of *be* + *not*, especially in spoken English.
(4) The lecture **begins** at 7:00 PM.	Use the **simple present** to talk about events scheduled in the future, such as events on a timetable or program.
(5) Once the lecture **starts**, each panelist will have 15 minutes to speak. Each panelist will have 15 minutes to speak once the lecture **starts**.	Use the **simple present** or **present progressive** in a time clause if a future form is used in the main clause. Some examples of time clauses include: *when, after, as soon as, until, while, once.*
(6) The City Museum **is about to exhibit** the world's greatest forgeries and restorations. (7) I'm just about to finish.	Use ***be about to*** (with the simple present form of *be*) + the base form of the verb to describe an action someone is ready to do in the immediate future. In spoken English we often use *just* to emphasize how soon the action will take place.

Grammar Practice

A Mary Johnson, the exhibition's curator and event organizer, is talking on her cell phone with Jack Ames, a friend and an art detective. Complete the conversation with the letters of the correct sentences.

a. You're coming to the lecture this evening, right?
b. As soon as I finish the welcome speech, I'll give her a personal tour.
c. I'm bringing my daughter along.
d. I'm just about to leave.
e. After she sees everything tonight, I won't be surprised if she becomes an art detective like you.
f. She's about to graduate high school, you know, and she plans to study art in college.
g. I'm hanging up now.
h. I know the exhibit opens tonight.

MARY: I'm so sorry, Jack. I'm running a little late.

JACK: It seems like you're busy on campus today **1.** _____ Do you want to cancel our lunch?

MARY: Not at all. **2.** _____ Do you mind waiting for me? The café is only a few minutes from here.

JACK: I'm in no rush, so I don't mind waiting.

MARY: **3.** _____

JACK: Of course. **4.** _____

MARY: Lydia?

JACK: Yes. **5.** _____

MARY: I'm sure she'll love the exhibit! **6.** _____

JACK: Thanks, Mary. Lydia understands my job, but tonight is a special opportunity. She'll encounter very well-done forgeries and get the chance to inspect them with tools that I use so often in my work.

MARY: **7.** _____ Then you two can work together fighting art crimes and distinguishing forgeries! . . . Aha! I'm here already, and I see you! **8.** _____

B Circle the best words to complete each conversation.

1. LYDIA: Dad, **is Ms. Johnson really giving / does Ms. Johnson really give** me a personal tour at the exhibit tonight? I can't wait!

JACK AMES: Yes. She promised. **She's about to make / She'll make** a short welcome speech at 6:30, and then she'll be free until the lecture at 7:00.

LYDIA: I'm so happy **you take me / you're taking** me to the exhibit. You know, Dad, maybe I'll work as an intern at the museum while **I study / I'm going to study** at the university.

2. VISITOR: The lecture **is beginning / begins** at 7:00. Is that right? Where will that be?

JENNY BLOOM: Yes, sir. 7:00. Go down this hall and **you'll see / you see** the auditorium on your right.

VISITOR: Will we have the chance to meet the speakers once the lecture **is over / will be over**?

JENNY BLOOM: Yes, sir. The guest speakers will stay until the exhibit **closes / will close.**

3. STUDENT A: Look at this painting. It looks just like van Gogh's "The Starry Night."

STUDENT B: Well, almost. Try using this instrument to inspect the brushstrokes. **You'll see / You're seeing** the difference.

STUDENT A: Let me look. Hmmm. You're right. Amazing! Hey, **are you coming back / do you come back** here tomorrow?

STUDENT B: **Is there / Is there about to be** another special event tomorrow?

STUDENT A: Yes. Mike LaMonte is giving a talk. Maybe **he's going to tell / he tells** us about the painting he's restoring for the university.

4. MARY JOHNSON: **I'm about to open / I open** the doors to the auditorium. Are you ready?

NICK ROSSI: Honestly? No. I still have the hiccups, and I'm really nervous! **You sit / You're sitting** on stage with us, right?

MARY: Calm down, Nick. Yes, **I'll be / I am** on stage. You're going to be fine. I'll introduce everyone and invite Professor Stevens to speak first. You'll have plenty of time to stop hiccupping before you **make / you'll make** your presentation. Relax.

Now choose one of the conversations and role-play with a partner.

Speaking

A Look at the schedule for Friday and the invitation.

You have a busy day Friday, but you also want to go to the art opening. Rearrange your schedule so that you'll be able to attend. Take notes. Remember: Your computer is at the computer repair shop. How will you let Amy know you'll be attending?

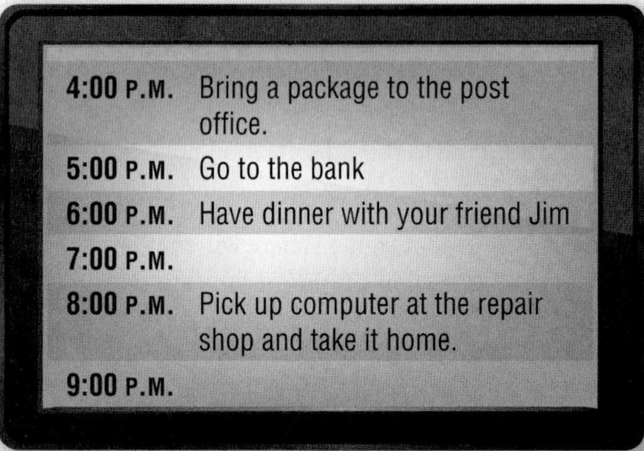

4:00 P.M.	Bring a package to the post office.
5:00 P.M.	Go to the bank
6:00 P.M.	Have dinner with your friend Jim
7:00 P.M.	
8:00 P.M.	Pick up computer at the repair shop and take it home.
9:00 P.M.	

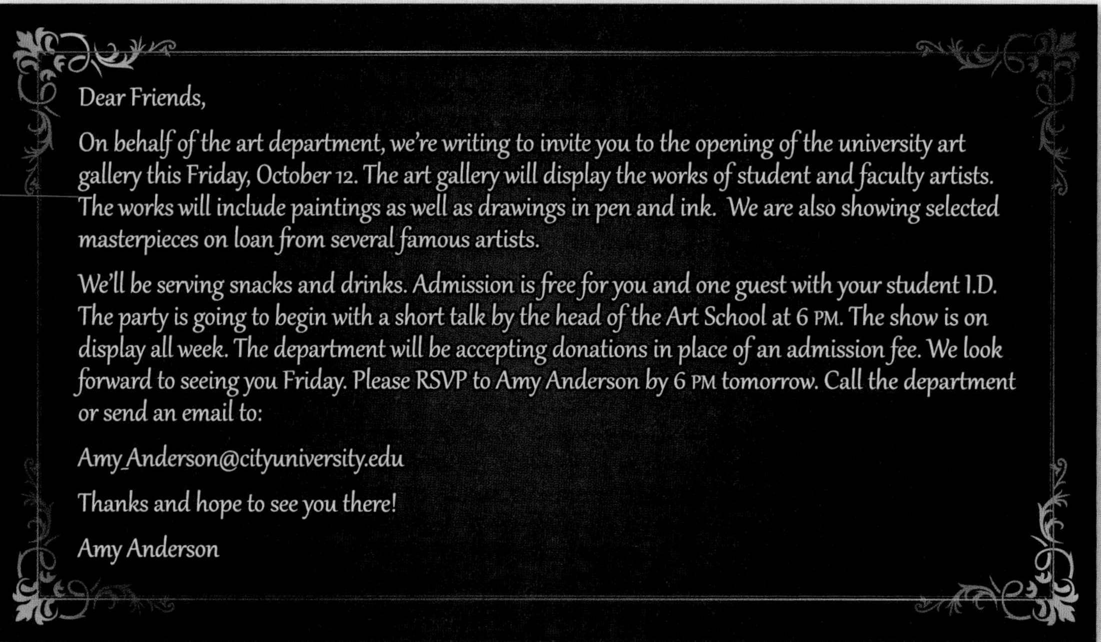

Dear Friends,

On behalf of the art department, we're writing to invite you to the opening of the university art gallery this Friday, October 12. The art gallery will display the works of student and faculty artists. The works will include paintings as well as drawings in pen and ink. We are also showing selected masterpieces on loan from several famous artists.

We'll be serving snacks and drinks. Admission is free for you and one guest with your student I.D. The party is going to begin with a short talk by the head of the Art School at 6 PM. The show is on display all week. The department will be accepting donations in place of an admission fee. We look forward to seeing you Friday. Please RSVP to Amy Anderson by 6 PM tomorrow. Call the department or send an email to:

Amy_Anderson@cityuniversity.edu

Thanks and hope to see you there!

Amy Anderson

B Talk to a group about your plans. Use the model. Discuss another time when you had to change plans because you were busy.

OK. I will call Amy and tell her that I'm going to change my plans.
First, I'll let her know what time I'm going to get there.
Then, I'll make sure I get to the post office before it closes.

MyEnglishLab

Listen for it.

Listening

A UNDERSTANDING MAIN IDEAS Listen to a reporter interview an art expert. What is the interview mainly about? Choose the best answer.

a. the process of a restoration **b.** how to use instruments in a restoration lab **c.** an art restorer's job

B UNDERSTANDING DETAILS Listen again. Number the steps in the correct order (1 to 7).

_____ **a.** Mr. Petersen lowers the eyepiece on the microscope.
_____ **b.** The X-ray spectrometer sees through layers of paint.
_____ **c.** The restorer adjusts the light on the microscope.
_____ **d.** The microscope focuses on the brushstrokes of the artist.
_____ **e.** You see the high-resolution photograph.
_____ **f.** The expert can detect if the painting is a fraud.
_____ **g.** The restorer uses the special camera to take a picture.

C AFTER LISTENING Imagine you bought a painting and have a meeting with an art expert. What questions would you ask?

Writing

A Talk to a partner about your favorite artists and styles of art. What do you like to see when you go to a museum or gallery? Do you like paintings, sculpture? Do you prefer modern art or earlier styles? Why?

B You just got an internship at your favorite art museum. One of your first projects is to arrange an exhibition. Plan the exhibition. Whose work will you display? What will be the theme of the exhibition? Create an invitation for the upcoming exhibit. Fill out the postcard with the dates, times, and what the guests will see at this show.

Exhibition date: ____________________

Where: ____________________

You are invited to an art exhibition.

What you will see:

____

____

____

C Exchange invitations with a partner. What additional information will you include to attract people to the exhibition? For example, some museums have music or food or other special events at exhibitions.

MyEnglishLab

Diagnostic Test

Grammar Summary

We use the **simple present** and the **present progressive** to talk about present events, states, or actions.

Verb forms	Notes	Examples
Use the **simple present**	for facts and general truths.	There **are** many forms of art.
	for existing states or conditions.	The painting **is** badly damaged.
	for habitual actions and regularly occurring events.	The museum **holds** an exhibition of student artwork every spring.
	to describe the plot of a movie or a book, or narrate a story.	The art thief **opens** the door, **listens** closely, and **determines** that the exhibit hall is empty.
Use the **present progressive**	to describe actions or events occurring now.	I am happy that he **is restoring** the painting to its original beauty. [**am** = state] [**is restoring** = action in progress]
	in time clauses with *when, while* to talk about a habitual action in progress.	He likes to listen to music when **he's working** on the painting.

We use both **future** and **present** tenses to talk about the future.

Verb forms	Notes	Examples
Use ***will***, ***be going to***, or the **present progressive**	to talk about future events, states, or actions.	Lydia **will graduate / is going to graduate / is graduating** from high school in May.
	to talk about future plans or state intentions. However, we use *will* when we decide on an action while we are speaking.	What **are** you **going to study** at the university? —I'm not sure. Maybe I'**ll take** an art history course.
Use ***will*** or ***be going to***	to make predictions, promises, or state intentions. However, we use *be going to* when a present situation leads us to a prediction.	The exhibit **will be** a great success!
Use ***will***	for invitations.	**Will** you **go** to the museum with me on Saturday?
Use the **future progressive**	to describe an event or action that will be in progress at a specific point in the future. To form the future progressive, use *will* or *be going to* and then *be* + present participle.	On Saturday the art students **are going to be helping / will be helping** at the museum all afternoon.
	with *will* to form polite questions (requests or inquiries).	**Will** you **be giving** any other lectures this year?
Do <u>not</u> use the **future** or **future progressive**	in time clauses if a future tense is used in the main clause.	**As soon as** the lecture **ends**, **I'm going to ask** Mr. Rossi a question.
Use the **simple present**	to talk about events scheduled in the future.	The talk by Mike LaMonte **is** on Saturday at 2:00 P.M.
Use ***be about to***	in the simple present to describe an action someone is ready to do in the immediate future.	The lecture **is about to** begin. Hurry! Let's find seats.

Self-Assessment

A (6 points) Complete the conversations with the correct form of the simple present, present progressive, or *be going to* and the verbs in parentheses.

A: 1. ____________ you ____________ (see) the criminal on the security camera?

B: Yes. We 2. ____________ (catch) him before he leaves the museum.

A: When 3. ____________ you ____________ (start) your internship?

B: Right after I 4. ____________ (graduate) from school.

A: I 5. ____________ (hang) this painting in the game room.

B: Why move it? I 6. ____________ (like) it better here in the living room.

B (5 points) Complete the sentences with the correct forms of *be going to, be about to,* or *will.*

1. What ____________ he ____________ to do tomorrow? Do you know his plans?
2. Please silence your cell phones. The lecture ____________ begin.
3. The gallery ____________ show the work of Matisse and Monet today.
4. The art department ____________ show the students' work until next Thursday.
5. The art detective just found the forger's thumbprint. He ____________ prove that the painting is a fake.

C (4 points) Correct the error in each statement.

1. The art detective is wanting to discuss the forgery case with the police.
2. She is about to starting her internship at the museum next week.
3. Are you familiar with the X-ray spectrometry instrument? It is helping the experts detect forgeries.
4. The museum displays the exhibit from March until December.

D (5 points) Circle the correct form of the verb in the present, present progressive, or future progressive.

1. Photography is an activity that **combines / is combining** many skills.
2. Criminals hope that their forgeries **are deceiving / will deceive** experts.
3. The gallery **will be displaying / displays** my work next month.
4. As a future art detective, I'm certain that I **am going to encounter / encounter** a few forgeries.
5. Over the next few months, the museum **is restoring / is going to be restoring** that painting.

Unit Project: Exhibition brochure

Work in a group. You are interns in a museum's restoration and authentication department. Your task is to create a brochure about a special exhibition to encourage people to visit the museum. Follow these steps.

1. As a group, discuss your favorite museums in your hometowns. Look at all of the websites, and choose one museum for your brochure.
2. Go to the museum's website and find an exhibit to feature in your brochure. You may want to use some images and descriptions from the museum exhibit.
3. Create a brochure describing the exhibit as well as other interesting things at the museum. Look at the model.

This original painting is famous for its mysterious background and the woman's half-smile.

This is a student's copy of the *Mona Lisa*. In this painting, the angle of her face and her hair are different. The color of her gown is brighter red and the mountains are not visible.

Come to City Museum for an Exhibition on Famous Forgeries!

Museum times:

The museum will be open Tuesdays through Thursdays 10 A.M. to 5 P.M., Fridays 10 A.M. to 7 P.M., and Saturdays and Sundays 10 A.M. to 6 P.M. The museum is closed on Mondays.

Join us for an evening of interesting discussion! Art expert Nick Rossi and Detective Mike LaMonte will be leading gallery talks.

You're going to be viewing twelve famous masterpieces next to works by expert forgers and masters of art reproduction.

Your challenge is: Can you tell the difference?

After the show there will be a reception. You'll be able to talk to the art experts and detectives in a question and answer session.

B Prepare a presentation of your brochure for the museum's restoration department. Follow the steps. Use the grammar from the unit in your presentation.

1. Deliver your presentation. Ask your classmates if they have any questions.
2. After all the groups have presented, discuss the exhibit. What kinds of challenges or questions would you ask visitors to get them to come to the exhibit? Would you include forgeries and authentic paintings? If so, which ones?

UNIT 2

Life in Pictures

OUTCOMES

After completing this unit, I will be able to use these grammar points.

CHAPTER 3

Grammar Focus 1
Simple past and past progessive

Grammar Focus 2
Used to

CHAPTER 4

Grammar Focus 1
Nouns: Proper, common, count, and noncount

Grammar Focus 2
Subject–verb agreement

MyEnglishLab

 What do you know?

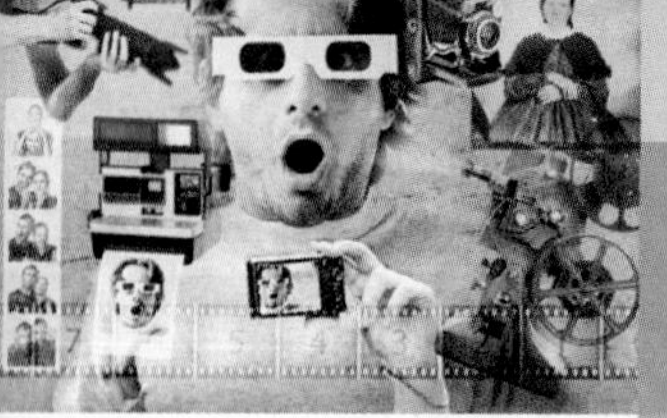

CHAPTER 3 Get the Picture!

Getting Started

A Read the information and talk to a partner. What do people in your country say when they are about to take a picture? What did photographers used to do in your country?

"Watch the birdie!" In the 19th century, portrait photographers used to use a little mechanical bird to get a child's attention when she was looking away. When a photographer was going to shoot a family portrait, he would hold up the birdie, squeeze it, and it would make a chirping sound.

"Say cheese!" Long ago, it was not common for people to smile when they were posing for a portrait. In England, people said "prunes" so their mouths would seem closed. There are many stories about why American photographers ask you to say "cheese" when they are about to snap your picture. When you say "cheese," your lips widen into a smile.

B Who took each picture? Read the statement and match the photo with its description.

_____ **1.** Margaret Bourke-White shot this close-up from a helicopter in 1952, as she was about to pass by a famous national symbol. Her photos appeared in many magazines and newspapers.

_____ **2.** In 2010, Astronaut Garrett Reisman created this photograph by pointing the camera lens at the reflection on his helmet visor.

_____ **3.** Eve Arnold took this picture while this actress was going over her lines. Arnold would often take portraits of Hollywood celebrities. She set up this shot during the filming of a movie.

_____ **4.** In 1860, James Wallace Black captured this aerial view of Boston as he was flying over it.

_____ **5.** A photographer captured this shot from one camera as he was about to use another large-format camera and cover its lens with a black cloth.

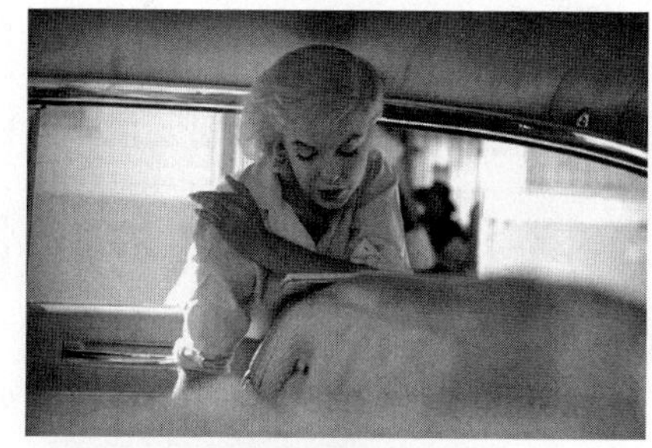
A

B

C

D

E

C Look back at Parts A and B. Complete the tasks.

1. Underline the **past form verbs** that describe a **completed action in the past.**
2. Double underline the **past progressive verbs** that describe an **action in progress at a specific time** in the past.
3. We use ***would*** and ***used to*** to describe **habitual actions** in the past. Circle them.
4. We use ***about to*** for events in the **immediate future.** Put parentheses around *about to* + verb.

MyEnglishLab

Vocabulary Check

Reading

A WARM-UP What do you think the people in the picture are about to do? How many generations of family members do you think are in the shot? Did you, or someone in your family, take "family reunion" pictures? What would you do at a family reunion? Talk to a partner.

B PREDICTING What kinds of questions do interviewers usually ask? What do you think the interviewer is going to ask the photographer? Now read the interview.

PHOTO BLOG Interview with Photographer Enrique Balaban

In 1975, Enrique Balaban's grandparents gave him a 35-mm camera for his twelfth birthday. At 15, he entered a photography contest and won first place. His recent project, *Generations*, is now on display in his hometown—Bronx, New York.

Did you always want to be a photographer?

EB: As soon as I got that first camera, I knew I wanted to be a photographer. My dad had an old "Brownie Hawkeye" camera—the kind that has the little flashbulb on the top. When he wasn't looking, I used to pretend I was snapping photos.

Tell me about the first picture you took.

EB: When I was 13, I took the camera to school. I was going to take pictures of everything. I remember that I shot pictures of everyone everywhere: in the cafeteria when we were eating our lunch, just before the school doors opened, or while we were running around on the playground. I didn't care what I was shooting . . . I just kept taking shots. My first photo was of my best friend. He was about to eat a plate of peas. And the way he was concentrating on getting each pea on his fork captivated me. I set up the shot at the table across from him.

Where did you have your first photography show?

EB: My first professional show took place in 1990, in New York. After I started to develop film, I realized that my images captured people in a moment when they were doing something interesting. I snapped things that were happening during the day. I explored the streets and took pictures of ordinary people. I wanted to depict everyday life in my show.

What is your current show about?

EB: Recently, I went to Puerto Rico to visit my grandparents. I was going to take their portrait and then go back to New York. But then, I got an idea to travel the world and create a series of shots of children and their grandparents—and I think I captured that essence of time really well. I went to Japan and photographed the oldest living man and his great-great-grandchildren. I tried to contrast the timeless beauty of youth and old age. That's what *Generations* is about.

C Read the sentences from the text and choose the correct meaning of the boldfaced words.

1. I **set up** the shot at the table across from him.
   a. posed **b.** planned **c.** fooled
2. I didn't care what I **was shooting**.
   a. taking pictures of **b.** throwing **c.** firing at
3. I **was going to take their portrait** and then go back to New York.
   a. tried to steal their picture **b.** planned to take their picture **c.** visited in order to paint their image
4. My images **captured** people in a moment when they were doing something interesting.
   a. trapped **b.** revealed **c.** caught
5. I **snapped** things that were happening during the day.
   a. bit **b.** took photos of **c.** broke

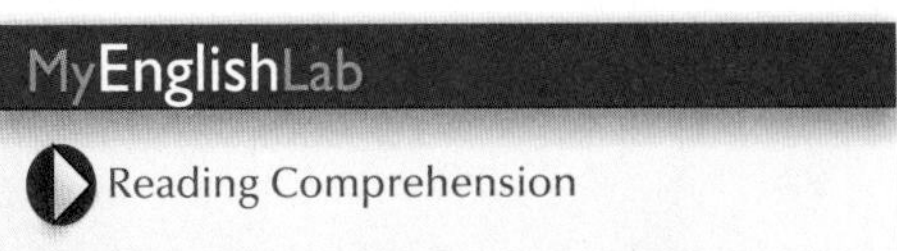

Grammar Focus 1 Simple past and past progressive

Examples	Language notes
(1) In 1975, Enrique Balaban's grandparents **gave** him a 35-mm camera for his twelfth birthday.	Use the **simple past** for actions or events that began and ended at a specific time in the past.
(2) As soon as I **got** that first camera, I knew I **wanted** to be a photographer.	Simple past verbs can be **regular** or **irregular**.
(3) After I **started** to develop film, I **realized** that my images captured people in a moment when they were doing something interesting.	**Adverbs of time**, such as *after, before, as soon as*, and *when*, help show the sequence of two completed actions or events in the past.
(4) He **was about to eat** a plate of peas.	Use *be about to* with a simple past form of *be* + the base form of a verb to describe an action someone was ready to do in the immediate future from a past point of view.
(5) I snapped things that **were happening** during the day.	Use the **past progressive** for actions that were in progress for a period of time in the past or that were interrupted by another action or event.
(6) **While** he **was looking** at his food, I **was setting up** my shot. **While** other children **played** games, I **studied** photography.	Use the adverb of time *while* + the past progressive to show two actions in progress at the same time in the past. Use the past progressive in both the main clause and the adverb clause. We may also use the simple past in both clauses to express actions performed at the same time within a finished period of time.
(7) He **was eating** when I **took** his picture. I **took** his picture while **he was eating**.	Use the **simple past and the past progressive together** in one sentence to describe how one action began earlier and was still happening when the second one occurred. Use *when* with the simple past and *while* with the past progressive. The action in the past progressive is the one that began first.
(8) I **was going to take** their portrait and then go back to New York. *(But then my plans changed so I didn't.)*	Do not confuse *was / were going to* with the past progressive. Use *was / were going to* + the base form of a verb to discuss future plans that changed or did not occur from a past perspective.

Negative statements	*Wh-* questions
I **didn't care**.	Where **did** you **have** your first photography show?
He **wasn't looking**.	What **were** the other children **doing** on the playground?
Yes / No questions	Short answers
Did you always **want** to be a photographer?	Yes, I **did**. / No, I **didn't**.
Were you **taking** pictures?	Yes, I **was**. / No, I **wasn't**.

See Appendix B on page A-1 for a list of irregular verbs and their past forms.

Grammar Practice

A Enrique Balaban is describing some of his favorite photographs. Complete the descriptions with the simple past forms of the verbs in the box.

be	begin	make	spend	stand	take

"I **1.** ______________ this shot when I **2.** ______________ 16. I **3.** ______________ that summer with my grandparents, and on that particular day I **4.** ______________ to explore their neighborhood. Everyone **5.** ______________ me feel welcome, and I was captivated by their friendliness. You can see a few of the people in this photograph. I **6.** ______________ at a distance to take this shot, but you can still feel their warmth and openness."

catch	forget	leave	rise	see	set up

"I **7.** ______________ my home early in the morning to get this shot. I **8.** ______________ my camera just before the sun **9.** ______________. When I **10.** ______________ the beauty of the colors as they appeared in the sky, I almost **11.** ______________ to start shooting. The tall buildings along the city skyline **12.** ______________ the sunlight in such an amazing way.

go	hide	know	light	put	sing

"This shot depicts New York as I know it: a city that never sleeps. I **13.** ______________ I could catch some interesting scenes of city life after midnight, so I **14.** ______________ walking one evening. Along the way, I captured this . . . some restaurant workers on break. Only one lamp **15.** ______________ the alley, but you can still see what was taking place. While some **16.** ______________ and clapped, others danced. They **17.** ______________ all their worries aside and enjoyed the moment. I **18.** ______________ in the shadows to catch them in action."

B Read the article about two professional photographers and correct the past form errors. Look at the example. There are nine more errors.

Deborah: "I ~~was becoming~~ *became* a wedding photographer right after my own wedding. We were hiring a photographer to shoot our ceremony and reception, but sadly he failed to capture many of the special moments of the most wonderful day of my life. He was catching us at odd moments. He took one photo while I was sneezing, and in another my parents argued about something! When I saw the photos, I was saying to myself, "I could take better pictures!" And now I do. I help other couples remember their most special moments in photographs."

Marcel: "I was beginning to take portrait photographs as a boy. My grandparents were buying me my first camera when I was 13. I didn't know much at first, but I was quickly learning. I liked to take pictures of my family. Friends and relatives started asking me to take family portraits. By the time I was 18, I was having a large collection of portraits. I was showing them to a photographer in town, and he invited me to work for him. After I learned all I could from him, I decided to open my own shop."

Grammar Focus 2 *Used to*

Examples	Language notes
(1) I **used to pretend** I was snapping photos.	Use ***used to*** + the base form of a verb to describe habitual actions or repeated events or situations in the past that are no longer true in the present.
(2) In my early years, I **would spend** (*also:* **I'd spend**) a lot of time on the city streets with my camera. I **used to be** interested in landscapes. [state] ***Incorrect:*** I ~~would be~~ interested in landscapes. My dad **used to have** a "Brownie Hawkeye" camera. [possession] ***Incorrect:*** My dad ~~would have~~ a "Brownie Hawkeye" camera. I **used to live** in Brooklyn as a boy. [location] ***Incorrect:*** I ~~would~~ live in Brooklyn as a boy.	We can also use ***would*** + the **base form of a verb** for habitual actions or repeated events in the past. Often, we can use either *used to* or *would*, but there are differences. • *Would* + the base form of a verb does not necessarily mean that an action or event no longer happens. It may continue in the present. • We cannot use *would* with stative verbs to describe a past state, possession, or location.
(3) I **used to set up** shots very carefully, but now I'm more spontaneous. I **used to plan** more, but I no longer need as much time to prepare for a shot.	**Adverbs of time** that refer to the present, such as *now* and *no longer*, help us to emphasize the contrast between *then* and *now*.
(4) Enrique **didn't used to take** many close-up shots. He **never used to do** that.	*Used to* is less common in **negative statements** than affirmative statements. Also, in conversation we use *never used to* more often than *didn't use to*. Do not use *would* in the negative to describe habitual actions that no longer occur in the present.
(5) **Did** you **used to take** more pictures of landscapes and skylines? —Yes, I did. / No, I didn't. (= *You **used to take** more pictures of landscapes and skylines, **didn't you**?* [more common])	***Yes / no* questions** with *used to* are not very common. In conversation, we often find other ways to form a question.
(6) Do you do portrait photography? —I **used to**. I stopped a few years ago. (= *I used to do portrait photography, but I don't anymore.*)	In conversation, short answers to *yes / no* questions in the present can use *used to* with no following base verb.
(7) Oh, you only recently started coming to this studio? Where **did** you **used to develop** your film?	***Wh-* questions** with *used to* are not very common, but with enough context they occur normally in conversation.

Note: In informal, spoken English and in some texts, *did / didn't* + ***use to*** is also used.

Grammar Practice

A Enrique has been a photographer for a long time. Over the years, he has changed the way he does some things. Complete the statements with the correct forms of *used to* and the verbs in the box. Use each verb only once.

be	have	not recognize	photograph	think
feel	include	not take	spend	work

1. Enrique __used to photograph__ people from a distance, but now he prefers to take close-ups.
2. Much of his recent work captures ordinary people on the street, but in the past the subjects of his photographs ________________ close friends and family.
3. Enrique prefers to make people appear natural in his photographs, but in the past he ________________ so many candid shots.

4. Enrique __________________ in a darkroom to develop photographs, but today most of his photos are digital.
5. Because Enrique mostly makes digital prints, he no longer needs a lot of film. He __________________ a good amount of money on film.
6. Enrique __________________ more photographs in print. Now he mostly keeps photos in digital form.
7. Enrique is successful now, so he owns three cameras and a dozen lenses. At one point in the past, his equipment __________________ only one camera and two lenses.
8. He __________________ that black and white photographs limited his art, but today he likes to use black and white, especially when his subjects are children.
9. Enrique __________________ shy at gallery events, but he doesn't get nervous anymore. In fact, he enjoys talking to new people about his work.
10. In the past, people __________________ his photographs very often, but thanks to the Internet his work is now familiar to many people around the world.

Work with a partner. Discuss which sentences can use either *used to* or *would*. Not all sentences can use *would*. Why?

B You are a reporter for a photography magazine. Write questions for an interview with Enrique Balaban. Use the correct forms of *used to* and the words in parentheses.

1. Can you please talk about your first professional photography equipment? What kind of camera and lens (you / use)?
____
2. You started your career with a traditional camera, and now you work mainly with a digital one. (you / set up) your shots differently before you went digital?
____
3. Where (you / keep) your photographs before computer storage became possible?
____
4. You recently launched your own website. How did (you / share) your photographs with potential clients in the past?
____
5. You talk quite a bit about your grandfather and his influence on you. (he / work) professionally as a photographer?
____

MyEnglishLab

Listen for it.

Listening

A UNDERSTANDING MAIN IDEAS Listen to a part of a TV documentary. As you listen, check (✓) the true statements.

☐ **1.** Jacob Riis was a German photographer.
☐ **2.** Before he became a photojournalist, he used to work in a police station.
☐ **3.** Riis used to take photos when he investigated the social conditions of the area.
☐ **4.** Before the invention of flash powder, Riis used to use candles to light his shots.
☐ **5.** Jacob Riis's photographs captured how people lived in the 19th century.
☐ **6.** Jacob Riis and Lewis Hine would shoot pictures of the worst neighborhoods in New York City.
☐ **7.** Hine published images of social reformers in his 1930s book.

B UNDERSTANDING DETAILS Listen again. Answer the questions.

1. Where did Jacob Riis used to live before he lived in New York?

____

2. What did Riis used to do before he became a photojournalist?

____

3. Where would Riis sometimes sleep?

____

4. What kind of conditions were people living in when Jacob Riis and Lewis Hine took their photos?

____

5. What would photographers like Riis and Hine do to set up for a photo?

____

6. What were Riis's and Hine's subjects doing when they took their pictures?

____

C AFTER LISTENING Talk to the class about famous photographers from your country. What are some famous shots of cities or tourist sites from your country? What kinds of photos do you like to capture when you visit a different country or city?

Speaking

A Look at photographs. Do you have any old photographs of your family? What era do you think these pictures are from? What did people used to wear? Why wouldn't they smile when they were getting their picture taken? Talk to a partner.

People used to use large format cameras, and today people use digital cameras. . . .
In the 19th century, when people posed for photos, they would not smile.
When people posed for a portrait they used to stand or sit very formally.

B Work with a partner. Look back at the photographs and talk about the similarities and differences between these photos and the photos we see today. What changes happened in how photographers use cameras and technology? What did your grandparents or parents use? What do you use to take pictures?

Photographers would use large format or box cameras, and today people use digital cameras. When photographers took pictures, they used to say "Watch the birdie" . . .

Writing

MyEnglishLab

Linking Grammar to Writing

A Find a favorite photograph of yourself. You can be alone or with somebody else. Choose a photo that has a "before and after" story.

B Write a one or two paragraph description of your photo. Use the questions below as a guide.

- Who took the picture?
- How old were you in the picture?
- What were you doing in the photo?
- What were you doing just before they took the picture?
- What did you do afterwards?

This is a picture of my brother Jimmy and me in 2000. I was 8 and Jimmy was 7. We were near the basketball court in a park. We used to play there almost every day after school. Our dad came over with the camera when we were about to shoot hoops against our neighborhood friends. We had about 10 guys from the neighborhood . . . they were coming to meet us. After our dad took that picture I got the ball and threw a basket. "Take a shot" means throw a basketball and it also means take a picture. So . . . I took the shot right after my dad "took the shot!"

C Exchange descriptions with a partner. Compare your descriptions, and ask and answer additional questions.

MyEnglishLab

Diagnostic Test

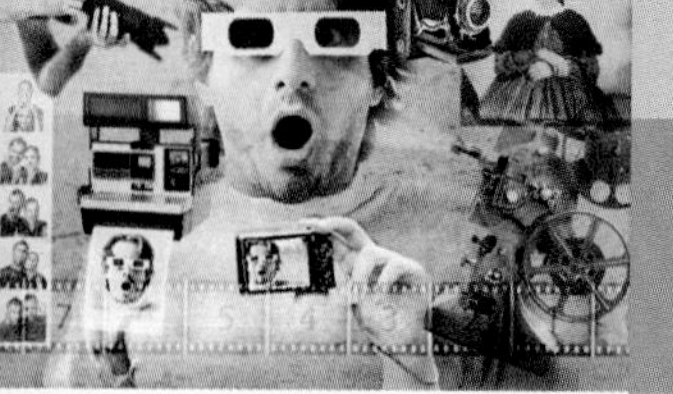

CHAPTER 4 Pictures—in Motion and Still

Getting Started

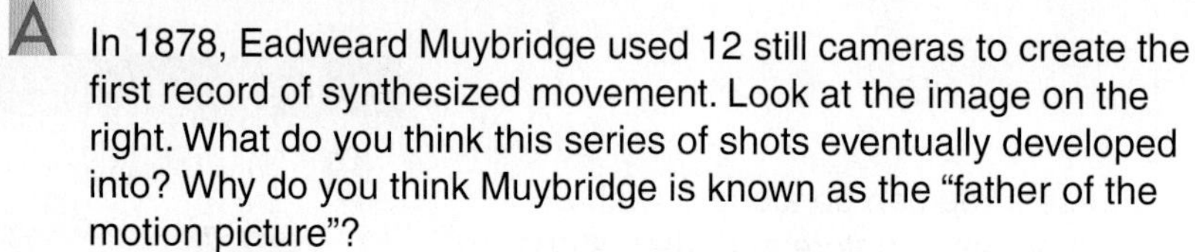

A In 1878, Eadweard Muybridge used 12 still cameras to create the first record of synthesized movement. Look at the image on the right. What do you think this series of shots eventually developed into? Why do you think Muybridge is known as the "father of the motion picture"?

B Between 1830 and 1900, inventors created various instruments for viewing images. These viewers had unusual names and were the early forms of the modern video camera. Read the descriptions and match them to the correct instruments.

A. Zoetrope

B. Zoopraxiscope

C. Kinteoscope

D. Thaumatrope

_____ **1.** This is an image attached to a round disk with strings on either side. As the disc rotates quickly around, the image appears to move.

_____ **2.** The name of this "toy" means "wheel of life." It spins quickly around like a top. When you look through vertical openings on the sides, the interior pictures seem to be in motion.

_____ **3.** This device was probably the first "movie projector." One machine projected stop-motion images through rotating glass disks to a smaller projection device. These disks rotated in quick succession to simulate movement.

_____ **4.** Tiny photographic images spin around in sequence on a cylinder. As the cylinder rotates, the angle of light gives the illusion of motion. Viewers used to use this special machine to watch a motion picture.

C A **concrete noun** refers to concrete or physical things (people, objects, or substances). An **abstract noun** refers to qualities or states. Write *C* next to the concrete nouns and *A* next to the abstract nouns.

__c__ angle	_____ glass	_____ light	_____ openings	_____ succession
_____ cylinder	_____ illusion	_____ machine	_____ picture	_____ toy
_____ device	_____ image	_____ movement	_____ projector	_____ viewer
_____ disk	_____ life	_____ movie	_____ sequence	_____ wheel

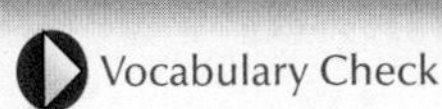

Vocabulary Check

Reading

A WARM-UP Work with a partner. Discuss these questions. When did studios release the first movie with sound? When was the first 3-D movie? What do you know about 4-D movies?

B SCANNING Scan the chronology of events in motion picture and television history. Find two events that happened 100 years apart. Then read the entire chronology.

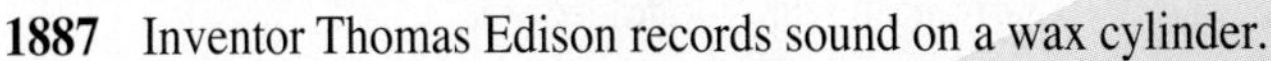

Great Events in the History of Motion Pictures and Television: What's Next?

1887 Inventor Thomas Edison records sound on a wax cylinder.

1895 The first public demonstration of motion pictures takes place in France.

1908 French director Émile Cohl creates *Fantasmagorie*, the first cartoon.

1922 An audience in L.A. enjoys the first-ever experience of 3-D movie glasses for *The Power of Love*.

1927 Warner Brothers studio releases the first movie with sound, *The Jazz Singer*.

1928 Mickey Mouse debuts in the first animated short film, *Steamboat Willie*.

1929 *On With the Show* is the first all-color full-length film with sound.

1936 The first black and white TV broadcast takes place in London.

1937 Walt Disney's company releases the first full-length animated film, *Snow White*.

1945 Nine TV stations are on the air across the United States.

1947 Audiences in the Soviet Union watch the first full-length, color 3-D film, *The Power of Love*.

1948 Americans view the *Ed Sullivan Variety Show* as it makes its debut.

1952 The *Adventures of Superman* airs as first live-action hero program on TV.

1953 TV stations broadcast programs in color; the Academy Awards show is on TV for the first time.

1960 The first presidential debates between John F. Kennedy and Richard Nixon are on TV.

1963 The Kennedy family's grief over President Kennedy's death gets worldwide media coverage.

1966 The DC comic book character *Batman* stars in his own TV show.

1969 Americans witness the Apollo 11 landing; Buzz Aldrin plants a U.S. flag on the Moon via live TV.

1977 The first VCR for VHS (Video Home System) reaches the United States.

1981 MTV airs the first music video: *Video Killed the Radio Star*.

1985 Pixar company produces the first "digital imaging processor" to create animation.

1993 Approximately 98% of all U.S. households own at least one television set.

2003 Electronics stores begin to sell the first DVD camcorder.

2005 DVDs replace VHS tapes; DVDs allow storage of hundreds of hours of video.

2008 Blu-Ray DVDs, and televisions with built-in Blu-Ray players become popular.

2010 After the release of *Avatar*, 3-D movies for 3-D High-Definition TVs arrive.

2011 The release of 4-D films allows audiences to experience special effects that give the illusion of smell, sound, touch, and movement.

C UNDERSTANDING FACTS AND DETAILS Answer the questions.

1. What did a French director show in 1908? ____________________
2. When was the first 3-D movie? ____________________
3. What did the audience wear during the first 3-D film in L.A.? ____________________
4. Who was the star of *Steamboat Willie?* ____________________
5. What was the first music video on MTV? ____________________
6. By 1993, what percentage of U.S. households owned a TV ____________________

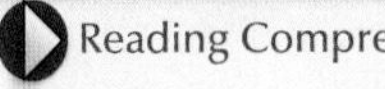

Reading Comprehension

Grammar Focus 1 Nouns: Proper, common, count, and noncount

Examples	Language notes
(1) An **audience** enjoys the first 3-D **movie**. DVDs allow **storage** of hundreds of **hours** of video.	Some nouns are **concrete**. They represent physical objects, people, or things that we experience with our senses. Some nouns are **abstract**. They represent ideas or things we cannot experience with our senses.
(2) **Edison** captures images on his first motion picture camera, the **Kinetograph**.	**Proper nouns** are names of particular people, places, or things. We write them with an initial capital letter.
(3) George Eastman invents celluloid **film** for **cameras**.	**Common nouns** are people, places, or things, but they do not begin with capital letters.
(4) Nine TV **stations** are on air across the U.S. Approximately 98% of all U.S. **households** own at least one television **set**.	Common nouns can be **count** or **noncount**. If we can count people, places, or things as separate units, we call them **count nouns**. These nouns have singular and plural forms.
(5) Digital satellite **dishes** become the most popular electronic device since the VCR. By 2005, **people** were beginning to buy more **DVDs** than VHS **tapes**.	We form the plural of most count nouns by adding *-s* / *-es*. ***Note:*** Never form a plural by adding an apostrophe + *s* (*'s*).
(6) <u>**An**</u> **audience** in Los Angeles enjoys <u>**the**</u> 3-D **film** *The Power of Love.* <u>**Those**</u> **debates** between Kennedy and Nixon aired in 1960.	We can use **indefinite articles** (*a* and *an*) and the **definite article** (*the*) before count nouns. We can also use **determiners**, such as *this, these, that, those, every, each,* and *one* to refer to specific units.
(7) The Kennedy family's **grief** over President Kennedy's death gets worldwide TV **coverage**.	**Noncount nouns** cannot be counted as separate units. These nouns do not have plural forms, but note that some noncount nouns end in *-s*. ***Examples***: *news, electronics.*
(8) The TV **coverage** <u>**was**</u> worldwide. <u>**It**</u> reached millions of homes.	Noncount nouns are generally <u>singular</u>. They require a singular verb, and we can refer back to them with singular pronouns.
(9) *Great Events in the **History** of Motion Pictures and Television: What's Next?*	Noncount nouns are also called ***mass nouns*** because they often refer to a whole group or mass rather than separate parts. For example, *history* is made up of many *events*.
(10) TV stations begin broadcasting in **(Ø) color**. Experts predict that Holographic TVs and movies will be the thing of **the future**.	We use the **zero article (Ø)** and **definite articles**, but we don't use indefinite articles immediately before noncount nouns. Also, we cannot use determiners that refer to specific units with noncount nouns, such as *this, that,* or *each*.
(11) DVDs record hundreds of <u>**hours of**</u> **video**. Film is a popular <u>**form of**</u> **entertainment**.	<u>Quantifying words and phrases</u> help to make noncount nouns countable.
(12) The **director** used several **cameras**. [count nouns] That period of **history** has not received a lot of **coverage** in **film**. During that time, Dr. Salk invented the **polio** vaccine. [noncount nouns]	Noncount nouns are generally more <u>abstract</u>, and count nouns are generally more <u>concrete</u>. However, a number of categories of noncount nouns include things that have a physical form.
(13) MTV was the first channel to show only music **videos** [count]. It aired the first music **video** [count], ***Video*** [noncount] *Killed the Radio Star,* in 1981.	Many common nouns can have a **count** or **noncount meaning**.
(14) Two thin pieces of **metal** covered the lens. (as material = noncount) It was a documentary about precious **metals**. (types = count)	The contrast between **abstract** and **concrete** often explains the difference in meaning. In other cases, the count meaning refers to different types of that thing.

See Appendix C on page A-4 to review spelling rules for regular plural nouns.
See Appendix D on page A-4 for a list of irregular plural nouns.
See Appendix E on page A-5 for a list of categories of noncount nouns with examples, including nouns with count and noncount meanings.

MyEnglishLab

Grammar Plus 1
Activities 1 and 2

Grammar Practice

A Complete the sentences with the words below. Use each word only once.

cartoons	picture	signals	technology
comics	popularity	sound	walk

1. Children were already watching ______________ like Mickey Mouse in the 1930s.
2. The 1927 film *The Jazz Singer* demonstrated the use of ______________ with motion pictures.
3. There was live TV coverage of Neil Armstrong's ______________ on the moon in 1969.
4. *Batman* and *Wonder Woman* are examples of TV shows based on ______________.
5. Just as video cassette recorders have become a thing of the past, newer electronic devices are gaining ______________ over DVD players.
6. The film *Avatar* with its 3-D ______________ used human actors and computer animation.
7. Most argue that Blu-Ray discs display a sharper ______________ than traditional DVDs.
8. Satellite television uses a process of sending and receiving ______________ from one dish to another through a satellite in space.

Sort the eight nouns in the box above into two groups: count and noncount. If a noun can have either meaning, choose the one that is used in the sentence in Part A.

Count		Noncount
singular	pural	

B Circle the correct count or noncount meaning to complete the text.

Avatar is **1.** (film / a film) that asks viewers to judge the necessity of taking land by **2.** (force / a force) and losing lives to gain riches. Director James Cameron uses **3.** (fiction / a fiction) to remind us of certain **4.** (truth / truths): Land and **5.** (life/ a life) are connected, war always leads to **6.** (death / a death), and love offers **7.** (chance / the chance) for personal growth.

Avatar takes place at **8.** (time / a time) far in the future, when it is possible to travel long distances in **9.** (space / a space) and reach alien worlds. The character Jake is one of a number of men and women who travel from Earth to Pandora to interact with the alien species, the Na'vi.

The more Jake discovers about the Na'vi, the more he respects them. He even falls in **10.** (love / a love) with one female, Neytiri. He begins to doubt his own purpose and his own people. The **11.** (work / works) of the military seems cruel. He begins to believe that the Na'vi have the right to live their lives.

Jake decides to side with the Na'vi in **12.** (war / the war) that comes. Cameron uses **13.** (art / an art) to force reflection on crises here on Earth, and his film gives us **14.** (hope / a hope) for our own future.

Look back at the text and underline five irregular plural nouns.

Grammar Focus 2 Subject–verb agreement

Examples	Language notes
(1) **French director Emile Cohl** creates *Fantasmagorie,* the first animated projection.	Use a **singular verb** with a **singular subject**.
(2) **The Earth** has many satellites around it.	Some nouns are always singular because they refer to something unique.
(3) **Economics** is a popular field of study.	Use a **singular verb** with **noncount nouns**, even when they end in -*s*.
(4) ***The New York Times*** covers presidential **debates**. ***The Adventures of Superman*** was the first live-action hero program on TV.	Use a **singular verb** with a **proper noun** that names a company or a work, even when the name or title includes a plural noun.
(5) **The Apollo 11 crew** lands on the Moon. The **Kennedy family** grieves over the death of the president.	A **collective noun** refers to a group of people or things, but because it is one group it usually takes a singular verb. Examples of collective nouns include: *army, class, club, company, committee, family, government, military, party,* and *team*.
(6) **Nine TV stations** are on air across the U.S.	Use a **plural verb** with a **plural subject**.
(7) **3-D glasses** are necessary to fully enjoy films like *Avatar.*	Some nouns always take a plural verb because they refer to an object with two parts. We call these nouns **binary nouns**, and they include: *binoculars, glasses, jeans, pants,* and *scissors*. They only take a singular verb when used with a singular quantifying phrase: **One pair of glasses** is broken.
(8) **Mass media** help people form opinions on different topics.	Some nouns always take a plural verb because they refer to something that has many separate parts or units. We call these nouns **aggregate nouns**, and they include: *data, media, goods,* and *works*. They may appear singular in form (*police*) or plural in form (*communications*), but they always take a plural verb.
(9) My **family** sits down to watch TV. [collective = known number of members] The **police** fight crime. [aggregate = unknown number of members]	One difference between aggregate nouns and collective nouns is that we do not know exactly how many parts or units are in an aggregate noun. Another difference is that we can have a singular and plural form of a collective noun (*family—families, team—teams*), but we cannot have singular and plural forms of an aggregate noun (police—~~polices~~).
(10) ***Steamboat Willie*** **and** ***Snow White*** are two of the oldest animated works. **Neither Edison nor Eastman** is responsible for the invention of 3-D glasses. **Neither the director nor the producers** were able to stop the bad weather.	Use a **plural verb** with a **compound subject**. The exception is a compound subject with *or / nor,* which requires the verb to agree with the subject that is closer to the verb.

See Appendix F on page A-5 for a list of collective and aggregate nouns.

Grammar Practice

A Circle the correct verbs to complete the sentences.

1. *Amazing Stories* **is / are** a TV series. These short works of science fiction **demonstrate / demonstrates** Steven Spielberg's ability to create films for both small and big screen audiences.
2. The news coverage of political world events **keep / keeps** people informed. TV audience size, however, **is / are** likely getting smaller as more people **turn / turns** to the Internet for up-to-date information.
3. Not every household in the U.S. **has / have** the latest electronic devices like 3-D TVs, DVD players, or DVRs (digital video recorders); however, there **is / are** TVs in nearly every home today.
4. *Truth or Consequences* began as a radio game show in 1940 and later became a TV game show. Today, neither the radio show nor the TV show **is / are** on the air. The majority of current TV game shows **follow / follows** a much different format.
5. The cast of *The Wizard of Oz* **is / are** not the same as the one that the producer originally wanted. In the film, Frank Morgan **play / plays** the Wizard, but the studio considered W.C. Fields for the role.
6. The film industry in Hollywood **know / knows** it must invent new technology to bring audiences back into the theaters. The process **has / have** already begun with 3-D and 4-D films.

B Read the text and correct the errors. Look at the example. There are nine more errors.

Big and Small TVs: Coming Full Circle with Screen Size

The size of television sets ~~have~~ *has* changed over time. Early television sets were large boxes with small pictures. RCA began selling fully-electronic television sets in 1939, and the picture were 5 by 12 inches (12.7 by 25.4 centimeters). Not only was the picture small, it was not clear or in color. Thankfully, technology advanced. Within twenty years, RCA were selling color TV sets with 21-inch screens.

Buyers continued to think, "Bigger are better." Inventors worked to meet that demand. In the 1990s and 2000s, large-screen technology entered many households. Today stores are selling HD television sets with screens as large as 80 inches. In fact, both Mitsubishi and Samsung has a model with an 82-inch screen.

However, not all people watches big screen TVs. As early as the 1960s, Japanese inventors realized that some people wanted a TV they could carry with them from place to place. In 1962, Sony were making portable TV sets with 5- and 8-inch screens. In 1982, Seiko came out with a 1 ¼ inch television screen on a wristwatch!

Electronics around the world continue to develop, but in different directions. Many programs and films are available through the Internet, so the large-screen television experience is not important. Audiences of TV shows and movies is finding it very convenient to watch video on mobile devices.

What is next? How will our needs determine how big our screens are in the future? Which size are we going to see more of in stores? Perhaps the answers lies in the growing popularity of Internet tablets with screens that are big enough to enjoy and small enough to be portable.

MyEnglishLab

Sounding Natural

Speaking

A Look at the photos. Write the name of the film genre under each image: 3-D action-adventure, comedy, drama, or thriller.

__________ __________ __________ __________

B Look at the words in the list. With a partner, discuss any words or phrases you do not know. Describe the audience members' expressions and the films. What was the audience doing? What was the film about?

excitement	fear	laugh their heads off	nail-biter	terror	special glasses	tear-jerker

The woman / man is terrified.
The audience screamed while watching a horror movie.
I see the look of terror on that audience member's face.

Listening

A BEFORE LISTENING Talk to a partner. Do you know what a hologram is? Do you think TV and films will be in 4-D in the future?

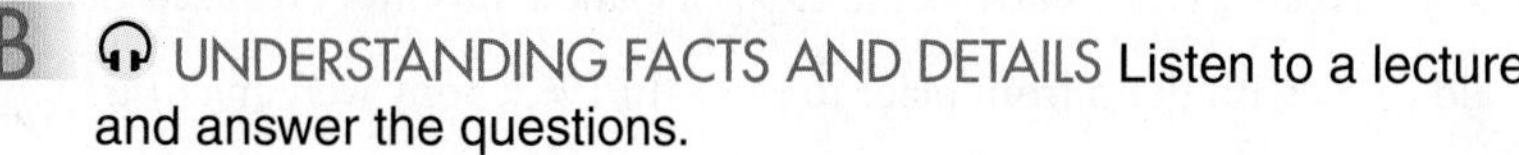

B UNDERSTANDING FACTS AND DETAILS Listen to a lecture and answer the questions.

1. What is the best title for the talk?
   a. The Progress of Electronics
   b. Two Hundred Years of Film Technology
   c. From Talkie to 4-D: The Evolution of the Motion Picture
2. In what year did Thomas Edison capture sound on a wax cylinder?
   a. 1861
   b. 1877
   c. 1907
3. What did the speaker say that people used to view 3-D films in 1915?
   a. stereoscopic lenses
   b. glasses with colored lenses
   c. pieces of red and blue film
4. What did the professor say about the future of film and TV?
   a. All movies will be 4-D.
   b. All TV stations will air holographic shows.
   c. Movies and TV shows could be holographic and 4-D.

C UNDERSTANDING SEQUENCE Listen again. Number the events in the correct order (1–6).

_____ **a.** Oliver Wendell Holmes created the stereoscopic viewer.
_____ **b.** The 4-D film *Dora and Diego's 4-D Adventure: Catch that Robot Butterfly* debuted in theaters.
_____ **c.** Thomas Edison captured sound on a wax cylinder.
_____ **d.** The Lumiere brothers said, "Cinema is an invention without any future!"
_____ **e.** The invention of 3-D glasses changed the way viewers saw movies.
_____ **f.** Many theaters had Sensurround but it did not work well.

Writing

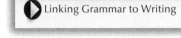

MyEnglishLab
Linking Grammar to Writing

A Brainstorm about your favorite movie or TV show. Use these questions as a guide. Think about why you liked the story or plot. Then talk with a partner about it.

- What do you know about its history?
- When did you first remember seeing it?
- When was the film first in the theater?
- Who starred in it?
- Did the movie win an Academy Award for "Best Picture" or "Best Actor"?
- Was the TV show on for many years?
- When did you used to watch it?
- What was it about?
- Who was your favorite character?
- Why did you like it?

B Write one or two paragraphs about your choice. Include the answers to the questions and any other interesting information.

When I was little, my favorite movies used to be the *Star Wars* series. I loved all the first movies with Harrison Ford and Mark Hamill, especially *Return of the Jedi*. My favorite characters were Chewbacca and Yoda. They were in the theaters in 1977, 1980, and 1983. Then there were new movies with the story starting from the time that Anakin Skywalker (Darth Vader), Luke Skywalker's father, was a child. Those movies came out in the 2000s. They were good, but I didn't enjoy them as much as I liked the original *Star Wars*.

Now my favorite movies of all are the *Harry Potter* series. I remember I read the books first, and then I went to see the films as soon as they debuted. I loved the action and the movie sets because they were very realistic. I felt like the books came alive. I used to order each *Harry Potter* book ahead of time so I would be the first to receive it. Then I would run out to the movie theater as soon as the movie debuted so I could see it. All the movies are great, in my opinion. My favorite character is Harry because he tries really hard to do the right thing and he is not afraid.

C Exchange paragraphs with a partner. Have you seen the movie or TV show that your partner wrote about? If so, do you agree with what your partner wrote? If not, do you want to see it now?

Grammar Summary

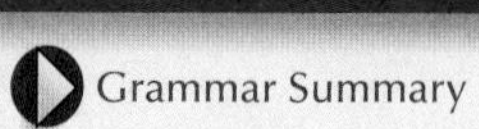

We use the **simple past**, the **past progressive**, ***was / were going to*** **+ base verb**, and ***used to*** **+ base verb** to talk about actions or events that happened at a past point in time.

Verb forms	Notes	Examples
Use the **simple past**	to describe completed actions or events that happened at a specific time in the past.	Ferdinand Braun **invented** the cathode ray tube in 1907.
Use ***be about to*** **with a simple past form of** ***be*** **+ the base form of a verb**	to describe an action someone was ready to do in the immediate future from a past point of view.	The producers arrived just as the director **was about to** shoot the next scene.
Use the **past progressive**	to describe incomplete or temporary past events and actions.	In the early 20th century, directors **were beginning** to explore the art of filmmaking.
Use ***was / were going to*** **+ the base form of a verb**	to discuss future plans that changed or did not occur from a past perspective.	The actor **was going to** accept the role, but his agent advised him not to appear in any more action movies.
Use ***used to / would*** **+ the base form of a verb**	to describe habitual actions or repeated events in the past that no longer occur in the present.	TV viewers in the 1980s and 90s **used to record** shows and movies with devices other than VCRs.

Subject and verbs must always agree.

<table>
<tr><td rowspan="7">Proper nouns
Names of particular people, places, or things.
Thomas Edison
Avatar
France</td><td colspan="4">Common nouns
People, places, or things, but not the name of one in particular.</td></tr>
<tr><td colspan="2">Count nouns
Things we can count as separate units.</td><td>Nouns with a count and noncount meaning</td><td>Noncount nouns</td></tr>
<tr><td>A singular noun takes a singular verb.</td><td>A plural noun takes a plural verb.</td><td rowspan="5">film (count = story that we watch)

film (noncount = the industry of filmmaking or the material we record pictures on)</td><td rowspan="5">grief
music
news

Use a singular verb even when the noun ends in -s.</td></tr>
<tr><td>device
demonstration</td><td>Regular nouns
experiments
processes</td></tr>
<tr><td>Unique nouns
the world
the universe</td><td>Irregular nouns
children
species</td></tr>
<tr><td rowspan="2">Collective nouns
A group with a known number of units
company
family</td><td>Binary nouns
One object with two parts
shorts
scissors</td></tr>
<tr><td>Aggregate nouns
A group with an unknown number of units
data
majority</td></tr>
<tr><td colspan="5">Compound subjects take a plural verb. The exception can be a compound subject with or / nor, which requires the verb to agree with the subject that is closer to the verb.</td></tr>
</table>

Self-Assessment

A (6 points) Complete the conversations. Write the correct form of the verb in the simple past or past progressive.

A: Wow, when ________________ your family ________________ (pose) for that photograph?
B: I think my grandfather ________________ (take) it in 1970.

A: What ________________ you ________________ (do) last night when I called?
B: I ________________ (watch) my favorite TV program.

A: I thought the *Wizard of Oz* ________________ (going to / be) on TV last night. What happened?
B: Oh yeah, the station ________________ (cancel) it because of a breaking news story.

B (4 points) Unscramble the sentences and rewrite them in the space provided. More than one word order is sometimes possible.

1. used to / a box camera / to take / use / Jacob Riis / his shots

____

2. have / our family / every three years / used to / reunions

____

3. Queen Victoria / every year / sit / would / for her portrait

____

4. until / Reisman's photo / my favorite image / the shot of the flag on the Moon / from space / I saw / used to be

____

C (5 points) Correct the mistake in each sentence.

1. I'm not very with good with an electronics. How does this device work?

2. The coverages of the Olympic Games is very good.

3. He was joking when he said we needed a binoculars to see my small TV screen.

4. I use DVR to record my favorite TV series when I'm not home to watch the live broadcast.

5. A good film has a good music.

D (5 points) Circle the correct form of the verb.

1. The movement of the animated characters **appear / appears** real and natural.
2. A pair of 3-D glasses **was / were** lying on the seat next to me.
3. The excited crowd **was / were** pushing through the doors of the movie theater.
4. Police **was / were** standing outside the theater to guard the celebrities.
5. Neither the producers nor the director **was / were** present at the debut of the movie.

Unit Project: Film and media festival

Work with a partner or in a group. Imagine that your school is going to have a media festival that focuses on a specific time period. Follow the steps:

1. Discuss what show or film you want to feature. The shows or films can be from the reading or you can include your group's favorites.
2. Create a poster board or Web ad and include three or more forms of media (TV shows, projection devices, and viewing devices) that would be suitable for projecting the film. Include a short explanation or tagline and images of the films or TV shows that you want to feature. Include one or two lines to persuade everyone to attend the festival. Look at the model.

Featured films

Steamboat Willie*, *The Jazz Singer*, and *The Power of Love

Did you ever wonder what movies used to be like when your grandparents or great- grandparents went to the cinema? This festival shows you feature films in their original format from 1922–1928.

In 1922, *The Power of Love* was the first 3-D film. Audiences saw the first cartoon, *Steamboat Willie*, in 1928. It was Mickey Mouse's screen debut. But in 1927, viewers were finally able to hear actors speak! *The Jazz Singer*, starring Al Jolson, came out in 1927. It was the first "talkie!"

B Prepare a presentation for the class. Follow the steps. Use grammar from the unit in your presentation.

1. Deliver your presentation to the class. Ask your classmates if they know the movie or show you presented. Ask them their opinion of it.
2. After all the groups have presented, discuss all the presentations. Ask and answer the other groups' questions about their films and methods of projection.
   - What did you learn about the films and the types of viewing devices?
   - What kind of films did people of the era used to like? What devices did they use?
   - What innovations happened during the era you chose?

UNIT 3

We Need a Hero

Outcomes

After completing this unit, I will be able to use these grammar points.

Chapter 5

Grammar Focus 1
Articles

Grammar Focus 2
Quantifiers

Grammar Focus 3
Adjectives

Chapter 6

Grammar Focus 1
Adjective clauses

Grammar Focus 2
Relative pronouns in adjective clauses

MyEnglishLab

 What do you know?

Chapter 5 The Bold and the Brave

Getting Started

A Read the opening statement from *The Adventures of Superman*. It describes characteristics of this famous superhero. What is a superhero? What are some other qualities superheroes have?

"Faster than a speeding bullet. More powerful than a locomotive. Able to leap tall buildings in a single bound . . . It's a bird! It's a plane! It's Superman . . . strange visitor from another planet who came to Earth with powers and abilities far beyond those of mortal men. Superman . . . who fights a never-ending battle for truth, justice, and the American way!"—*The Adventures of Superman*, 1952.

B Read each statement about a superhero. Then match it to its correct restatement.

_____ **1.** "If she can't save the world, no one will."
—*Wonder Woman*

_____ **2.** "With great power comes great responsibility."
—*Spider-Man*

_____ **3.** "No fear."—*Black Canary and the Justice League*

_____ **4.** "This time, the suit makes the man."—*Iron Man*

_____ **5.** "A hero for all generations."—*Captain America*

a. The clothes create the hero.
b. Great leaders should be dependable.
c. The only defender of the world.
d. The hero for all time.
e. Don't be afraid of anything.

C Look back at Parts A and B. Complete the tasks.

1. Underline the nouns or noun phrases with the **indefinite article *a*** or ***an***.
2. Circle all the nouns with the **definite article *the***.
3. Draw a box around all the nouns with **zero article (Ø)**.
4. Complete the chart. Include five or more examples of zero (Ø) article nouns from Parts A and B.

Nouns with *a* / *an*	Nouns with *the*	Nouns with zero article (Ø)

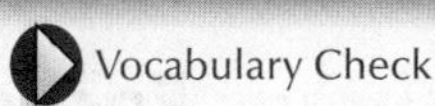

Reading

A Work with a partner. Decide which qualities are 1) super powers, 2) positive personality traits, or 3) weaknesses.

a deafening voice	being out of the water	invisibility	morals
always telling the truth	bravery	Kryptonite mineral	speed
anger / rage	confidence	mind-reading	X-ray vision

B SCANNING Scan the article on superheroes. As you read, find the answers to the questions. Then read the entire article.

1. Who was the first comic book superhero? ______________________
2. What is one type of superpower? ______________________
3. Where do superheroes usually live? ______________________

The BOLD and the BRAVE: The Formula for a Superhero

America's fascination with superheroes began in the 1940s when the world was in chaos and people lived in fear. Most people know the first superhero: "Superman," the defender of "Truth, Justice, and the American Way." DC Comics later introduced other superheroes to their fans: Batman, Aquaman, the Green Lantern, Wonder Woman, Black Canary, and Flash. These early comic book characters inspired men, women, and children to have strength and courage during troubled times. From the 1950s to the 1980s, more superheroes appeared. Stan Lee, the artist and creator for Marvel Comics, featured characters such as Spider-Man, the Hulk, the X-men, and the Fantastic Four. Both Marvel and DC Comics created characters who would be examples of high moral standards. There is one thing that all comic book stories have in common—a formula.

The formula for creating a superhero is simple: all superheroes require extraordinary powers, such as super strength, the ability to fly, telepathy (mind-reading), a deafening scream, X-ray vision, or the ability to climb walls. A superhero had to have a secret identity or "alter-ego"—the person they would be from day to day. Some superheroes were reporters by day, and put on their costumes to transform into defenders of justice. A nerd became a champion; an underdog became a success. The hero or heroine had a brightly colored costume made of special fabric that was fire or bullet-resistant.

All superheroes had a "hideout"—a safe place to hide from people or villains. The hideout could be a tree house in the air, a cave, or a castle. Some heroes used a vehicle, like a special car or an invisible plane. Some had tools or gadgets, like Wonder Woman's golden lasso of truth. But most superheroes had a "weakness"—something that made them lose their powers and become vulnerable to their enemies. Superman was vulnerable to Kryptonite, a kind of radioactive material from his home planet. Aquaman could not spend much time out of the water. Without their costumes, Spider-Man and Batman were just regular guys. But most importantly, the traits of superheroes were traits that Americans and many people desired: confidence, strength, bravery, and the determination to be better people.

C UNDERSTANDING DETAILS Write four superhero features from the text.

1. ______________________
2. ______________________
3. ______________________
4. ______________________

Grammar Focus 1 Articles

Examples	Language notes
(1) **A** superhero had to have **an** alter-ego.	Use the **indefinite articles *a*** and ***an*** before an **indefinite noun**: a singular count noun with no reference to any one person or thing in particular. Use ***a*** before a consonant sound and ***an*** before a vowel sound.
(2) Lex Luther is **a** villain and **an** enemy of Superman.	We can use the indefinite article + singular noun to classify something or someone.
(3) Superman has **a** civilian job that is part of his secret identity.	We use the indefinite article for the first mention of a singular common noun.
(4) Superman has a vulnerability to **a** mineral called Kryptonite. Exposure to **the** mineral robs him of his powers.	An **indefinite noun** usually becomes **definite** after the first mention. Use the **definite article** when your listener understands that you are talking about a particular person or thing.
(5) **The** formula for creating a superhero was simple. (*Which formula?—The formula for creating a superhero.*)	A first mention is not always needed to make a noun definite. Other information in the sentence sometimes answers the question *which one* and makes that noun specific.
(6) Our fascination with superheroes began in **the** 1940s when **the** world was in chaos and people lived in fear.	Use the definite article with unique nouns (the only one of its kind).
(7) All superheroes had **a** "hideout." People and villains could not find them in those places. These early comic book characters inspired men, women, and children to have strength and courage during troubled times.	**Generic nouns** refer to all members of a group. The choice of article for a generic reference depends on the type of noun. We can use: indefinite article + singular noun zero article + plural noun zero article + noncount noun
(8) Batman cannot fly, but he gets around easily and quickly in **the** Batmobile.	Use the definite article before a singular noun to refer to inventions, species of animals, and musical instruments in general.
(9) **The** Kryptonians' powers increase on Earth. Superman learned this when he met others from his home planet.	To make a generic reference to most nationalities, you can use the definite or zero article + plural noun. Use only the definite article before nationalities ending in *-ese, -sh, -ch,* and *-s.* ***Examples:*** the Japanese, the British, the French.
(10) You can find comics at **the** bookstore or at **the** library.	Use *the* + singular noun to refer to public places.
(11) Stan Lee, the artist and creator for Marvel Comics, introduced characters such as, Spider-Man, the X-men, and **the** Fantastic Four.	Use **zero article** (Ø) before names of people, most companies, most cities, most countries, and names of planets. Use the **definite article** before a collective name (a name that particular people use to identify themselves as a group).
(12) Spider-Man can probably climb **the** Rocky Mountains faster than any other superhero. Peter Parker worked as a photojournalist for **the** *Daily Bugle*.	Use the **definite article** before names of newspapers and other regular publications, governing bodies, geographical regions, mountains, rivers, and oceans.
(13) Not all superheroes were born on **Earth**; Superman comes from **Krypton**. Can our brave superhero save **the** Earth from evil aliens?	Use the **zero article** before names of planets. Use the **definite article** before "Earth" to refer to it as a unique world, different from other worlds.

See Appendix G on page A-6 for a list of nationalities.

Grammar Practice

A Complete the blog's plot summaries with the correct articles: *a / an* (indefinite), *the* (definite) or Ø (zero article).

Superman Comics – My Top Picks

Here are three of my favorite stories from older issues. In case you haven't read them, I'll include plot summaries.

1. [DC Comics, Number 295—January 1976] "Costume, Costume—Who's Got the Costume?"
   In __________ fight with __________ Father Time, Superman loses his costume. When __________ fight ends, will Superman have his costume—and superhuman strength—back? Who will __________ final victory belong to?
2. [Action Comics, Number 494—April 1979] "The Secret of the Super-S!"
   Someone sends __________ letter to __________ office of __________ *Daily Planet*, and __________ mystery writer promises to tell everyone all of Superman's secrets. As newspaper reporter Clark Kent, Superman travels with his partner __________ Lois Lane to his hometown of __________ Smallville. Together they search for answers, but along __________ way they encounter __________ ghosts and __________ ancient Kryptonian warrior!
3. [Action Comics, Number 582—February 1982] "Star-Killer—The Universe Killer"
   New adventures put our hero in __________ danger. Superman and Brainiac combine their strengths to stop __________ evil device from destroying __________ Earth and __________ whole universe. Can they do it?

B Read the Web directory and correct the errors. You will need to add, delete, or change articles to make the corrections. Look at the example. There are 13 more errors.

Real name: Peter Parker

Place of birth: ~~The~~ New York City

Occupation: Photographer

Superpowers: Spider-Man has the superhuman strength, amazing speed, and spider-like balance. He can stick to and climb the walls. He also has special sense and knows when the danger is near.

Super gadgets: As gifted high school student, Peter Parker used his knowledge of science to invent the device that could form and throw spider-like webs. He wears "webshooter" on each wrist.

Origin of powers: Peter Parker received his superpowers from spider bite. This took place at the demonstration at a science center. A spider was radioactive.

Character traits: Peter Parker was unlikely choice for a superhero. He was a shy teenager with little confidence or physical strength. His high intelligence separated him from others. Becoming the Spider-Man turned the underdog into popular hero.

Grammar Focus 2 Quantifiers

Examples	Language notes
(1) **One** feature was noticeable in all of the comic book stories.	**Quantifiers** describe the quantity or amount of a singular noun or noun phrase. They answer the questions *how much* or *how many*.
(2) **Every** superhero has a hideout. (= *All superheroes have hideouts.*) **Each** superhero has a hideout. (= *There isn't one superhero without a hideout.*)	***Each*** and ***every*** are similar in meaning, but *each* refers to a single member and *every* refers to all members of a group.
(3) My uncle has **each and every** issue of the Superman comic book series.	In less formal English, ***each*** and ***every*** can emphasize the individual people or things in a group.
(4) The heroes had **several** characteristics in common. **A number of** superheroes are able to fly. ***Incorrect:*** *A number of superheroes* ***is*** *able to fly.*	Some quantifiers can only be used with plural nouns. They include: ***many, a great many, a number of, few, fewer, both, several,*** and cardinal numbers greater than *one*.
(5) **A few** superheroes come from alien planets. (= *Some superheroes.*) (6) **Few** people know Clark Kent's true identity—Superman. (= *Not many people.*)	***A few*** has a neutral meaning and refers to a low number that is not exact. ***Few*** emphasizes a low number that is not exact. *Very* limits the number even more: *very few* superheroes.
(7) Which superhero wears a cape, Superman or Batman? —**Both** do.	We can often use a quantifier for plural nouns by itself, but its reference must be clear to the listener.
(8) In the 1940s people experienced **a great deal of** chaos and fear.	Some quantifiers can only be used with noncount nouns. They include: ***little, much,*** and ***a great deal of***.
(9) Even superheroes need **a little** help sometimes. (= *Some help.*) Peter Parker was a shy teenager with **little** confidence. (= *Not much confidence.*)	***A little*** has a neutral meaning and refers to a small amount that is not exact. *Little* emphasizes a small amount that is not exact. *Very* limits the amount even more: *very little confidence.*
(10) **A lot of** superheroes can fly. Superheroes spend **a lot of** time fighting villains.	Many quantifiers can be used with noncount nouns and plural nouns. They include: ***all of the, most, a lot of, no, enough,*** and ***a piece of***. ***Note:*** *Lots of* and *a lot of* are less formal than *much* and *many*.
(11) **Some** superheroes, like Spider-Man, marry a regular person. Did the Hulk have **any** girlfriends?	***Some*** and ***any*** can be used with plural or noncount nouns. Use *some* in affirmative statements. Use *any* in negative statements. Both may be used in questions.
(12) Stan Lee created **many of the** superheroes that we know and love today.	For specific people or things in a group, we can use: quantifier + *of* + *the* (plural noun) An object pronoun can also appear in this structure: *Stan Lee created* ***many of*** *them*.
(13) **Most of** Stan Lee's superheroes from the 1940s have been given a modern look and a modern lifestyle.	There must be agreement between the verb and the subject that appears in a quantifying phrase with *of*.
(14) Rob Callender, one of Batman's earliest villains, used a **pair of** special goggles to rob banks.	Because **binary nouns** refer to an object with two parts, we commonly use ***pair of*** to quantify them.
(15) Between the 1950s and 1980s **a bunch of** new superheroes appeared.	Some common **collective nouns** that express quantity include: *a **group** of, a **set** of,* and a ***bunch** of*.
(16) Superheroes often fight **a series of** battles with the same villain. [Collocation: *series of + battles*]	Many collective nouns have very limited usage to express quantity. For example, we can refer to *a herd of sheep* but not *a herd of birds*. We say *a flock of birds*.
(17) There was a **trace of** radiation left from the spider bite on Peter Parker's hand.	**Unit nouns** also have collocations. Unlike collective nouns, which refer to a mass, unit nouns can refer to separate parts of something.

See Appendix F on page A-5 for a list of collective nouns.
See Appendix H on page A-7 for a list of quantifiers for count and noncount nouns.
See Appendix I on page A-7 for a list of quantifying collective nouns.
See Appendix J on page A-8 for a list of unit nouns.

Grammar Practice

A Circle the correct quantifier to complete each statement.

Who is The Hulk?

1. The Hulk, a large green-skinned giant, has (**a number of / much**) superpowers, which include superhuman strength, great speed, and the ability to heal fast.
2. Thanks to the Hulk's superhuman strength, when he jumps, he covers a distance of (**few / a few**) miles.
3. Doctor Bruce Banner was present at the testing of a nuclear bomb, and by accident (**a great many / a great deal of**) radiation entered his body. Soon after that, he began changing into the Hulk.
4. Unfortunately, Banner becomes the Hulk whenever he becomes very angry. There is (**little / a little**) of Banner's intelligence, memory, or personality in the Hulk.
5. For (**some / any**) time, Banner lived outside society because he was unable to control himself.
6. In later comics, the Hulk develops (**one / no**) very unusual ability. He is able to see ghosts.
7. Like (**no / every**) superhero, the Hulk has enemies with the power to hurt him.
8. The Hulk has joined forces with others from time to time. He was a part of the original team of Defenders, and (**all / all of the**) members wanted to stop the villain Yandroth.

The Hulk

B Choose the correct quantifiers to complete the statements.

an act of	a bolt of	a period of
an article of	a matter of	a piece of

1. In a comic book story called "The Other," Bruce Banner (the Hulk) gives Peter Parker (Spider-Man) ____________________ advice on treating a particular illness from radiation.
2. Jennifer Walters, the She-Hulk, was at first very wild as a green-skinned giant, but after ____________________ time she gained her normal level of intelligence and was better able to control her superhuman strength.
3. Audiences easily recognize the Penguin, one of Batman's most famous villains, because of his short build and his formal way of dressing. ____________________ clothing that the Penguin is rarely without is his black top hat.
4. Jay Garrick, the original Flash superhero, displayed ____________________ courage when he fought the evil character Superboy-Prime. Others died in that great battle, but Jay lived on.
5. Barry Allen was the second man to call himself the Flash. Allen received his superhuman speed through a mix of chemicals, which spilled on him after ____________________ lightning struck his laboratory.
6. For the majority of characters in comic book stories, becoming a superhero was not ____________________ choice.

Grammar Focus 3 Adjectives

Examples	Language notes
(1) Superman is a **strange** visitor from another planet.	A **descriptive adjective** (also called a *qualitative adjective*) modifies a noun. It gives information about a quality of a person or thing. It often comes before the noun or pronoun it modifies and becomes part of a noun or pronoun phrase.
(2) Superheroes are **strong** and **brave**. Most superheroes had something that made them lose their powers and become **vulnerable** to their enemies.	Many descriptive adjectives can also follow a linking verb and refer back to the subject. Some descriptive adjectives appear more often in this position than as part of a noun or pronoun phrase.
(3) Superman is faster than a **speeding** bullet. These early comic book characters inspired people to have strength and courage during **troubled** times.	You can recognize some descriptive adjectives that appear before nouns because they often have ***-ing*** or ***-ed*** endings. They are called **participial adjectives**. Those with an *–ing* ending express an **active meaning**. Those with an *–ed* ending express a **passive meaning**.
(4) Superman is very **courageous**. He is rather **handsome**, too. He is more **powerful** than a locomotive. He's **stronger** than humans. He's one of the **oldest** superheroes.	Descriptive adjectives can have degrees. We can express a stronger or weaker degree by using adverbs with adjectives, including: *very, rather,* and *quite*. We can also use comparative and superlative forms of descriptive adjectives.
(5) **Afraid** for their own safety, superheroes keep their real identity a secret.	Descriptive adjectives are very common in fiction. In writing, they can appear somewhat separate from the main part of the sentence as a single word or adjective phrase.
(6) **The Bold** and **the Brave**: A Formula for a Superhero **The strong** are responsible for **the weak**.	We can make generic statements about a group of people with *the* + descriptive adjective. This generic reference takes a plural verb because the plural noun *people* is understood.
(7) Peter Parker's birth as a superhero proves that **the unlikely** can happen. Comic book readers like surprises; **the unexpected** is expected.	We can also use *the* + descriptive adjective to make a generic reference to things or events. This generic reference takes a singular verb because it is uncountable and abstract.
(8) "Alexander **the Great**" would be a good name for a superhero.	**Titles**, especially of kings and queens, often appear as first name + *the* + descriptive adjective.

See Appendix K on page A-8 for adjectives that follow linking verbs.

Grammar Practice

A Match the descriptions to the characters. Look at the words in bold.

_____ **1.** The **Amazing** Spider-Man
_____ **2.** The Incredible **Hulk**
_____ **3.** The Fantastic **Four**
_____ **4.** The Dynamic **Duo**
_____ **5.** Maximus the **Mad**

a. This **pair** of superheroes has kept Gotham City safe for many years. Their friendship began when Batman saved a young Dick Grayson from danger and then taught him to fight crime. Grayson then became known as Robin.

b. This villain is highly intelligent, but he also has **serious psychological problems**. One of his most interesting gifts is the ability to create devices from simple materials.

c. As a **giant** with surprising **strength**, this superhero can lift extremely heavy objects. It's too bad that he is not as smart as he is powerful.

d. Reed, Sue, Johnny, and Ben received their superpowers through an accident while onboard their spaceship. More like a close family, this **team** works together to protect society from evil.

e. This **great** superhero is loved for his ability to swing and climb over the streets of New York. He accepts that his powers make him responsible for those weaker than him.

Circle all the qualitative adjectives in the names and the descriptions. There are 21 in total.

B Complete the sentences with the definite article *the*, if necessary. Write Ø if *the* is not needed. Then role-play the conversation with a partner.

A: Why do you still have your comic book collection? Aren't you too old for that kind of reading?

B: Comics aren't just for **1.** _____________________ young. The stories can be very exciting and complex. Most stories are very well written. These aren't picture books for **2.** _____________________ uneducated.

A: I don't see how a man in a bright red and blue suit can be **3.** _____________________ complex.

B: You don't get it. The stories tell about amazing adventures. It's fun to read comics. The stories also inspire. Everyone needs a hero, even **4.** _____________________ old. When I'm 100, I'll still be reading about victory over **5.** _____________________ evil.

A: But these are very old comics. The stories are **6.** _____________________ old. Why should you keep reading old stuff? Why don't you throw these out and make room for new ones?

B: You mean out with **7.** _____________________ old and in with **8.** _____________________ new? Never! Do you know how much money these older books are worth?

A: Are you saying that comic books are also for **9.** _____________________ rich?

B: You have a lot to learn, little brother.

MyEnglishLab

Listen for it.

Listening

A UNDERSTANDING MAIN TOPICS Listen to a program on a radio talk show. What is the main topic of the talk show?

___

B CLASSIFYING INFORMATION Superheroes often have a "secret identity" or "alter-ego." Listen again to the talk show and then write the name of the superhero next to his or her alter-ego. Then write the alter-ego's profession below the image.

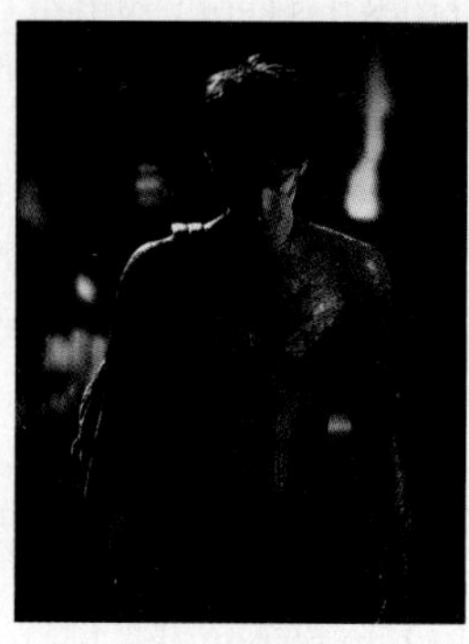

a. Clark Kent, ___
b. Diana Prince, ___
c. Peter Parker, ___
d. Jean Grey-Summers, ___

C AFTER LISTENING Talk with a partner. Why do you think superheroes had alter-egos? Do you think the alter-ego is the opposite of the superhero? Why?

Speaking

A Talk with a partner. Discuss the formula and characteristics of superheroes from the reading. What are some other personality traits or weaknesses that superheroes might have?

B What comic book superheroes are popular in your culture? What characteristics do they have? Are they similar to or different from American superheroes? Take notes in the chart.

There is a popular superhero in my country called Samurai X.
He is an anime character who has great fighting skills.
He is different from American superheroes because he fights with swords.

Superhero: ___

Characteristic 1	Characteristic 2	Characteristic 3

Now discuss the superhero with a group or the class.

MyEnglishLab

Linking Grammar to Writing

Writing

A Taglines usually compare the superhero to an animal or thing. For example, Superman is compared to speeding bullets or train engines.

"Faster than a speeding bullet. More powerful than a locomotive. It's a bird, it's a plane, it's Superman."

Choose one or two superheroes and compare your hero to an animal or thing. Create a tagline. Write notes in the box.

B Work with a partner. Create an original superhero.

- Look at the example. Use the information to decide what powers and characteristics your hero will have.
- Create a tagline for your new superhero. Think about the taglines for other superheroes, such as Superman *("It's a bird, it's a plane, it's Superman!")*.

Superhero's name: Aquaman

First comic book appearance: 1941

Title: The Sea King

Origins: The lost kingdom of Atlantis

Superpowers: communicates with and commands fish and other marine life, breathes underwater, swims at very fast speeds, exceptional vision

Known for: bravery, a sense of adventure, curiosity, a love of ocean life

Costume: blue one-piece suit (like a wetsuit) with letter "A" on the chest

Weakness: air (he cannot survive for long out of the water); loss of his right hand

Hideout: a castle / palace under the sea

Tools or weapons: super sea weapons and tools, ability to hurl bolts of hardened water

Tagline: Defender of Earth's Oceans!

C Imagine your character is going to appear on a radio or TV show. Write an introduction for him or her. As a guide, look at the description of Superman from the popular TV show *The Adventures of Superman* on page 44. Start out with a "hook," then mention where the superhero is from and his or her characteristics. Present your character to the class. You can use a recording device or read the description aloud to the class. Make your presentation in the style of a TV or radio announcer.

Chapter 6 Myths, Folklore, Fairy Tales, and Legends

Getting Started

A What is your favorite fairy tale or folktale? Write the title, some important characters, and a short summary about the tale. Then talk to a partner about it. Does your partner know the story? Is there a similar story in his or her culture?

Title: ______________________

Characters: ______________________

Summary: ______________________

B Work with a partner. Match the heroes and heroines from popular fairy tales, mythology, and folklore with their descriptions. How many characters are familiar to you?

Hua Mulan

Aladdin

a. Cinderella **b.** Aladdin **c.** Hercules **d.** Paul Bunyan **e.** Frog Princess **f.** Hua Mulan

_____ **1.** is a legendary giant and lumberjack of North America whose footprints created the Great Lakes.

_____ **2.** is the heroine of an epic Chinese poem who was a warrior in an all-male army.

_____ **3.** is the heroine of a Russian saga whom the witch Baba Yaga transforms because she disobeys her father.

_____ **4.** is a Roman-deity who became a champion by successfully completing 12 difficult tasks.

_____ **5.** is a poor girl in a German fairy tale who loses her shoe on the night she meets her prince.

_____ **6.** is the boy that finds a magic lamp and is the hero in a famous Middle Eastern folktale.

C Rewrite the sentences in Part B. Then circle the phrases that describe nouns. Follow the example:

Example: Aladdin is the boy (that finds a magic lamp) and is (the hero in a famous Middle Eastern folktale.)

1. ______________________

2. ______________________

3. ______________________

4. ______________________

5. ______________________

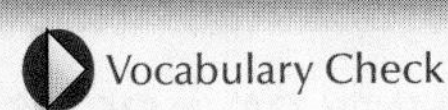

Vocabulary Check

Reading

A WARM-UP Talk to a partner. Why do you think fables and fairy tales have a moral or lesson?

B SCANNING Scan the article and identify the main differences between a fairy tale and a myth. Write two or three characteristics of each type of literature. Then read the entire article.

____

Tell Me a Story about the Princess who. . .

Storytelling is an activity in which people all over the world engage. Fairy tales are probably the first kind of story most people hear as children. All children know at least one story about a hero who defeats a giant, or the formulaic tale of a princess whom a brave prince must rescue. And most people know the popular phrase that begins these tales: "Once upon a time . . ." which always inspires a child's imagination.

The stories we know today as *Cinderella* or *Sleeping Beauty* evolved over many centuries from an oral tradition. Parents passed the stories down to their children for many generations. In Europe, it was not until the early 1800s that these tales actually appeared in book form. The most famous tales are probably those of brothers Jacob and Wilhelm Grimm, whose collection of fairy tales exists in translation in more than 160 languages.

Long before the Brothers Grimm's *Children's and Household Tales*, an oral tradition also existed in which people told fables of the Greek and Roman deities (gods and goddesses). Mythology has both folkloric and religious origins. Myths developed from ancient tales that helped people explain the creation of the world and forces of nature. In ancient Greek and Roman myths, people feared the deities. For example, Zeus's anger could transform a human being into an animal or stone. Hera, his wife, on the other hand, was a goddess who could not only change her appearance but could also transform a person into an animal or stone as a punishment.

The stories of these deities played an important part in the evolution of the fairy tale. Fairy tales and the sagas of deities often hold a hidden message—a moral to the story, a lesson to learn. The intention behind these stories is to entertain but more importantly, to instruct.

Unlike mythological deities, the heroes and heroines from folk and fairy tales do not have superpowers. They are common people or "folk." They represent the rich and the poor. Many times, the hero learns that selfish actions may lead him into danger. He may suffer a punishment from someone he offended—like an evil sorcerer or a witch. The heroine may be unfairly punished for her beauty—like *Snow White*, whose evil stepmother tried to kill her.

Fairy tales or legends, or ancient Greek fables are stories that have similar formulas. Like the Greek writer Aesop's fable of the *Tortoise and the Hare*, in which the turtle is slow and steady, while the rabbit is careless and proud, there is always a lesson, like, "slowly but surely wins the race." Fables caution, instruct, and often, end with the phrase . . . "and the moral of the story is. . . ."

C UNDERSTANDING FACTS AND DETAILS Write facts about each person or character. Then next to each name write *M* for *myth*, *FT* for *fairy tale*, or *F* for *fable*.

_____ **1.** Grimm brothers ____________________

_____ **2.** Cinderella ____________________

_____ **3.** Snow White ____________________

_____ **4.** Stepmother ____________________

_____ **5.** Zeus ____________________

_____ **6.** Hera ____________________

_____ **7.** Aesop ____________________

_____ **8.** the Hare ____________________

Grammar Focus 1 Adjective clauses

Examples	Language notes
(1) *Two simple sentences:* All children have their favorite story of a hero. **The hero** defeats a giant. *Changed to a complex sentence with an adjective clause:* All children have their favorite story of a hero [head noun] **who defeats a giant**. [adjective clause]	An **adjective clause**, like a single word adjective, modifies—that is, describes, identifies, or gives additional information about—a noun. The clause closely follows the head noun (the noun it modifies). Adjective clauses are dependent (subordinate) clauses and cannot appear alone. They must be connected to an independent (main) clause.
(2) Snow White ran from her stepmother, **who was a jealous, evil witch**. [*who* = her stepmother] Most children know the popular phrase **that begins these tales**. [*that* = the popular phrase]	We use a **relative pronoun** to form an **adjective clause**. The most common relative pronouns are *who, which,* and *that.* Use *who* or *that* for people. Use *which* or *that* for things.
(3) Cinderella is the poor girl in a German fairy tale, **who lost her shoe on the night she met her prince.** [subject of adjective clause = *who;* verb of adjective clause = *lost*]	An adjective clause must have a subject and a verb. The relative pronoun is sometimes the subject.
(4) *Two simple sentences:* Storytelling is an activity. People all over the world engage in **this activity**. *Changed to a complex sentence with an adjective clause:* Storytelling is an activity **in which people all over the world engage**. [more formal] Storytelling is an activity **which people all over the world engage in.** [less formal] [subject of adjective clause = *people;* verb of adjective clause = *engage;* object of preposition *in* = *which*]	The relative pronoun is sometimes the object of a verb or preposition. In more formal English, the preposition comes before the relative pronoun. In less formal English, the preposition appears after the verb.
(5) Aladdin is the hero in a Middle Eastern folktale, **which tells about his adventures after he finds a magic lamp**. Aladdin, **who found a magic lamp**, is the hero in a Middle Eastern folktale.	The head noun of an adjective clause is often the final word of the main clause, so the adjective clause appears in a final position. However, a middle position for an adjective clause is also possible, especially when the head noun is the subject of the main clause. When possible, we often avoid the middle position because it can be difficult for the listener to connect the main subject to the main verb. Look at the two examples. The first has a better flow because of the final position of the adjective clause.
(6) Hercules was a Roman deity **who became the champion of Mycenae by successfully completing 12 difficult tasks**.	Adjective clauses can be restrictive or non-restrictive. A **restrictive adjective clause** identifies a head noun and does not have commas. The listener needs this information to understand the overall meaning.
(7) *Sleeping Beauty*, **which tells about a princess under a bad magic spell**, evolved from oral tradition.	A **non-restrictive adjective clause** gives additional information about a head noun and needs commas to separate it from the main clause. The information is not necessary to understand the overall meaning. ***Note:*** The relative pronoun *that* cannot be used in a non-restrictive adjective clause.

MyEnglishLab

Grammar Plus 1
Activities 1 and 2

Grammar Practice

A Complete the text with the correct adjective clauses.

that they named Shiro	who had no children
which he received through Shiro's help	who had seen everything
which means "white"	who then gave great riches to the old man
which the awful neighbor never learned	

Once upon a time in the mountains of Japan there lived a kind old couple **1.** ____________. They did, however, have a dog **2.** ____________, **3.** ____________. There was much love between the couple and the dog, and Shiro even helped the man work in the field.

One day, the good dog led the old man to a place and barked to tell the man to dig. When the man dug in the ground, he found gold. A greedy and mean neighbor **4.** ____________, asked to borrow Shiro. The evil man wanted to find gold, too. When he did not, he became angry.

Twice more, Shiro brought riches to the old couple. Twice more, the wicked neighbor remained with nothing. At one point, the old man received the magic power to transform dead trees into beautiful cherry trees. This amazing gift **5.** ____________, caught the attention of a great lord, **6.** ____________.

The moral of Hanasaka Jiisan **7.** ____________, is that true friendship brings rewards and greed brings none.

Go back and circle the head nouns for the seven adjective clauses.

B Combine the two ideas to make one sentence with a main clause and an adjective clause. Use the relative pronouns given. The head nouns are underlined. Use commas for non-restrictive clauses.

1. Some view folklore as fantasy, but the <u>tales</u> are important because they reflect culture. The tales often tell about ancient deities and brave adventures. [which] *Some view folklore as fantasy, but the tales, which often tell about ancient deities and brave adventures, are very important because they reflect culture.*
2. According to Hawaiian legend, a boy named Haupu was born under a <u>rainbow</u>. A rainbow is a sign of great power. [which] ____________
3. Haupu was a strong, brave <u>warrior</u>. Everyone on the Hawaiian islands knew and respected this warrior. [that] ____________
4. One night, the Oahu chief Kaena organized a <u>fishing trip</u>. The trip took his people toward Haupu's island of Kauai. [which] ____________
5. Haupu woke to see <u>Kaena's people</u>, and he prepared to protect his land. He thought the people were warriors. [whom] ____________
6. Haupu ran to high ground and picked up a large <u>boulder</u>. He then threw the huge rock into the sea between the two islands. [which] ____________
7. <u>Chief Kaena</u> suffered along with many of the fishermen. The chief was standing bravely in his canoe when the rock fell. [who] ____________
8. Onto the shore, the big boulder sent waves of <u>sand</u>. That sand formed a point. [that] ____________
9. Today those <u>people</u> understand the names Kaena Point and Rock of Kauai. They know the legend of Haupu and Kaena. [who] ____________

Grammar Focus 2 Relative pronouns in adjective clauses

Examples	Language notes
(1) Jacob and Wilhelm Grimm are the brothers **who compiled *Children's and Household Tales*.** "Is Cinderella the girl **that lost her glass** slipper?" the boy asked the teacher.	Use the **subject relative pronouns *who*** and ***that*** for head nouns that are people. In speaking, *that* is more common as a subject relative pronoun. In more formal writing, *who* is more common as a subject relative pronoun.
(2) Fairy tales are probably the first kind of story **which most people hear as children.** "What was the first fairy tale **that you remember hearing?**" I asked my friend.	Use ***that*** and ***which*** for head nouns that are things. In speaking, *that* is more common as a subject relative pronoun in restrictive clauses. In more formal writing, *which* is more common as a subject relative pronoun in restrictive clauses.
(3) *The Frog Princess*, **which originally came out of Russian folklore**, is a well-known story around the world.	We cannot use the relative pronoun *that* in a non-restrictive adjective clause.
(4) Paul Bunyan is a legendary giant and lumberjack of North America **whose footprints created the Great Lakes.** (= *footprints of the legendary giant and lumberjack*) Our teacher uses the fairy tales of one publishing company **whose goal is to give old characters modern lives and make old stories interesting to new generations.**	When head nouns are people, use the relative pronoun *whose* to show possession. We also use *whose* with an animal or a group of people, such as a company or team.
(5) The Frog Princess is the heroine in a Russian saga **whom the witch Baba Yaga transformed because she disobeyed her father.** [Most formal and not common in conversation.] The Frog Princess is the heroine in a Russian saga **who the witch Baba Yaga transformed because she disobeyed her father.** [Serious writers avoid using *who* as an object relative pronoun.] The Frog Princess is the heroine in a Russian saga **that the witch Baba Yaga transformed because she disobeyed her father.** [Appropriate in less formal writing and common in conversation.]	In formal English, use the **object relative pronoun** *whom* when the head nouns are people. *Whom* can be the object of a verb or preposition. In less formal English, *who* and *that* can replace *whom* as an object relative pronoun.
More formal: (6) The children drew pictures of the hero **about whom they read.** [Very formal and not common.] The children drew pictures of the hero **whom they read about.** *Less formal:* The children drew pictures of the hero **that they read about.** The children drew pictures of the hero (Ø) **they read about.** [Most common choice.]	In formal, academic, or legal English, we often use a preposition before *whom* or *which*. This is not common in everyday English. In contrast, it is common to omit an object relative pronoun in a restrictive adjective clause in speaking and writing because it makes our speech less wordy. The omission of a relative pronoun is called the **zero relative pronoun (Ø)**. Note the progression from formal to informal in the examples. Also, note that we never place a preposition before the relative pronouns *who* or *that*.

Grammar Practice

A Choose the correct relative pronoun.

_____ **1.** According to Maori legend, three brothers used a magic fishhook to pull up Te Ika a Maui or "the fish of Maui," **which / who** today we know as the Northern Island of New Zealand.
_____ **2.** The Incas, **whom / who** lived up high in the mountains, had many legends about llamas.
_____ **3.** Princess Aurora, **which / who** audiences also know as Sleeping Beauty, has been the heroine of a book, a film, and a ballet.
_____ **4.** One legend from the West African country of Benin tells of Ezomo, a hero **who / which** gained victory over a greedy chief **which / that** had the power to change into an elephant.
_____ **5.** Pinocchio, the Italian tale about a boy **whose / whom** nose grows with every lie, teaches the value of honesty.
_____ **6.** A Finnish friend told me about Lintukoto, a land **that / whose** birds flew to for the winter.
_____ **7.** Gabrielle-Suzanne Barbot de Villeneuve published her version of *Beauty and the Beast*, a traditional tale in **which / that** a woman learns to love a kind prince, although he looks like a monster.
_____ **8.** The dragon is a popular mythological creature **which / who** many ancient peoples feared and respected.

Go back and write Ø before any sentence with an adjective clause in which the zero relative pronoun can be used.

B Read the story and correct the errors. Look at the example. There are nine more errors. You can add, delete, or change words. You can also add or delete commas.

Baba Yaga is a popular character ~~whom~~ *who* often appears in Russian folklore. Although she is a witch and can be terrible to look at, she occasionally helps heroes which are brave and have a pure heart.

Baba Yaga is not like most other witches get around on a broom. This witch flies in a deep bowl that is used for grinding food. Her home also makes her unique. Baba Yaga lives in the woods, and her house stands on large chicken legs, that can walk and turn the whole house around.

One well-known story with Baba Yaga is the tale of Vasilisa the Beautiful. Vasilisa is a young girl who's stepmother sends her to request light from the scary witch. The cruel stepmother thinks that Vasilisa will not return, but she does not realize the amount of courage and goodness whom Vasilisa has.

Vasilisa faces the witch asks the girl to do several tasks, from cooking to cleaning. Some of the tasks are tricky to perform, but Vasilisa is brave enough to try. The witch, which must admit Vasilisa is a good and honest worker, gives the requested light.

In the end, the light from Baba Yaga changes Vasilisa's life that used to be full of sadness and difficulty. The witch's magic enters the family's home with a power, that drives the evil stepmother away, and Vasilisa begins to know a peaceful, happy life.

Listening

A UNDERSTANDING MAIN IDEAS Listen to a documentary TV show. What is the narrator discussing? Choose the title that best represents the topic.

☐ The Legends of Great Kings
☐ The Companions and Champions of Heroes
☐ The Differences between Legends and Myths
☐ The Importance of Storytelling

B UNDERSTANDING DETAILS Listen again. Choose the correct answers.

1. According to the speaker, many fairy tales began with an introduction about which of the following?
   a. Someone who was a hero
   b. Someone who was an evil villain
   c. A villain who had a special power
2. Based on the documentary, which of the following is true about heroes?
   a. They had villains who were their companions.
   b. They were not safe from people who wanted to hurt them.
   c. They had companions who protected them from villains.
3. What does the speaker say about Merlin?
   a. That he was the one who helped King Arthur find his famous sword.
   b. That Merlin was the reason that Camelot disappeared.
   c. That King Arthur did not know who Merlin really was.
4. According to the speaker, who were King Arthur's loyal supporters?
   a. They were other kings who lived close by.
   b. They were warriors who traveled from faraway places.
   c. They were knights that were loyal to other kings.
5. Why was Robin Hood called an "outlaw"?
   a. Because people thought Robin was dishonest.
   b. Because Robin Hood did things that were against the law.
   c. Because Robin Hood was a man who defied the evil Sheriff.
6. According to the documentary, what did Robin Hood and his Merry Men do?
   a. They waited in Sherwood Forest and robbed the Sheriff of Nottingham.
   b. They took money from people who were wealthy and gave it to those who were not.
   c. They stole a lot of property and kept it in the forest for themselves.

C AFTER LISTENING Who are the legendary heroes that you know? Are there any popular legends from your country? Talk to a partner and compare legends.

MyEnglishLab

Sounding Natural

Speaking

A Think of any character from a legend, fable, folktale, or fairy tale. Try and pick a popular character that other people would know. Write notes about the character.

B Work with a partner. You are going to ask ten questions to help you guess the character your partner chose. Use the models below as a guide.

> *Is this story about someone who was a prince?*
> *Is this story set in a place where there was magic?*
> *Is this person someone who could use magic?*

Your partner can only answer *yes* or *no*. If you do not guess after ten questions, your partner wins. Then switch roles.

Writing

A Think about three stories you know well. They can be legends, folktales, or fairy tales. Do you see ways that the stories could be changed to make them more interesting? For example, for *Cinderella*, think about what the story would be like with a kind stepsister and a cruel Cinderella. Write notes about some ways you could change the three stories.

B Now choose one of the stories. Rewrite the complete story with a "twist." What happens now in the end? Use the information below as a guide.

- Remember to include where the characters live, who they are, what happens, what they do, and if they have magical powers.
- You can use the phrases below to begin or end your story.

Introduction: Once upon a time. . . Once there was a [man / woman / princess / prince / witch] who . . . In a land full of mystery, there was . . .

Endings: And, they lived happily ever after . . . And, the moral of the story is . . .

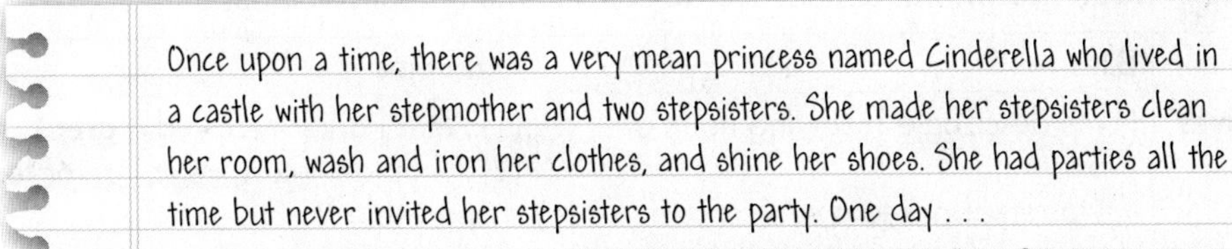

Once upon a time, there was a very mean princess named Cinderella who lived in a castle with her stepmother and two stepsisters. She made her stepsisters clean her room, wash and iron her clothes, and shine her shoes. She had parties all the time but never invited her stepsisters to the party. One day . . .

Grammar Summary

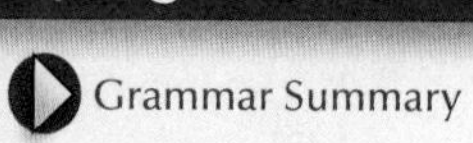

There are three types of **articles**: indefinite, definite, and zero article (Ø).

Type of article	Uses	Examples
Indefinite article = ***a*** (before a consonant sound) = ***an*** (before a vowel sound)	(1) first mention of a singular noun (2) before a singular noun to make a generic reference	(1–2) It's a common **belief** that a **child** needs a **hero**. (1–2) *Adventures of Superman* was an exciting **TV show**.
Definite article = ***the***	(1) mention of a particular person or thing (2) with unique nouns (3) before a singular noun to refer to inventions, species of animals, and musical instruments in general (4) before nationalities ending in *-ese, -sh, -ch,* and *-s* (5) before a singular noun to refer to a public place	(1–2) The **creator** of Superman invented other superheroes for the **world** to enjoy. (3) The **webshooter** helps Spider-man swing from building to building. (4) The **French** have their own comic book heroes. (5) Clark Kent sees Lois Lane every day at the **office**.
Zero article (Ø) **= no article**	(1) before most proper nouns (2) before plural nouns and noncount nouns to make a generic reference	(1) **Clark Kent** is **Superman**. (2) **Superheroes** have superhuman **strength**.

Quantifiers describe the quantity or amount of a singular noun or noun phrase.

With count nouns	Singular nouns: *one, each, every*
	Plural nouns: *many, (a) few, fewer, both, several, a good number of*
With noncount nouns	Count and noncount nouns: *all, some, any, no, plenty of, a lot of, lots of*
	Noncount only: much, *(a) little, less, a great deal of, a bit of*
With binary nouns	*a pair of*
As collective nouns = to refer to a mass	Common quantifying collective nouns: *a* ***group*** *of, a* ***set*** *of, a* ***bunch*** *of* Quantifying collective nouns with restricted use: *a* ***flock*** *of, a* ***series*** *of*
As unit nouns = to refer to a part of a group	*an* ***act*** *of, a* ***grain*** *of, a* ***trace*** *of, a* ***speck*** *of, a* ***piece*** *of*

There are two types of **noun modifiers**: descriptive adjectives and adjective clauses.

Type of noun modifier	Uses	Examples
Descriptive adjectives	(1) to describe a following noun or pronoun (2) to refer back to a subject and describe it (comes after a linking verb) (3) to make a generic statement about a group of people	(1) Peter Parker received a **great** gift. (2) As Spider-Man, Peter Parker feels **responsible** for others. (3) Robin Hood, a classic hero, stole from **the rich** and gave to **the poor**.
Adjective clauses	(1) to identify a person or thing = restrictive (no commas) (2) to give additional information about a person or thing = non-restrictive (commas)	(1) [thing] Honesty is a value **(which) that saves heroes from evil.** (2) [person] Pinocchio, **who learned the lesson of honesty**, transformed from a puppet to a human boy.

Self-Assessment

A (6 points) Complete the conversations with the correct article: *a, an, the,* or *Ø* (zero article).

AUNT MAY: Do you have **1.** ______ date with Mary Jane?

PETER PARKER: Yeah, we're going to dinner and **2.** ______ theater.

LOIS LANE: Why can't you use your X-ray vision to see through **3.** ______ walls of the bank?

SUPERMAN: I can see through most materials, but I can't see through **4.** ______ lead.

JENNIFER WALTERS: You must use your strength to help **5.** ______ weak.

DR. BRUCE BANNER: I want to, cousin. But sometimes I think my anger makes me more of a danger to **6.** ______ world.

B (5 points) Complete the sentences with the correct quantifier. Use each quantifier once.

a little	a good number of	any	a piece of	little

1. Can ______________ superhero defeat the Green Goblin?

2. ______________ Kryptonite, even as small as your fist, can hurt Superman.

3. There is ______________ in the universe that moves faster than the Flash, who is as fast as lightning.

4. A superhero must face ______________ villains in his or her lifetime.

5. "Batman!" cried Robin. "I need ______________ help."

C (4 points) Correct the four adjective errors.

Paul Bunyan is a hero legendary in the American Midwest and Northwest. One tall tale tells how it took five giants storks to deliver him as a baby to his parents. As a giant, Paul cleared forests and cut wood better than any other lumberjack. His size and strength allowed him to perform acts fantastic. He and Babe the Blue Ox, his companion, were so much big than all other people and animals that their footprints created lakes.

D (5 points) Combine the two ideas to make one sentence with an adjective clause.

1. Ariel, the mermaid, first saw the prince during a storm. The storm threw the prince into the sea.

____

2. In a very brave act, Ariel saved the prince. She quickly fell deeply in love with the prince.

____

3. The mermaid made a deal with the Sea Witch. The witch had the power to make Ariel human.

____

4. Ariel drank a magic potion. The potion gave her two human legs.

____

5. Ariel does not win the prince's love, but she passes an important test. The test proves the strength of her love and the goodness in her heart.

____

Unit Project: Commerical ad

A Work with a partner or a group. Imagine that you are going to create a new product and write an advertisement for it. Follow these steps:

1. Discuss this idea: Many corporations and advertisers often use the names of characters from Greek and Roman mythology or legendary heroes to sell their products. Because of the special powers or personality traits these characters have, they can inspire the product's name or qualities. Here are some examples. Can you think of any others?

   Cupid's Dating Service, *Venus* Beauty Products; *Neptune* Swimming Pools, *Robin Hood* Baking Flour, *Hermes* bags/fashion line; *Apollo* space program; *Atlas* Map Company, *Poseidon's* Beach Resort, or *Johnny Appleseed* Furniture and Seed Company.

2. Now choose a character from fairy tales, mythology, or legends. Create a new product and then write a slogan or advertisement based on the traits or characteristics of the hero. Look at the model.

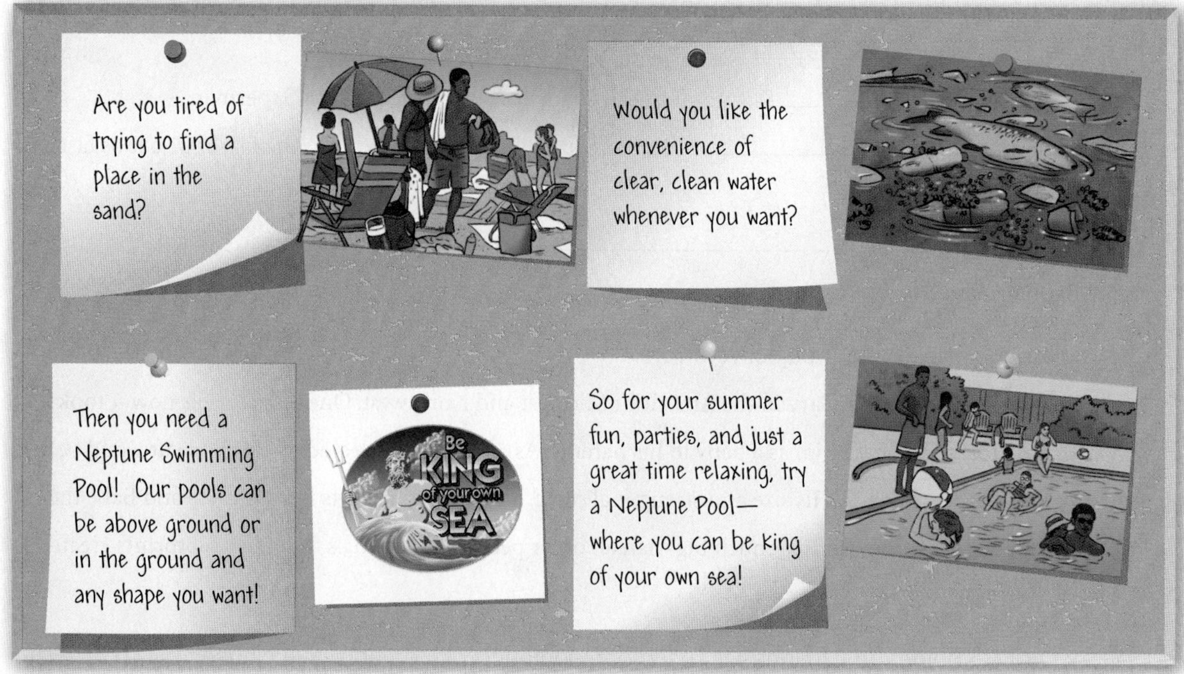

B Prepare your presentation for the class. Follow the steps. Use grammar from the unit in your presentation.

1. Present your advertisement to the class. Read the script aloud and show images on a presentation board, or make a video and show it on the class computer.
2. Ask the class if they have questions about the product. Would they buy it and use it? Why or why not? What would make your commercial better?

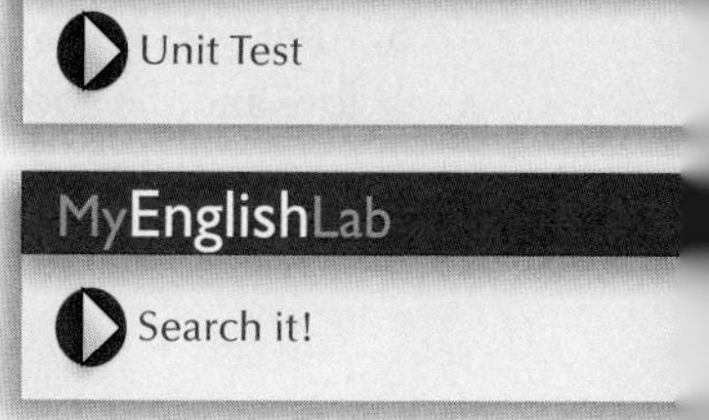

UNIT 4

Animal Instinct / Extinct Animals

Outcomes

After completing this unit, I will be able to use these grammar points.

Chapter 7

Grammar Focus 1
Present perfect

Grammar Focus 2
Present perfect progressive

Grammar Focus 3
Adjective clauses with *where* and *when*

Chapter 8

Grammar Focus 1
Past perfect

Grammar Focus 2
Past perfect progressive

MyEnglishLab

 What do you know?

CHAPTER 7 The *Real* Horse Whisperer

Getting Started

A Take the survey. Which activities have you seen or experienced? Talk to a partner. Ask and answer questions to compare your surveys.

Have you ever gone to a rainforest?

Yes, I have... No, I haven't...

- ☐ been to a horse show
- ☐ visited a zoo
- ☐ seen a beehive
- ☐ ridden on a camel
- ☐ worked on a dairy farm
- ☐ hiked in a wildlife preserve

B Read the description of falconry. Underline the words that follow the auxiliary verb *has* or *have*. These words are **participles**.

Falconry is one of the oldest professions in the world. In fact, humans have been keeping falcons for nearly 4,000 years. These magnificent raptors—birds of prey—have learned to fly away and instinctively return to their master's special glove. For centuries, falconers have been training hawks and falcons to help control pests, like rats or mice, which often invade farms and property.

C Look back at Parts A and B. Complete the tasks.

1. We form the **present perfect** with the auxiliary verb *have* or *has* + the past participle of the verb. Circle the examples of the present perfect.
2. We form the **present perfect progressive** with the auxiliary verb *have* or *has* + the participle of *be (been)* + the present participle of the verb. Underline the examples of the present perfect progressive.
3. Complete the chart.

Present perfect	Present perfect progressive

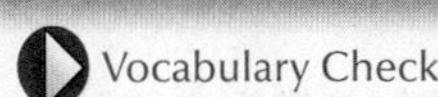

Reading

A WARM-UP Have you ever thought about a career working with animals? What are some animal-related careers that you know? Talk with a partner.

B SKIMMING Skim the job descriptions of three people who have unusual careers with animals. As you read, write how long each person has been doing his or her job. Who has been working the longest? Then read the entire text.

Unusual Careers with Animals

Emma Ford has been training and flying hawks and falcons since she was a small girl. She has always been passionate about these beautiful birds of prey. Emma grew up in a small cottage on the estate of Chilham Castle, in Kent, England. In 1982, when she was 18, Emma married fellow falconer Steve Ford. That same year, the Fords opened the British School of Falconry, where they have been instructing other enthusiasts on this ancient art. They also have established schools in Scotland and in the United States (in the state of Vermont). Emma has written several books on falconry, as well as an autobiography, *Fledgling Days: Memoir of a Falconer*. She has appeared in many nature films and commercials since her teens and was also the subject of the British TV show, *Countrywoman*.

Born in 1935, **Monty Roberts** has spent most of his life with horses. Monty has been observing and listening to them since he was 13 years old. Monty found that horses have a predictable body language and way of communicating with humans. For many years, he has helped these majestic animals to calm their instinctive fears. He has been using his special techniques to tame wild horses. In 1996, Monty published *The Man Who Listens to Horses*. He has won numerous awards, and his life has been portrayed in the documentary, *A Real Horse Whisperer*.

In the field of animal-related jobs, few people would probably choose to work in an *apiary*—a bee yard. But beekeeping is a profession even older than falconry—it dates back 12,000 years. A beekeeper, also called an *apiculturist*, becomes an expert on bees, their hives, and their behavior. Though traditionally, most beekeepers have been male, there has recently been a rise in the number of female apiculturists in North America. **Liz Lindsey** is among this new generation of beekeepers. She lives in North Carolina, where she has been tending the swarms in her backyard since 2007. Collecting and processing honey takes time and patience. Beekeepers also process beeswax, which has been a key ingredient in candle-making and even lip balm. Beekeepers have often sold bees for their pollen, which helps with growth of flowers and other plants. Liz says, "Keeping bees has brought me back to my love of science."

C CLASSIFYING INFORMATION Check (✓) the statements that are true for each person.

Emma	Monty	Liz	
			has always worked with raptors.
			has been collecting honey and selling pollen for years.
			has been instructing students in the profession for many years.
			has been married since age 18.
			has developed methods to communicate with animals.
			has been very patient and fearless.
			has written books and been the star of TV programs or movies.

Grammar Focus 1 Present perfect

Examples	Language notes
(1) Keeping bees **has brought** me back to my love of science. Emma Ford, Monty Roberts, and Liz Lindsey **have found** unusual animal careers.	We form the **present perfect** with: *have / has* + past participle We often use contractions with subject pronouns (*he has—he's / I have – I've*), especially in spoken English.
(2) *Present perfect:* Emma Ford **has established** falconry schools in the U.K. and in the U.S. *Compare to simple past (specific past point):* In 1982, Emma **married** fellow falconer Steve Ford.	Use the **present perfect** for completed actions at a non-specific past point in time.
(3) *Present perfect:* Monty Roberts **has spent** most of his life with horses. *Compare to present progressive (at this moment):* He **is riding** a horse right now.	The present perfect can describe actions that began in the past and continue to the present.
(4) *Present perfect:* Monty **has won** numerous awards. *Compare to simple past (no connection to present or future):* **He** won **numerous awards**.	Use the present perfect for past actions that may repeat in the future.
(5) The baby falcon **hasn't (has not) left** its mother.	For **negative statements** use: *have not / has not* + past participle
(6) I have **never** ridden a horse. She **still** has**n't** learned to ride a horse. She has**n't** learned to ride a horse **yet**. / She has**n't yet** learned to ride a horse. (*Less frequent word order*)	Use the adverb ***never*** to express a **past action** that didn't happen at any time in the past. The adverbs ***still*** and ***yet*** can express a similar meaning, but they also suggest that the speaker expects the action or event to happen in the future.
(7) Filmmakers have **already** told Monty's story in their documentary, *A Real Horse Whisperer.* Filmmakers have told Monty's story in their documentary **already**, *A Real Horse Whisperer.*	The present perfect is often used with various **expressions of time**. Use the adverb ***already*** to emphasize the completion of an action at a non-specific past point in time.
(8) The mother bird has **just** returned with food for its young.	Use the adverb ***just*** to describe an action completed in the recent past. The action may have an effect on the present.
(9) She has **always** had an interest in bees.	In **affirmative statements**, use the adverb ***always*** to emphasize that a state or condition has continued up to the present time.
(10) Liz Lindsey has been a beekeeper **for several years**.	Use ***for* + amount of time** to say how long a state has existed.
(11) She has kept bees in her backyard **since 2007**.	Use the adverb ***since*** to say when a present action or state began.
(12) **Have** you ever **seen** a beehive? —Yes, I **have**. / No, I **haven't**. **Has** he done this before? —Yes, he **has**. / No, he **hasn't**.	Use the present perfect to ask about one's **general past experience**. We often use the adverbs ***ever*** and ***before*** to emphasize any time before now.
(13) How many falcons **have** you **trained** so far?	Use the present perfect to ask ***how many*** or ***how many times*** for past actions that may repeat in the future. We often use the adverbs ***so far*** and ***up to now*** in these questions.

MyEnglishLab

Grammar Plus 1
Activities 1 and 2

Grammar Practice

A Complete the text with verbs in the present perfect and the words given.

Interview with Matthew Holt, Zookeeper

1. ________________________ (how long / you / work) **as a zookeeper?**

MH: Since 2004, but **2.** ________________________ (I / be) passionate about animals my whole life.

What kind of experience did you have with animals before you became a zookeeper?

MH: I spent my summers on my uncle's farm, and he taught me to tend animals. In college, I worked as a volunteer at the zoo. I'm glad that I can work here full-time now. It's really only at the zoo that **3.** ________________________ (I / learn) to work with wild animals.

How did you decide on a career in zookeeping?

MH: 4. ________________________ (I / always / know) that I wanted to work with animals. I studied biology in college, and like I said, I volunteered at the zoo while I was a student. This is truly a magnificent place to work. **5.** ________________________ (the staff / become) like a family to me.

6. ________________________ (your work / ever / put) **you in danger?**

MH: 7. ________________________ (I / experience) only one serious injury, and it happened when I was lifting a very heavy bag of animal feed! [*laughs.*] We interact with the animals, but we don't actually handle all of them, so I'm not often in any danger.

Are there any skills that 8. ________________________ (you / not / master / yet)**?**

MH: I think between my background in science and my true love for animals **9.** ________________________ (I / manage) quite well so far.

10. ________________________ (what / you/ learn) **from doing this kind of work?**

MH: More than anything, I think **11.** ________________________ (I / come) to appreciate the similarities and differences among all creatures in the world.

B Circle the verb forms that best complete the sentences.

1. As a wildlife rehabilitator, Anita **has helped / helped** baby squirrels successfully return to nature. People bring her lost squirrels throughout the year, and she cares for them on her own property.
2. Anita **has prepared / is preparing** a warm box for a baby squirrel, and the animal is already resting in it.
3. Right now Anita **is using / has used** an eyedropper to give milk to the baby squirrel.
4. This baby squirrel **doesn't grow / hasn't grown** big enough to be released into nature, but in a few weeks it will be time to let it go.
5. Squirrels **open / have opened** their eyes at five weeks. They can be released at 12 weeks.
6. Anita **has rescued / rescued** many squirrels since she received her license as a wildlife rehabilitator.
7. The baby squirrel **was / has been** in Anita's care for several weeks. Tomorrow she will let it go.
8. Anita volunteers her time to care for wildlife. She **has never accepted / isn't accepting** money.

Grammar Focus 2 Present perfect progressive

Examples	Language notes
(1) He **has been using** his special techniques to calm and tame wild horses.	We form the **present perfect progressive** with: *have / has + been* + the present participle We often use contractions with subject pronouns (*he has—he's, we have – we've*), especially in spoken English.
(2) Liz **has been tending** beehives since 2007. Emma **has been** a falconer for over 30 years. ***Incorrect:*** Emma **has** ~~been being~~ a falconer for over 20 years.	Use the present perfect progressive for an action that began in the past and continues to the present. The present perfect progressive emphasizes that the action is not completed and is in progress now. ***Note:*** We do not usually use non-action verbs in the progressive.
(3) Matthew **has been caring** for a baby elephant.	The present perfect progressive can describe an activity that was recently started and is still in progress, but it may not necessarily be happening at the time of speaking. This use is similar to the present progressive when we refer to temporary actions.
(4) The new mother bird **hasn't been flying** far from the nest.	For **negative statements,** use *have not / has not + been* + the present participle.
(5) Monty **has been observing and listening** to them **since** he was thirteen years old. Emma Ford **has been working** as a falconer **for** over 30 years.	The present perfect progressive can express the duration of an activity (how long it is), from a past point in time to the present. Use ***since*** + a starting point of an activity. Use ***for*** + the duration of an activity.
(6) Monty **has yet** to meet a horse he couldn't calm. (= *He **hasn't** met a horse **yet** . . .*)	***Has / have yet*** + **infinitive** has the same meaning as ***has not / have not*** + ***yet.***
(7) **Have** you **been working** with any new horses? —Yes, I **have**. / No, I **haven't**. **Has** the book **been selling** well? —Yes, it **has**. / No, it **hasn't**.	Use the present perfect progressive to ask about actions that began in the past and continue to the present.
(8) What **have** you **been doing lately**?	When asking about recent activities still in progress, questions often include the adverbs ***lately*** and ***recently***.

Grammar Practice

A Complete the text with verbs in the present perfect progressive and the words given.

Farm Animals in Need of Care: Are there any Doctors to Answer the Call?

The U.S. farm industry **1.** ____________________ (experience) a drop in the number of veterinarians. Graduates from veterinary schools **2.** ____________________ (choose) city and suburban locations over rural ones. Why **3.** ____________________ (the U.S. / see) fewer and fewer farm vets? Sadly, it's not necessarily a lack of passion but a need for money and comfort. Large animal vets receive less compensation and often work in tough conditions.

This is a difficult situation for farmers. In California alone, several rural areas **4.** ____________________ (depend) on a single farm vet. One recent vet school graduate explains that she **5.** ____________________ (give) advice to some farmers over the phone since they live so far away. In other parts of the United States, farm animals have no veterinarian at all to tend them.

One medical school **6.** ______________________ (try) to attract students into its farm veterinarian program by going into high schools and talking to young people about work in rural areas. The U.S. government **7.** ______________________ (not / turn) a blind eye toward the issue either. Politicians **8.** ______________________ (work) hard on a law that would give financial help to graduates who practice in rural areas which are in need of farm veterinarians.

B

Circle the verb forms that best complete the sentences.

Guide-Dog Trainers Wanted: 1. Have you been thinking / Did you think about a career with animals? Would you like your work to have meaning? Consider becoming a guide dog trainer! Our school **2. needs / has been needing** patient people who have passion and respect for animals and a sincere interest in helping others.

3. Have you been working / Have you worked with dogs before? Experience with animals helps, but our program will teach you to train dogs for a very specific purpose. For more than 25 years, we **4. have been teaching / are teaching** trainers to form healthy, productive relationships between guide dogs and their blind partners.

Do you think you **5. have / have been having** the right skills? Strong candidates will demonstrate confidence in public speaking and knowledge of animal behavior. The job of a guide dog trainer combines physical work, communication skills, and a knowledge of animal psychology. If you **6. were looking / have been looking** for the right program to help you start a career in dog training, contact us at dogscansee.org.

C

Complete the sentences with the correct words. Use each answer only once.

already	before	ever	for	never	since	up to now	yet

EMPLOYER: Tell me about your experience. Have you **1.** ______________ trained a horse?

JOB CANDIDATE: No, but I've been riding horses **2.** ______________ I was nine years old. I'm very comfortable around them, and I know how to tend to their needs.

EMPLOYER: Have you led any kind of tour **3.** ______________ ?

JOB CANDIDATE: No, I haven't. But I've been tutoring some school children **4.** ______________ over a year now, and I think being a tutor and being a tour guide are a bit similar. I've **5.** ______________ been a tour guide, but I'm good with people.

EMPLOYER: Well, I'll be honest. We've **6.** ______________ had about a dozen other people come in to interview, but I've **7.** ______________ to meet one who has people skills and real experience with horses. You seem to be the first.

JOB CANDIDATE: I'll be honest, too. I've been interviewing for different jobs, but **8.** ______________ I haven't found one that combines so many of my passions: animals, nature, and teaching. This seems to be the first.

EMPLOYER: I think we can both end our search. You're hired.

Now role-play the conversation with a partner.

Grammar Focus 3 Adjective clauses with *where* and *when*

Examples	Language notes
(1) She lives in North Carolina, **where she has been tending the swarms in her backyard since 2007.** Her career began in 2007 **when she set up an apiary in her backyard.**	An **adjective clause** is a dependent clause that modifies a noun (called the head noun). An adjective clause closely follows the head noun. Use the **relative pronoun *where*** to form an adjective clause that modifies a place. Use the **relative pronoun *when*** to form an adjective clause that modifies a time.
(2) In 1982**, when she was 18,** Emma married fellow falconer Steve Ford. [non-restrictive] Monty Roberts clearly remembers the day **when he first began to understand horses.** [restrictive] Monty Roberts clearly remembers the day Ø **he first began to understand horses.** [restrictive]	Adjective clauses with ***where*** and ***when*** can be restrictive (identifies head noun and doesn't use commas) or non-restrictive (non-identifying and needs commas). In restrictive adjective clauses, it is common to omit *where* and *when* and use the zero relative pronoun (Ø).
(3) A person must carefully choose the place **where he or she wishes to practice apiculture.** In cases **where there is little distance from a neighbor's yard**, a backyard apiary may not be welcome.	Some common head nouns with ***where*** include: *place, area, room, house, point, spot.* Other common place head nouns, such as *situation* and *case,* make a logical rather than physical reference.
(4) Liz Lindsey began her work as a beekeeper at a time **when female apiculturists were just beginning to appear in greater numbers.**	Some common head nouns with ***when*** include: *time, day, occasion, moment, period, season.*
(5) Yes, I've read *The Man Who Listens to Horses.* I love the part **where (when)** Roberts talks about his failure with the horse named "Fancy Heels" and all that he learned from it.	Some head nouns can be used with either *where* or *when* and include: *part, bit, case.*

Grammar Practice

Combine the two sentences. Use the second sentence to form an adjective clause using the relative pronoun *where* or *when.*

1. I want to spend my vacation in a place. I'll see lots of nature and wild animals there.
   I want to spend my vacation in a place where I'll see lots of nature and wild animals.
2. I've been saving money for a plane ticket to Australia, and in particular, Kangaroo Island. There's a wildlife preserve on the island.
   ____
3. The preserve is on a large piece of property. Kangaroos and other animals move about freely there.
   ____
4. Because I've chosen to go there as a volunteer, I'll stay in the staff quarters. Other volunteers will be living there.
   ____
5. I'll take my vacation during the Australian winter. The weather is much drier but still warm then.
   ____
6. I know there will be those days. On those days I'll do simple and unexciting tasks, like gardening or collecting firewood.
   ____
7. However, there will also be exciting times. During those times my work will bring me closer to the wildlife.
   ____
8. I believe the experience will help me after graduation. At that time, I'll be looking for a way to use my degree in zoology.
   ____

Correct the errors with adjective clauses. Follow the example. There are four more errors. You will need to add or change words.

Believe it or not, there are people who choose to work with poisonous snakes every day. But why would they place themselves in a situation ~~that~~ *where* a dangerous reptile could bite them? The answer is simple: to save the lives of others.

Snake milkers handle the most dangerous snakes in the world because the venom from the snakes' sharp fangs is very valuable. Venom is necessary, for example, to create *antivenom*, the medicine who can act against a bite from a poisonous snake. There are other medicines that also make use of snake venom. We live in a time new medicines and cures are constantly sought after, so the need for venom is strong.

Fortunately, a snake milker doesn't have to go out in the wild every day to search for snakes. A snake milker tends to these reptiles in a serpentarium, where is a place that poisonous snakes live.

One common way to extract the venom involves three steps: removing a snake from its home, milking the venom from the fangs, and then freeze-drying the venom. During the second step, there is a dangerous moment where the snake must bite the covering of jar and not the snake milker's hands.

Do you think you might enjoy such work? Those interested in a career as a snake milker must have a degree in chemistry, biology, biochemistry, or herpetology (the study of reptiles)—and, of course, a passion for snakes.

MyEnglishLab

Listen for it.

Listening

A 🎧 UNDERSTANDING MAIN IDEAS Listen to an interview on a talk show. Who has the host been interviewing? What have they been doing most of their lives?

____

B 🎧 UNDERSTANDING FACTS AND DETAILS Listen again. As you listen, check all the true statements. Then write new sentences to correct the false statements.

☐ **1.** Jane and Andy have been living in Hollywood since 1998. ____________

☐ **2.** Andy has owned parrots, a horse, and a chimpanzee. ____________

☐ **3.** Jane has never touched a snake because she doesn't like them. ____________

☐ **4.** Koalas have always been difficult to train. ____________

☐ **5.** Jane has recently injured her arm while working with an elephant. ____________

☐ **6.** Jane traveled a lot in South America. ____________

☐ **7.** Jane has been working in a wildlife sanctuary since 2000. ____________

☐ **8.** Andy and Jane have been married since 2004. ____________

☐ **9.** The couple has worked on 12 movies and nearly 25 television shows. ____________

C AFTER LISTENING Look back at Part B. The speakers have mentioned several animals that they have worked with. Which animals have you seen in nature or "the wild?" Which animals have you seen in zoos or sanctuaries? Discuss with a partner or in a group.

Speaking

MyEnglishLab

Sounding Natural

A One of the most famous TV shows in the U.S. has been Jeff Corwin's show *Animal Planet.* Work with a partner. Imagine you are a talk show host and you are going to interview Jeff Corwin or one of the animal experts in the reading. Read the information below or return to the reading passage. Then role-play with a partner.

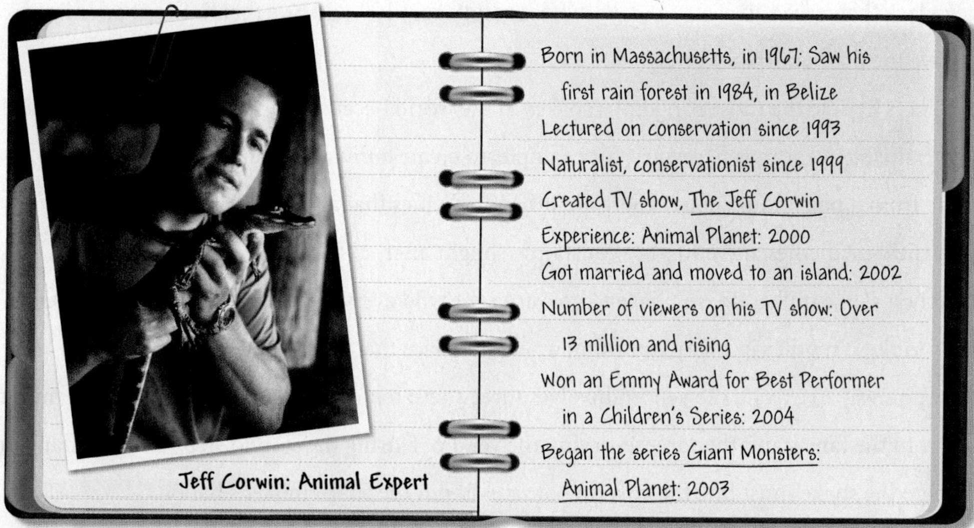

Jeff Corwin: Animal Expert
Born in Massachusetts, in 1967; Saw his first rain forest in 1984, in Belize
Lectured on conservation since 1993
Naturalist, conservationist since 1999
Created TV show, The Jeff Corwin Experience: Animal Planet: 2000
Got married and moved to an island: 2002
Number of viewers on his TV show: Over 13 million and rising
Won an Emmy Award for Best Performer in a Children's Series: 2004
Began the series Giant Monsters: Animal Planet: 2003

Hello, Mr. Corwin. Welcome to the show. What have you been doing lately?

Hi! Thanks for having me.

B Talk in a group or with a partner. Which shows have you seen about wildlife or animals? What TV shows are popular in your country?

MyEnglishLab

Linking Grammar to Writing

Writing

A Read these magazine titles. What do you think they are about? Try to match each title with its description. Then talk to a partner about which you have read or would like to read.

____ *Birds and Blooms*	**a.** Takes readers all over the globe with color photographs of rare and endangered animals and the efforts to save them and their wild habitats
____ *Equus Magazine*	**b.** Inspiring people to care about the planet since 1888
____ *National Geographic*	**c.** Beauty in your own backyard
____ *Wildlife Conservation*	**d.** The horse owner's resource

B You are a reporter for a famous wildlife magazine. You have just done research on and interviewed Jack Hanna and Temple Grandin. Use the information below to write a short article.

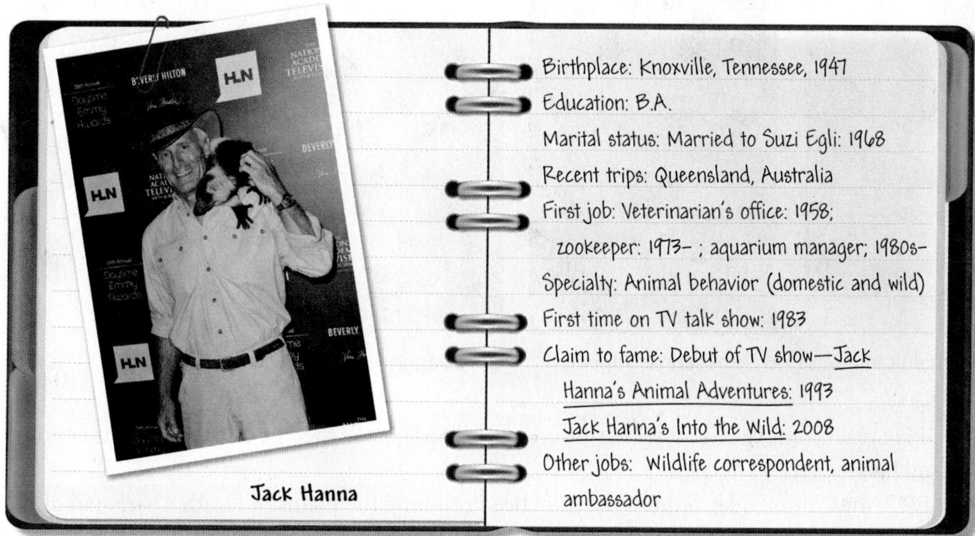

Jack Hanna
Birthplace: Knoxville, Tennessee, 1947
Education: B.A.
Marital status: Married to Suzi Egli: 1968
Recent trips: Queensland, Australia
First job: Veterinarian's office: 1958;
zookeeper: 1973– ; aquarium manager; 1980s–
Specialty: Animal behavior (domestic and wild)
First time on TV talk show: 1983
Claim to fame: Debut of TV show—Jack Hanna's Animal Adventures: 1993
Jack Hanna's Into the Wild: 2008
Other jobs: Wildlife correspondent, animal ambassador

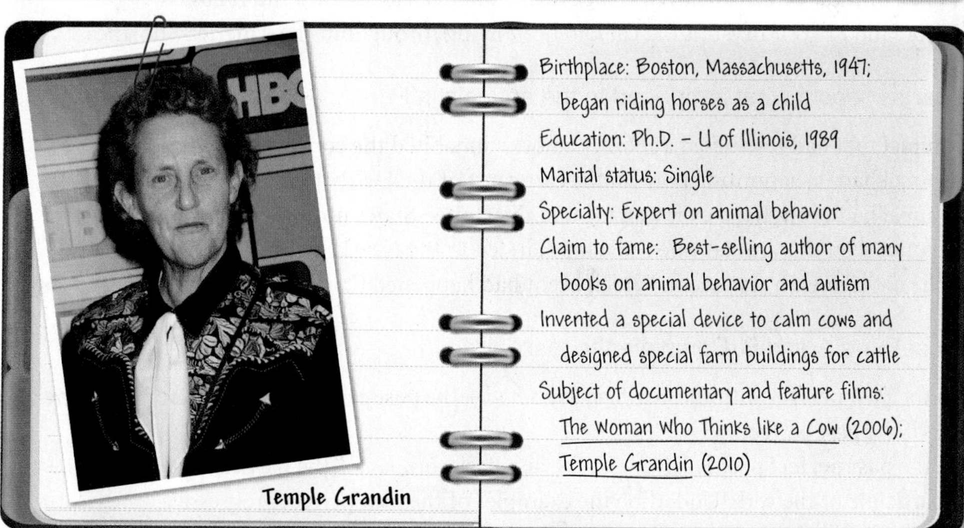

Temple Grandin
Birthplace: Boston, Massachusetts, 1947; began riding horses as a child
Education: Ph.D. – U of Illinois, 1989
Marital status: Single
Specialty: Expert on animal behavior
Claim to fame: Best-selling author of many books on animal behavior and autism
Invented a special device to calm cows and designed special farm buildings for cattle
Subject of documentary and feature films: The Woman Who Thinks like a Cow (2006); Temple Grandin (2010)

Jack Hanna has been working with animals since he was 11 years old. Hanna has had a life-long fascination with both domestic and wild animals. Once an assistant to a veterinarian, he has since . . .

C Exchange essays with a partner. Compare your essays and their similarities and differences.

CHAPTER 8 On the Verge of Extinction

Getting Started

A Extinction is part of the natural cycle of the Earth. Animal species may die out because of predators, because they lose their habitats (homes) or due to human activities, such as hunting. Can you identify these extinct creatures? Match the description with the picture.

A Eastern Mountain Lion

B Passenger Pigeon

C Quagga

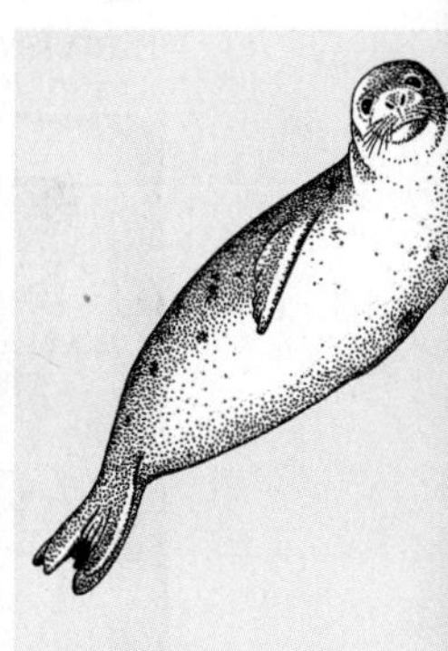

D Caribbean Monk Seal

_____ **1.** In 1494, Columbus called these marine creatures "Sea Cow" when he had first seen them on their island habitat.

_____ **2.** By 1883, these horse-like animals that had been roaming the plains of South Africa had died out.

_____ **3.** Flocks of these birds had covered the North American skies until the 1950s.

_____ **4.** Before the 21st century, this big cat had been living throughout the American northeast.

B Talk to a partner about what happened to the animals in Part A. Answer the questions.

1. Which animal that had resembled a zebra, had once inhabited the continent of Africa?
2. Which animal had been hunting prey on the east coast of the U.S. before it became extinct?
3. Which animal had been flying over Canada and the United States until it disappeared?
4. Who had once seen this animal when his ships landed in the New World?
5. Look at the dates in each statement. Which event had happened first? Which event happened last?

C Look back at Parts A and B. Complete the tasks.

1. We form the **past perfect** with the auxiliary verb *had* + the past participle of the verb. Circle the examples of the past perfect.
2. We form the **past perfect progressive** with the auxiliary verb *had* + the participle of *be* (*been*) + the present participle of the verb. Underline the examples of the past perfect progressive.
3. Complete the chart.

Past perfect	Past perfect progressive

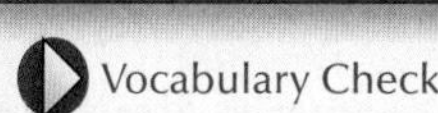

Vocabulary Check

Reading

A WARM-UP Look at the photos of animals in Part B that are extinct or near extinction. Where do you think each animal had once lived? Talk to a partner.

B PREDICTING Look again at the animals. Why do you think they are extinct or near extinction? Read the article and check your predictions.

News | Maps | Science | Education | Games | Events | Blogs | Explorers | Apps

And then there was one . . .

Until 1972, the scientific world had assumed that the Pinta Island tortoise was extinct. This was the belief until a park ranger discovered one tortoise that had been living alone on this desert island in the Galapagos. Until June 2012, "Lonesome George" resided at the Charles Darwin Research Center, where he had been living for over 30 years. Biologists had hoped to find a female tortoise to mate with him but their efforts were unsuccessful. The Pinta Island tortoise is now considered extinct. Lonesome George was about 100 years old when he died.

In 2006, scientists declared the Baiji white dolphin functionally extinct. Baiji dolphins had been the victims of fishermen's nets, which played a large part in their disappearance. Scientists believed this dolphin had completely vanished from the Yangtze River, until recently, when a fisherman believed he had spotted one. The group of scientists returned to the river and has been searching for this "sole survivor" ever since.

Biologists have also turned their attention to birds like the Bengal florican. Called the "whispering bird," it has practically vanished from the grasslands of Cambodia where it had been nesting for centuries. Now, fewer than 1,000 survive. A similar fate has afflicted the Bactrian camel of the Gobi Desert. Large numbers of these amazing two-humped creatures had once roamed the rocky Gobi Desert of Mongolia. Now, there are fewer than 800 of them left in the world, which places them on the endangered species list. Conservationists also monitor the golden lion tamarin monkey of the Amazon rain forest, whose numbers have dropped to fewer than 2,000 in the wild.

The first animal to become extinct in the 21st century was the Pyrenean ibex—an animal that resembled a goat. Herds of ibex had been living in the Spanish mountains until recently. The last one died in 2006, the same year when the West African rhinoceros disappeared from its grassy habitat. Though there is no hope for the return of the majestic ibex or magnificent rhino, we have not yet abandoned efforts to revive populations of animals like the Pinta tortoise or the Baiji dolphin. Future generations may never see any of these amazing animals unless conservationists make an effort to revive their numbers.

C Read the criteria for animal extinction from the International Union for Conservation of Nature. Find the status of each animal in the reading and use the information to complete the chart.

Extinct	No animals have been seen	
Functionally extinct	None capable of breeding	
Endangered	High risk of extinction because too few exist	
Vulnerable	Population is fewer than 1,000	
Threatened	Population is between 1,000 and 3,000	

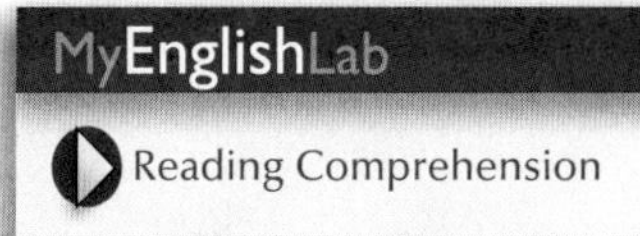

Grammar Focus 1 Past perfect

Examples	Language notes
(1) Until 1972, the scientific world **had believed** the Pinta Island tortoise to be extinct.	To form the **past perfect**, use: *had* + the past participle We often use contractions with subject pronouns (*he had—he'd / I had—I'd*) in spoken English.
(2) By 2006, the Baiji white dolphin **had become** functionally extinct.	Use the past perfect to express that an action took place before a specific past point in time. We can use the preposition ***by*** to state that specific past point.
(3) Before that time, the dolphin population **had been** much bigger.	In conversation, we often use the verb *be* and *go* in the past perfect, but other verbs do not often appear in this form. The past perfect most frequently appears in writing.
(4) They **believed** it **had completely** disappeared from the Yangtze River.	We often see the past perfect in statements with the simple past. The two tenses show a relationship in time. The past perfect refers to the earlier of two actions or events.
(5) **By the time** the last ibex died in 2006, the West African rhinoceros **had** also **disappeared**. The West African rhinoceros **had** also **disappeared by the time** the last ibex died in 2006.	The adverb phrase ***by the time*** makes the relationship between two past actions or events clearer by emphasizing the completion of that earlier time period. Use *by the time* + simple past + past perfect. (Either clause can appear first.)
(6) A fisherman **spotted** a Baiji white dolphin, and then a group of scientists **went** back to the river and **searched** for it.	The use of the past perfect and simple past together contrasts with a series of verbs all in the simple past, which expresses that all the actions and events took place in a past time period and they occurred one after the other.
(7) Scientists **hadn't (had not) known** about the sole Baiji white dolphin.	For **negative statements**, use: *had not* + the past participle
(8) Until the scientist visited the Charles Darwin Research Center, he**'d never seen** a Pinta Island tortoise. The scientist walked to the Center with excitement; he **hadn't seen** "Lonesome George" **yet**.	Use the adverb ***never*** to express a past action that didn't happen at any time in the past. The adverbs ***still*** and ***yet*** can express a similar meaning, but they also suggest that the speaker expects the action or event to happen in the future.
(9) When conservation efforts began, the animal's numbers **had already become** dangerously low. When conservation efforts began, the animal's numbers **had become** dangerously low **already**. [less common word order]	Use the adverb ***already*** to emphasize the completion of an action before a specific past point in time. We often see a time clause, (*when* + simple past) with a main clause using *already* + past perfect.
(10) When I arrived, the staff **had just finished** tending the animals.	Use the adverb ***just*** with the past perfect to describe an action completed immediately before a specific past point in time.
(11) Until 2000, numerous herds of Bactrian camels **had roamed** the Gobi Desert **for** centuries.	Use ***for*** + **amount of time** with the past perfect to express how long a state has existed before a specific past point in time.
(12) **After** the scientist **had studied** the animal, he **recorded** his thoughts in careful detail. (= ***After*** *the scientist* ***studied*** *the animal, he* ***recorded*** *his thoughts in careful detail.*)	The adverbs ***after*** and ***before*** can appear in statements with both the past perfect and simple past.

Yes / no questions and short answers	*Wh-* questions
Had you **seen** this kind of animal? Yes, I **had**. / No, I **hadn't**.	Where **had** the animals **lived**? How **had** they **survived**?

Grammar Practice

A Complete the text with verbs in the past perfect and the words given.

Why have certain fish vanished from the waters? The Blackfin Cisco is one of several fish that are now extinct in North America. Before overfishing, the Blackfin Cisco **1.** ____________________ (live) in the Great Lakes. By the 1960s, it **2.** ____________________ (also / fall) prey to sea lamprey and other predatory fish.

By 1985, another type of cisco **3.** ____________________ (disappeared) from the Great Lakes region. People **4.** ____________________ (not / realize) their own threat to the fish until it was too late. Overfishing **5.** ____________________ (slowly / decrease) the populations of the Shortnose Cisco to the point of no existence.

The condition of lake water itself can also threaten fish. Between worsening conditions in Lake Erie and overfishing, the Blue Pike **6.** ____________________ (go) into extinction by 1983.

It isn't too late to protect other fish. Understanding threats and taking steps to control them is key. For example, although it was human activity that **7.** ____________________ (allow) sea lamprey to invade the Great Lakes in the 1920s, the U.S. government is now taking action to control their population.

B Complete the text with verbs in the past perfect or simple past and the words given. In some cases, either form is correct.

When an animal or insect population nears extinction, is any hope left? Luckily for the Large Blue Butterfly, biologist Jeremy Thomas **1.** ____________________ (believe) the answer was yes. Across northern Europe this beautiful blue butterfly **2.** ____________________ (nearly / disappear) by the 1970s, and it was not clear why. **3.** ____________________ insect collectors ____________________ (capture) too many for the population to survive?

Thomas **4.** ____________________ (determine) the cause only after he **5.** ____________________ (study) a group of Large Blue Butterflies in the U.K. for six summers. He **6.** ____________________ (prove) that the butterfly's survival depended on a kind of red ant. In turn, the red ants needed short grass to allow the sun to warm the soil they lived in. Sadly, with fewer rabbits or cattle to eat the grass, it **7.** ____________________ (grow) too high to ensure the ants' survival. A threat to the red ants resulted in a threat to the Large Blue Butterfly.

By the time Thomas **8.** ____________________ (be) ready to take action, the species **9.** ____________________ (die) out in Great Britain. But Thomas **10.** ____________________ (have) a plan to revive its population. In Sweden, he found Large Blue Butterfly caterpillars, and he **11.** ____________________ (bring) them home. He also brought cows to the same area where he released the caterpillars. It was a conservation success. The herd of cows kept the grass low, the ants lived, and the caterpillars **12.** ____________________ (grow). The Large Blue Butterfly has recently returned to the U.K.

Grammar Focus 2 Past perfect progressive

Examples	Language notes
(1) The ibex **had been living** in the Spanish mountains.	To form the **past perfect progressive**, use: *had* + *been* + the present participle Especially in spoken English, it is common to use contractions with subject pronouns (*he had—he'd, we have—we'd*).
(2) Until 2006, scientists **had been looking** for surviving Baiji dolphins.	Use the past perfect progressive to express that an action was in progress *before* a specific past point in time. This contrasts with the past progressive, which refers to an action in progress *at* a past point in time: *In 2005, they **were** still **looking** for these dolphins.*
(3) The scientists were disappointed. They **had been searching** all morning with no sign of the dolphin.	The past perfect progressive can explain the result of an earlier action in a later time period. The earlier action took place not long before the second past point in time.
(4) The tortoise **had been living** alone in the desert of the small Galapagos Island **for many years**.	Use ***for*** + **amount of time** with the past perfect progressive to express the duration of an activity (how long it was) up to a past point in time.
(5) By the time she **earned** her master's degree in biology, she **had been working** at the research center for over three years.	We can use the past perfect progressive with the simple past to express the duration of a past activity up to a specific past point in time. Use of ***by*** or ***by the time*** makes the timeline clearer. Remember that non-action verbs do not normally appear in the progressive. (*She **had been** a volunteer at the research center.*)
(6) As a volunteer, she **hadn't been receiving** compensation for her work.	We form **negative statements** in the past perfect progressive with *had not* + *been* + the present participle. Especially in spoken English, it is common to use the contraction *hadn't.*

Yes / no questions and short answers	*Wh-* questions
Had invaders **been preying** on the animals? Yes, they **had.** / No, they **hadn't.**	Where **had** "Lonesome George" **been hiding**?

Grammar Practice

MyEnglishLab

Grammar Plus 2
Activities 1 and 2

 Circle the verb forms that best complete the text.

Ten to twelve thousand years ago mastodons, early ancestors of the elephant, **1. had roamed / roamed** Earth. Until the Ice Age, they **2. had lived / had been living** in the Great Lakes region of North America. One male mastodon that weighed five to six tons **3. had chosen / chose** its final resting place in the area we know today as Livingston County, New York. This fact **4. had remained / had been remaining** unknown until 1991, when a crew of construction workers **5. had discovered / discovered** the site about five feet underground. They **6. had dug / had been digging** at the time of their surprising find.

Soon people **7. had been talking / were talking**, and the news **8. had reached / reached** local scientists. The workers **9. had already taken / had already been taking** some of the bones home as souvenirs by the time scientists from a nearby university arrived on the site. Nevertheless, most of the skeleton **10. had still remained / still remained** so the scientists **11. had had / had** much to study and appreciate. The workers **12. had removed / had been removing** the skull of the mastodon from the ground with the help of a bucket. Of course, the university-led excavation **13. had required / required** more patient and careful digging.

This **14. had been / was** a true treasure! Although people **15. had found / had been finding** mastodon bones before, not many **16. formed / had been forming** a complete skeleton. Fortunately for scientists, the bones of the New York State mastodon **17. had been lying / were lying** in a bog, which was a bed of sticky, wet clay that helped keep the bones in good condition.

B Read the article and correct the errors with the past verb forms. Look at the example. There are 10 more errors.

Before director Steven Spielberg had brought his dinosaurs to the big screen, author Michael Crichton entertained readers with the tale of Jurassic Park. Relive the excitement as you read this plot summary.

Only a short time ago, Dr. Alan Grant and Dr. Ellie Sattler have been working on a dig in Montana. They were experts on dinosaurs and plants that has become extinct. Now as guests of the billionaire John Hammond, Drs. Grant and Sattler were seeing the impossible: a world where live dinosaurs had roamed. In front of their eyes a huge Brachiosaurus was eating from a tree, and a herd of Parasaurolophus ran. They had arrived at Jurassic Park, a place where Mr. Hammond had hoped to attract tourists and scientists alike. In addition to Drs. Grant and Sattler, Mr. Hammond's guests included his lawyer, a mathematician, and his two grandchildren. Before they had arrived on Mr. Hammond's island, none of them had been seeing real dinosaurs.

On a safari-like tour, the guests began to ride through the park. At first, there was little to see because the dinosaurs didn't show themselves to the guests. Then trouble had appeared. One of the workers has been planning for some time to steal Hammond's creations. The worker shut down security on the island so he could carry out his crime, but then everything that protected the guests on the tour disappeared.

What had Mr. Hammond been thinking when he had revived these large and dangerous dinosours? Had it been a mistake to create the park? In the end, there is only one question that the audience must answer: Just because science says we can do it, does it mean we should?

MyEnglishLab

Sounding Natural

Speaking

A Look back at the reading and grammar activities. Work with a partner. Find all the animals that are extinct. Discuss what had happened to each of the animals by the time something else happened. Use the expressions with the past perfect or past perfect progressive forms.

after	already	before	by	by the time	for
Mastodon	Passenger Pigeon	Monk Seal	Large Blue Butterfly	Pyrenean Ibex	Baiji Dolphin
millions of years ago	hundreds of years ago	1920–1930	1950–1970	1990–2000	2010

B Look back at the reading, or think about an animal in your home country. Talk about the animals with a partner or in a group.

I'm going to talk about the status of the Quagga.
The Quagga is an animal that has become endangered. Scientists thought it had vanished by . . .

Listening

A BEFORE LISTENING Look at the map. Where do you think most dinosaurs and other prehistoric animals had lived before they became extinct?

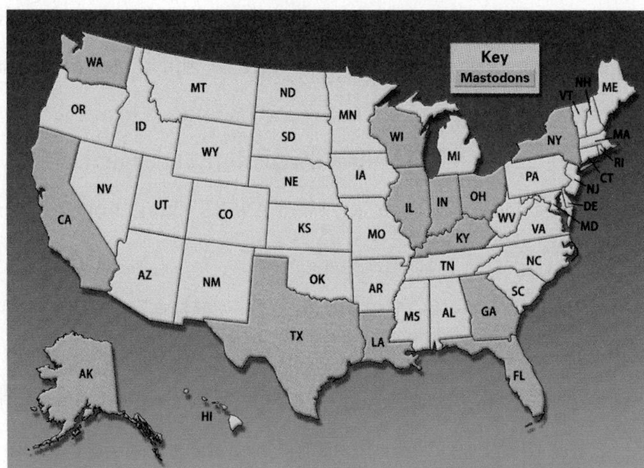

B UNDERSTANDING MAIN IDEAS Listen to a short lecture. Where is the speaker? What do you think the speaker had just discussed? ______________________________

C UNDERSTANDING FACTS AND DETAILS Listen again. Check (✓) all the things that the speaker mentioned.

☐ **1.** Columbus had seen the North American mastodon.
☐ **2.** The Caribbean monk seal had become extinct by the time Columbus landed.
☐ **3.** Lonesome George had been living on Pinta Island before he moved.
☐ **4.** The mastodon became extinct because of its dangerous habitat.
☐ **5.** The mastodon had been living in North America for millions of years by the time humans appeared.
☐ **6.** Mastodons had been predators of humans.
☐ **7.** Mastodons had weighed about 3 tons.
☐ **8.** There is evidence that the North American mastodon had lived in New York State.

MyEnglishLab

Linking Grammar to Writing

Writing

A Vanishing Cats are big cats, like tigers and lions, which have become extinct or endangered. Look at the map and make notes about these cats. Then write a short essay on the Vanishing Cats. You can refer back to Reading Activity C for information about extinction.

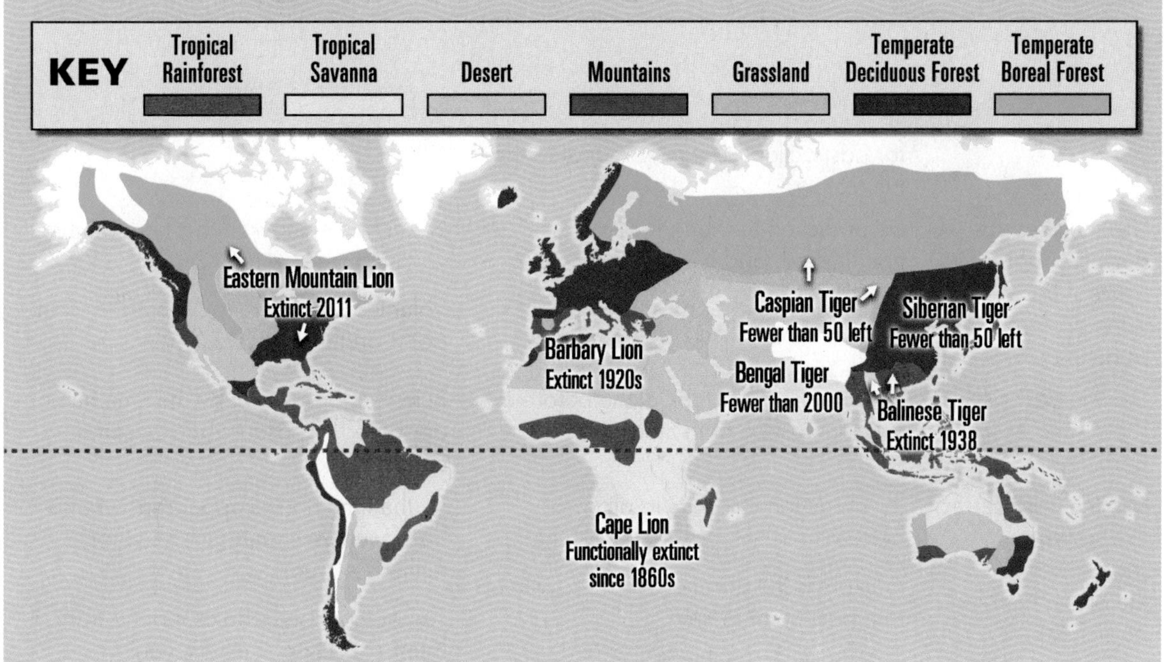

B Answer these questions in your essay.

1. Where had the big cats been living before they vanished?
2. Which had become extinct first?
3. Officials have declared which animal extinct in the 21st century?
4. What kind of terrain had the animal been inhabiting?
5. What is the official classification of the animal?
6. What had humans done to the animals' habitats?

The Vanishing Cats

In many countries in Africa, big cats had been living in the mountains and deserts. They had roamed the grasslands of Africa. Unfortunately, over the past centuries, many of these animals have become extinct.

C Exchange essays with a partner. Compare your essays and talk about their similarities and differences.

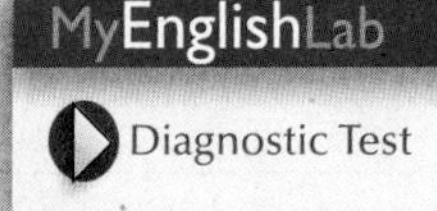

Grammar Summary

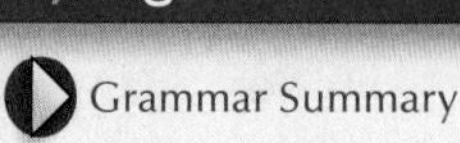

Grammar Summary

We use the **present perfect** and **past perfect** for actions that happen before another time or event. We use the **present perfect progressive** and the **past perfect progressive** for actions that are in progress before or until another event.

Verb forms	Notes	Examples
Use the **present perfect** [*have / has* + the past participle]	for completed actions at a non-specific past point in time. for actions that began in the past and continue to the present. for past actions that may repeat in the future.	She **has earned** a degree in zoology. I'**ve cared** for animals all my life. We'**ve visited** Australia two times.
Use the **present perfect progressive** [*have / has* + *been* + the present participle]	for an action that began in the past, is not finished, and is in progress now. for temporary actions at the present time.	Nigel **has been working** here on the wildlife preserve for 12 years. Volunteers **have been helping** to clear paths on the preserve.
Use the **past perfect** [*had* + the past participle]	for an action that took place before a specific past point in time.	Scientists agree that by the time humans appeared, dinosaurs **had become** extinct.
Use the **past perfect progressive** [*had* + *been* + the present participle]	for an action that was in progress before a specific past point in time. to express the duration of an activity up to a past point in time.	By the time horses appeared, whales **had been swimming** the seas for millions of years. The author used photos that he **had been collecting** since his youth.

We use **adverbs of time** to describe when an action occurred.

The adverbs *ever* and *before* commonly appear in questions with the present perfect and past perfect.	Have you **ever** worked with guide-dogs? Had you trained guide-dogs **before**?
The adverb *already* commonly appears in affirmative statements in the present perfect and past perfect.	My training course has **already** begun. I had already **met** the instructor.
The adverbs *never, yet,* and *still* commonly appear in negative statements with the present perfect and past perfect.	I've **never** met a more patient instructor. I hadn't mastered all the skills **yet**. The guide-dog that I'm training **still** hasn't learned to follow all my commands.
Use *for* to express duration and *since* to state the starting point of a present activity.	I've been working with the same guide-dog **for** three weeks. The dog has been in our care **since** June.
Use *by* or *by the time* to emphasize that an action or event finished before a specific past point in time.	**By** the end of the course, the guide-dog had learned all the commands.

An **adjective clause** is a dependent clause that modifies a noun. Adjective clauses with ***where*** modify a place. Adjective clauses with ***when*** modify a time.

Use the relative pronoun *where* for place nouns.	Common place nouns: *place, area, room, house, point, spot, bit, part, case*	Even experienced riders have gotten lost in those parts **where trails are not clearly marked**.
Use the relative pronoun *when* for time nouns.	Common time nouns: *time, day, occasion, moment, period, season, bit, part, case*	There are days **when the weather makes it unsafe to go horseback riding**.

Self-Assessment

A (6 points) Complete the conversations. Write the correct form of the verb in the present perfect or present perfect progressive.

EMMA: I **1.** ______________________ (wear) this falconer glove for so long that it is worn out. I need a new one.

CLERK: This glove **2.** ______________________ (be) our most popular for the past few years. Try it on.

SUE: I **3.** ______________________ (hear) that some species of honey bees are under threat of extinction.

LIZ: That's true! But many associations of beekeepers **4.** ______________________ (work) to protect them.

INTERVIEWER: Jeff, how long **5.** ______________________ (you / star) in your popular TV show?

JEFF: I **6.** ______________________ (have) this program since 2003.

B (6 points) Combine the two sentences. Use the second sentence to form an adjective clause using the relative pronoun *where* or *when*.

1. Liz Lindsey has found much happiness in her apiary. She tends her beehives there.

____

2. Emma watched the magnificent birds in the air. They were searching for prey and other pests on the ground. ____

3. Monty shared his special experience with horses in 1996. In that year, he published a book.

____

C (4 points) Correct the mistake in the each sentence.

1. The animal rescuer is taking care of the injured tiger for several months before he returned it to its native habitat.

2. Dinosaurs have been extinct long before humans inhabited the Earth.

3. Scientists not yet determine the cause of the dolphin's disappearance.

4. After it becomes prey for the sea lamprey, the Blackfin Cisco was extinct.

D (4 points) Write a sentence with the past perfect or the past perfect progressive and the words given. Use the words in the order that they appear.

1. Bactrian camel / in the Gobi Desert / for 1,000 years ______________________________

____

2. Scientists / declare / Siberian tiger / near extinction / until recently ______________________

____

3. Before / Baiji dolphin / became extinct / be / swim ______________________________

____

4. In 1993 / paleontologists / discover / a mastodon fossil ______________________________

____

Unit Project: Wildlife TV show

Work with a partner. Imagine you are working for a popular TV production company. Your team is going to create a weekly TV show based on the people and endangered or extinct animals you have read about in this unit. Follow these steps.

1. With your partner, discuss these questions.

- Who is going to host the show? (A famous person? You or your partner?)
- Describe the qualifications or experience your host has had.
- Explain why you have chosen this host, what the person has done, and why he or she would be the best candidate for the show.
- What animals would you research for the first show?
- What has happened to this animal? What will you tell them about it?
- What area of the world will you cover in your first show? Why have you chosen it?
- What do you want viewers to know about these animals?

2. Write a proposal for your show. Use the information above and add anything else that you think would be interesting. Think about similar shows that you know. What else do they have that would work for your show?

3. Now create a storyboard to prepare your presentation. You can use images, charts, statistics or other information to make your presentation colorful and interesting to your audience. Look at the model.

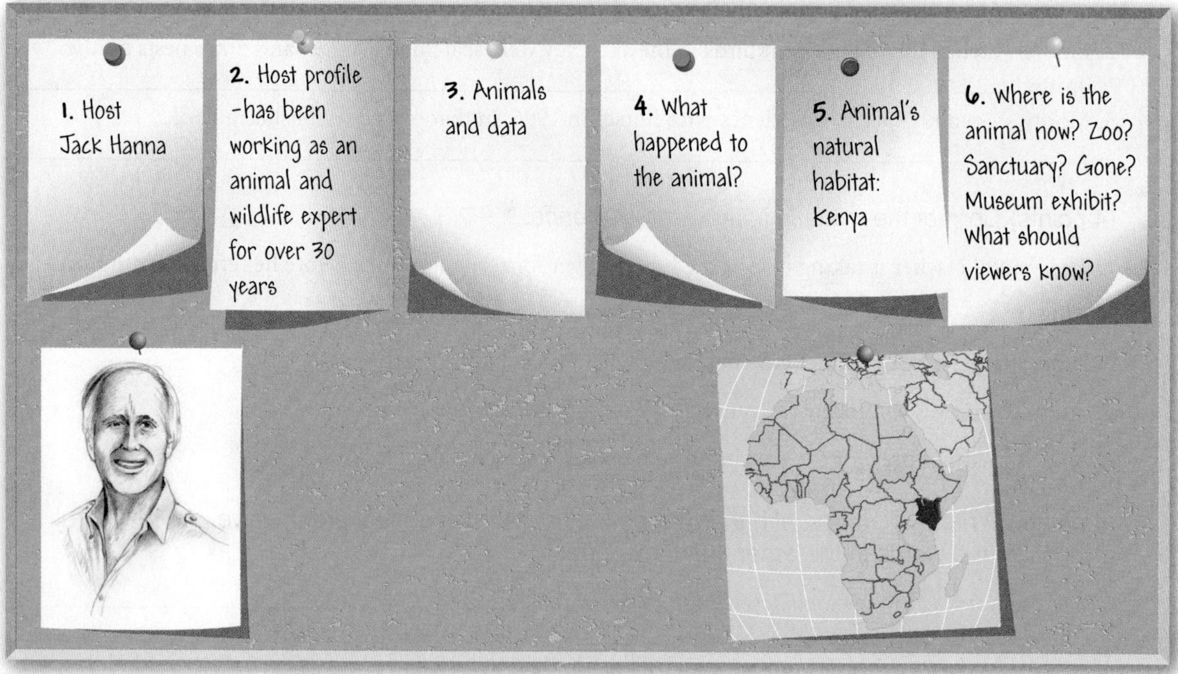

B Make your pitch! Present your storyboard to your class. Follow the steps. Use the grammar from the unit in your presentation.

1. Deliver your presentation. Ask the class if they have any questions.

2. As a class, imagine you are on the official "Board of Directors" of the TV station. Then, as a class, cast your votes for the show.

I'm here to present our idea for the show, "Instinct or Extinct?"
The host of our show will be Jack Hanna, who has been working as an animal and wildlife expert for over 30 years. . . .

UNIT 5

Trending and Spending

OUTCOMES

After completing this unit, I will be able to use these grammar points.

CHAPTER 9

Grammar Focus 1
Phrasal verbs: Overview and separable

Grammar Focus 2
Multi-word phrasal verbs

CHAPTER 10

Grammar Focus 1
Phrasal verbs: Inseparable

Grammar Focus 2
Intransitive phrasal verbs

MyEnglishLab

What do you know?

CHAPTER 9 What's in Your Closet?

Getting Started

A Look at the images and talk with a partner. Do you think these fashions are in style now? Which ones do you like?

B Something that is *trendy* is fashionable and popular right now. Are you trendy, or do you create your own style? Complete the questionnaire. Then compare answers with a partner.

TREND QUIZ

☐ T ☐ F 1. I never throw anything out—you never know what might come back into fashion.
☐ T ☐ F 2. I can't pass up a bargain—I buy all my clothes on sale.
☐ T ☐ F 3. I pick out the newest styles in magazines.
☐ T ☐ F 4. Before I make an expensive purchase, I like to think it over first.
☐ T ☐ F 5. I look forward to seeing the new styles every season.
☐ T ☐ F 6. I can't keep up with current fashion trends.
☐ T ☐ F 7. I always try on clothes at the store before I buy them.
☐ T ☐ F 8. I like thrift shops where I can buy or give away my old clothes.
☐ T ☐ F 9. I often read fashion magazines so I never miss out on the latest trends.
☐ T ☐ F 10. I often wear clothes that have gone out of style.

More odd-numbered questions "True?" You're trendy.
More even-numbered questions "True?" You have your own style.

C Look back at Part B. Complete the tasks.

1. **Phrasal verbs** consist of a verb followed by a particle (a preposition or an adverb). Some phrasal verbs take a noun as a direct object and are *separable.* That means we can place a noun or a pronoun between the verb and the particle. Look at the example. Then, underline all the phrasal verbs in Part B.

   I always **try on** clothes before I buy them. I always try clothes on. I always **try** them **on**

2. **Multi-word phrasal verbs** consist of a verb and two or more particles. Multi-word phrasal verbs are usually *inseparable*. The pattern is verb + adverb + preposition. We cannot place the object between the verb and its particles. Look at the example. Then, circle all the multi-word phrasal verbs in Part B.

   I often wear clothes that have **gone out of** style.

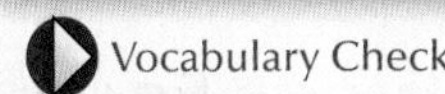

MyEnglishLab

Vocabulary Check

Reading

A WARM-UP Talk to a partner. What is a fashion forecaster? What do you think a fashion forecaster does? What clothing styles do you think people will still wear in the future?

B PREDICTING Before you read, look at the images in the article below and in Getting Started. Which decade does each "look" represent? Then read the article and check your answers.

When Fashion Trends Make a Comeback

When you go shopping, what do you do? Do you just try on whatever looks comfortable? Or, do you **think** it **over** carefully and **pick out** clothing that not only looks good but is also the latest fashion? Have you ever considered that someday that new dress or suit might go out of style? Well, that's what fashion forecasters do.

Fashion forecasters keep up with the latest trends. They pay attention to colors and fabrics and try to predict what people will be wearing in the next few years. They know which looks will go out of style. Some trend forecasters insist that they 'need to know what the customer wants before the customer knows they want it.' Fashion, they say, is transitory—what you're wearing today might not be trendy tomorrow. However, it could come back into style in the future. If you **missed out on** wearing them the first time, here are some fashions that have made a comeback.

1960s: The "waif" look—a "pixie" haircut, dramatic makeup style; turtleneck shirts, skinny jeans, low-rise jeans. Made a comeback: 2001 and 2011.

1970s: The "Hippie" style: Loose, natural fabrics; peasant skirts; bell-bottom jeans. Made a comeback: 2012.

1980s: The "preppy" look –oxford shirts, Izod sweaters, penny loafers, khaki pants. Made a comeback: 2004 and 2010.

1990s: The "grunge" look—natural fabrics, plaids; short, messy hair; leggings, boots. Made a comeback: 2009.

2000s: "Hip hop and Hipster" look—tracksuits, kangol hats; cropped tops and skinny pants. Made a comeback: ?

The clothes of the 1960s and '70s may have an advantage over clothes from the 2000s. We associate trends with the people who wore them—like fashion icons Audrey Hepburn or Jackie Onassis. Their styles were "classic." Forecasters say that you should never give away classic pieces of clothing because they will never go out of style. If you see a little black dress or a tailored men's suit on sale, that's an opportunity you should never **pass up**. So don't throw out those skinny jeans yet: you can look forward to wearing them in this decade and beyond.

C UNDERSTANDING VOCABULARY IN CONTEXT Read the passage again and answer the questions.

1. In paragraph 1, what is a synonym for ***think over***?
   a. consider **b.** forget **c.** not know
2. Look at ***pick out*** in paragraph 1. What is the best synonym for *pick out*?
   a. take **b.** select **c.** remove
3. In paragraph 2, what does ***miss out on*** mean?
   a. not see **b.** not want **c.** not experience
4. In the last paragraph, what does ***pass up*** mean?
   a. refuse **b.** meet **c.** not succeed

MyEnglishLab

Reading Comprehension

Grammar Focus 1 Phrasal verbs: Overview and separable

Examples	Language notes
(1) Forecasters say that classic pieces are the clothes you should never **give away**.	**Phrasal verbs** are a type of multi-word verb with two parts. They consist of a **verb** and a **particle**—a preposition or an adverb. The most common prepositions in phrasal verbs are *in, on, about,* and *for.* The most common adverbs in phrasal verbs are *up, down, off,* and *on.*
(2) Do you **think about** what is trendy? [very literal = give thought to; *consider*] Those are the items you should never **pass up**. [more idiomatic = not use one's chance; *refuse*]	A **particle** changes the meaning of the verb. However, sometimes the definition of the phrasal verb remains very literal, that is, clear and easy to understand. When the meaning is very different from the original definition of the verb and not immediately clear, we say it is idiomatic.
(3) "That's a beautiful dress. Do you want to **try** it **on**?"	We use phrasal verbs more often in conversation than in writing. Greater use of phrasal verbs generally makes one's speech more informal, so while phrasal verbs are common and very natural in spoken English, we don't usually see them in formal writing.
(4) When I was **growing up**, I used to love to **try on** my mother's hats and shoes. (grow up = *intransitive;* try on = *transitive*)	Phrasal verbs can be transitive or intransitive. **Intransitive** phrasal verbs do not have an object. **Transitive** phrasal verbs have an object.
(5) Did you **pick out** something trendy? Did you **pick** something trendy **out**?	Many transitive phrasal verbs are **separable**. That means the object can come after the particle *or* between the particle and the verb.
(6) Do you always **pick out** something that not only looks good but is also the latest in fashion?	With transitive separable phrasal verbs, long objects are best placed *after* the particle.
(7) Why did you **give** it **away**? ***Incorrect:*** Why did you ~~give away it~~?	When the object of a separable phrasal verb is a pronoun, it must come *between* the verb and the particle.
(8) **Keep** that lovely hat **on**. You look great in it! (keep on = *not remove*)	A small number of separable phrasal verbs require the object to appear *between* the verb and the particle.

See Appendix M on page A-9 for a list of separable phrasal verbs.
See Appendix P on page A-11 for a list of intransitive phrasal verbs.

Grammar Practice

Circle the 10 transitive separable phrasal verbs.

A Fashion Comeback

Regina knew that her great-grandmother's house was full of interesting things. The older woman never threw anything out, and that included old clothes from her youth back in the 1920s. Regina thought it would be fun to wear one of her great-grandmother's old swing-era outfits to the costume party at her school. She wanted to pick out a dress from one of the trunks in the attic. Who knows what other generations had left there for her to discover?

Regina asked her friend Diane over, and together they explored the top floor of the old house. "Let's check out this trunk first," suggested Regina. They laughed as they each tried on very old and very large hats. Regina and Diane decided to keep them on their heads as they abandoned the first trunk and turned to a second trunk. Under layers of tissue, Regina soon found a beautiful dress. Short in length, it seemed perfect for dancing.

Surely the dress would fit her, she thought. "How stylish!" said Diane. "Oh, you have to talk her into letting you wear this dress to the party."

That's just what Regina did, but it wasn't hard because her great-grandmother was a very generous woman. And when Diane was ready to give back the old hat on her head before she left, Regina's great-grandmother said, "I'd rather give it to a friend of the family than give it away to a stranger. Please take it and enjoy!" Diane happily accepted the gift.

The following week Regina and Diane made their entrance at the costume party. They simply couldn't pass up the chance to revive an old fashion.

Match five of the circled verbs with the definitions below.

a. look closely at with great interest ____________________

b. make someone agree to something or believe something ____________________

c. return to someone ____________________

d. invite as a guest to one's house ____________________

e. not remove ____________________

B

Circle the correct particles to complete the text.

1. A: Why did you ask me **over / out**?

B: I need your fashion advice. Come upstairs, okay? Let me get a few things from my closet. I'm going to try **on / out** different outfits, and you can tell me which one I should wear to my job interview.

2. A: What do you think about this business suit? It looks expensive, but the store was almost giving it **up / away** for free! I couldn't pass **on / up** such a great price, so I bought it.

B: Hmm. It fits you well, but it's so formal. Let's see another outfit.

3. A: I don't know what to choose. I want to look professional but friendly and interesting. I want to say, "Hey! I can do this job, and you'll enjoy working with me." Can you help me pick **out / on** an outfit which sends that message?

B: Well, I think you need a business casual look. You know, relaxed but still professional. Hmm. Keep those pants **up / on**. They look good, but try wearing something different on top.

4. A: Hey! Check this hat **out / in**. What do you think?

B: I think you have it on backwards. Turn it **on / around**. Uh . . . it certainly says, "I'm interesting," but it doesn't make you look professional.

5. B: The hat looks like it's from the 1980s. Out-of-date fashion can really turn people **off / down**. You need to throw it **out / on** and keep only things that are in style. Here. Try this shirt with those pants. The look is trendy and fun, but formal enough for the workplace.

A: Yeah. This works. Thanks!

Now role-play the conversation with a partner.

Grammar Focus 2 Multi-word phrasal verbs

Examples	Language notes
(1) Your favorite dress or suit might **go out of** style one day.	**Multi-word phrasal verbs** have three parts. They consist of **a verb** and **two particles** and take one object. Most multi-word verbs are **inseparable** and generally follow the pattern: verb + adverb + preposition + (object) The object must come *after* the second particle.
(2) I **handed** the hat **over to** the salesperson. My cousin tried to **talk** me **out of** it.	A few multi-word phrasal verbs are **separable**. They take two objects. They generally follow the pattern: verb + (direct object) + adverb + preposition + (indirect object)

See Appendix N and O on pages A-9 and A-10 for lists of multi-word phrasal verbs.

Grammar Practice

MyEnglishLab
Grammar Plus 2
Activities 1 and 2

A What is a fashion icon? Fashion icons are trendsetters. They are the people whom we associate certain styles with. Choose the correct phrasal verbs to complete the descriptions of six fashion icons. The underlined word in each item has the same meaning as the phrasal verb. Use each phrasal verb only once and pay attention to verb tense. Then, write the letter of the name of each fashion icon next to the description of his or her style.

A. Cher

B. Jackie Kennedy Onassis

C. Michelle Obama

D. James Dean

E. George Clooney

F. Michael Jackson

come back into	keep up with	miss out on
go out of	look forward to	play around with

_____ **1.** The public always ________________ seeing this amazing entertainer, who had great musical talent and a strong fashion sense. Everyone anticipated his appearances in the clothes he made popular, from the red leather jacket with a black-V on the front to the single shiny silver glove.

_____ **2.** Her beauty remains timeless, and the styles she made classic will never leave the world of fashion. Other first ladies in the United States have copied her use of tailored suits and simple, elegant dresses. Clean lines, soft colors, and a confident display of fashion know-how never ________________ style.

_____ **3.** This is one woman who has never been afraid to experiment and have fun with fashion. Fans of this singer and actress have enjoyed seeing her ________________ clothing over the decades. She's worn artful headpieces, flashy dresses, and cool bell-bottom pants.

_____ **4.** He became a movie legend in the 1950s, and the image he created has often ________________ fashion. Many shots depict him as confident, casual, and a bit dangerous. His cool look usually consisted of jeans, a white t-shirt, and a black leather jacket. Indeed, his style has often appeared again on and off the screen.

_____ **5.** When women wish to ________________ the times and dress fashionably, they study the styles of both popular entertainers and women on the political scene. This beautiful, tall, athletic wife of a U.S. president has set the pace for others to follow. She often mixes classic outfits with unique and memorable pieces, such as colorful belts or interesting shoes.

_____ **6.** Women rarely ________________ seeing one of his films. Both his acting and his fashion style are smooth, cool, rich, and natural. Men don't ignore his fashion sense either. Many men have combined tailored suits with casual shirts and left their faces unshaven to look like this actor.

B Circle the correct particles to complete the text.

How to Be a Trendsetter

1. You can look **back on / up to** fashion icons of the past and present, but never copy the style of another. Come **up with / out of** your own unique look.
2. Listen to the fashion advice of a friend, but don't feel you have to go **along with / back over** it. Friends should be able to get **through with / along with** each other without agreeing on every fashion choice.
3. Is someone wearing the same article of clothing as you? No worries. Get **together with / out of** the awkward situation by doing something unusual with that piece. Turn a hat backwards, for example, or roll up the sleeves of a shirt. Don't be afraid to play **around with / along with** a favorite look.
4. You may not have much money to spend on clothes, but you can always get **away from / by on** creative combinations. Ask an older relative to recall past fashions. You can bring something **back into / up to** style, but combine it with something modern. For example, wear a new shirt with a cousin's old jacket.

Match the phrasal verbs you chose above with the definitions below.

1. agree or accept ________________
2. return ________________
3. admire or respect________________
4. have a good relationship ________________
5. think of an idea or answer ________________
6. escape ________________
7. survive with little money ________________
8. experiment with ________________

Speaking

MyEnglishLab
Sounding Natural

Work with a partner. Imagine you are a reporter for a fashion magazine. Choose a decade from the reading and take turns asking and answering questions about the styles from that time period. Include questions and answers about your personal style.

REPORTER: Do you keep up with fashion trends from the <u>1960s</u>?
INTERVIEWEE: Yes, I like to wear <u>skinny pants and turtlenecks</u>.
REPORTER: Why do you think <u>turtleneck sweaters</u> are back in style?
INTERVIEWEE: Because people think <u>turtleneck sweaters make them look good</u>.

B Work with a partner or in a group. Discuss the questions about trendsetters.

1. Think about the styles you discussed in Part A. What trendsetters do you associate with different styles?
2. What celebrity trendsetters or designers have influenced your personal style?
3. Who are the celebrities in the photos? Why are they famous?
4. Whose looks do you think will never go out of style?
5. Whose looks have come back into style?

____

____

____

____

____

Listening

MyEnglishLab
Listen for it.

BEFORE LISTENING Look at the images in Speaking Part B. Which of the people are actors? Which are musicians? Which have crossed over into fashion design? Can you think of any others?

B UNDERSTANDING MAIN IDEAS Listen to a news podcast. What is the best title for the program?

☐ Trendsetters and Fashion Icons
☐ Keeping up with Celebrities
☐ Mixing up Music Blends with Fashion Trends
☐ The Comeback Kids—Musicians Who Launched Fashion Careers

C UNDERSTANDING DETAILS Listen again. Then answer the questions.

1. What does the host say they've been talking about?
____
2. What issue has the host asked the audience about?
____
3. What does the male caller say about his fashion sense?
____
4. What does the female caller say she cannot keep up with?
____

MyEnglishLab

Linking Grammar to Writing

Writing

A Imagine you are a fashion forecaster. You are meeting with the buyer at a department store and need to make recommendations about which fashions to bring back and which should never be worn again.

Look back at the reading and find all the articles of clothing listed under one or two decades. Then make two categories in your notebook: *Never bring it back!* and *Bring it back! Keep it in your closet: it will never go out of style.* Write one or two sentences about each piece. Why would you keep it? Why would you throw it out? Should designers bring it back? Will the piece ever go out of style?

B Now think about what is in your closet. Write a three-paragraph article about clothing trends. Make recommendations based on your personal style. Use the questions as a guide.

Paragraph 1. What do you like to wear? Why?
Which articles of your clothing have gone out of style?
Which styles are you wearing that you missed out on the first time around?
Which of your clothes are in style now?
What do you recommend your friends keep or give away?

Paragraph 2. What trends are famous or popular among your friends or in your country?
Are there any styles that recently came back into fashion? (1980s? 1960s?)
Which trendsetters do you and your friends keep up with?

Paragraph 3. What is your prediction for the fashion of the future?
What clothes do you think are going to make a come back?
What pieces do you hope that designers will bring back?
Which clothes do you think will never go out of style?

I like to wear a lot of classic pieces because I know they will never go out of style. For example, I think women should always keep little black dresses or skinny pants from the 1960s. Those pieces will never go out of style. I missed wearing those articles of clothing the first time around, but I think they will always be in fashion.

Some people like the styles from the 1980s. Those clothes went out of style for a while, but rappers and hip hop artists like Sean John and Usher brought them back. The oxford button-down shirt and khaki pants were popular in the 1980s, and made a comeback when Usher and other singers started to wear them. . . .

I predict that fashion from the 1980s will make another comeback. I think so because there are a lot of remakes of movies from the 1980s. However, I'm also pretty sure that the hairstyles from the 1980s are not going to come back into style. It's mainly because nobody likes "big hair!"

C Exchange papers with a partner. Ask and answer questions about your partner's article. What styles would you try? Which are not your style?

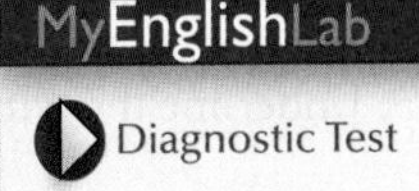

CHAPTER 10 Why We Buy What We Buy

Getting Started

Work with a partner. Look at the names of the following items. Do you know what the product looks like? What do you think of when you hear the words "Tiffany®" or "LEGO®" or "Chanel®"?

1. Do you know the colors or logos of these famous brands?
2. Do you think color plays a role in helping a customer decide on any of these products?
3. How do you react to the shapes, textures, and colors of these products? (positively? negatively?)
4. Which of these products immediately switches on your sense of touch, smell, taste, hearing, or sight?
5. Could you get by without most of these products?
6. Would you give in to buying any of these products?

B Some products can fail for different reasons. Some reasons include: consumers responded negatively, the products consisted of unappealing ingredients, or the products came across as strange. In the end, consumers felt that they didn't get what they bargained for. Read the product names in the chart. What do you think was the problem with each product? Rate the products on a scale of 1 to 3. Do you agree or disagree with the companies' final decisions to take the products off the shelves?

	3 I agree with them.	2 I don't care about it.	1 I disagree with them.
Lifesavers Soda (1912)			
Clairol's "Touch of Yogurt" Shampoo (1979)			
Colgate Kitchen Entrees Microwave Dinners (1982)			
Harley-Davidson Perfume (1990)			

Talk to a partner. Why do you agree or disagree with the companies' decisions? Do you have a negative or positive feeling about the taste, texture, smell, or look of these products?

Look back at Parts A and B. Complete the tasks.

1. As you saw in Chapter 9, some phrasal verbs are <u>transitive</u>. The direct object follows the preposition or a noun or pronoun can be placed between the verb and the preposition. Put parentheses around the verbs in Parts A and B that are followed by a preposition.

   I pick out **my clothes**. I pick **my clothes** out. I pick **them** out.

2. Some phrasal verbs and multi-word verbs are <u>intransitive</u>. There is not a direct object after the verb. An adverb often follows the preposition. Circle the phrasal verbs in Parts A and B that have an object.

   I like to **shop around**. The store **stocked up on** popular video games.

3. Underline the phrasal verbs that do not have an object.

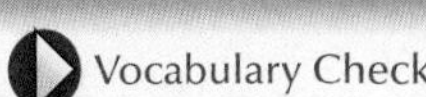

Vocabulary Check

Reading

A In his book *Buyology: Truth and Lies about What We Buy*, Martin Lindstrom explores "neuromarketing"—the science behind the choices we make. Look at the images. How do you think most people react to each of them? Write two or three words for each image.

______

______

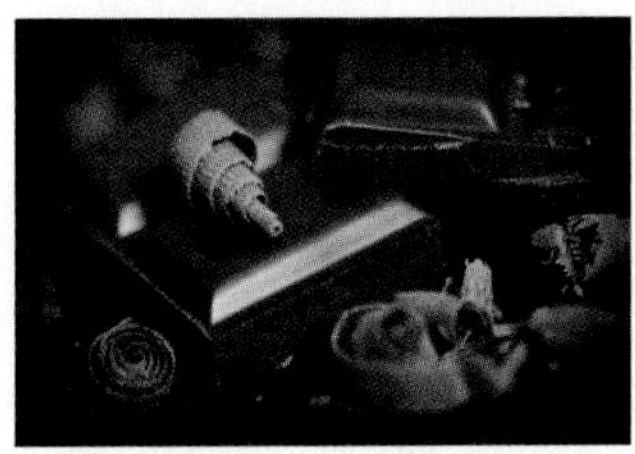
______

B PREDICTING What do you think happens in the brain when we see products we like or dislike? Read the passage and check your prediction.

News | What's Hot! | Fashion | Celebs | Games | Events | Blogs

Why We Buy What We Buy

Is there a reason why you buy certain things? Author Martin Lindstrom knows the answer to this question. Lindstrom has conducted a study on what happens in the brain when we see things we want to buy. This is called "neuromarketing." Neuromarketing refers to how marketers focus on patterns of consumer thinking. It is a scientific process that deals with fMRIs and EEGs—two types of scanning machines that can peer into the brain and give scientists specific information about how the brain works.

Neuromarketing is a way to access the hidden desires we lock away in our brains. Before a patient enters the scanner, a technician injects him with a special dye. As the person goes through the fMRI machine, the scanner lights up areas of the brain that respond to different images. As the patient sees these images, the brain immediately responds. The responses show up on the scanner because of the dye. Finally, the scans point out four "spots" in the brain that become active when the person has seen certain images:

The Cool Spot → activates when we see an electronic device or fancy car, which we believe enhances our social status.

The Collection Spot → shows the desire to accumulate objects or money.

The Craving Spot → turns on when we have strong desires for things like chocolate or video games.

The Fear Spot → lights up when marketers target something we fear—like gaining weight or not "fitting in."

Lindstrom uses this data in his work as a "brand futurist," to predict which brand strategies will pay off. He claims that 9 out of 10 new products fail because of poor marketing. By 2020, he predicts that most movies and television programs will contain intentionally placed products, like Mac laptops. Lindstrom doesn't actually believe in product placement in advertisements. He says that when movie viewers come across actors holding famous brand products, it turns off the viewers and they feel disinterested.

Not all marketing experts agree with Lindstrom's studies, but neuromarketing is a new trend that marketers depend on for collecting consumer data. The experts pick up where the brain scans leave off. They don't exclusively rely on neurological data to target consumers, but they have to understand how the data may affect their marketing plans.

C UNDERSTANDING FACTS AND OPINIONS Read each statement. Write *F* for the facts and *O* for the opinions.

_____ **1.** The fMRI scanner can peer into the brain.
_____ **2.** When we see a product that we like, we think about buying it.
_____ **3.** Lindstrom uses data as a "brand futurist" to make predictions about products.
_____ **4.** Neuromarketers depend on collecting consumer data.
_____ **5.** Many marketing experts disagree with Lindstrom's research.

Grammar Focus 1 Phrasal verbs: Inseparable

Examples	Language notes
(1) It is a scientific process that **deals with** fMRIs and EEGs.	Some transitive phrasal verbs are **inseparable**. That means the object must come *after* the particle.
(2) It **turns off** the viewer. [Also possible: It **turns** the viewer **off**.]	A dictionary will tell you whether a phrasal verb is separable or inseparable. However, placing a noun object *after* the particle is usually correct.
(3) Movie viewers **come across** actors holding famous brand products. (= *meet by chance* [phrasal verb]) The ship **came across** the Atlantic. (= *travel* (where?) [verb + preposition])	Remember that a **particle** changes the meaning of a verb; a preposition does not. Do not confuse the particle of an inseparable phrasal verb with a preposition that follows a verb simply to add information to the sentence.
(4) Marketers pick up where the brain scans **leave off**. (= *ends*) It **turns off** the viewer. (= *stops any interest*)	A particular particle often expresses the same basic idea in different phrasal verbs: *off* = stop or end (*leave off, turn off*) *on* = continued action (*go on, carry on*) *up* = completion (*use up, grow up*) *around* = action without a purpose (*play around, hang around*) *out* = refusal or fighting (*keep out, hold out*)
(5) It **turns off** the viewer and they feel disinterested. (= *stop any interest*) Please don't forget to **turn off** the lights when you leave. (= *stop using or operating*)	Many phrasal verbs are **idiomatic**, so they can have multiple meanings. Pay attention to the context of a phrasal verb (the words around it) to understand the definition. This is true of both separable and inseparable phrasal verbs.
(6) Marketers **focus on** patterns. (focus (Latin root) = *center, central point*; focus on = *center one's attention* on)	The verbs of many inseparable phrasal verbs are of Latin origin.
(7) The scans **point out** these four "spots" in the brain. ***Compare:*** The scan indicates these four "spots" in the brain. [more formal]	Phrasal verbs with a very idiomatic meaning often have a one-word equivalent that is more formal or academic.
(8) **Physical activity**: *get on, get off, wait for, look at* **Communication**: *talk about, refer to, write to, respond to* **Mental activity**: *think about, believe in, focus on, decide on* **Cause-effect**: *depend on, rely on, result in* **Happening**: *come across, happen to, occur in*	It is useful to learn sets of phrasal verbs that share a common activity or purpose. Note how these inseparable phrasal verbs can be grouped based on meaning.

Grammar Practice

MyEnglishLab

Grammar Plus 1
Activities 1 and 2

A Identify the sentence in each pair with a transitive phrasal verb. Underline the phrasal verb once and the object twice. Then circle the correct definition of the phrasal verb.

1. **a.** Audiences come across product placement not only in films but in TV shows as well.
   b. In one scene, the actor comes across a busy street by jumping from car roof to car roof.
   This phrasal verb means [meet by chance / buy].

2. **a.** Advertising agencies enter into contracts with film studios so that products can appear in films.
   b. A patient enters into the fMRI machine after a technician injects the person with a special dye.
   This phrasal verb means [make something official / have an argument].

3. **a.** The two teams of technicians will switch shifts on Friday.
   b. The technician switched the machine on.
   This phrasal verb means [organize / start operating].

4. **a.** As a patient goes through the machine, the scanner shows the brain's response to stimuli.
   b. Marketers go through all the data and determine the consumer's wants and needs.
   This phrasal verb means [argue strongly / examine carefully].

5. **a.** Not all marketers think Lindstrom's research is key, but they are willing to look it over.
   b. The actress looks over the heads of the crowd and sees the hero enter the room.
   This phrasal verb means [examine quickly / replace completely].

6. **a.** The advertisers got a good price through their personal connections at the TV studio.
   b. The patient was nervous at first, but she got through the scanning with no difficulties.
   This phrasal verb means [survive/ question].

Write the six phrasal verbs in the correct column.

Separable	Inseparable

B Replace the words in bold with the phrasal verbs below to make the text less formal. Pay attention to the verb form.

carry on	get off	get through	go through	talk about
come across	get on	get to	~~look for~~	think of

Looking for

~~Seeking~~ a Way to Reach Today's Consumer

Advertisers must continually **invent** new ways to show products to consumers. In the past, advertisers placed commercials at key points in the programming, and viewers patiently watched a chain of ads until their show came back on the air. Each advertiser had about 30 seconds to deliver their message.

Today advertisers are working with a new generation. Viewers are not as willing to watch when they **encounter** an ad, because they have a choice. As soon as an ad starts, a viewer can use the remote control of the DVR to **reach** the next part of the program. Younger viewers wonder how their parents ever **survived** all those commercials!

It's no surprise that product placement came into existence. Advertisers **examined** all their options and decided that intentional placement of their products within a program could work better than a commercial which viewers would likely skip. TV show producers were willing to **discuss** product placement because they needed the advertisers' money to **continue** production.

But just as TV audiences grew tired of the commercials that interrupted their shows in the past, viewers today have already started to complain about frequent and obvious product placement. Is it time for everyone to **leave** the product placement train they all so excitedly **boarded** several years ago? Perhaps advertisers are on the wrong track.

Grammar Focus 2 Intransitive phrasal verbs

Examples	Language notes
(1) We might experience fear when we don't **fit in.**	**Intransitive** phrasal verbs do not take an object.
(2) Those responses **show up** on the scanner because of the dye. ***Compare:*** Those responses appear on the scanner because of the dye. A successful ad has a message that **doesn't go away.** It stays in the customer's mind. ***Compare:*** A successful ad has a message that remains.	Remember that **phrasal verbs** with idiomatic meanings often have a one-word equivalent that is more academic and formal.
(3) Nine out of 10 new products don't **work out** because of poor marketing. (work out [intransitive] = *work successfully in the end*) The staff **worked out** their differences and were able to create a very marketable product. (work out [transitive] = *fix (a problem); make something stop being a problem*)	Some phrasal verbs can be both intransitive and transitive. In these cases, the definitions can change slightly or greatly.

See Appendix P on page A-11 for a list of intransitive phrasal verbs.

Grammar Practice

MyEnglishLab
Grammar Plus 2
Activities 1 and 2

A Read the pairs of sentences. Write *T* if the phrasal verb is transitive. Write *I* if it is intransitive.

1. a. Every evening advertisements **light up** in New York's Times Square. ______
b. The scanner **lit up** the area of the brain which corresponds to fear. ______

2. a. An fMRI technician can see an area of our brain "**turn on**" when we experience a craving. ______
b. Almost any time you **turn on** the TV, you see a commercial within a few minutes. ______

3. a. Oh, no! This piece **came off** the scanner when I tried to move it. Did I break it? ______
b. Don't worry. That piece **came off** before. It's easy to put back on. ______

4. a. Scanners can **pick up** certain human responses to products that marketers might miss. ______
b. Let's finish looking at the data. We can **pick up** where we left off this morning. ______

5. a. We don't know which ads viewers will respond to better, but scanners will help us **find out.**
b. The goal of neuromarketing is to **find out** patterns of consumer thinking. ______

6. a. All the marketing research **paid off** when the TV ad began to attract new clients. ______
b. As a new business, we needed three years to **pay off** the bank loan. ______

Look again at the six phrasal verbs: *light up, turn on, come off, pick up, find out, pay off.* Compare the transitive and intransitive meanings. Do any of the verbs have a significant change in meaning? Which one(s)? Match the verbs with their definitions.

______________ = discover (information)	______________ = shine light
______________ = completely pay	______________ = start working
______________ = become unattached	______________ = be successful in the end
______________ = start again	______________ = notice or detect

B Complete the text with the phrasal verbs below. Three phrasal verbs will not be used. Pay attention to verb form.

carry on	come off	fit in	leave off	pick up	show up
come in	find out	go away	pay off	shop around	work out

A company can have a good product, but efforts to sell it may not **1.** ____________________ if the marketing strategy is weak. Why **2.** ____________________ if an ad campaign isn't working? Set up a good strategy from the beginning and everything will **3.** ____________________ in the end.

In their book *Neuromarketing: Understanding the "Buy Buttons" in Your Customer's Brains*, Patrick Renvoise and Christophe Morin instruct companies to learn how customers make decisions. What determines a *yes* or *no* answer to the question, "Should I buy this?" Do buyers rely on their hearts or their minds? Is it possible to **4.** ____________________ ?

Renvoise and Morin used neuroscience to get answers, and they explain that the Old Brain is the true decision-maker. The Old Brain switches on our need to survive. If anything endangers our well-being, the Old Brain becomes interested in getting something that helps everything return to normal. This concept is the starting point of a four-step plan to successful marketing:

- First, you must identify the customers' pain. What do they need? Do they feel unpopular and want to **5.** ____________________ better? Did they buy paint that doesn't cover the old color and **6.** ____________________ when you touch it? Tell the customer you understand the problem and your product can fix it.

- Second, your product must **7.** ____________________ on the market and in the customer's mind as unique and clearly the best. If you can't prove this to be true, people will **8.** ____________________ and consider buying a competitor's product.

- Third, don't stop with the message that you can make the pain **9.** ____________________. Give a demonstration of your product. Show the results to the customer.

- Fourth, remember that a marketing plan can fail at any stage when you don't successfully send the message to the Old Brain.

The main message to marketers: Understand your customers' brains and you'll understand how to sell to them.

MyEnglishLab

Sounding Natural

Speaking

A Look at the image. In 1957, Vance Packard published the book, *The Hidden Persuaders*. It described how companies try different ways of persuading people to buy products. What message was the advertiser trying to send to movie viewers? Talk to a partner.

I think that the advertiser was trying to get people to buy popcorn.

B Talk with a group. How do you feel about seeing your favorite actor or actress using a popular product in a television show or movie? Does this turn you off or make you think about the product?

When I see my favorite actor drinking Coke ®, I feel connected to him because I drink Coke, too.

Listening

MyEnglishLab

Listen for it.

A LISTENING FOR MAIN IDEAS In his 1980 book, *Great Expectations: America and the Baby Boom Generation*, Landon Jones categorized people born after WW II as "Baby Boomers." This was a time when a high number of children were born, which helped this group gain a lot of "buying power" as they got older and became more successful. It also marked the first time a particular generation was identified in terms of marketing. Look at the names of the different groups and the years they were born: Baby Boomers: born 1946–1964, Generation X: born 1965–1980, Generation Y: born 1981–mid-90s, and Generation Z / Net Generation: born mid-90s–2010

Listen to an excerpt from a documentary and answer the questions.

1. Why is Generation Z called the "Internet Generation?"
2. What products do Gen Xers like to use?
3. What things do Generation Y people love?

Now, talk with a partner. What products did your generation grow up with? What about your parents' generation?

B COMPARING INFORMATION Listen again. Check (✓) the statements that relate to Generation X. Then listen again and check the statements that relate to Generation Y.

Gen X	Gen Y	Statements
		are comfortable and savvy about technology
		value family more than their jobs
		enjoy social networking but prefer meeting up with friends in person
		support environmental and social causes
		enjoy pop culture, being part of the latest trends, things that are cool
		are the first to buy new devices (PDAs, eReaders, cell phones, MP3 players)
		show off a lot—post pictures on social networks and text activities to friends
		do not like advertising that focuses on printed material
		rely on word-of-mouth for advertising
		are always looking for a bargain because they don't have brand loyalty

C AFTER LISTENING Talk to a partner. Look at the qualities you selected for each category. Compare the information to distinguish similarities and differences. Where do you fit in?

Writing

MyEnglishLab

Linking Grammar to Writing

A Marketers use neuromarketing to target consumers of specific age groups—generations of people who have "buying power." Studies show that Generations X and Y respond differently to different marketing strategies. One marketing strategy focuses on a "Sensory Approach" while the other concentrates on a "Social Approach." Read the chart.

	Sensory approach	Social approach	Most effective marketing strategies	Least effective marketing strategies
Gen X	• rely on seeing facts and proof of superior quality • suspicious of "slick" marketing • open to new tastes, sounds • are skeptical about advertising	• meet up with friends or attend business-related gatherings • use text /IM, online social communities, interpersonal networking, email. • very family-oriented	1. Internet advertising 2. online social networks 3. online news 4. viral marketing 5. discount coupons 6. contests 7. mobile advertising	1. direct mail (flyers, post cards, etc.) 2. TV 3. radio 4. newspapers 5. telemarketing (phone calls)
Gen Y	• like tangible products • like bright digital images • want music connected with a product • are optimistic about the future • impatient—want things "now."	• use text/IM, blogs, online social groups • use video sharing • connect to friends through networks • spend time on college campus	1. mobile advertising 2. Internet advertising 3. viral marketing 4. paid Internet searches 5. street signs or shopping malls	1. direct mail 2. TV 3. newspapers 4. telemarketing

Now look at the marketing campaigns for two products. Who do you think the campaign was focusing on: Gen X or Gen Y? Do you think they achieved success or did they fail? Why?

Campaign 1 All Right Soda.
Logo: Red and black with All Right in the center
Slogan: "Everything's gonna be all right!"
Media: Print and video advertisements; no Internet presence; had telephone marketing with 1-800 phone number

Campaign 2 Smith's Soda.
Logo: Keeps changing its colors. Has many flavors.
Slogan: "Run with the little guy . . . create some change."
Media: Contests, radio advertisements, website sales; product placement in films; no TV commercials

B Write an essay about one of the products and the generation it targets. Use ideas from the chart. Explain the effect of different types of marketing on different age groups. Include examples.

> I think Smith's soda focused on Gen Y to attract the youth market. The company changes the logo colors because they thought a design that stayed the same would turn off customers.

C Exchange essays with a partner. Talk about how you would market the same product to a different target audience. How would the product change if you marketed it to a different group?

Grammar Summary

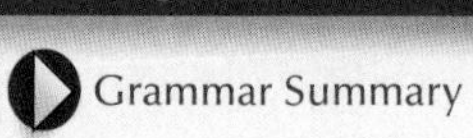

Phrasal verbs are a type of multi-word verb with two or more parts.

Phrasal verb = verb + particle(s)	Particles change the original meaning of the verb. **pass** (single-word verb) = go past **pass up** (phrasal verb) = decline; not use one's chance to do something

In a phrasal verb, particles come after the verb. A **particle** changes the meaning of the verb.

Particles can be **prepositions**.	The most common prepositions in phrasal verbs are *in, on, about,* and *for.*
Particles can be **adverbs**.	The most common adverbs in phrasal verbs are *up, down, off,* and *on.*

We can understand the **meaning of phrasal verbs** in three ways.

Learn the Latin verb.	The verb of many inseparable phrasal verbs is of Latin origin. ***Example***: What does your decision **depend on**? *-pend-* = hang, support → *depend on* = need the support of, the existence of
Learn the meaning of the particle.	Some common meanings of particles: *on* = continued action (*go on*); *up* = completion (*use up*); *around* = action without a purpose (*play around*); *out* = refusal or fighting (*keep out*)
Learn sets of phrasal verbs based on their common use.	**Physical activity**: *peer into, get on, get off, wait for, look at* **Communication**: *talk about, refer to, write to, respond to, enter into* **Mental activity**: *think of, believe in, focus on, decide on, react to, go through* **Cause-effect**: *depend on, rely on, result in* **Happening**: *come across, happen to, occur in*

Some phrasal verbs have **objects** and some do not.

Transitive phrasal verbs	The company **profited from** that decision.	These verbs take an object.
Intransitive phrasal verbs	I like to **shop around** and not visit one store only.	These verbs have no object.
Transitive-Intransitive verbs	The marketing team **worked** the problem **out**. Advertising online **worked out** well.	Some phrasal verbs can be both transitive and intransitive.

Objects can have different **positions** in sentences with phrasal verbs.

Separable phrasal verbs	Let's **give away** those old clothes. Let's **give** those old clothes **away**. Let's **give away** the clothes you no longer wear. Did you **give** them **away**?	Noun objects can appear after the particle or between the verb and particle. Place long noun objects after the particles. Place pronoun objects between the verb and particle.
Inseparable phrasal verbs	You can **pay for** the product in one payment or multiple payments.	Noun and pronoun objects must appear after the second particle.
Multi-word phrasal verbs	Successful advertising makes you feel like you don't want to **miss out on** a good opportunity. She **talked** her partner **out of** buying the product.	Most multi-word phrasal verbs are inseparable. A few multi-word phrasal verbs are separable because there are two objects, an object of the verb and an object of the preposition.

Self-Assessment

A

(5 points) Circle the correct phrasal verb to complete the sentence.

1. I plan to go shopping this weekend. I don't want to **miss out on / go out of** the holiday sales.
2. Advertisers need to **play around with / keep up with** the trends and learn what people want today.
3. The marketing specialist **kept his glasses on / gave away his glasses** as he studied the data.
4. The TV ad made the hotel look great, so I was **coming back into / looking forward to** my stay there.
5. I really admire the people who **pass up / come up with** interesting ideas for commercials.

B

(6 points) Complete the sentences with the correct phrasal verbs. Use the objects in parentheses to help you. Pay attention to verb form and word order.

check out	pass up	talk out of	turn around
give away	pick out	throw out	turn on

A: Look! The candy store over there is **1.** ________________________ (free samples).

B: Ooh, let's not **2.** ________________________ (that opportunity)! Just remember, they're doing it to make us want to buy something!

A: We need to **3.** ________________________ (a few things) to make room for the new exercise bike.

B: Do we really need the bike? I know it looks great on TV and all, but . . .

A: Yeah, and the people in that commercial look great, too. You can't **4.** ________________________ (me / it). We both could use the exercise, so I'm buying it!

A: How do you **5.** ________________________ (this music box)?

B: If you **6.** ________________________ (it), there should be an on-off switch on the other side.

C

(4 points) Circle the two phrasal verbs (verb + particle). Underline the two (verb + preposition) combinations.

1. The inventor demonstrated how to switch on the device.
2. The fMRI technician looked over the top of the scanner and got the doctor's attention.
3. The course on neuromarketing was challenging, but John got through it and passed the exam.
4. The nurse told me to go through the double doors and turn right.

D

(5 points) Complete the sentences with the correct particles.

1. The advice of fashion forecasters can help you fit ____________ by looking stylish.
2. It's best to shop ____________ before you make a big purchase. Take the time to find bargains.
3. One electronic device could break ____________ and advertisers would still reach you on another.
4. The green button lit ____________ to indicate that the scanner was ready for use.
5. Smart choices in expensive clothing stores can pay ____________ over time.

Unit Project: Designing a product

Work with a partner. Imagine that you are product designers who are going to create a proposal for a new product, service, or fashion line. Follow the steps.

1. Discuss how you will come up with your idea. Many product designers look at the world around them. They have to think about what people want, what they need, and what they will buy because it's trendy or useful, or both. Sometimes, designers get their inspiration from products that already exist, and improve upon them. Some designers create products that are completely new and innovative.
2. Decide on your product or fashion line. What have you based your idea on?
   For example: You can create a new kind of mobile device, or a personal shopper website.
3. Describe your product or service. What is it? How is it new or what other product does it improve on?
4. How will you create your brand and logo? What name or symbol will represent your product / service?
5. Come up with a short storyboard before you make your presentation. Remember to:
   - Decide on a catchy name for your product and brand
   - Pick out colors that represent your product and concept
   - Figure out a slogan to represent your product
   - Create a logo or symbol

Prepare your presentation for the class. You can use PowerPoint, PDF, or any type of presentation software. Your presentation should be three to four minutes.

1. Deliver your presentation. Keep these points in mind.
   - <u>Visuals:</u> Use images, photos, or illustrations of your idea to prepare your presentation. Images will help your audience understand your ideas more easily.
   - <u>Number of slides:</u> For a 3-minute presentation, you should have between 10 and 12 slides.
   - <u>Timing:</u> You should speak for between 15 and 30 seconds per slide.
   - Keep the amount of text on the slide to a minimum. People want to listen to you, not read text.
   - Make sure your presentation has a hook, body, and conclusion that appeals to your audience.

Are you tired of carrying around heavy books for class? Then you need "Light-Reader!"

I decided to create a new type of digital e-reader because I had several heavy textbooks to carry every day. I wanted to be able to bring my books to class, but many times I would feel overwhelmed by their size. I thought about a new kind of reader and came up with the name "Light-Reader. . . ."

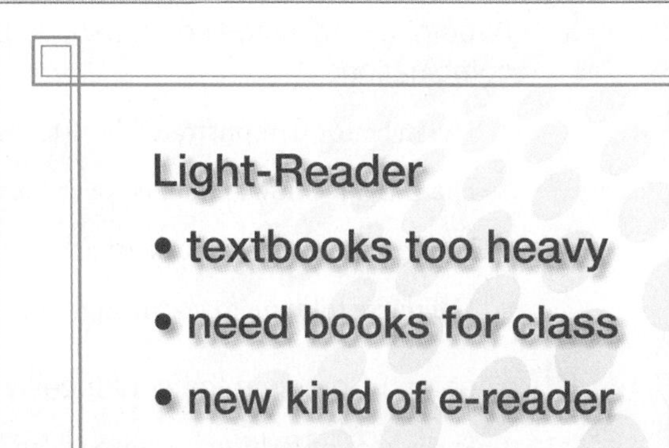

Light-Reader
• textbooks too heavy
• need books for class
• new kind of e-reader

2. After all the groups have presented, discuss or evaluate the presentations.
   - Did the presentation have a hook? Did they have images and other visuals in the presentation?
   - Did the presenters have an appeal to the audience?
   - Would you buy their product? Why or why not?

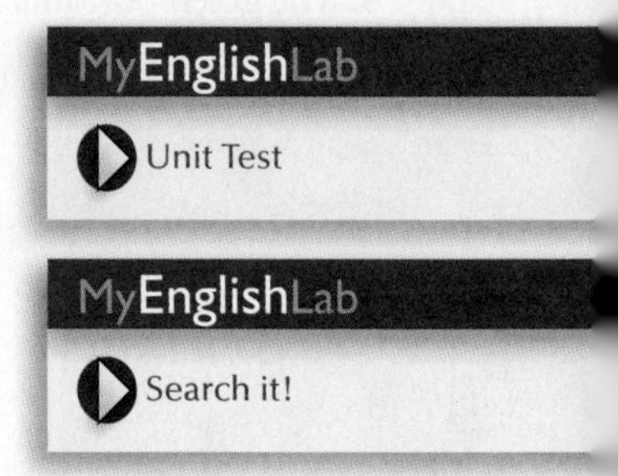

UNIT 6

Get the Message

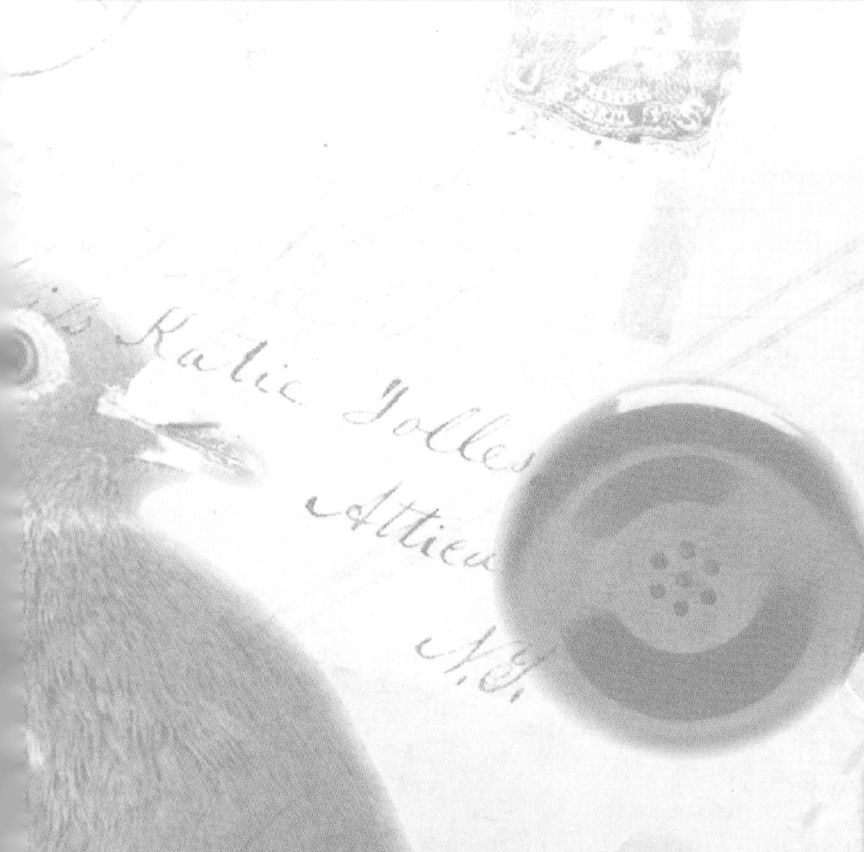

OUTCOMES

After completing this unit, I will be able to use these grammar points.

CHAPTER 11

Grammar Focus 1
Modals and semi-modals

Grammar Focus 2
Modals and semi-modals: Necessity

Grammar Focus 3
Modals and semi-modals: Certainty

CHAPTER 12

Grammar Focus 1
Modals and semi-modals: Necessity in the past

Grammar Focus 2
Modals and semi-modals: Certainty in the past

MyEnglishLab

 What do you know?

Chapter 11 From Diaries to Blogs

Getting Started

A Talk with a partner. What is communication? How would you define it? How many methods of communication can you think of? Which methods usually happen between two or more people? Which forms of communication might be kept private and individual?

B What's your communication style? Take the survey and discuss your responses.

1. Which methods of communication do you need to use every day? (Check all that apply.)
   ☐ email ☐ text ☐ phone
   ☐ video-chat ☐ instant messenger (IM)
   ☐ social networking
2. Do you have to use some methods of communication because there is no other way to stay in touch with your friends or family?
   ☐ Yes ☐ No
3. Do you believe there is an "etiquette" (social behavior) you must follow when you write a letter or an email or send a text?
   ☐ Yes ☐ No
4. Are you less formal in texts or emails than you ought to be?
   ☐ Yes ☐ No
5. How often do you think people should talk or write to friends or family? (Check one.)
   ☐ more than once a day ☐ once a day
   ☐ once or twice a week
6. Have you ever written a blog, journal, or diary?
   ☐ Yes ☐ No If No, you may skip Question 7.
7. Have you ever thought you had better delete something from a diary, blog, or video log (vlog) because you were worried that someone might read it?
   ☐ Yes ☐ No
8. Would you dare to blog, text, email, or chat by IM when you were not supposed to (for example, in class at a movie, at a lecture)?
   ☐ Yes ☐ No

C Work with a partner. Look back at Parts A and B. Complete the tasks.

1. Some of the verbs above have modals before them. **Modals** are **helping verbs** that express specific ideas when they combine with a main verb. Find seven modals and underline them.
2. Look at the categories in the chart. Discuss their meanings with your partner. Then write the modals in the correct place in the chart. Some categories may take more than one modal.

advice or suggestion	*should*
assumption or speculation	
certainty / near certainty	
high / low expectation	
necessity / no necessity	
possibility / impossibility	
warning	

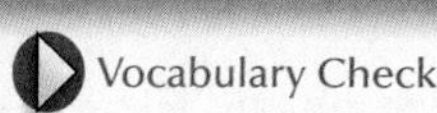

Reading

A WARM-UP Diaries, journals, and personal letters look different from other forms of writing. What features do they have in common? What are they supposed to look like? Discuss with a partner.

B PREDICTING Look at these examples of 19th century writing. Can you guess which one started with "Dear Sister"? Which one do you think is a diary entry? Which one is a personal letter? Which author do you think wrote the novel *Tom Sawyer?*

October 1853

—I have not written to any of the family for some time . . . firstly, due to the fact that I didn't know where they were, and secondly, because I have been fooling myself with the idea that I was going to leave New York every day for the last two weeks. . . .

*I have not received a letter from home lately, but got a "Journal" the other day, in which I see the office has been sold. I suppose Ma, Orion, and Henry are in St. Louis now. If Orion has no other project in his head, he ought to take the contract for getting out some weekly paper, if he cannot get a foremanship *. . . .*

*If my letters do not come often, you need not bother yourself about me . . . and if I don't manage to take care of No. 1**, be assured you will never know it. I am not afraid, however; I shall ask favors from no one, and endeavor to be (and shall be) as "independent as a wood-sawyer's clerk."*

* **foremanship:** position as a supervisor of a boat or in a carpentry shop / ** **No. 1:** oneself

23 July 1847

We have arrived in Buffalo. What a treacherous trip! When I travel next, it shall be by the Erie Canal and a slow mule-hauled passenger boat. I will never get used to the rumbling sound of a locomotive as it thunders across our great state. Even the pigeons could not escape the eerie sound of its screeching brakes as the monstrous engine enters into the station, their flock darkening the sky. I would wish for these beasts to go away, but in truth, I absolutely dare not do so, for then I would defy progress. And as the child of an engineer, I ought to enjoy the benefit of my father's labours. Father says we must embrace progress or the world will stop turning.

The sky is so dark . . . storms must be brewing on the horizon. I shall wait for them to pass, being without any coat and still easily chilled. I should hire a coach, instead of walking to the Dingham's home. They have invited me to lunch, and for that, I truly need to bring a small token of appreciation. Perhaps if time allows, I will buy sweets in town. Then I am supposed to stop in the post office to send off a telegram to mother so she knows of my safe arrival.

C UNDERSTANDING INFERENCE Read the texts again and answer the questions.

1. What did the writer of the first text plan to do soon?
2. What do you think a "wood-sawyer" might be?
3. According to the second author, for whom do you think the father works?
4. Based on information in the readings, which text do you think might be written by a woman?
5. Where do you think the second author could have been writing the text?
6. What form of communication do you think a telegram might be? Why do you think so?

Grammar Focus 1 Modals and semi-modals

Examples	Language notes
(1) I **should hire** a coach. [first-person plural] He **should write** more often. [third-person singular] They **should send** a reply. [third-person plural]	**Modals** are a type of auxiliary (helping) verb. They do not change forms to agree with the subject. subject + modal + base form of the main verb
(2) Even the pigeons **could not escape** the eerie sound. We **had** (we'**d**) **better not travel** today.	Modals have **negative** forms. modal + *not* + base form of the main verb
(3) The author **might be writing** somewhere in town.	Modals have **progressive** forms, but only the main verb changes. modal + *be* + main verb with *-ing* ending
(4) The occupants **are supposed to** be there. (with modal = *The occupants* ***should be*** *there.*] You'**ll (you will) have to visit** us soon. (with modal = *You* ***must visit*** *us soon.*)	**Semi-modals** are multi-word constructions that express the same ideas as modals, but semi-modals change forms to agree with the subject and show time.
(5) I **cannot find** the address. [ability] You **have to be** more careful. [necessity] It **must be** here somewhere. [certainty]	When modals and semi-modals combine with the main verb of a sentence, they express **specific ideas**, such as **ability**, **necessity**, and **certainty**.
(6) He **must take** the contract. [necessity] He **ought to take** the contract. [advice] He **could take** the contract. [suggestion]	Many modals and semi-modals express the **same idea but in different degrees**.

Grammar Practice

A Correct the errors in the text. Look at the example. There are eight more errors.

The Lost Girls: A Travel Journal about Inner and Outer Discoveries

Are you living as you want to live or as you think you ~~be~~ *are* supposed to live? This is what three young women asked themselves back in 2006. With their thirtieth birthdays not far off in the future, Jennifer Baggett, Holly Corbett, and Amanda Pressner knew they had better not wasted any time. They took a good look at their lives as media professionals in New York and questioned their life goals. Did they really want a career and marriage, or did society tell them that every person musts have these things in order to be happy?

To find answers, the three friends felt they should to travel the world. Self-discovery, they thought, oughts to come through experience outside the familiar. Their journey took them 60,000 miles across twelve countries and four continents, from Kenya to Southeast Asia. The women began to blog about their adventures as a way to stay in touch with family and friends back home. Quickly, many others also took interest in *The Lost Girls.* Baggett, Corbett, and Pressner returned with a deeper understanding about the world and themselves. They also realized their new-found knowledge might helps other young people. A publisher agreed. In 2010, the women authored *The Lost Girls: Three Friends. Four Continents. One Unconventional Detour Around the World.* Young women can also turns to the Lost Girls' blog for travel and lifestyle advice. Baggett, Corbett, and Pressner may not to have all the answers, but there is one lesson they are happy to share with others: You not have to worry about feeling lost. Accept it. Experience it. That's what life is about.

B Circle the correct meaning of each modal or semi-modal.

The Ins and Outs of Instant Messaging

1. To save time when you're texting, you **should learn** common symbols. For example, @ means *at*.
   Should expresses **a.** warning **b.** advice **c.** permission
2. You **can** also **use** abbreviations, such as *u* for *you*.
   Can expresses **a.** permission **b.** prediction **c.** possibility
3. The receiver **might not know** all the symbols you are using, especially the emoticons, like :-o (which some use to say they are surprised).
   Might expresses **a.** strong expectation **b.** speculation **c.** ability
4. A quick chat by IM **could be** more appropriate than a phone call when at least one person is in a quiet place, such as a library or doctor's office.
   Could expresses **a.** suggestion **b.** necessity **c.** willingness
5. You**'d better not start** a text chat when you're in class or at a lecture.
   Had better expresses **a.** ability **b.** unwillingness **c.** urgent advice
6. You**'re** really **not supposed to use** IM for important professional correspondence.
   Be supposed to expresses **a.** prediction **b.** expectation **c.** impossibility
7. To ensure safety, some workers **are never to engage** in instant messaging while on the job.
   Be to expresses **a.** speculation **b.** prohibition **c.** certainty
8. If you've never used IM, then you **must not have** a cell phone.
   Must expresses **a.** near certainty **b.** necessity **c.** warning

Grammar Focus 2 Modals and semi-modals: Necessity

Examples	Language notes
(1) Father says we **must embrace** progress. Passengers **are to wait** here until further notice. We **have to wait** for the storms to pass. We **can't leave**. / We'**re not allowed** to leave.	We use **modals of necessity** ***must*** and ***be to*** for rules, orders, and laws. In other less formal situations, we express necessity with ***have to*** in the affirmative and ***can't*** or ***not be allowed to*** in the negative.
(2) We **have to travel** by train. [strong necessity] We **don't have to travel** by train. [no necessity]	The degree of necessity changes significantly when ***have to***, ***can***, ***may***, and ***be allowed to*** are in their **negative** forms.
(3) You'**ve got to believe** me. / You **got to believe** me. You'**d better send** word. / You **better send** word. **I'm supposed to stop** in the post office. You **shouldn't worry**.	We often use modals and semi-modals in <u>conversation</u>. Speakers commonly use **contractions** with ***have got to***, ***had better***, and ***be supposed to*** in the affirmative and with many modals and semi-modals in the negative. Note that you can say, but never write, *gotta*. Instead, write ***got to***.
(4) **Do** we **have to wait** here? You **don't have to wait**.	We use ***have to*** more often than ***must*** in questions and in the negative.
(5) **May** I please **write** to you? **Can** I **write** to you?	We use ***may*** in polite questions. In everyday English, we prefer ***can*** to ask <u>permission</u>.
(6) I **have to tell** you how much I'm looking forward to your visit. I **should warn** you about Mark. Perhaps I **could make** a suggestion or two.	Modals of necessity often combine with verbs that are related to speaking to <u>express the need to share certain information</u>: ***have to*** = strong necessity to speak ***should*** = obligation to speak ***could*** = polite introduction to opinion
(7) I **couldn't** possibly **ask** you to do that. Thank you, but I **can't accept** such a gift.	We often use modals to express our unwillingness to accept the generosity of another. **Polite refusals** use ***can't*** and ***won't***. The modals ***couldn't*** and ***wouldn't*** are even more polite.
(8) It **may not be** a bad idea to send a letter. You **might** want to reconsider.	Use of the weaker modals ***might***, ***may***, ***could***, and ***can*** make a suggestion sound less forceful.

	Degrees of necessity			
	affirmative		negative	
Necessity 100%	*Necessity*	must	*Prohibition*	must not (mustn't)
				cannot
				not be allowed to
				may not
		be to		be not to
		(will) need to		
		(will) have to		
		have got to		
			Unwillingness	will not (won't)
				would not (wouldn't)
				cannot (can't)
				could not (couldn't)
	Challenge	dare	*Warning*	dare not
	Urgent advice	had better		had better not ('d better not)
	Expectation	be supposed to		not be supposed to
	Advice	ought to		ought not to
		should [shall, *in questions*]		should not (shouldn't)
	Suggestion	could		
		might		
			No necessity	(will) not have to
				(will) not need to
		shall [*in questions*]		shall not
	Permission	may		
		be allowed to		
	Willingness	will		
		would		
		can		
0%		could		

Grammar Practice

Circle the verbs that best complete the dialogue about email etiquette.

A: You're pretty Internet savvy. Let me ask you something. **1. Are you supposed to / Do you dare** respond to a message when you're only copied?

B: You mean, cc'd? Well, if someone cc's you, the message isn't really for you. The sender just wants you to be aware of the situation. It's FYI, you know, just for your information. You **2. mustn't / don't have to** respond, but it's okay to. Let's say you want to add a comment or ask a question. Then you **3. can / shall** write to the others. Why do you ask?

A: A few of my co-workers often cc me on multiple messages. I don't know why they feel I **4. could / should** be aware of absolutely everything. Some messages refer to projects I'm not even working on. All those emails just fill up my inbox.

B: You **5. might / would** ask them to cc you only when the information concerns you. I **6. dare to / should** imagine they would respect your request. Just send a short friendly note about it.

A: That's a good idea. You know, email is so common, but certain practices aren't clear. **7. They'd better / They ought** to have lessons on email etiquette.

B: Actually, there are many articles on netiquette, you know, guidelines for online behavior, but some people **8. don't need to / won't** ever read them. They'll always do things their way.

A: That's true. You know, one rule of netiquette that I wish people would follow is using greetings in email. **9. We've got to / We needn't** slow down and take the time to say hello. I **10. have to / might** admit it really bothers me when I get messages without any *Hi* or *Hello*. It's like once people stopped using regular mail, polite expressions, like *Dear* and *Regards*, just vanished.

B: I know what you mean. The thing that bothers me the most is how others share my contact info when they forward a message to people that I don't know. **11. I'd better not / I'd never dare** share another person's contact info without their permission.

A: I agree, but how do you send a message to a group without showing everyone's address?

B: You **12. have to / would** enter all their addresses in the bcc field. A blind carbon copy protects their privacy.

A: I didn't know that. I **13. could / should** thank you for the free netiquette lesson!

B Complete the text with the modals of necessity below and the words in parentheses. Some sentences have more than one correct answer.

aren't supposed to	don't have to	need to	've got to
can't	had better	ought to	will
could	must	~~should~~	would dare to

Are Diaries a Must?

Who keeps a diary? Is it the teenager who pours her hurt, love, and excitement onto the pages of a notebook every night? Or perhaps it's the hopeful writer who one day plans to use events from his own life to write a best-selling novel.

The better question to ask is this: who ___should keep___ (keep) a diary? The answer is everyone. Here's why:

We all **1.** ________________ (have) a friend who is a good listener. But maybe you ________________ **2.** (easily share) your feelings with others. If that's the case, then express your thoughts on paper. Any psychologist **3.** ________________ (tell) you that you **4.** ________________ (hold) everything inside. Opening up is healthy, and a diary encourages this.

Unlike a blog, a diary kept on paper remains private. You **5.** ________________ (worry) about unwanted attention or readers who **6.** ________________ (judge) you. Let others think you're not keeping up with the times because you use old-fashioned pen and paper. They're the ones who **7.** ________________ (be) careful because their overly personal blogs might one day appear before the eyes of their teachers or employers.

Everyone **8.** ________________ (try) their hand at writing. "But I have no plans to be a novelist," you say. That's okay. The writing practice will keep your mind sharp and help you look more closely at your views and values. Just relax and write. There are no writing rules or social etiquette you **9.** ________________ (follow).

10. ________________ (you leave) something for future generations? "But you said a diary remains private!"—True; no one will invade your privacy during your lifetime. But you **11.** ________________ (admit) you wouldn't pass up the chance to read your great-grandmother's diary, right? Let the kids know about the adventures, passions, fears, and fantasies you had.

So what are you waiting for? Start writing!

Go back and circle the three weakest modals or semi-modals of necessity.

Grammar Focus 3 Modals and semi-modals: Certainty

Examples	Language notes
(1) Storms **must be** brewing on the horizon. [near certainty] ***Compare:*** A storm **is brewing**. [complete certainty]	**Modals of certainty** can express different degrees of certainty, but even the strongest modals do not express 100% certainty. ***Must, have to,*** and ***have got to*** express that the speaker is almost certain.
(2) Her father **could be** a famous engineer. [possible] Her father **couldn't be** a famous engineer. [impossible]	The degree of certainty changes significantly when ***can*** and ***could*** are in their **negative** forms.
(3) A storm is on its way, so travel **is going to be** difficult. Travel **will become** difficult if a storm starts.	We use both ***be going to*** and ***will*** for predictions, but when we base a prediction on specific events or facts use *be going to.*
(4) **Shouldn't** the **reply** arrive within the hour? It **ought to take** only a few minutes.	We use ***should*** and ***ought to*** to express expectation. *Should* is more frequent, especially in questions and in the negative.
(5) There **may not be** any reply. They **might not send** a reply today.	We use ***may*** and ***might*** to speculate. *May* can suggest a slightly higher level of certainty.
(6) Diaries **can** (or **could**) help a person discover his or her true nature.	***Can*** and ***could*** help express the strength of an opinion. *Can* suggests more agreement with the stated idea. *Could* simply presents the idea as a possibility.
(7) I **should think** you'd benefit from keeping a diary. I **should imagine** the letter would be there by now.	We can use ***should*** with verbs that are related to thinking to express a degree of doubt about one's opinion or speculation.
(8) You **certainly** could come over if you have time.	We use adverbs called **amplifiers** to emphasize or increase the certainty of a statement, an assumption, or a suggestion.
Stronger adverbs: (9) You **absolutely** must see that exhibit! I **definitely** had better buy some stamps today. She might be **completely** exhausted from the long trip. I would **truly** like to meet your family. You **simply** must read his letter. You **really** shouldn't write all that in your diary. What if someone reads it? *Weaker adverbs:* I'm **quite certain** the train is supposed to leave at 6:15. I'm **pretty sure** I can call you tomorrow. I'm **just not sure** I can take the time to write a letter.	Amplifiers are not unique to modals, but we often hear and see them used with modals. Like modals, amplifiers have different degrees of strength.

Certainty	Degrees of certainty		
		affirmative	negative
100% ↑	*Present impossibility*		cannot (can't)
			could not (couldn't)
	Near certainty about present	must	must not
		have to	
		have got to	
	Strong prediction	be going to	not be going to
	Prediction	will	will not (won't)
	Expectation about future	should	should not (shouldn't)
		ought to	
	Speculation about present or future	may	may not
		might	might not
↓	*Present or future possiblilty*	can	
0%		could	

Grammar Practice

 Circle the modal or semi-modal that best completes the sentence.

Here are several things you can do to establish a better Internet connection.

1. There are several browsers to choose from. Try a new one. It **might / must** prove to be faster or easier to use than your current browser.
2. Close windows and quit applications that you aren't using. This **should / cannot** speed up your connection.
3. Turn off auto-updates of installed software because they **have to / may** be wasting available bandwidth.
4. Use anti-virus and other software to protect your computer. Malware **ought to / can** invade your workspace and use your Internet connection for its own purposes.
5. Use a good download manager. Downloading a large file **can / should** slow down other Internet activities, but a good download manager will limit bandwidth use and allow easier browsing.
6. Empty your Recycle Bin regularly. Any computer **ought to / might** work better after the user deletes old files and makes more memory available.
7. Consider your setup. You **will / might** move your router to a better location to improve your wireless connection.
8. Is your computer still slow? Try rebooting. You**'re almost certainly going to / certainly aren't going to** see an improved connection after you restart your system.

B Complete the text with the modals of certainty below. Some sentences have more than one correct answer.

aren't going to	could	might	will
cannot	has got to	shouldn't	won't

Winston Wins!

Some **1.** ________________ think that the Internet is the fastest way to deliver information. One small bird in South Africa has proved that to be untrue. An experiment determined what form of delivery was faster for data transfer: broadband Internet or Winston, a homing pigeon. Winston used wind and instincts to deliver a USB memory stick from one office to another, some 50 miles away. In what **2.** ________________ be one of the greatest victories of nature over technology in recent years, Winston was able to complete the task in two hours.

The financial services company which set up the experiment knows that it **3.** ________________ improve communications in order to save money. In the past, they've waited between 6 and 48 hours to transfer data over the Internet. They certainly **4.** ________________ waste time on slow data transfers anymore when another method is faster. Winston and other homing pigeons **5.** ________________ now be making weekly trips between their two offices.

Of course, the company has to protect the information the birds are carrying. There's a small possibility that the memory sticks **6.** ________________ fall into the wrong hands. But outsiders **7.** ________________ be able to read the encrypted data without breaking the code.

Despite all the new technology we now have, Winston reminds us not to rush to declare older forms of communication extinct. Homing pigeons have been delivering information since the days of the first Olympic Games, when Greeks released these birds with messages that announced the winners. People all over the world have continued to use them in times of war and peace. Homing pigeons definitely **8.** ________________vanish anytime soon.

MyEnglishLab

Listen for it.

Listening

A UNDERSTANDING MAIN TOPICS Listen to a conversation. What is the main topic of the conversation?

a. How to use Internet video chat
b. The importance of helping family
c. Helping someone with a new computer

B UNDERSTANDING INFERENCE Listen again. Then answer the questions.

1. What can be inferred about the man?
   a. He is not comfortable with the computer.
   b. He is knowledgeable about the Internet.
   c. He has never seen the woman before.
2. What can be assumed about the woman?
   a. She is very young.
   b. She is not familiar with instant messaging or video chat.
   c. She has never used a computer before.
3. What is true about the speakers?
   a. This is their first conversation.
   b. They are talking on the telephone.
   c. They always use video chat to communicate.
4. What might happen the next time they speak?
   a. They will send each other email.
   b. They might use video chat.
   c. They are planning to talk on the phone.

C AFTER LISTENING Talk to a partner about a time when you had to show or explain to someone how to use the Internet or a computer program. Did the person need you to explain everything step by step?

Speaking

MyEnglishLab

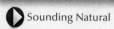

Sounding Natural

A Work with a partner. Imagine that you have met someone who has never used video chat, social networking sites, email, or texts. Take turns giving advice about these communication methods. Include information about different types of Internet browsers, social media, and cell phones.

First, you are supposed to have an Internet connection.

You should buy a good modem and get cable or DSL (direct service line). . . .

You absolutely must have the most recent browser installed on your computer.

B Talk to a partner. What methods of written communication did people use in your country 20 or 30 years ago? How did people used to communicate? How were people supposed to deliver or receive letters? Could they use telegrams? Could they use email?

What do you think technology might be like 20 years from now? What types of communication devices (cell phones, video chat capabilities) do you think we might be using? Do you think we will still be using the same technology as we are using today? Will the technology change?

MyEnglishLab

Linking Grammar to Writing

Writing

A Many people use a journal to write down the things they observe, or things they have to do and must do. Some people blog or write in a diary every day to express their feelings and experiences, or to talk about things that they have done. Have you ever kept a journal or diary? Talk with a partner. What kinds of things would you write in a journal or diary? Are there things you would not write? Why?

B Write a blog, diary, or journal entry for today and tomorrow. Make sure to use dates, places, and other information to make it as detailed as you can.

- What things are you supposed to do today?
- What do you have to do?
- What should you do?
- What do you think you had better do before the day is over?
- What do you think you will do later today or tomorrow?
- What things do you think you might do later or before you go to sleep?

This evening, I went to a movie. I just got home. Now, I'm supposed to be studying for a French test but I don't feel like it. But I really should study. I should stay up all night to prepare for this test. But I think I had better sleep and get up early tomorrow morning to review for the test. I know I might not pass the test. But I think I might study better tomorrow morning. I'll probably need to talk to my teacher tomorrow after class if I don't pass.

C Exchange entries with a partner. Compare your entries and talk about their similarities and differences. Ask your partner for more information about things you find interesting.

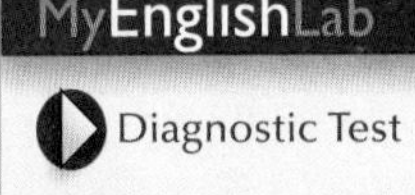

CHAPTER 12 Across the Wires

Getting Started

A Look at the communication methods used during the 19th and 20th centuries. Guess which methods people must have used to communicate in writing. Which do you think they had to use as a way to communicate by speaking?

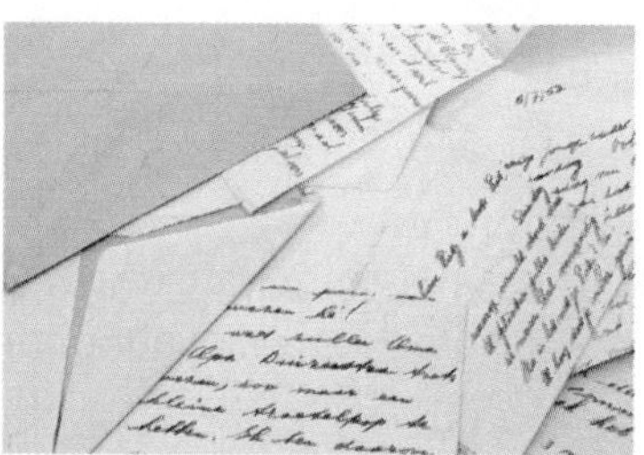

B Imagine what life was like in the United States in the late 19th and early 20th centuries. How might people have kept in touch with friends and family? Look at the images in Part A. Write the correct communication method for each type of message. Then decide which methods could have been in use during the 19th or the early 20th century. Which might still be used today?

1. Which methods of communication do you think would have been for personal use?
2. Which system might have been better for sending formal or business messages? Why?
3. Which system was supposed to have been the fastest? Which was probably the slowest?

C Look back at the directions and activities for Parts A and B. Complete the tasks.

1. Are there modals and semi-modals with ***have*** + **past participle** that express certainty, possibility, necessity, or speculate about past events? ______________________
2. Underline the modals or semi-modals that express **certainty in the past.**
3. Circle the modals or semi-modals that express **possibility in the past.**
4. Draw a box around modals or semi-modals that express **necessity in the past.**
5. Put a question mark over modals that express **speculation in the past.**

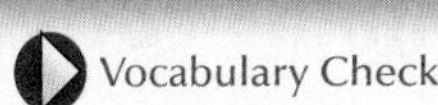

Reading

A WARM-UP Have you ever "dropped in" on someone without calling first? How do you feel when people drop in unexpectedly? What do you think people must have done before there were telephones?

B PREDICTING What do the words *wireless*, *make a call*, and *calling cards* mean today? What do you think these terms might have meant in 1875? Read the texts and find the answers.

Place Your Calling Card . . . here

Long before the invention of the telephone in 1877, people "made calls"—in person—to speak with one another. If no one was home, you were supposed to leave your "calling card"—a small paper card with your name on it, on a silver tray; much like leaving a voicemail message today. Calling cards were plain or very detailed. You had to go to the local printer and he would make you a set of cards.

GOING WIRELESS

In June 1826, Robert Stephenson, the "father of the railways" sent a telegram from Euston to Camden stations in England. The message contained one word: "BRAVO." Almost 200 years later, the telegram, a former icon of communication, has become extinct. Western Union sent its last telegram in 2006. Blame email, faxes, and even the telephone for the demise of the "wireless." Inventor Samuel F. B. Morse would have been very disappointed. COMPLETED MESSAGE STOP.

Ham It Up!

It might be hard to believe, but Ham (amateur) radio operators are still on the airwaves. In fact, the number of operators today is almost as high as when Ham radio reached its peak in the 1920s and '30s, around the same time the telegram was popular. First you had to have a "call sign" like, W6FZZ (the call sign of Samuel F. B. Morse's grandson) and a license from the Federal Communication Commission (FCC). Then, an amateur Ham operator in the U.S., for example, could have easily communicated with an operator in Greenland or Australia without placing a long-distance call. To request a conversation, all you had to do was tap out the same code: "CQ CQ CQ," to alert listeners that W6FZZ was calling in Morse code. With telegraph wires gone, most ham operators today only use the telephone lines to communicate—W6FZZ (. . . SIX . . . FOXTROT ZULU . . . ZULU) . . . over and out.

CB or Not CB . . . what's your handle?

We may never know if the Citizens Band, or CB, radio was supposed to outlive the Ham radio. Unlike the Ham operators, a CB radio operator didn't have to get a licence to communicate. Though CB radio became a popular hobby with both truck and car drivers during the 1970s until the '80s, there might only be a handful of truckers still using the Citizens Band lingo today. The CB must have been a source of comfort for lonely truckers. Drivers had "handles" (nicknames) like "Big Ben," and spoke in code: "Breaker 1-9, Breaker 1-9, you've got a bear on your tail." All that, just to say: "watch out for the police car behind you."

C UNDERSTANDING INFERENCE Read the text again and answer the questions.

1. What can be inferred about people who owned silver trays and had detailed calling cards?
2. According to the second paragraph, what can be inferred about Robert Stephenson's one-word message?
3. What does the author imply about how Ham operators communicate today?
4. Based on the last paragraph, how might the CB radio have made police work more difficult?

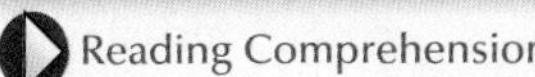

Grammar Focus 1 Modals and semi-modals: Necessity in the past

Examples	Language notes
(1) He **should have left** his calling card, but he forgot.	To express **necessity in the past**, **modals** use a **perfect** form: modal + *have* + past participle
(2) They **should have been paying** more attention in order to understand the code.	Modals in the past can have a **progressive** form, but it is less common than the perfect form: modal + *have been* + present participle
(3) When you **needed to** see or speak with friends you "made calls" to one another.	To express necessity in the past, semi-modals use their **past** forms.

Necessity	Degrees of necessity in the past			
	affirmative		negative	
100% ↑	*Necessity*	had to needed to		
	Challenge / Risk	dared	*Avoidance of negative consequences*	did not dare (didn't dare)
	Warning	had better have		had better not have
	Strong expectation	was / were to		was / were not to
	Expectation	was / were supposed to		was / were not supposed to (wasn't / weren't supposed to)
	Advice	should have		should not have (shouldn't have)
	Suggestion	might have could have		
	Willingness	would have	*Regret*	would not have (wouldn't have)
↓ 0%			*No necessity*	did not need to (didn't need to) did not have to (didn't have to)

Grammar Practice

Circle the modal or semi-modal that best completes the sentence.

TEACHER: Western Union completed the first telegraph line across the United States in 1861. Before that, how did communication take place among the U.S. states and territories?

STUDENT 1: People on one coast simply **1. didn't have to wait / had to wait** until someone from the other coast visited and brought news with them.

STUDENT 2: Didn't they have mail trains in the 1800s?

TEACHER: Well, yes. The postal service started putting mail on trains in the 1830s, but its service didn't reach all regions and it needed better organization.

STUDENT 3: They **2. could have used / were supposed to use** horses to carry mail out to the West and then back East. I mean, wasn't that possible?

STUDENT 4: They had those big stagecoaches back then. They **3. should have used / would have used** single horses. Just one horse with one rider.

TEACHER: Ah-ha! A fine idea! Let me explain how politics and the need for faster communication led to the creation of the Pony Express. Around 1860, talk of a war between the northern and southern states was building. California out in the West had entered the Union in 1850. With the knowledge that a civil war might be coming, the northern politicians **4. had better have lost / didn't dare lose** one of its newest and largest states to the South. To strengthen its hold on California and the remaining Western territories, the U.S. government **5. needed to find / was supposed to find** faster and more direct communication.

STUDENT 1: But how much mail could a single rider carry? They probably had a lot of riders, and I'm sure they **6. should have used / needed to use** a lot of horses to run the Pony Express.

TEACHER: A good observation. The Pony Express was a trail of 2,000 miles from Missouri to California. Riders **7. were supposed to deliver / could have delivered** the mail from one end to the other in 10 days. That was fast delivery back then. To achieve this, the Pony Express required around 80 riders and up to 500 horses.

STUDENT 4: I wonder who worked harder, the riders or the horses.

B Complete the text with the modals of necessity below and the verbs in parentheses. You must use the correct forms of the modals and semi-modals. Some sentences have more than one correct answer.

be supposed to	have to	not have to	should
had better	need	ought to	would

STUDENT 2: I bet it was hard on the horses to ride fast. **1.** ________________ the riders ________________ (change) horses often?

TEACHER: Yes. Riders **2.** ________________ (change) horses every 10 to 15 miles. The young men **3.** ________________ (change) as often—about every 100 miles or so. There were over 100 stations, but riders **4.** ________________ (spend) much time at any of those points because they were always on a tight schedule.

STUDENT 4: Did riders receive good pay?

TEACHER: Riders' wages were around $100 a month, which was good money, but it was dangerous work. Riders **5.** ________________ (leave) their fears at home when they hit those rough trails in the old West.

STUDENT 3: How long did the Pony Express last?

TEACHER: Not long. As I said, Western Union set up the transcontinental telegraph in 1861. The Pony Express lasted from April 1860 to October of 1861. Despite serious financial problems, the owners **6.** ________________ (probably keep) the horse line running a bit longer, but the telegraph brought it all to an end. Still, with successful delivery of over 34,000 pieces of mail and only one piece lost, the owners and riders **7.** ________________ (be) proud.

STUDENT 1: The Pony Express riders **8.** ________________ (be) legends.

Grammar Focus 2 Modals and semi-modals: Certainty in the past

Examples	Language notes
(1) Samuel Morse **would have been** very disappointed.	To express **certainty in the past, modals** use a **perfect** form: modal + *have* + past participle
(2) They **might have been using** a CB radio.	Modals in the past can have a **progressive** form, but it appears less frequently: modal + *have been* + present participle
(3) They **had to have known** Morse code.	To express certainty in the past, semi-modals use their **past** forms.
(4) An amateur Ham operator in the U.S. **could have easily communicated** with an operator in Greenland or Australia. (= *It was possible for them to chat. Maybe they did. Maybe they didn't.*) My grandfather **could have been** a radio announcer because he had such a great speaking voice. Instead, he was a manager in a factory. (= *He missed the opportunity to be on the radio. He regrets this.*)	***Could have*** + main verb can express two different ideas: **past possibility** and **past opportunity** (regret).
(5) Before the telegraph, news traveled slowly, and Americans in the West **would wait** for months to receive mail. (= *used to wait*) At one point in my childhood, I thought I **would be** a radio announcer. (= *was going to be*)	***Would*** can express more than one meaning. It may have a meaning similar to *used to* and refer to **known past habits**. It can also refer to **the future in a past context**.

Certainty	Degrees of certainty in the past			
	affirmative		negative	
100%	*Near certainty*		*Impossibility*	
		must have		must not have
		had to have		
	Known intentions	was / were going to		was / were not going to
	Known past habits	used to		did not used to
		would		would not (wouldn't)
	Speculation	may have		may not have
		might have		might not have
0%	*Possibility*	could have		could not have

Grammar Practice

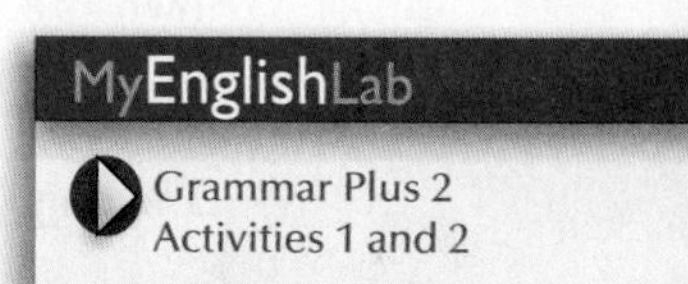

Match the descriptions of past forms of communication to the correct statements of speculation.

a. That **may have been** the system of the telegraph.

b. That **had to have been** a demonstration of the scanning phototelegraph.

c. That **must have been** the practice of the Railway Mail Postal Service.

d. That **could have been** the first wireless telegraph message.

e. That **might have been** an early version of the international flag signaling system, which modern ships still rely on for communication.

_____ 1. The clerk at the door of the moving car had to move the "catcher" arm in order to pick up the mail pouch, which was hanging outside the station.

_____ 2. Sailors could exchange 70,000 signals using this code, which the British Board of Trade created in 1857.

_____ 3. Operators had to send and receive messages in a code of dots and dashes.

_____ 4. The inventor should have been more careful when he showed his device during a storm at sea, but he successfully sent his message from the ship to his lab in St. Petersburg, Russia.

_____ 5. The audience had to wait for 20 minutes to see the black-and-white image of a butterfly appear on paper, after someone had sent it as an electronic signal.

Look back at statements a–e. Write the modals of speculation in the correct column in the chart.

Strong certainty	Weak certainty
	may have been

B

Complete the text with modals and semi-modals to speculate or express necessity about the past.

In 2009, a graduate student at the University of Delaware discovered an old letter in an archive box. This box contained various diaries, letters, and other *ephemera*—newspaper clippings, photographs, official documents, and property deeds from the 17th to 20th centuries. At first glance, she thought it *could have been* _____ (*speculation*: be) from the late 1800s. She **1.** _____ (*necessity past*: handle) the letter very carefully. First, she **2.** _____ (*necessity*: put on) special archival gloves. When she read it, she **3.** _____ (*past probability*: not) believe her eyes. The signature on the letter was from Thomas Jefferson, the third president of the United States! It appeared to be a letter that Jefferson had written in 1808 to a physician, expressing his sadness about the death of a prominent hero from the Revolutionary War.

Her first thoughts were that she **4.** _____ (*necessity*: to get in touch with) the head of the archives immediately. They **5.** _____ (*necessity*: to authenticate) the letter and make sure it wasn't a forgery. Since it **6.** _____ (*speculation*: be) in the box for a long time, the historians **7.** _____ (*probability*: determine) where it had come from and how long it had been "lost."

The historians believe that the letter **8.** _____ (*speculation*: be) in a private collection a long time ago, before the library acquired it.

Listening

A BEFORE LISTENING Talk to a partner. What are some ways that we create and send messages today? From the chapter, what other methods do you know about?

B UNDERSTANDING SEQUENCE Listen to a lecture. Number the items in the order that the professor mentions them (1–8).

_____ Belinograph (wirephoto machine)	_____ Morse code
_____ Carrier pigeon	_____ Semaphore
_____ Ham radio	_____ Telegraph
_____ Messenger	_____ Telephone

C CONNECTING IDEAS Listen again. Match each older technological device (1–4) with its modern equivalent (a–d)

_____ 1.

_____ 2.

_____ 3.

_____ 4.

a. computer code **b.** ham radio **c.** fax machine **d.** mobile telephone

Speaking

A Sam found a large sea chest in his grandmother's attic. It once belonged to his grandmother's father. When he opened it, he couldn't believe his eyes. Inside it, he found a newspaper from 1912 and several photos. He also found pieces of a message that someone must have written in code. He has been trying to decipher it. With a partner, decode the message using the following information and clues:

An SOS is a distress signal. It is Morse Code for "Save Our Ship" or "Save Our Souls." Look at the code. What do you think "D" must stand for? What was the name of the ship that sunk?

The Daily News
Final edition
April 15, 1912
World's Greatest Liner Strikes Iceberg

CQD CQD SOS SOS CQD DE MGY MGY

The "D" must mean . . .

This must have been . . .

CQD means:
C = come
Q = quick
MGY is the call (identification) sign for the ship

B Work with a partner. Look again at the items that Sam found in his great-grandfather's trunk. They are clues about his past. Use the information in Part A to answer these questions.

Who was the great-grandfather? What must his job have been?
Why do you think he might have received the message?
Why do you think he might have kept these items?

Writing

A In 1945, the U.S. post office was supposed to deliver a letter to the home of Mrs. S. E. Lawrence in Gloucester, Massachusetts. But something went wrong. Read about a lost letter and analyze the facts.

1. The original sender, Mr. H. Grimsland, lived in Chicago, Illinois.
2. However, Mr. Grimsland sent the letter from New Hyde Park, NY on July 26, 1945.
3. He used a new Franklin D. Roosevelt Memorial envelope and new one-cent stamps.
4. The envelope was empty.
5. Stamp collectors often met up in the city of a new postage stamp's origin.
6. It was common to send a letter with the new postage stamp to other collectors.
7. Hyde Park, New York was F. D. Roosevelt's home for many years.
8. There is also a Gloucester, England.
9. The letter was delivered in 2011, 66 years later.
10. It was turned over to the Annisquam Historical Society.

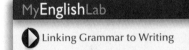

Roosevelt Memorial
Franklin D. Roosevelt
President of United States 1933-1945
Born Jan. 30, 1882
Hyde Park, New York

B Write one or two paragraphs to interpret and speculate about what might have happened. What could have been the relationship between the sender and the recipient? Why could Mr. Grimsland have sent the letter?

I think that . . . sent the letter. It seems that . . . might have happened. The sender was probably . . . and the recipient of the letter might have been . . . It is possible that Mr. Grimsland sent the letter because . . .

C Exchange paragraphs with a partner. Did you have the same ideas about what might have happened?

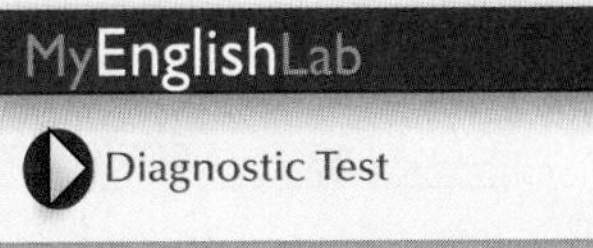

Grammar Summary

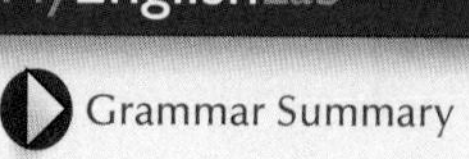

Modals and semi-modals express particular ideas when they combine with a main verb.

Notes	Example
Modals have affirmative, negative, progressive, and perfect forms, but they do not change form to agree with the subject.	(1) You **should include** your signature in an email. (2) You **shouldn't leave** the subject heading blank. (3) You **should be studying** now, not sending email to friends. (4) You **should have checked** your spelling before you sent the email. (5) You **should have been studying** instead of doing a video chat last night.
Semi-modals change form to show subject-verb agreement and time.	(6) I'**m supposed to be** on a conference call right now. (7) **Were** we **supposed to** meet earlier today?

We use modals and semi-modals to express different degrees of **necessity**.

Necessity	Need in the past	Need in the present or future	Need in the future only
100% ↑		can / cannot	
		would (not)	
	needed to	must (not)	will need to
	had to	am, is, are (not) to	will have to
		need to	
	dared not / didn't dare	have to	would (not) dare
	had better (not) have	have / has got to	
	was / were (not) supposed to	dare (not)	
		had better (not)	
	should (not) have	am, is, are (not) supposed to	
		ought (not) to	shall (not)
	might have	should (not) to	
	could have		
	didn't need to	might	won't need to
		can	
	didn't have to	could	won't have to
		not need to	will (not)
↓ 0%	would (not) have	not have to	

We use modals and semi-modals to express different degrees of **certainty**.

Certainty	Certainty about the past	Certainty about the present	Certainty about the future
100% ↑		cannot / can't	
	could (not) have	couldn't	
	must (not) have	must (not)	
	had to have	have to	
		have got to	
	was / were going to		am, is, are going to
	used to / didn't used to		
	would (not) [*for known habits*]		will (not)
		ought to	ought to
	should (not) have	should	should (not)
	may (not) have	may (not)	may (not)
	might (not) have	might (not)	might (not)
		can	
↓ 0%	could have	could	could

Self-Assessment

A (6 points) Circle the verbs that best complete the sentences.

1. Because the Internet is free, people **should / don't have to** pay to use email.
2. You **can / dare to** own a CB radio without a license.
3. Homing pigeons **have to / had better** fly during the day because they need sunlight to navigate.
4. Today you **aren't supposed to / don't need to** have a desktop computer to access the Internet.
5. According to FCC rules, every Ham radio operator **is to / ought to** have a license.
6. You **have got to / could** have good listening skills to understand Morse code.

B (4 points) Complete the dialogs with modals of certainty from the box.

can't	could	must	should

1. **A:** What's wrong?
   B: It simply ____________ be true! My favorite group just tweeted that they're canceling their tour.
2: **A:** Let's talk again next Monday. I'll be out of town, but can we do a video call?
   B: I ____________ be at the office by 9. It depends on traffic. Let's aim for 9:30. Does that work?
3. **A:** Take a look. Lily just sent a text from the resort. She also sent a photo of herself on the beach.
   B: I got the same photo. I've never seen her so happy. She ____________ be having the time of her life.
4. **A:** My favorite blogger hasn't written anything for a few days. I wonder what's wrong.
   B: I ____________ be wrong, but my guess is that he's just having computer problems. It happens.

C (5 points) Rewrite the sentences to express necessity in the past.

1. Pony Express riders must weigh less than125 pounds. ____________
2. Riders don't have to be a certain height. ____________
3. All Pony Express riders have to take an oath. ____________
4. Riders are not to drink alcohol, fight, or use foul language. ____________
5. Pony Express riders dare not ride too slowly. ____________

D (5 points) Complete the speculations about past possibilities with the words in parentheses.

In the early days of the telephone, there were "party lines" that allowed multiple users in different locations to speak on the same line. This was mainly a way to save money.

1. It ____________ (could / be) the first form of conference calls, but businesses didn't see the possibility.
2. It ____________ (had to / be) difficult to have a private conversation on that kind of line.
3. Speakers ____________ (need to / shout) over one another to make themselves heard.
4. Without the party line, some people ____________ (may not / know) as much about their neighbors.
5. Surely someone knew there ____________ (be going to / be) conference calls in the future.

Unit Project: Presentation on ephemera

A Work with a partner or in a group. You are going to make a presentation about ephemera. Follow the steps.

1. Antiques and other collectibles we see in flea markets and antique stores are called *ephemera*. Ephemera can be obsolete or out-of-use devices, old wind-up watches, or even old photographs. Many collectors of ephemera might specifically buy things such as telegraphs, stereoscopes, or old cameras.
2. Choose items from the list below or think of your own ideas. Take notes about the ephemera and its modern equivalent.

YESTERDAY	TODAY
Old original typewriter (Remington)	Computer keyboard
Wireless facsimile cylinder	Scanner-Fax
Mimeograph	Fax machine
Telegraph	Photocopy machine
Old telephone	Cell phone
Calling card	Voicemail message / email / text

3. Create a Powerpoint presentation or make a poster. Make sure you contrast two different centuries. (For example, 2000s vs. 1900s or 1900s vs. 1800s.) Look at the model.

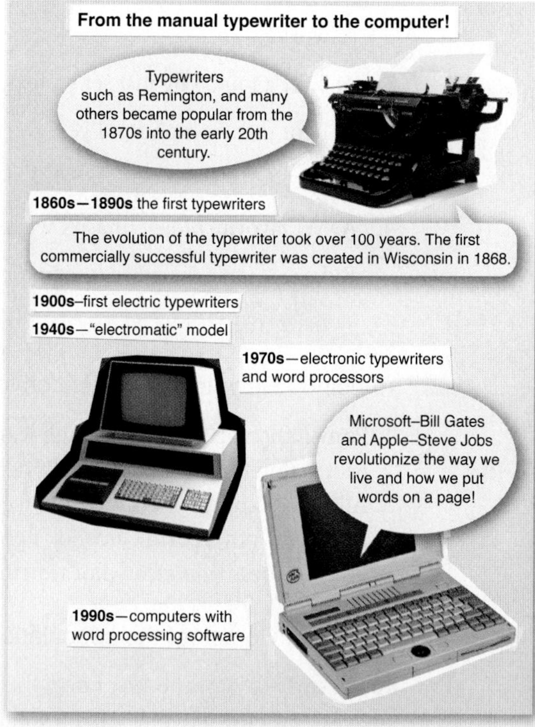

From the manual typewriter to the computer!
Typewriters such as Remington, and many others became popular from the 1870s into the early 20th century.
1860s—1890s the first typewriters
The evolution of the typewriter took over 100 years. The first commercially successful typewriter was created in Wisconsin in 1868.
1900s–first electric typewriters
1940s—"electromatic" model
1970s—electronic typewriters and word processors
Microsoft–Bill Gates and Apple–Steve Jobs revolutionize the way we live and how we put words on a page!
1990s—computers with word processing software

B Prepare your presentation for the class. Follow the steps. Use grammar from the unit.

1. Deliver your presentation. Explain to your classmates what it must have been like for someone to use the device from the past. For example, you can talk about:
   - how long must it have taken to use the device.
   - what it must have been like when people had to use the older device.
   - what they had to do to operate the device.

We must admit that the computer is one of the most important devices in the history of communication. . . .

In the 1900s, before the invention of computers, people could have communicated in a few ways.

It must have taken a long time to type a letter by using the . . .

2. After all the groups have presented, discuss how the devices evolved. Which devices do you think paved the way for modern devices? Do you see similarities and differences between some of the devices that your classmates presented? Discuss them with a partner or in a group.

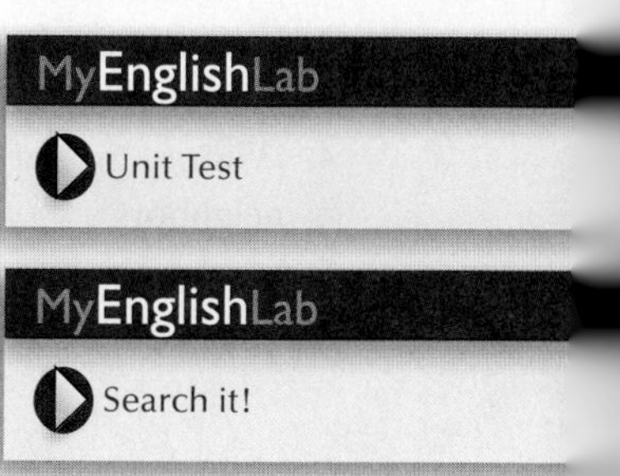

UNIT 7

Echoing Voices

OUTCOMES

After completing this unit, I will be able to use these grammar points.

CHAPTER 13

Grammar Focus 1
The passive: Simple present and simple past

Grammar Focus 2
The passive: Perfect forms

CHAPTER 14

Grammar Focus 1
Stative passive

Grammar Focus 2
Participial adjectives

MyEnglishLab

 What do you know?

CHAPTER 13 The Book that Has Never Been Read . . .

Getting Started

A Look at the images of some of history's most famous cryptographers and decipherers. Read the descriptions of the mysterious texts that each worked with and match the man with his work.

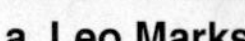

a. Leo Marks

b. Hermes Trismegistus

c. Jean-François Champollion

d. Leon Baptista Alberti

_____ **1.** The Emerald Tablet was created by this ancient Egyptian scientist, who claimed it held the secrets of spirituality, health, and the sum of all knowledge in the universe. The text has never been completely translated.

_____ **2.** The Cipher Disk, the first "encryption" disk, was created by this mathematician and philosopher. It was written in alpha-numeric code. This code remained unbroken for nearly 300 years, until it was deciphered by Charles Babbage in 1854.

_____ **3.** During WW II special poems had been created to pass undetected by spies. Those poems were rewritten in a new code, which was devised by this Chief Cryptographer of Special Operations.

_____ **4.** The Rosetta Stone had been carved in three languages—Greek, Demotic, and Egyptian Hieroglyphs—and was buried in the sand for centuries. It was discovered in 1799 by Napoleon's soldiers and has been exhibited in the British Museum since 1802. In 1822, its hieroglyphs were finally deciphered by this man.

B Look at the information about the texts above. Some have been written on paper or textile; others had been carved on stone. Discuss these questions with a partner.

1. Which text do you think has been considered the greatest linguistic discovery of all time?
2. What do you think the Emerald Tablet was used for?
3. Why were hieroglyphs not deciphered until the early 19th century?
4. How do we know that the Cipher Disk was created in the Middle Ages?

C Read the information about the passive voice. Then look back at Parts A and B. Complete the tasks.

We use the **passive voice** when the agent (doer) of an action is unknown or non-specific, or, to shift the focus to the object. We form the **present** or **past passive** with *be* + the past participle. We form the **present** or **past perfect passive** with the correct form of *have* + *been* + the past participle.

1. Underline the **simple present of *be* + the passive participle.**
2. Double underline the **simple past of *be* + the passive participle.**
3. Circle ***be* + *have* or *has* + the past participle.**
4. Draw a box around ***be* + *had* + the past participle.**

Reading

A WARM-UP Talk with a partner. Why do you think a book might never be read? A mysterious text was given to a code-breaker, who was also an expert in many subjects, and he could not figure out what it said. Why do you think he was unable to decipher it?

B SKIMMING Linguists and code-breakers have long been puzzled by a mysterious manuscript. Why was it called the "Voynich manuscript?" Skim the text and find out.

The book that wasn't judged by its cover

In 1912, a book was found in a trunk in an old Italian castle; its author was unknown. It was unremarkable; an "ugly duckling" among a stack of beautiful manuscripts that had been found in a monk's unique collection. Wilfred Michael Voynich, a rare books dealer, purchased the manuscript. He said that the book's intentional lack of outward beauty was the characteristic that had captured his attention the most.

Voynich was astounded not only by the manuscript's encrypted text but by its many detailed illustrations as well. This 234-page tome, which had been printed on special folding paper, contained illustrations of astronomical charts, plants, and other sketches. Some of the images depict human figures that appear to be bathing in a "fountain of youth." But the text itself is definitely the most mysterious part of the book—it was written in a puzzling, unrecognizable alphabet—neither Latin, Cyrillic (Russian), nor Greek, but something that was completely unknown. It was impossible for Voynich—or anyone else—to detect the meaning of its characters. The only clue to its geographic origins was its handwritten calligraphy which was slanted in a script known as *italic,* a style common to early 14th-century Florence, Italy. Some letters look like numbers, others appear to be a mix of the three alphabets. Voynich found only one clue: a letter from its previous owner had been hidden between the book's pages. It stated that it was bought by a duke, who had acquired it from friar and cryptographer Roger Bacon in the 13th century. Some experts speculate that it might have been Bacon's work. Others think it could have been a fraud by Voynich himself.

Linguists and cryptanalysts have been baffled by the Voynich manuscript. Originally, its age was estimated to be from the 16th century, until physicists used the science of carbon-dating and a special spectrometer to analyze its age. It was probably created between 1404 to 1438—making it almost 100 years older than had been previously thought.

Its contents have still not been deciphered, though teams of cryptanalysts and even military code-breakers have been working on ways to decode its hidden meaning. Over the past 100 years, the Voynich manuscript has passed from place to place—through various networks of individual buyers and antiquarian dealers. In 2006, it was purchased by the Yale University library, in Connecticut, where it has been ever since.

C UNDERSTANDING SEQUENCE Number the events in the correct order (1–6).

_____ The manuscript's age was determined to be 100 years older than its original estimation.
_____ The book's cover was intentionally created to be plain.
_____ A letter was hidden in the book by a previous owner.
_____ The book was discovered by someone and then purchased by Michael Voynich.
_____ Experts considered that the manuscript might have been created by Roger Bacon.
_____ The book was given to code-breakers and cryptanalysts for evaluation.

Grammar Focus 1 Simple present and past passive and use of the *by*-phrase

Examples	Language notes
(1) Some of the images **depict** human figures. [transitive verb + object] It **was** unremarkable. [intransitive verb + no object]	Verbs can be transitive or intransitive. **Transitive** verbs have an object. **Intransitive** verbs do not have an object.
(2) **Active:** A duke bought it. **Passive:** It was bought by a duke.	Transitive verbs can have an active or passive meaning. An **active** sentence places the focus on the agent (the doer of the action) by making it the subject. In a **passive** sentence, the focus shifts to the object (the receiver of the action), so the receiver is the subject. Because a passive verb can still express an action, we can also refer to this structure as the **dynamic passive**.
(3) Linguists, cryptanalysts, and code-breakers all over the world **are puzzled** by the manuscript.	We form the **passive in the simple present** with: *am, is, are (not)* + past participle.
(4) In 1912, a book **was found** in a trunk in an old Italian castle.	We form the **passive in the simple past** with: *was / were (not)* + past participle.
(5) In 2006, **it** (*the manuscript*) was purchased **by the Yale University library** (*the people who own the library*).	The **subject** of a passive sentence is usually an inanimate thing—an object, concept, or event. We use ***by*** to name the **agent**, which is often a person. The ***by*-phrase** follows the passive verb.
(6) It stated that it was bought **by a duke** who had acquired it from cryptographer and astronomer, Roger Bacon. (*The pronoun "it" refers to old information. "Duke," the agent, is new information.*)	A passive sentence with a *by*-phrase **identifies the agent as new or important information** in the context of the specific discussion. Additional information about the agent can follow in a relative clause.
(7) The book's cover **was** intentionally **created** to be plain. *(Agent is unknown.)* For all the scholars who **were asked** to study the manuscripts, the code remains unknown. *(Agent is not important.)* The manuscript is in a special collection at the Yale University library. That purchase **was made** in 2006. *(Agent is obvious. = Yale University library.)*	We often use passive sentences when the agent is unknown, not specific, or not important. Sometimes the agent is obvious, so the *by*-phrase is unnecessary. Include a *by*-phrase only when it is important to tell the listener who the agent is.

Active sentence		
agent / subject	action / verb	receiver/object
A duke	bought	it.

Passive sentence		
receiver / subject	action / verb	agent / *by*-phrase
It	was bought	by a duke.

Grammar Practice

A Read the sentences. Look at the boldfaced verbs. Write *T* for *transitive* and *I* for *intransitive*. Then rewrite the transitive sentences in the passive. Not all the passive sentences need a *by*-phrase. Name the agent only when the information is important.

T 1. Napoleon's army **discovered** the Rosetta Stone in 1799.
The Rosetta Stone was discovered by Napoleon's army in 1799.

_____ 2. Their discovery **was** significant.

_____ 3. They **sent** the fragment of carved stone to scholars in Cairo.

_____ 4. Someone **named** it the Rosetta Stone, after the discovery site.

_____ 5. Many scholars from different countries **translated** the writings on the stone.

_____ 6. It **was** a long process to decipher the code.

_____ 7. The writer **inscribed** the text in three languages: Greek, Demotic, and Egyptian hieroglyphs.

_____ 8. In time, people **understood** all the inscriptions, even the difficult hieroglyphic writings.

_____ 9. Other historical documents from ancient Egypt **became** readable thanks to the Rosetta Stone.

_____ 10. Today we **give** the name *Rosetta Stone* to anything that serves as a key to break a code.

B Circle the words that best complete the text. Should the focus be on the agent or the receiver of the action?

What is known about the Emerald Tablet?

Many legends surround the Emerald Tablet. Where did it come from? Who wrote it and **1. why did this person write it / why was it written**? Was the author Hermes Trismegistus, the ancient Egyptian teacher who some considered a deity? One story tells how **2. Hermes carved the legendary text on emerald tablets / the legendary text was carved on emerald tablets by Hermes** and **3. placed them / they were placed** in the King's Chamber of the Great Pyramid. Did that really happen? The truth remains unknown. However, many people believe that **4. someone found the tablet / the tablet was found** in a secret room under the pyramid of Cheops in 1350 B.C.

What great wisdom does the tablet offer? **5. The text contains a guide / A guide is contained by the text**, which medieval scientists followed with great respect. Some believed **6. the Emerald Tablet held the secret formula for making gold / the secret formula for making gold was held by the Emerald Tablet.** But mostly **7. people see it / it is seen** as a set of teachings on the relationship between people and the universe—a key to the most basic mysteries of nature.

Grammar Focus 2 Perfect forms and other uses of the passive

Examples	Language notes
(1) The Voynich manuscript **has been passed** from place to place. Its contents **have** still not **been deciphered**.	We form the passive in the **present perfect** with: *have / has* (*not*) *been* + past participle We place adverbs after the first auxiliary verb.
(2) This 234-page tome **had been printed** on special paper.	We form the passive in the **past perfect** with: *had* (*not*) *been* + past participle
(3) Authorities **had given** the book to cryptanalysts and code-breakers for evaluation. [*Active = focus on agent*] **The book had been given** to cryptanalysts and code-breakers for evaluation. [*Passive = focus on direct object*] **Cryptanalysts and code-breakers had been given** the book for evaluation. [*Passive = focus on indirect object*]	Sometimes the subject of a passive sentence is not the direct receiver of the action. The **subject** of the passive sentence can actually be the **indirect object** of the equivalent active sentence.
(4) What**'s** it **called**? —The Voynich manuscript.	We frequently see some passive forms in all contexts, including, ***be made, be called,*** and ***be used.***
(5) Scholars speculated that the manuscript **had been created by Roger Bacon**.	We often use the passive in the past to **recognize people** for their inventions, creations, or discoveries. Common passive verbs that function this way include *be written by, be invented by,* and *be discovered by.*
(6) Voynich had been astounded **not only by the manuscript's encrypted text but by its many detailed illustrations as well**.	When the agent is a long noun phrase, we often name the agent in a passive sentence rather than begin an active sentence with a long noun phrase.
(7) **Our team had used** carbon-dating and a special spectrometer to analyze its age. [*Active = personal tone*] **The science of carbon-dating and a special spectrometer had been used** to analyze its age. [*Passive = objective tone*]	Passive sentences are common in **academic writing, scientific reports, and news reports**, where the author must present only facts. Common passive verbs for reporting research include *be determined, be expected, be found, be seen,* and *be shown.*
(8) **It is speculated by many that** Roger Bacon, a famous cryptographer, is the author. **It was estimated to be** from the fifteenth century.	We often use the passive with *it* as the subject to state information, such as a belief, prediction, or assumption: *It* + *be* + past participle + (*by* whom) + *that*-clause *It* + *be* + past participle + (*by* whom) + infinitive Past participles that commonly appear in this structure include *said, thought, believed, considered, known,* and *regarded.* This structure is common in formal English, where the information should not suggest agreement or disagreement with the stated idea.

Grammar Practice

A Circle the verbs that best complete the text.

Some languages **1. have been created / have created** more for fun rather than for communication. Such languages as Pig Latin **2. are not considered / don't consider** official languages. They **3. are seen / see** as games. They usually **4. are applied / apply** playful patterns to existing languages. In the case of Pig Latin, the first consonant sound of a word is moved to the end, and the syllable "ay" **5. is added / adds** on. For example, *language* becomes *anguagelay*. What use does Pig Latin have? Sometimes it **6. is used / uses** to keep information private from those who do not understand the pattern. In short, it can serve as a code, that is, a secret language.

Gibberish and Verlan are two more examples of code languages. In comparison with Pig Latin, these **7. are considered / consider** more complex. Gibberish has developed in different countries, and in English alone many variations exist. The basic concept is to add a nonsense sound to every syllable of a word. For instance, using "uddag," *learn* becomes *luddagearn*. Obviously, it **8. is called / calls** Gibberish for a good reason! Verlan is even more difficult for listeners to decipher. Verlan **9. was invented / invented** in Paris in the 1980s, and it **10. has been grown / has grown** in popularity. As with Gibberish, Verlan **11. is mainly spoken / mainly speaks** by younger generations. Words **12. are taken apart / take apart**, syllables **13. are reversed / reverse**, and new words are formed. *Hello* turns into *lohel* (or if you prefer French, then *jourbon* for *bonjour*). Uddagunduddagerstuddagand?

B Rewrite the boldfaced sentences to have a more appropriate focus. Change the active sentences to passive and the passive sentences to active. Word order will sometimes change as well.

1. My uncle works with secret codes. **You call him a cryptanalyst.** ________________________________

2. **Different retail companies and even some military agencies have hired him.** ________________________________

3. The work of a cryptanalyst is very important. **Professional cryptanalysts secure many information systems, such as online banking and email.** ________________________________

4. There is no direct educational path leading to a career in cryptanalysis. **However, degrees in computer science or mathematics are held by most professional cryptanalysts.** ________________________________

5. The military is aware of the need to strengthen existing information systems. **The military has hired the best cryptanalysts to improve national security.** ________________________________

6. Indeed, cryptanalysts are in demand. However, one cannot enter the profession with only a casual interest in puzzles and codes. **Expert knowledge of math and computers along with experience in the field strengthen the work of a cryptanalyst.** ________________________________

Talk with a partner about the changes you made. Why have the texts become stronger?

MyEnglishLab

Sounding Natural

Speaking

 Read the texts about language. What else do you know about Latin, Esperanto, and artificial languages from movies?

1. When classical Latin, which was spoken in the age of the Roman Empire, began to die out, it was replaced by a less standard form of Latin, known as "Vulgar Latin." Although classical Latin can still be read, it is no longer a living, spoken language. In the Middles Ages (8th to 13th centuries) Vulgar Latin became the "lingua franca" of a much smaller world population. Over time, spoken Vulgar Latin evolved into the Romance languages that are spoken worldwide today.
2. Do you know what Esperanto is? Esperanto is an artificial language, which was designed in the 20th century to become the "lingua franca." It is derived from Romance, Germanic, and Slavic languages and has a very simple grammar. Esperanto is used in more than 110 countries and has close to two million speakers.
3. Have you ever wondered how actors and actresses in science fiction films learn "alien or artificial languages" like Na'vi (from *Avatar*), Klingon (from *Star Trek)* Parseltongue (from *Harry Potter),* or, Elvish (from *Lord of the Rings*)? There is a group of linguists who belong to "The Rosetta Project," whose job is to create artificial or "invented" languages. These languages have been constructed not only for use in fictional media, like movies, but also in the real world.

Ayfizayu plltxuye
(means "Once upon a time" in Na'vi)

tlhIngan maH!
(means "We are Klingons!" in Klingon)

Heru i Million_ in Quenya
(means "Lord of the Rings" in Elvish)

B Answer the questions with a partner.

1. Why do you think Latin became a "dead" language? What do you think "lingua franca" means? Can you think of examples of languages that evolved from Latin? Do you know any other languages that have been derived from another language?
2. Why do you think Esperanto has not become a more popular spoken language?
3. Why do you think the group is called "The Rosetta Project"? How do you think these languages have been created? Why were the alien languages invented?

I think Latin became a dead language because it wasn't studied formally by a lot of people.

I think Esperanto has not become a more popular language because it is not taught anywhere.

"The Rosetta Project" is probably called that because it was named after the famous stone.

Listening

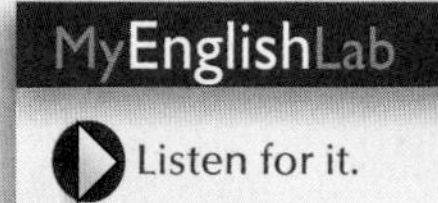

 UNDERSTANDING MAIN IDEAS Listen to an interview. What does the woman do?

____

____

B  UNDERSTANDING DETAILS Listen again. Check (✓) the statements that are true.

☐ **1.** The cipher had been planted in one of William Shakespeare's texts.
☐ **2.** It is possible that the cipher had been placed there by Shakespeare himself.
☐ **3.** The true Prince was thought to be Roger Bacon.
☐ **4.** The Prince's name was hidden in the pages of the texts.
☐ **5.** In order to decipher the message, a special machine was created.
☐ **6.** No one knows exactly why Bacon had been denied his status as "Prince."
☐ **7.** Though the messages were decoded, the mystery has not yet been solved.

C AFTER LISTENING Talk to a partner. What do you think about the hidden cipher? Do you believe the story? Do you think you would enjoy decoding and analyzing hidden messages? Why or why not?

Writing

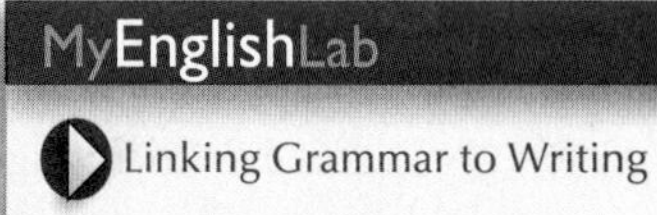

A Review the reading on page 133. Make notes in the chart to analyze the information. Then read the text below and complete the chart.

Recently some fortunate discoveries of ancient texts have provided interesting clues to a language that was believed to be dead. A very complex language known as Pictish was recently identified on stones in Scotland. Some of the symbols provide intriguing clues to the grammar and sound of the language, even though the text has not been deciphered yet.

The stones were highly stylized and engraved with images of soldiers, riders on horseback, and even hunting dogs. These engravings were once thought to be simple "rock art," but are now believed to be tied to the major languages spoken in Britain in 730 A.D. The eighth-century historian Bede described the major languages as: British, Scottish Gaelic, Pictish, and English. It is interesting to modern linguists that Pictish was classified by Bede as a separate language. They believe there may have been a particular accent or dialect of Pictish that was spoken in the British Isles and existed along with the other languages. Linguists still do not understand its complex structure. In order to understand its actual spoken language, modern linguists need to examine its characteristics compared to other ancient languages, such as Old Irish, Old Anglo-Saxon, and many others. One linguist stated: "We may need to wait for . . . the Pictish equivalent of the Rosetta Stone."

Book or stones	Where were the texts discovered?	How are the texts compared?	What images were included?	Were the languages spoken, written, or both?
Voynich manuscript	in a trunk in Italy			
Pictish stones	in Scotland			

B Compare what happened when these languages were discovered. Use the information to write about where and when the texts were discovered. How are the texts alike? How are they different? Which do you think will be deciphered first?

The Voynich manuscript was discovered in . . . while the Pictish stones were found in . . . The images in the Voynich manuscript were drawn, but the images on the Pictish stones were engraved . . .

C Exchange papers with a partner. How are your ideas similar and different?

CHAPTER 14 Enduring Voices

Getting Started

A Work with a partner. Sentences *a–e* all mean the same thing, and the word for "language" is in bold. Try to read the sentences aloud; don't worry about making mistakes. Do you recognize any of these languages? Guess what the sentences mean and match your guess to the questions.

_____ **1.** Which was originally only a spoken language in Africa and has been influenced by Arabic?

_____ **2.** Which is now considered a "dead" language of the Romans?

_____ **3.** Which might be an endangered or dying dialect of French?

_____ **4.** Which was once the unifying language of 15 republics?

_____ **5.** Which is spoken in a very isolated part of Spain?

a. Una **lingua** numquam satis est.

b. Один **язык** недостаточно. (Odin **yazyk** nedostatočno.)

c. **Lugha** moja haitoshi.

d. **Hizkuntza** ez da nahikoa.

e. Una soleta **lenga** basta pas jamai.

B Look at the world map. Write the number of the country or area that answers each question.

1. Which country do you think has the most spoken languages but one national written language?
2. Where do you think there are more than 100 vanishing languages?
3. In which area of the world was a lost language discovered in 2010?
4. In which country is there a language that has not been heard in almost 1000 years?
5. Which country is home to a language that now has just 80 surviving speakers?
6. Which country has many spoken languages but no official language?

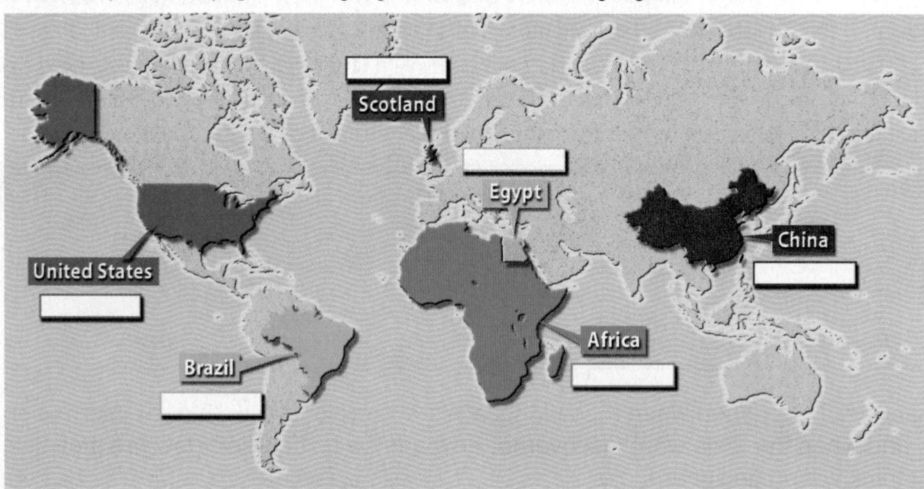

C We use the past participle as an adjective. It often acts like an adjective because it follows an intransitive verb, such as *to be* or *to feel*. We form the **stative passive adjective** from the past tense *-ed* form of a regular verb, or the passive participle of an irregular verb. We form the **participial adjective** from the verb + *-ing*.

translated [regular participle]; ***done*** [irregular participle]; ***interesting*** [participial adjective]

Look back at Parts A and B. Complete the tasks.

1. Circle the **stative passive adjectives.**
2. Underline the **participial adjectives.**

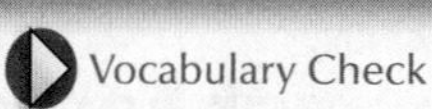

Reading

A WARM-UP How do you think a writing system for a language is decided? Do you know how written- and spoken-language dictionaries are created? Do you know of any cultures that have no written method of communication? What "living" languages do you speak, read, or write?

B PREDICTING What happens to a language when there is only one surviving speaker? What can be done to rescue a dying language or dialect? Read the text and find the answers.

Rescuing an Endangered Language

Dying Languages

There are more than 7,000 languages on the Earth. Some experts believe that by 2100, nearly half of them might become extinct. Like vulnerable animal species, there are also many endangered languages—linguists say that one language dies every two weeks. The main problem that humanity faces with disappearing languages is not just the loss of the language itself, but also of the culture, traditions, and the historical knowledge about the environment and people associated with that language.

Spoken vs. Written Language

In 1993, there was only one 93-year old woman left in Canada who spoke Tuscarora—a language of the Iroquois tribes of North America. There are still a few remaining speakers in the U.S., but it is a nearly extinct language. When the last known speaker of Nushu—a mysterious language in China spoken exclusively by females—passed away at the age of 94, the language died with her. Nushu had not been written down, leaving linguists and other cultural anthropologists unable to recreate its vocabulary, grammar, or syntax.

In contrast, when a written language is no longer spoken, it may also be declared a "dead" language. Many ancient languages are no longer spoken—such as Latin or Egyptian hieroglyphs—though texts in these languages and writing systems still survive.

Dialects are variations of a spoken language that carry a region or city's cultural identity and heritage, like Shanghainese in China, or Provençal, in France. Many dialects are considered endangered because most of the speakers are now elderly. According to the United Nations, more than 50 of China's minority languages and dialects are disappearing. Occitan, a language spoken in France, has six different dialects. Four of these six dialects are now endangered, mainly because they are not taught in schools or spoken among younger generations.

A Chance for Revival

Linguists often find that it is easier to revive an endangered spoken language than a written one. Is it possible to save a dying language? K. David Harrison and Greg Anderson, two linguists who have taken on the task of researching and documenting vanishing languages all over the world, seem to think so.

In the summer of 2005, a project was begun through a government initiative to save some of the world's dying languages. This project spans the globe from the Americas to the farthest reaches of the South Pacific Islands. Time is of the essence, for, as many linguists believe, when there is only one speaker of a language left, the language is already extinct.

C UNDERSTANDING CONCLUSIONS Write *T* for the true statements and *F* for the false statements.

_____ **1.** By 2100 there may be approximately 3,600 languages left on Earth.
_____ **2.** Culture and tradition can be separated from language.
_____ **3.** The Tuscarora language is extinct in Canada.
_____ **4.** Latin is only used as a spoken language.
_____ **5.** Saving a dying language is challenging.

Grammar Focus 1 Stative passive

Examples	Language notes
(1) Some dialects **are** only **found** in isolated areas.	The **stative passive** describes a situation or state. It has the same form as the dynamic passive, but it does not refer to an action received. To form the stative passive, use: subject + *be* + past participle of the main verb
(2) Language **is composed** of sounds and symbols. ***Incorrect:*** ~~**People compose** language of sounds and symbols.~~	We are not usually able to rewrite stative passive sentences as active ones.
(3) Nushu **is classified as** an extinct language since the last speaker in China recently died.	In the stative passive, we can use **prepositions other than *by***. This is because the past participle functions as an adjective, so we use common adjective + preposition combinations, such as *be found in, composed of,* and *classified as*.
(4) Gibberish and Verlan **are** not **used in** academic circles. Those code languages **are associated with** young speakers.	We can group common **adjective + preposition** combinations by their function: To name a location: *be found in, be located in, be shown in, be surrounded by* To classify or define: *be classified as, be considered as, be known as, be known for, be listed as, be measured by, be named as, be recognized as, be regarded as, be referred to as* To explain composition: *be composed of, be divided into, be filled with, be made up of* To express a relationship: *be associated with, be based on, be linked to, be related to* To explain a use or purpose: *be intended for, be required for, be restricted to, be used in*

Grammar Practice

A Complete the text with the prepositions below. You will use some prepositions more than once.

as	for	in	of	with

Hawaiian: An enduring or vanishing language?

Hawaii, the 50th state in the United States, is located **1.** ______________ the central Pacific Ocean. It is the only state made up entirely **2.** ______________ islands. It is also the only state with two official languages. English, of course, was the first to be named **3.** ______________ the official language when Hawaii became a state in 1959. Hawaiian, or *Olelo Hawaii*, was listed **4.** ______________ the other official state language later in 1978. It had not been used by the government or in schools before that time, but the new law helped revive the native language. In the second half of the twentieth century, the people were filled **5.** ______________ new interest in the native language in big and small ways. The University of Hawaii opened a Hawaiian language graduate studies program, and street signs appeared with Hawaiian names. The language was becoming familiar once again.

What are the characteristics of Olelo Hawaii? It is an oral language that is centuries old, but a written system developed with the appearance of westerners on the islands in the 19th century. This same writing system is used today by the Hawaiian government. The written alphabet, which was originally intended **6.** ______________ teaching purposes, is composed **7.** ______________ 12 letters. The letter *W* has two pronunciations: /v/ and /w/. In total, there are only five vowel sounds and eight consonant sounds, which explains why Hawaiian is known **8.** ______________ repetitive sounds in words, like *wiki-wiki* (fast).

Statistics show that there are far more English speakers than Hawaiian speakers today, but because Olelo Hawaiian is taught in schools and because it is associated **9.** ______________ strong cultural traditions, like music and dance, there is hope that the native language will not vanish any time soon.

Look back at the text and underline the six passive sentences that can be rewritten as active sentences.

B Complete the sentences using the words in parentheses in the stative passive along with the correct prepositions.

Facts about Endangered Languages

- Endangered languages **1.** ________________________ (divide) five categories: *vulnerable, definitely endangered, severely endangered, critically endangered*, and *extinct*. These classifications **2.** ________________________ (base) research and statistics.
- When a language **3.** ________________________ (classify) *vulnerable*, it means that speakers include children, but the use of the language **4.** ________________________ (restrict) certain places, for example, the home.
- The degree of endangerment **5.** ________________________ (carefully / measure) the size and age of the population. For a language that is *severely endangered*, the children likely don't use it and the parents may understand it, but few of them speak it. In contrast, a *critically endangered* language is only spoken by the grandparents, whose generation is growing smaller in number.
- Research on endangered languages **6.** ________________________ (not only / intend) scholars. The findings are collected and published in order to make all of society aware of the need to protect the integrity of dying languages as well as the culture and human knowledge they contain.

Grammar Focus 2 Participial adjectives

Examples	Language notes
(1) Some languages **are endangered** by increasingly small populations. [passive verb]	The **past participle** appears in passive constructions. We have used it to form passive verbs.
There are many **endangered** languages. [adjective]	We can also use the past participle as a qualitative adjective called a **participial adjective.**
Many languages are **endangered**. [adjective]	Like other adjectives, a participial adjective may appear either before the noun it modifies or after a linking verb to refer back to the subject.
(2) Humanity faces problems with **dying** languages. [modifier] The statistics are **frightening**. [complement]	**Present participles** are also used as participial adjectives. They, too, can be **modifiers** and appear before a noun or they can be **complements** and appear after a linking verb to refer back to the subject. We usually see participial adjectives before nouns.
(3) The study of the world's languages is **interesting**. (active meaning = *this study interests people*)	Present participles have an **active meaning.** They describe people or things that perform an action or have an effect on something.
He is **interested** in the study of the world's languages. (passive meaning = *something interested him*)	Past participles have a **passive meaning.** They refer to the condition or state people are put in.
(4) This is a **frightening** situation. Linguists are **frightened** by the loss of culture when a language dies.	Many transitive verbs form participial adjectives with **active and passive meanings** (*-ing* / *-ed* forms). However, some participial adjectives are more common in one form and not another. Present participial adjectives that are more common than their past (*-ed*) forms: *following, encouraging, increasing, leading, threatening, working* Past participial adjectives that are more common than their present (*-ing*) forms: *written, spoken, known, educated, determined, complicated, unexpected*
(5) The audience was **surprised** at (by) the findings.	There are many prepositions that **follow past participial adjectives**. These prepositions refer to the person or thing that caused the particular condition or state.
(6) As the last speaker of the language, she **appeared** (**looked, seemed, became, grew**) very **concerned** about the loss of her people's culture and traditions. The work to save dying languages **seems** (**appears, looks**) **challenging**, but it is doable.	***Be*** is the most common linking verb we see before a participial adjective. Other common linking verbs include: *become, look, seem, grow,* and *appear.*
(7) Who **was involved** in the research? *(= be in a state of involvement)*	***Get*** before some passive participial adjectives expresses the meaning of *become.*
Many scientists **got involved** in the research. *(= enter a state of involvement)*	***Get*** + **past participle** contrasts in meaning with the more common passive structure with *be.* It is more common in informal English, especially in conversation.

See Appendix S on page A-12 for more adjective + preposition combinations.

Grammar Practice

A Circle the adjectives that best complete the text.

A Determined Protector of the World's Languages

Dr. K. David Harrison is a **1. leading / led** specialist in endangered languages. He is deeply **2. concerning / concerned** about the number of **3. vanishing / vanished** languages and is working hard to save them from extinction. Dr. Harrison is much **4. respecting / respected** as are his **5. publishing / published** works. In *When Languages Die: The Extinction of the World's Languages and the Erosion of Human Knowledge*, Dr. Harrison details the loss of languages and what that loss means to society. The book is both a careful scientific study and a **6. fascinating / fascinated** depiction of the human experience that is connected to language.

Dr. Harrison's reach has been growing in recent years. He appeared in the 2008 documentary film *The Linguists*, which earned **7. glowing / glowed** reviews at many film festivals. He and his co-star, Professor Gregory Anderson, prove to be very **8. dedicating / dedicated** linguists as they travel around the world in an effort to document endangered languages by interviewing **9. surviving / survived** speakers. While the professors' on-screen adventures may not compare in excitement to the action of a Hollywood movie, their initiative is truly **10. amazing / amazed**. They are scientists in their approach, but they are also **11. interesting / interested** in personal experiences. They are **12. committing / committed** to telling the whole story of human communication.

B Circle the correct prepositions to complete the texts.

1. Hanna Koper is one of eight remaining speakers of N|u, a South African language. She recalls past gatherings that were crowded **1. in / of / with** other N|u speakers. They would sit, talk, and laugh together—in their native language. Hanna says she hears their voices in her dreams now; she gets annoyed **2. about / at / of** them, though, and tells those voices to be quiet. She is tired and wants to sleep.

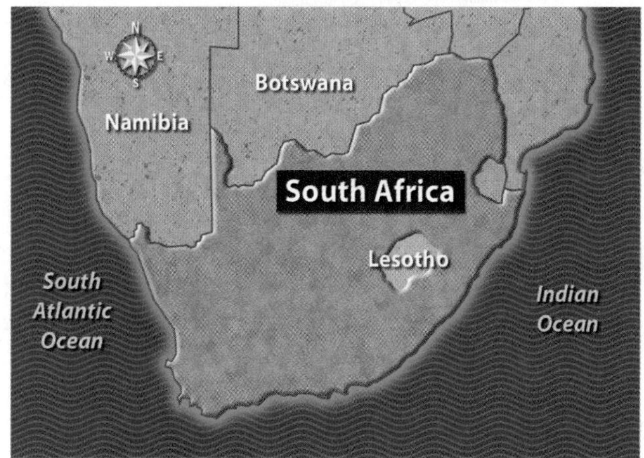

2. Kilash and Ishuz Ehnawanan are two of the fifteen surviving speakers of Thao, a dying language in Taiwan. They are worried **3. about / for / with** the future and the loss of their language. They would be pleased **4. about / for / with** the opportunity to teach Thao to the younger generation, but the young people, they say, are not interested **5. at / for / in** learning.

MyEnglishLab

Sounding Natural

Speaking

A What is your first language like? How would you analyze it? Use the chart to find your first language's place in the linguistic tree.

Major linguistic families of the world's languages

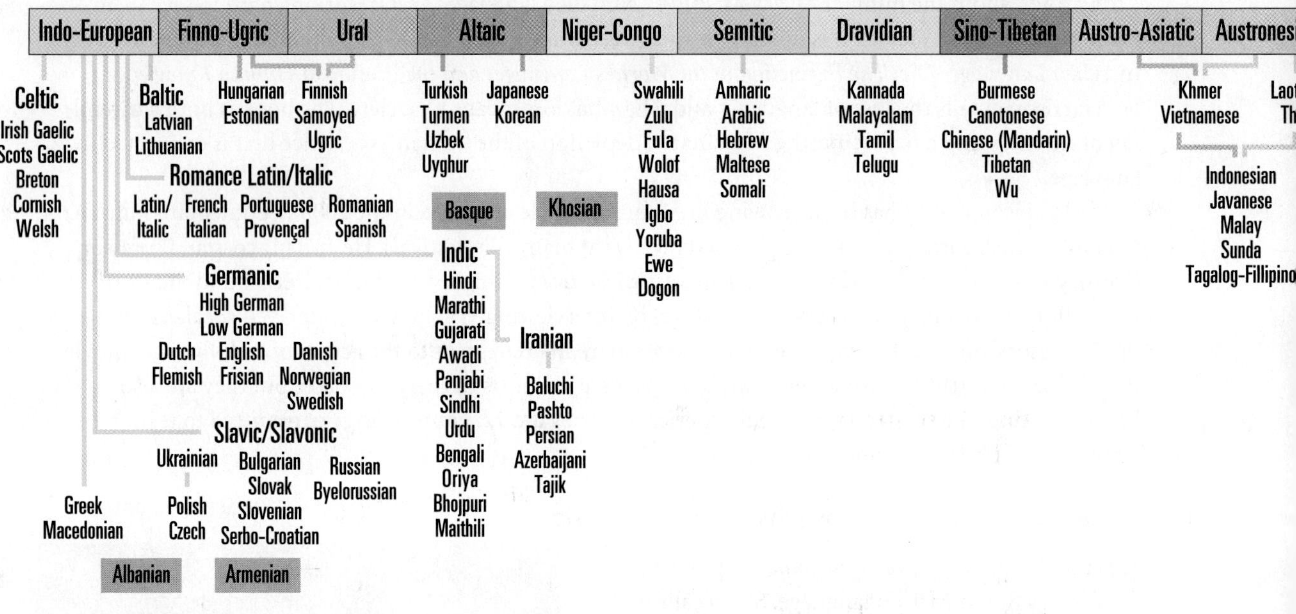

B Answer these questions with a partner.

1. Which languages do you find to be the most interesting?
2. Which languages would you be interested in learning (other than English)?
3. Which languages do you think will be the most spoken in the world by 2020?
4. How does the spoken form of your first language differ from its written form?
5. Are there any threatened languages in your country?

Listening

MyEnglishLab

Listen for it.

A UNDERSTANDING MAIN IDEAS What do we call a person who speaks more than two languages? Have you heard the word *polyglot*? Listen to the beginning of the lecture and check another word or phrase used for polyglot.

- ☐ Multi-linguist
- ☐ Multiple language speaker
- ☐ Bilingual speaker
- ☐ Speaking in tongues

B CATEGORIZING INFORMATION Listen again and answer the questions.

1. What are three or four of Professor Arguelles's spoken languages? ______________________
2. In what languages that are no longer spoken does Professor Arguelles have reading and writing ability?

____

C AFTER LISTENING Talk to a partner. What did the speaker say about Professor Arguelles's language learning techniques? Does he speak your first language? Do you agree or disagree with his techniques? Would you try them?

Writing

A Read the case studies about two dying languages. Think about these questions as you read. Do you think it is important to save dying languages? Should researchers document these languages / dialects and record them? What do you think about accents and dialects? Why do you think the languages / dialects might be endangered?

1. At the Living Tongues Institute for Endangered Languages, linguists K. David Harrison and Greg Anderson have been researching the world's dying languages. Recently, they identified an isolated language in a small district of India. This "hidden" language, which is called Koro, is a new discovery for linguists. While Harrison and Anderson were searching for two other endangered languages—Aka and Miji—they heard this third language being spoken. As they listened, they realized that Koro was distinct from both other languages in the area, and not related to the other two languages in the linguistic tree. Although all people of the village are integrated, (meaning that they work and live together) and do not see themselves as ethnically or culturally different, these three different languages are spoken by each different group. Only about 800 to 1,200 people speak Koro, which means that the language is in danger of becoming completely extinct in the near future.

2. In the United States, regional accents seem to shift frequently due to immigration and technology. In contrast, many dialects—which have different vocabulary words, sentence structure (syntax) and pronunciation—still exist in places like Louisiana, the Appalachian Mountain regions, and the Outer Banks (small islands off the coast of North Carolina). For example, the "Ocracoke Brogue" is spoken on the isolated island of Ocracoke. In the past, its residents did not have much interaction with people from the mainland. With more tourism and technology, this has changed. It may now be endangered because the older residents use the dialect and the younger generations are influenced by media, visitors, or newcomers to the island. Linguists say that losing a language means losing a culture, and losing a dialect means losing a subculture.

B Write a short opinion essay on one of the languages or dialects. State your opinion about what linguists and anthropologists should do to save endangered languages and dialects. Use information from this text as well as from the reading on page 141. Support your opinions with facts and examples from the texts.

Use the sentence starters and key words below to guide your writing.

I was surprised / shocked / not surprised by . . .
I'm very interested in . . .
Endangered languages are important to study because . . .
This is a fascinating topic because . . .
I thought it was very interesting because . . .
The . . . language / dialect is vanishing because . . .
The information about . . . is surprising due to the fact that . . .
Linguists may have a complicated task because . . .
They are not satisfied with the results because . . .

C Exchange your essay with a partner. Which languages did you write about? How are your facts and opinions similar or different?

Grammar Summary

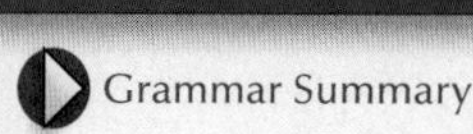

Transitive verbs can have an active or passive meaning. An **active sentence** places the focus on the agent. A **passive sentence** focuses on the receiver of the action.

simple present passive	*am, is, are* (*not*) + past participle	(1) Gibberish **is spoken** by many.
simple past passive	*was / were* (*not*) + past participle	(2) Hawaiian **was** not **taught** in schools in the first half of the twentieth century.
present perfect passive	*have / has* (*not*) *been* + past participle	(3) Hieroglyphs **have been studied** by many linguists from different countries.
past perfect passive	*had* (*not*) *been* + past participle	(4) The words **had been carved** carefully in stone.
Include the *by*-phrase	• When it is important to tell the listener who the agent is. • When the agent is a long noun phrase. • To identify the agent as new information in the context of the discussion.	
Omit the *by*-phrase	• When the agent is unknown, non-specific, or not important. • When the agent is obvious. • When the speaker wants to avoid naming the agent.	
Verbs that often appear in the passive	• In all contexts: *be made, be done, be called, be told,* and *be put.* • To give recognition: *be written by, be invented by, be developed by,* and *be discovered by.* • To report research: *be determined, be expected, be found, be seen,* and *be shown.* • To make neutral statements [*It* + (*be*) + past participle]: *be said, be thought, be believed, be considered, be known,* and *be regarded.*	

The stative passive does not refer to an action received. The **stative passive** describes a situation or state. The past participle functions as an adjective, so prepositions other than *by* can follow.

be associated with	be located in	be composed of
be known as	be divided into	be related to

When present and past participles function as adjectives, we call them participial adjectives. **Participial adjectives** can be modifiers and appear before a noun or they can be complements and appear after a linking verb to refer back to the subject. It is more common for participial adjectives to appear before nouns.

present participle = active meaning	(1) Look at these **interesting** inscriptions. (2) The study of ancient texts is **interesting** to many.
past participle = passive meaning	(3) The listeners all wore **surprised** expressions. (4) You seem **surprised** by the conclusion.

Linking verbs other than *be* can appear with participial adjectives: *become, look, seem, grow,* and *appear.*

Self-Assessment

A (5 points) Complete the sentences. Use the verbs in parentheses and the correct forms of the passive voice.

1. A complex coded message ______________________ (receive) by our military one week ago.
2. The code ______________________ (not break) yet by cryptanalysts.
3. It was obvious from the beginning, however, that a combination of languages ______________________ (use) to create the code.
4. It ______________________ (believe) that the code was deliberately sent to test our military.
5. It ______________________ (expect) that cryptanalysts will meet with success in the near future.

B (6 points) Choose the correct sentences to complete the conversation.

A: What language is spoken in your home?

B: My parents speak only Portuguese, but they understand Banawá. **1. My grandparents speak Banawá. / Banawá is spoken by my grandparents.**

A: **2. Do you understand Banawá? / Is Banawá understood by you?**

B: No, not really. **3. My sister and I know more English than Banawá. / More English than Banawá is known to my sister and me.** Banawá isn't really heard all that much. **4. People consider it a dying language. / It's considered a dying language.**

A: What's the language of instruction at your school?

B: **5. They give instruction in Portuguese and English. / Instruction is given in Portuguese and English.** The use of English increases with each grade level.

A: So some classes are held in English?

B: Yes. **6. They teach some classes completely in English. / Some classes are taught completely in English.**

Circle the two intransitive verbs in the conversation.

C (5 points) Correct the stative passive error in each sentence.

1. Tetlin, which is a small community of just over 100 people, is located at Alaska.
2. Cora David, a Tetlin elder, has published a book that is filled by stories of her people.
3. Athabascan, a Tetlin dialect, is used by this collection of stories.
4. Because the book is intended to a broad audience, English translations are given as well.
5. David's book, along with the audio recording of her reading, can be considered for a publication of linguistic, cultural, and historical importance.

D (4 points) Choose the correct participial adjectives to complete the sentences.

1. Some people find ancient carvings **intrigued / intriguing.**
2. Their **amazed / amazing** initiative has earned the respect of many.
3. The code is **complicated / complicating.** It will take much time and effort to understand it.
4. The cryptanalyst is very **dedicated / dedicating** to her work.

Unit Project: Language phrasebook

A Work in a group. You are going to research a dead, extinct, endangered, or invented language and make a phrasebook of useful words and expressions. If possible, form a group with classmates who speak several different languages. Follow these steps:

1. Choose from one of these languages or do research to find one that you are interested in:

   Dead languages (no longer written): *Latin, Sumerian, Egyptian hieroglyphs*
   Extinct languages (no longer spoken): *Tonkawa* (U.S. Native American); *Sakhalin Ainu* (Japan)
   Endangered languages: *Vod* (Russian Fed; near border of Estonia); *North Frisian* (spoken near Netherlands and Denmark); *Cornish* (UK)

   You can also look online for other dead, extinct, or endangered languages.

   Invented languages: *Elvish, Klingon, Na'avi. Parseltongue,* or others.

2. Research the history or background of each language. Be sure to answer these questions:
   - How is the language grammatically organized?
     For example: Subject-verb-object (English)
     Subject-object-verb? Verb-object-subject?
   - How were words pronounced?
   - Where was it spoken?
   - Was it a written language as well as spoken? If so, which alphabet is used?
   - What happened to its speakers?
   - What has been done to save it (as a dying language)?

B Prepare a presentation of your phrasebook to the class. Follow the steps.

1. First, do a standard presentation of the completed phrasebook. Use some of these phrases to start your presentation.

   The language was spoken in . . .
   It was not a written language . . .
   It was only a spoken language . . . This language was discovered in . . . by . . .
   This language was never translated because . . .

2. Now teach the class how to say *hello*, and a few other phrases. Have one member of your group be the interpreter or hold up cards with "subtitles."
3. After the presenters have spoken, talk in a group. Discuss the similarities and differences you might see between the languages. Do any languages have words in common? Do any words sound like words in languages you speak or are familiar with?

UNIT 8

Brain Power

OUTCOMES

After completing this unit, I will be able to use these grammar points.

CHAPTER 15

Grammar Focus 1
Gerunds as subjects

Grammar Focus 2
Gerunds as objects and possessive gerunds

Grammar Focus 3
Other uses of gerunds

CHAPTER 16

Grammar Focus 1
Infinitives as subjects and objects

Grammar Focus 2
Infinitives of purpose

Grammar Focus 3
Other uses of infinitives

MyEnglishLab

 What do you know?

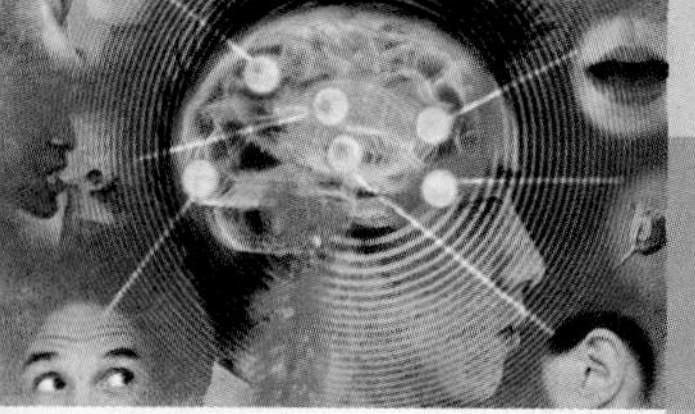

CHAPTER 15 Unlocking Your Brain's Potential

Getting Started

A What do you know about the brain? Look at the images and read the descriptions. Match the activity with the part of the brain that is the most necessary for performing it.

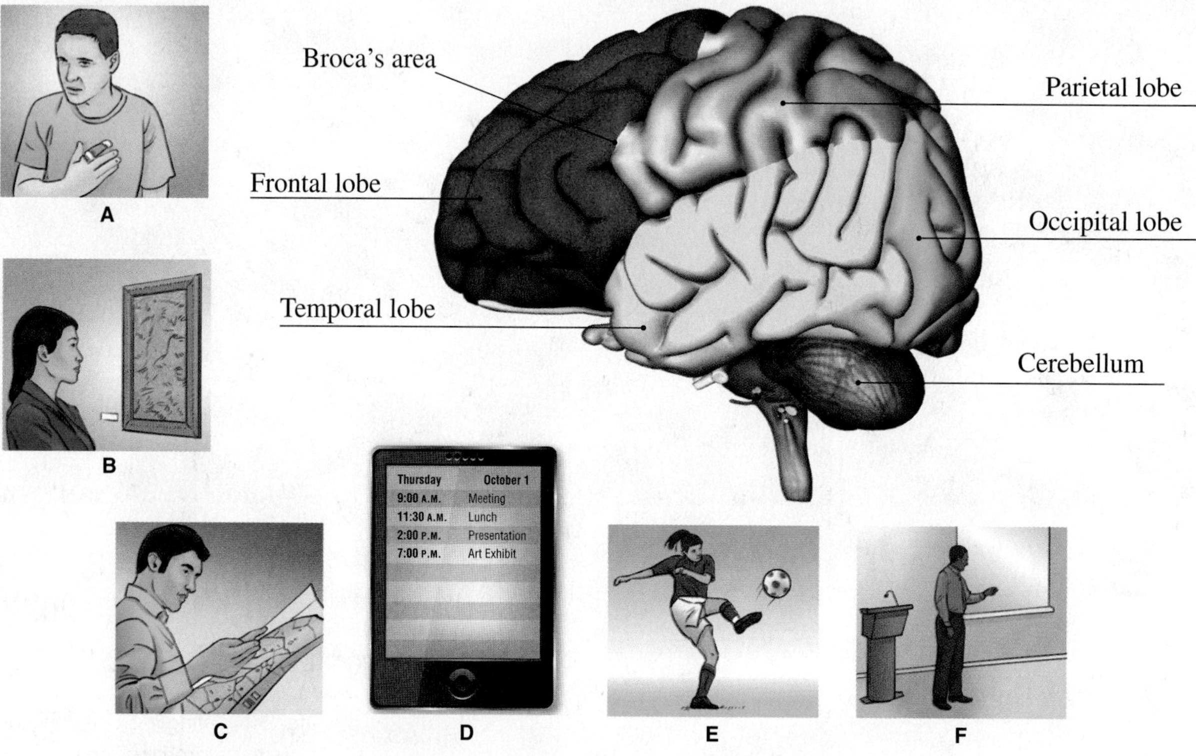

_____ **1.** The **occipital lobe** is at the back of the brain and controls seeing.

_____ **2.** The **cerebellum** is involved with many functions, such as controlling pain, breathing, regulating sleep, and managing digestion.

_____ **3.** Moving body parts (such as your arms and legs), problem solving, hearing, paying attention, talking, and remembering are all managed by the **frontal lobe**.

_____ **4.** The **parietal lobe** helps us with reading maps, locating things, sensing hot and cold, and touching.

_____ **5.** The **temporal lobe** is the largest area of the brain and is situated at the front and sides of the head. It is in charge of planning things, controlling emotions, and reasoning.

_____ **6.** The frontal lobe includes the **Broca's area**, which is for speech and language.

B Talk to a partner about some activities you enjoy doing. Look at the images in Part A again. Guess which parts of the brain are associated with your hobbies and activities.

C Look back at Parts A and B. A **gerund** is a verb plus the suffix *–ing*. A gerund acts like a noun, as the subject or object of a verb. A gerund can also be the object of a preposition after a verb. Complete the tasks.

1. Circle the **gerunds** that are **subjects**.

2. Underline the **gerunds** that are **objects of verbs**.

3. Draw a box around **gerunds** that are **objects of a preposition**.

MyEnglishLab

Vocabulary Check

Reading

A WARM-UP Talk to a partner. What is a neuroscientist? What is a neuroscientist interested in finding out? What questions would you ask a neuroscientist?

B UNDERSTANDING MAIN IDEAS Are our brains hard-wired or are they capable of adapting? Do you think learning a new language or training for a sport can change your brain? How do scientists use brain mapping to discover what happens in the brain? Read the text to find the answers.

Mapping the Brain and Unlocking Its Hidden Potential

Just like a computer's processing unit, our brains are hard-wired to perform certain activities, from sleeping to swallowing. The brain has two hemispheres, and the different parts of each hemisphere play a role in how various tasks are completed. Each part of the brain has a specific function; some functions are involuntary and some are voluntary. Involuntary actions, such as breathing, hearing, and seeing, are actions that we don't decide to do; they just happen. These actions are mainly controlled by the cerebellum at the back of the brain. We make conscious decisions about performing voluntary actions, such as raising an arm or kicking a ball, and these actions are controlled by other parts of the brain.

Another interesting area of study is determining which areas of the brain control creativity and logic. Neurologists and neuroscientists can use scanning devices like the fMRI for peering into the brain to get information about these areas. By combining use of the fMRI with other scanning machines, like the PET scan (Positron Emissions Tomography), neuroscientists are able to see more of the brain's activities and have a better understanding of its mysteries. While scanning the brain, neuroscientists can also map the brain to find out what happens to our memory when we learn or relearn certain tasks. Brain mapping allows them to connect a part of the brain's structure to its function. It aids with detecting what parts of the brain give us certain abilities and how the brain retrains itself if it becomes damaged or injured. During the scanning process, scientists can watch as the brain works on various tasks or does different activities.

Brain mapping also looks from the outside into the brain's functions. It examines how our environment changes our brain's structure by studying the physical changes in the brain. Scientists can understand how the brain changes under different conditions, such as learning or aging. Brain mapping also helps doctors understand what happens physically in the brain—after brain injuries, as a part of superior thinking or when performing certain tasks.

Have you ever wondered how a gymnast performs a complex, highly technical tumbling move so flawlessly? Or how a violinist can move the fingers on his left hand so quickly over the strings while bowing efficiently with his right hand? Practice, also known as "mind-training," results in the ease of performing these tasks. By mapping the brain, neurologists can better understand how to unlock the brain's hidden potential.

C RECOGNIZING PURPOSE AND TONE Answer the questions in your notebook.

1. Why does the author compare the brain to a computer processor?
2. How does the author define the areas of the brain in charge of breathing or moving?
3. What are neuroscientists interested in discovering?
4. What do neurologists and neuroscientists find out when they map the brain?
5. What things can PET and fMRI scans be useful for?
6. Which of the following best describes the author's tone: informative, persuasive, skeptical, or curious?

Grammar Focus 1 Gerunds as subjects

Examples	Language notes
(1) think + **-ing** = *thinking* agree + **-ing** = *agreeing*	A **gerund** is the *-ing* form of a verb that acts like a noun. To form a gerund, use: base verb + *-ing*
	Some verbs follow special spelling rules.
(2) believe + **-ing** = *believing*	For verbs that end with *e* after a consonant, drop the *e* and add *-ing*.
plan + **-ing** = *planning*	For verbs with a short vowel before the final consonant *b, d, g, l, m, n, p, r, s, t*, or *v*, double the final consonant and add *-ing*.
forget + **-ing** = *forgetting* visit + **-ing** = *visiting* ***NOT:*** ~~*visitting*~~	For verbs with two syllables and ending with a short vowel before a final consonant, double the final consonant and add *-ing* when the second syllable is stressed. If the second syllable is not stressed, do not double the final consonant.
(3) not + knowing = *not knowing*	Use *not* to form a negative gerund.
(4) **Breathing** is an involuntary function. [subject = gerund] **Brain mapping** allows them to connect the brain's structure to its function. [subject = gerund phrase (modifier + gerund)] **Mapping the brain** helps doctors understand brain injuries. [subject = gerund phrase (gerund + direct object)] **Bowing efficiently** is a skill that violinists must master. [subject = gerund phrase (gerund + adverb)]	Just like nouns and noun phrases, gerunds and gerund phrases can be the **subject** of a sentence.
(5) **Detailed mapping** of the brain explains how the brain functions. [adjective + gerund]	**Descriptive adjectives** can modify gerunds, just as they modify nouns.

Grammar Practice

A Complete the sentences with gerunds. Use the verbs in parentheses. You may look back at the spelling rules on page 154.

1. ________________ is one of the five senses. (touch)
2. ________________ and ________________ are two others. (hear, smell)
3. ________________ a map requires use of the parietal lobe. (read)
4. ________________ emotions is a function of the frontal lobe. (control)
5. ________________ detailed plans is not easy for everyone. (outline)
6. ________________ some animals relaxes the mind and can reduce stress. (pet)
7. ________________ our body, from our legs to our little finger, is a function of the temporal lobe. (move)
8. ________________ a baseball requires use of three different lobes, from the moment one sees the ball to the second one swings the bat. (hit)
9. ________________ is not a conscious activity, that is, it's automatically regulated. (breathe)
10. ________________ is possible with help from the temporal lobe. (remember)
11. ________________ down and ________________ up involve the temporal lobe, which helps us move, and the brain stem, which controls our pain. (fall, get)
12. ________________ problems and ________________ decisions are not skills that everyone is good at. (solve, make)

B Unscramble the words to form sentences with gerunds or gerund phrases as subjects. Do not confuse the gerunds with verbs in progressive tenses.

1. the brain / helps / us / locate / scanning / pain
   Scanning the brain helps us locate pain.
2. function / sleeping / a / is / of / the brain stem
   ____
3. not sleeping enough / causing / was / health problems
   ____
4. a problem / often / solving / two or more / takes / brains
   ____
5. may be / an injury to / the occipital lobe / not being able to see / a result of
   ____
6. becoming / easier / understanding the brain / is / with new research and technology
   ____
7. by / reasoning / planning and / the frontal lobe / are controlled
   ____
8. singing / requires / beautiful / several parts of / the use of / the brain
   ____
9. is / mind mapping / doctors / helping / treat / brain injuries
   ____
10. the brain / understand / us / its many functions / helps / mapping
    ____

Grammar Focus 2 Gerunds as objects and possessive gerunds

Examples	Language notes
(1) The brain controls **breathing, sleeping,** and other involuntary activities.	Gerunds and gerund phrases can also be the **object of a verb** (the **direct object**).
	There are many verbs that take a gerund as the direct object. Here are some of the most common ones.
(2) Gymnasts enjoy **tumbling** very much.	Verbs that express emotion: *like, enjoy, love, (not) mind, dislike, can't stand, hate, feel like*
The violinist stopped **moving** his fingers and bow, and silence filled the room.	Verbs that describe physical or verbal actions: *keep, start, stop, quit, finish, discuss, suggest, mention*
The neurologist considered **retraining** the patient's injured brain.	Verbs that refer to a thought process or mental state: *consider, imagine, postpone, forget, remember, recall*
(3) You should wear a helmet to protect your head when you **go cycling** or **rollerblading**.	We use ***go + gerund*** to describe many recreational activities, such as swimming and shopping.
	Gerunds can also be the **object of a preposition** (the **indirect object**). Common patterns include:
(4) The patient responded positively to the **mind-training**. [verb + preposition + **gerund**]	a) verb + preposition + gerund **Examples**: *decide on, look forward to, help with, respond to*
The middle brain is responsible for **controlling** language. [linking verb + adjective + preposition + **gerund**]	b) linking verb + adjective + preposition **Examples**: *good at, afraid of, happy about, responsible for*
We're very interested in **mapping** the brain. [past participle (as adjective) + preposition + **gerund**]	c) past participle (as adjective) + preposition **Examples**: *concerned about, remembered for, interested in*
(5) We can regulate our **breathing**. The neurologist's **training** was excellent.	We use a **possessive noun or possessive adjective** before a gerund to express possession.
(6) I don't mind my roommate (him) **snoring** because it's not too loud, and I'm a heavy sleeper.	In informal speech, we often use a name or object pronoun before a gerund to express possession. This practice is more informal than use of a possessive noun or adjective.

See Appendix Q on page A-11 for a more complete list of verbs followed by the gerund.
See Appendix R on page A-11 for more go + *gerund phrases.*
See Appendix S on page A-12 for more verb + preposition + gerund and adjective + preposition + gerund combinations.

Grammar Practice

Complete the sentences. Choose verbs from the boxes and change them to gerunds.

cycle	do	exercise	jog	move	sit

1. MARC: I enjoy **1.** ________________ physical activities. I go **2.** ________________ every morning. On the weekends I like **3.** ________________, and I usually ride for at least ten miles each day. I can't stand **4.** ________________ in one place for very long. Sometimes I watch TV, but after twenty or thirty minutes I feel like **5.** ________________. I just can't sit still! I don't think I'll change much as I get older, especially because **6.** ________________ keeps me healthy. I want to live until I'm 100!

be	have	learn	play	play	study

2. LIDA: I'm a very musical person. I can't imagine not **7.** ________________ music in my life. I began **8.** ________________ to play the piano when I was six. I remember **9.** ________________ so happy because I felt like I had been given a gift, the gift to create music. I practiced **10.** ______________ the piano every day. At nine, my parents recognized my musical potential, so I started **11.** ______________ at a special school for the arts. I can't say that everyone would love to hear my **12.** ______________, but it certainly brings me a lot of joy.

do	feel	lose	solve	spend	take

3. Rasool: I love puzzles of any kind. There's nothing like a good brain teaser. I enjoy **13.** ______________ riddles, and I'm also pretty good at crosswords. I admit **14.** ______________ a strong sense of pride and satisfaction as soon as I complete a really difficult crossword. I realize it takes a lot of brain power to create complex puzzles in the first place, and I truly appreciate someone **15.** ______________ the time to provide me with the challenge! I consider my **16.** ______________ puzzles to be mental exercise. That's how I justify **17.** ______________ so much time on what some people call games. It's not just fun. Puzzles are a proven way to increase brain power. If you want to avoid **18.** ______________ some of your own, go find a good puzzle to solve.

Go back and circle the three gerunds that appear with a possessive adjective or object pronoun. Which one uses an object pronoun to express possession?

B Complete each sentence with the correct preposition and the gerund form of the verb in parentheses.

1. The athlete was worried ______________ able to play because of his injury. (not be)

a. of **b.** about **c.** over

2. He was concerned ______________ full use of his sight. (regain)

a. with **b.** for **c.** about

3. It seems he was afraid ______________ blind. (go)

a. for **b.** about **c.** of

4. The patient was complaining ______________ frequent headaches. (experience)

a. about **b.** from **c.** for

5. The technician spoke calmly to the patient, who was nervous ______________ a brain scan. (have)

a. of **b.** from **c.** about

6. The skilled staff was capable ______________ the scan without any discomfort to the patient. (complete)

a. about **b.** of **c.** with

7. Some patients admit ______________ claustrophobic—they don't like feeling closed in. (feel)

a. to **b.** about **c.** of

8. The staff succeeded ______________ the patient's fears by playing music during the scan. (reduce)

a. by **b.** in **c.** with

Grammar Focus 3 Other uses of gerunds

Examples	Language notes
(1) We have great interest in **mapping** the brain. [noun + preposition + **gerund**] We make conscious decisions about **performing** voluntary actions. Practice results in the ease of **performing** these abilities.	We often see gerunds after **noun + preposition** combinations.
(2) The next step is **analyzing** the brain scan. [subject + linking verb + **gerund phrase**] (= ***Analyzing*** *the brain scan is the next step.*) The doctors are having trouble **determining** the source of pain. [have trouble + **gerund**] The specialist spent a good amount of time **studying** the scans. [spend time + **gerund**]	Gerunds can function as **complements**: a) after linking verbs b) after special expressions with verb + noun object: have difficulty / have fun / have trouble / have a hard time / have a difficult time / spend time + gerund
(3) **Tumbling** requires skill. [gerund] The gymnast is **tumbling**. [present participle in a progressive verb] That's a complex **tumbling** pass. [present participle as an adjective]	Remember that gerunds act as **nouns**. They function as subjects, direct object, indirect objects, and complements. Do not confuse gerunds with **present participles**: Present participles are used in progressive verbs. Present participles are used as adjectives.

See Appendix T on page A-12 for a list of noun + preposition + gerund combinations.

Grammar Practice

Read the text. Circle the gerunds and underline the present participles.

The doctor who is famous for his innovative scanning

The first full body scan was performed in 1977 by Dr. Raymond Vahan Damadian. He successfully built and used the Magnetic Resonance (MR) scanning machine to diagnose medical conditions without going into the human body. Dr. Damadian knew he was making a significant contribution to medicine. Through dedication and hard work, he succeeded in creating one of the most amazing tools in modern medicine.

As early as 1969, Dr. Damadian became intent on giving doctors a unique window into the entire human body. He proposed the idea of a whole body scan, but he had a hard time convincing the scientific community it was possible. Dr. Damadian was up for the challenge. He spent a great deal of time proving his opponents wrong. Nearly a decade later, his dream was realized, and doctors around the world showed interest in using his invention. The first MRI scanner was introduced for commercial use in 1980.

Dr. Damadian's ideas and his device led to other advances in medicine. Today doctors regularly use the functional MRI (fMRI). This kind of imaging allows one to detect and measure changes in the active part of the brain. Thanks to brain scanning we have obtained more knowledge of the human mind than was ever thought possible.

Respect and credit go to Dr. Damadian for all that doctors are able to do with an MRI. Perhaps it is not so surprising that this man was the one to realize something that seemed impossible. Although he had trouble making a career in music as a violinist or in sports as a tennis pro, that background along with his degrees in math and medicine proves he is a man of many skills, a man with creativity, and a man who is not worried about taking risks—he knows when they are worthwhile.

B Complete the chart with gerunds and present participles from the text in Exercise A, including its title.

Present participles used as participial adjectives	Present participle used in a progressive verb tense	Gerunds used as complements
1.	1.	1.
2.		2.
3.		3.

Gerunds used as objects of prepositions		
verb or verb phrase + preposition + gerund	adjective + preposition + gerund	noun + preposition + gerund
1.	1.	1.
2.	2.	2.
	3.	3.

MyEnglishLab

Sounding Natural

Speaking

A Look back at the reading on page 153. Summarize the information about mapping the brain in your own words. Pay attention to the explanations of scientific terms and think of ways to explain it to someone who doesn't know how the brain works. Talk to a partner about the major points in the reading. How can mapping the brain be helpful to physicians and patients?

B Work with a partner. Talk about activities that you are each interested in learning. Decide which activity might take the longest or be the most difficult, and which could be the easiest to learn and why: learning a new language, mastering a dance step, painting, knitting, cooking a dish without a recipe, reading a 200-page book in a new language, or learning a computer programming language.

Look back at the image of the brain on page 152. Which parts of your brain do you think are most active when you are performing these tasks?

I like to play tennis. So when I hit a ball or serve a ball, I know that the . . . part of my brain is most active.

When I'm reading, the . . . and . . . parts of my brain are probably the most active.

Listening

A UNDERSTANDING MAIN IDEAS Listen as a talk show host interviews a medical doctor. What is the doctor's specialty?

____

____

B UNDERSTANDING DETAILS Listen again. As you listen, check (✓) all the things that are true.

☐ **1.** All parts of the brain control movement.
☐ **2.** Playing sports requires coordination.
☐ **3.** The temporal lobe has more control than the cerebellum.
☐ **4.** People cannot train the brain by doing repeated activities.
☐ **5.** Planning is a physical action.
☐ **6.** A PET machine is used for scanning the brain.
☐ **7.** Scanning the brain can help scientists create a map of the brain.
☐ **8.** The frontal lobe and the brain stem control sensations.
☐ **9.** By finding the source of pain, doctors can help patients control it.

C AFTER LISTENING Talk to a partner. What was the interviewer's attitude toward brain mapping? How do you feel about brain mapping?

MyEnglishLab

Linking Grammar to Writing

Writing

A Read the text about mapping the brain and memory.

Centuries ago, great scientific thinkers like Galen (200 AD) and Leonardo da Vinci (1500 AD) explored the brain and its inner workings. Galen found that the brain—not the heart—is the seat of human senses. Leonardo was one of the first to realize it was in control of our mental activity, and later produced drawings of it. Following in the footsteps of Galen and Leonardo, two neuroscientists at the University of California, Los Angeles, (UCLA), Dr. John Mazziotta and Dr. Arthur Toga, have used the concept of brain mapping to create a realistic and comprehensive 3-D map of brain activity.

The scientists have mapped the normally developing brain in order to track its maturation from childhood to adulthood and investigate the changes in memory, problem-solving, reasoning, and other functions. They can use the 3-D images to understand how a test subject's brain reacts to seeing different patterns or images. The brain "lights up" during the scanning process when the person views an image and recalls it.

Have you ever wondered why you remember doing something in your childhood but cannot remember what you ate for breakfast this morning? Scientists categorize memory in two ways: long-term memories—those memories we store from many years ago, or memories of repeated activities (like swinging a baseball bat or playing a piece on the piano)—and short-term memories (like a grocery list or something we just saw five minutes ago).

Read the list. Write *L* for *long-term memory* or *S* for *short-term memory* for each description.

_____ **1.** Reciting a phone number
_____ **2.** Remembering a list of words
_____ **3.** The action of an actor, memorizing lines from a script
_____ **4.** Riding a bicycle
_____ **5.** Learning a new song
_____ **6.** Solving a math problem
_____ **7.** Your sixteenth birthday party
_____ **8.** The name of someone you just met
_____ **9.** Telling someone what you just heard on the news

B Write about a memory from your childhood: a class, a party, a sports event, a school trip.

- What do you remember doing? What have you forgotten about that event? Has your memory of that event changed as you've gotten older?
- Now, think about things you were interested in doing as a child that you are no longer interested in doing today. Were you good at playing sports as a child? Are you still good at that sport today? Did you enjoy drawing? Were you good at it? Compare your childhood abilities with what you are good at doing today.

You can use sentence starters, such as:

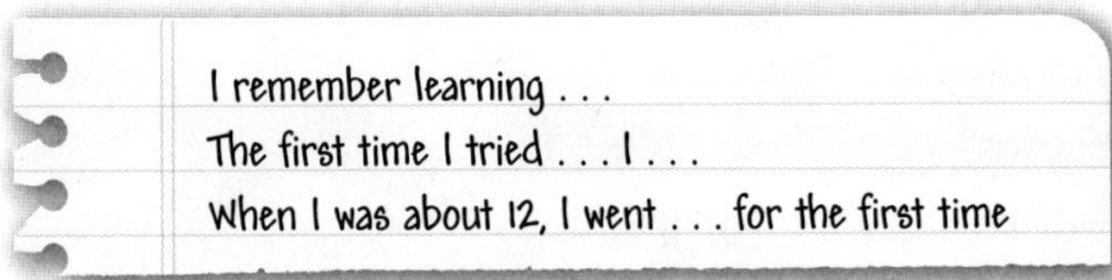

I remember learning . . .
The first time I tried . . . I . . .
When I was about 12, I went . . . for the first time

C Exchange papers with a partner. Talk about similar or different experiences you have had.

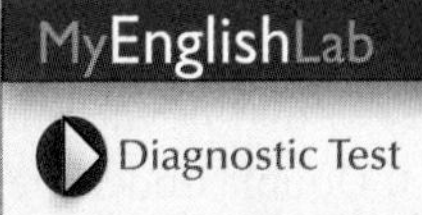

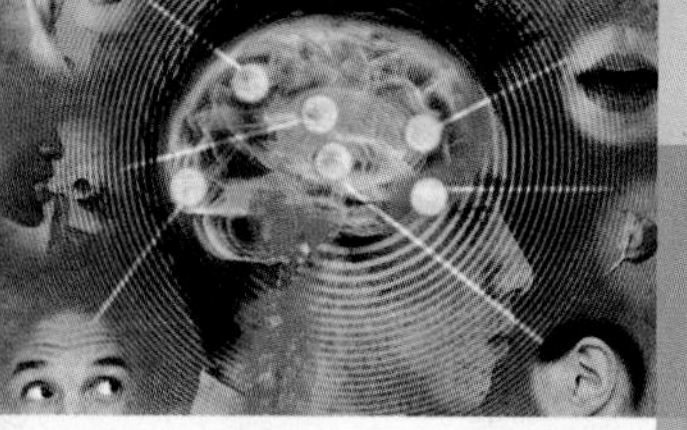

Chapter 16 How to Think Like a Genius

Getting Started

A As you read in Chapter 15, the brain has four lobes plus the brain stem and cerebellum. Each of the lobes has two sides, called the left and right hemispheres. Read each question and check (✓) *True* or *False*. Total your answers to see which hemisphere is more dominant for you.

True	False		Left brain vs. right brain
		1	I need to wear a watch so I always know what time it is.
		2	I like to solve puzzles and answer riddles.
		3	It is important to read a map and follow directions.
		4	I'm able to solve math and logic problems very easily.
		5	I'm not musical or artistic—I don't know how to play an instrument.
		6	I keep a "to do" list.
		7	It is more natural for me to express myself with words than with images.
		8	If I have to make a decision, I like writing down "pros" and "cons."
		9	I wouldn't want to be a detective because I am not intuitive.
		10	I like to research things before I decide to try them out.
		11	It is easier for me to remember names than faces.
		12	I have no desire to write poetry or take dance lessons.
		13	I do not like to take risks.
		Total: True _____ Total: False _____	

Answers: If more than half of your answers are True, you are left-brain dominant. If more than half of your answers are False you are right-brain dominant.

B Read the statements. Compare them with your answers from Part A. Then check (✓) the statements that describe left- or right-brain dominance.

Activity	Left-brained	Right-brained
People who are logical like to do crossword puzzles.		
Musical people are usually not afraid to sing in a karaoke contest.		
To learn a new language is easy for verbal people.		
Volunteering to paint a large mural on a wall sounds interesting.		
Mathematical types are quick to figure out a restaurant bill.		
To read a novel is one way to simulate imagination.		
Intuitive people try to assemble furniture without reading the directions.		

C Look back at Parts A and B. The infinitive is formed with *to* + a base verb. The infinitive can be the subject, infinitive of purpose as subject, or the object of a verb. Complete the tasks.

1. Circle the **infinitive as subject** or **infinitive of purpose as subject**.
2. Underline the **infinitive that is an object of a verb**.
3. Double underline the **infinitive that is an object of an adjective** or **participial adjective**.

Reading

A WARM-UP Who is Leonardo da Vinci? What was he famous for? Check (✓) the things you think Leonardo da Vinci knew how to do well.

☐ build a machine	☐ paint	☐ play sports	☐ run an art school
☐ build bridges	☐ play a musical instrument	☐ read	☐ write

B PREDICTING Do you think Leonardo da Vinci was left-brained or right-brained? Read the text to find the answer.

BRAINSTORMING:
How to Think Like a Genius

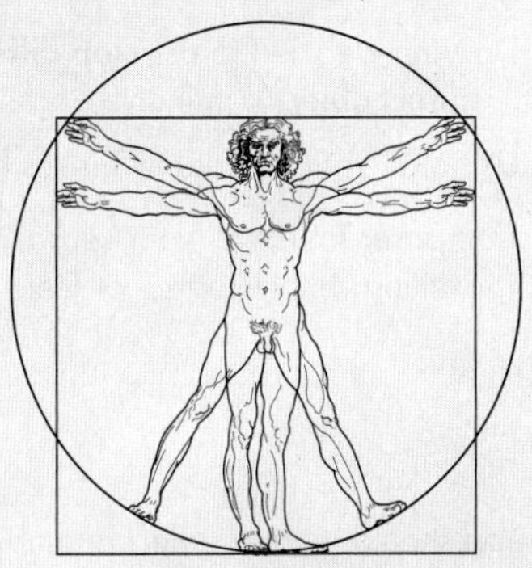

Little is known about the personal life of the great artist, thinker, and engineer, Leonardo da Vinci, but historians have credited him with the idea of "brainstorming"—getting ideas quickly down on a page. It has been said that Leonardo often got distracted because he liked to multi-task; he often abandoned one project in order to explore another idea. He is most famous for his drawing of *Vitruvian Man* and his paintings, the *Mona Lisa* and *The Last Supper*. Yet, his greatest gifts were his journals—they contained everything from drawings of animals and mapping the brain to sketches of bridge designs and a prototype of aircraft.

In Leonardo da Vinci's journals—like the *Codex Atlanticus* and the *Codex Madrid*—there are thousands of pages containing his notes, sketches of people, musical instruments, machines, plants, or animals, and ideas for engineering projects. Perhaps the most intriguing thing about his notes was his backwards handwriting. Though scholars believed Leonardo wanted to be secretive, most historians now attribute it to the fact that Leonardo simply preferred to write with his left-hand. However, Leonardo was ambidextrous—having the ability to write or paint with either hand. He believed that we are more able to understand life and the world by using the "whole brain" and "seeing the big picture." Leonardo was a rare individual who was as good at creating visual images as he was at writing. When he had completed one notebook, he immediately started a new one. He continued to write until he was an elderly man and had completed twenty unpublished journals before he died in 1517. The journals now reside in libraries all over the world.

In his book, *How to Think Like Leonardo da Vinci*, Michael Gelb analyzes and categorizes Leonardo's way of thinking into seven steps, in order to learn and better understand how the mind works.

1. **Curiosity:** Use curiosity to improve creative thinking and self-expression.
2. **Demonstrate** an ability to learn from your mistakes.
3. **Sensations:** Use your senses of taste, smell, sight, touch, and hearing to make life more exciting.
4. **"Gray areas of life":** Learn to **tolerate ambiguity**. Don't be afraid to take risks.
5. **Art and Science:** Try to develop "whole-brain" thinking and imagination by combining art and science.
6. **Total body-awareness:** Balance your entire body and mind to develop fitness and better health.
7. **Connection:** Think about how to interact and connect with the world.

By following Leonardo's steps to master our abilities and to improve our skills in all areas, it seems that anyone can learn to think like a genius.

C UNDERSTANDING DETAILS Write *T* for the true statements and *F* for the false statements.

_____ **1.** The article is about Leonardo da Vinci's brain.
_____ **2.** Leonardo believed people should use their whole brain.
_____ **3.** To be ambidextrous means you are able to write with your left hand.
_____ **4.** To balance the entire body, you should develop a good health plan.
_____ **5.** Leonardo's journals inspired Michael Gelb to write his book.

MyEnglishLab
Reading Comprehension

Grammar Focus 1 Infinitives as subjects and objects

Examples	Language notes
(1) **To multi-task** means to do several things at the same time. [**subject** = infinitive] **To think like da Vinci** is an attainable dream. [**subject** = infinitive phrase]	An **infinitive** (*to* + base verb) or **infinitive phrase** can be the **subject** of a sentence. This kind of sentence structure is used more in formal, literary, or academic writing than in conversation.
(2) **Not to take risks** means fewer opportunities to learn.	Use *not* to form a negative infinitive.
(3) Da Vinci learned **to multi-task**. [**direct object** = infinitive] Da Vinci decided **to develop different interests**. [**direct object** = infinitive phrase]	Many verbs can only be followed by an infinitive, and not a gerund. The infinitive is the **direct object**. Some of the most common ones are ***appear, decide, hope, manage, need,*** and ***want***.
(4) **Using** all your sensations makes life more exciting. ***Compare:*** **To use** all your sensations makes life more exciting. [more formal or literary]	It is more common in everyday English to use a gerund as a subject. The **gerund as a subject** expresses an activity. The **infinitive as a subject** can focus more on one's intent. However, the difference in meaning is usually insignificant. There is a greater difference in the level of formality.
(5) You should learn **to tolerate** ambiguity. Da Vinci practiced **writing** with both hands. He continued **to write** until he was an elderly man. OR He continued **writing** until he was an elderly man.	Both infinitives and gerunds are frequently direct objects. However, there are some fixed patterns: Some verbs can only be followed by an infinitive. Some verbs can only be followed by a gerund. Some verbs can be followed by either a gerund or an infinitive and there is no difference in meaning.
(6) I was tired, so I stopped **reading** my book. (stop + *gerund* = *stop an activity*) I stopped **to answer the phone**, and I went back to my reading later in the evening. (stop + *infinitive* = *stop to do another activity*)	Some verbs can be followed by either a gerund or an infinitive, but there is a major difference in meaning: *stop / quit* + gerund = stop an activity completely *stop / quit* + infinitive = stop one activity in order to do another *forget* + gerund = forget something that happened in the past *forget* + infinitive = forget to perform a necessary task, usually with a negative impact *remember* + gerund = remember something that happened in the past *remember* + infinitive = remember to perform an action *try* + gerund = experiment with something new to see if it works *try* + infinitive = make an effort to do something difficult *go on* + gerund = continue an activity without stopping *go on* + infinitive = start a new activity after finishing another *regret* + gerund = feel sorry about what you have done *regret* + infinitive = regret to say bad news

See Appendix U on page A-12 for a more complete list of verbs followed by the infinitive.

Grammar Practice

Rewrite the proverbs. Change all the gerunds to infinitives.

1. Thinking well is wise; planning well, wiser; but doing well is the wisest and best of all. (Persian proverb)
   To think well is wise; to plan well, wiser; but to do well is the wisest and best of all.
2. Teaching is learning. (Japanese proverb)
3. Erring is human, forgiving is divine. (Alexander Pope, English poet)
4. Traveling hopefully is a better thing than arriving. (Robert Louis Stevenson, *Virginibus Puerisque*)
5. Knowing is nothing at all; imagining is everything. (Albert Einstein)

Discuss the meaning of each proverb with a partner.

Correct the one error in each statement. One statement has two errors.

1. Leonardo da Vinci grew being famous for more than his art. He also worked as an engineer and a writer.
2. Gelb's book recommends to follow Leonardo's model and develop our ability to use the whole brain. For example, we can practice being more tolerant of ambiguity.
3. Consider to unlock your hidden potential as a thinker. Don't hesitate to try new activities.
4. Don't fail to use every opportunity to grow as a thinker. One can always manage learning something from a mistake.
5. People need to ask questions. Curiosity helps developing self-expression and creative thinking.
6. Don't refuse taking a risk. You can't always avoid entering one of the so-called gray areas of life.

C Circle the correct gerund or infinitive to complete the text. If both are correct, circle both.

Consider Being a Person of Many Interests

You may remember **1. seeing / to see** Condoleezza Rice in newspapers or on television after the 2000 U.S. presidential election. She served as the 66th Secretary of State under President George W. Bush. Did you also know that some people have seen her on stage seated at a piano? Dr. Rice also happens to be a concert-level pianist. She is an excellent example of a modern polymath.

A *polymath* is a multicareerist, a person who succeeds in mastering one field and then goes on **2. to master / mastering** at least one other. The existence of polymaths proves that some hobbies can turn into second careers. It isn't wrong to dedicate yourself to a single career, but if you love doing other things and know you're good at doing them, why stop? Go on **3. enjoying / to enjoy** these activities and try **4. gaining / to gain** even greater skill at them. Neurologists confirm that behavior can shape the brain, so if multiple skills are mastered, the mind is able to transfer them to other contexts. For example, the creative mind of a poet can find solutions to problems in the business world, and the stage presence of a pianist can transfer to a political speech before millions.

None of us want to enter old age and regret **5. not living / not to live** life more fully, so take a lesson from polymaths. Don't feel you must quit **6. spending / to spend** time on a hobby. Don't stop **7. exploring / to explore**, and never limit your interests. We each have one lifetime. Don't forget **8. making / to make** the most of it.

Grammar Focus 2 Infinitives of purpose

Examples	Language notes
(1) Leonardo da Vinci often abandoned one project **(in order) to explore** another idea.	**Infinitives of purpose** express intention or reason. They answer the question *why?* or *what for?* The full form uses *in order*, but we often omit this phrase, especially in spoken English.
(2) **In order not to lose** a skill, you must practice using it.	To form a negative infinitive of purpose, use: *in order not* + infinitive.
(3) **To develop** "whole-brain" thinking, try combining art and science in your life. [**infinitive of purpose** + imperative] **To appreciate** Leonardo's greatness, you must recognize his contributions as an artist, engineer, and thinker. [**infinitive of purpose** + modal of necessity]	Infinitives of purpose can appear at the beginning of the sentence. In this position, the infinitive phrase is followed by a comma. An imperative or a modal of necessity often follows.
(4) The seven steps were listed **to teach** people how to develop their whole minds. [explains reason for action] Leonardo used notebooks **in order to sketch** ideas for engineering projects. [explains the purpose of the object] ***Incorrect:*** Leonardo used ~~**in order to sketch** ideas for engineering projects~~ notebooks.	Infinitives of purpose can also appear after the main verb to explain the reason for the action or after a direct object to explain its purpose. ***Note:*** Do not separate the main verb from the direct object with an infinitive of purpose.
(5) Use your sensations **to make** life more exciting. [infinitive of purpose] ***Also possible:*** Use your sensations **for a more exciting life**. [*for* + noun phrase] ***Incorrect:*** Use your sensations ~~**for to make**~~ life more exciting. / Use your sensations ~~**for make**~~ life more exciting.	Do not use the preposition *for* with an infinitive of purpose or only a base verb. You can explain the reason for an action with either an infinitive or *for* + noun or noun phrase.

Grammar Practice

A Check (✓) the sentences with infinitives of purpose.

☐ **1.** To be better at any skill, you need to practice.
☐ **2.** Being artistic means to have skills in painting and drawing.
☐ **3.** You should experiment with different techniques to find the best way to learn.
☐ **4.** Even gifted artists need formal training to develop the talents they were born with.
☐ **5.** In most professions, one must learn to multi-task.
☐ **6.** Remember to set realistic goals in order not to fail.

B Correct the errors with infinitives of purpose.

1. Violinists need bows for make smooth music from their strings.

2. One must gain knowledge of economics for to have a career in banking.

3. Gymnasts stretch to avoiding injury.

4. Public speaking skills are required in order be a politician.

5. An army officer in order to control the soldiers under his or her command demonstrates leadership.

6. Pianists need to spend many hours at the keyboard for training their fingers to move quickly, accurately, and gracefully.

Grammar Focus 3 Other uses of infinitives

Examples	Language notes
	Infinitives can function as **complements**:
(1) The challenge in most people's lives is **to multi-task**. [subject + linking verb + **infinitive**]	a) After linking verbs
This chapter has convinced me **to read** Gelb's book. [verb + object + **infinitive**]	b) After some verb + noun object combinations that express requirement or persuasion: ask / convince / expect / need + (whom) + infinitive
Being ambidextrous means having the ability **to write** with either hand. [noun + **infinitive**]	c) After some nouns: ability / decision / opportunity / plan / time + infinitive
(2) It is truly amazing **to realize the depths of Ms. Rice's talents**. (It = *place holder for "to realize the depths of Ms. Rice's talents"*)	Infinitives can also function as **adjective complements**. In this role they directly follow the adjective. The subject pronoun *It* often functions as a "place holder" for an infinitive or infinitive phrase. *It* signals that the true subject will appear later in the sentence. This pattern is common with participial adjectives and other descriptive adjectives.
Compare: **To realize the depths of Ms. Rice's talents** is truly amazing. [more formal]	The role of the infinitive as the true subject becomes clearer when we see the infinitive at the beginning of the sentence without the place holder.
(3) Condoleezza Rice was lucky enough **to perform** with the famous cellist Yo-Yo Ma. ***Incorrect:*** Condoleezza Rice was lucky enough **performing** with the famous cellist Yo-Yo Ma.	Infinitives follow many descriptive adjectives: ***right, wrong, sorry, happy, sad, glad, lucky, ready, easy, hard, difficult, necessary,*** and ***important***. In this pattern, the infinitive generally expresses intent or completion.
	Infinitives follow many present and past participial adjectives.
(4) It was exciting **to hear** them play. (= *The very opportunity to hear these musicians was exciting.* (The situation was characterized by excitement.))	a) Present participles used as adjectives have an active or transitive meaning and usually refer to a situation. The infinitive complement explains the action that is having an effect on someone.
It excited me **to hear** them play. (= *Hearing them play excited me.* (Their playing caused this feeling in me.))	b) Past participles used as adjectives have a passive meaning and usually refer to a person's state or feelings. The infinitive complement explains the action that led to that state.

See Appendix V on page A-13 for more verbs followed by object + infinitive.
See Appendix W on page A-13 for more nouns followed by an infinitive.
See Appendix X on page A-13 for a list of adjectives followed by an infinitive.

MyEnglishLab

Grammar Plus 3
Activities 1 and 2

Grammar Practice

A Circle the correct words to complete the text.

To: Doctor Andrew Howard, Department of Neuroscience <howard.andrew@US.school.edu>
From: istudythebrain@homebase.com
Subject: Inquiry regarding research opportunity

Dear Dr. Howard,

I am writing **1.** to let / for letting you know I am interested **2.** to work / in working with you. I have recently returned to the university **3.** for receive / in order to receive my Ph.D. It is my wish **4.** to become / becoming a researcher in the field. One reason why I chose **5.** to apply / in order to apply to this program was because of your work in the field. Like you, I believe some of our abilities are natural, and there are others we need **6.** learning / to learn.

During my time here at the university, I intend **7.** to continue / continuing my focus on right-brained and left-brained skills. I have already conducted studies, and although I agree with some of the results, I believe it is necessary **8.** in order to conduct / to conduct more research. I would like **9.** finding out / to find out more about how our brains function.

10. In order to participate / To participate in a brain-mapping study has always been one of my goals.

I **11.** look forward to hear / look forward to hearing from you.

Sincerely,

Janice Valente, Ph.D. Candidate

B Correct the seven errors with gerunds and infinitives / infinitives of purpose.

To: istudythebrain@homebase.com
From: Doctor Andrew Howard, Department of Neuroscience<howard.andrew@US.school.edu>
Subject: Re: Inquiry regarding research opportunity

Dear Janice,

Thank you for writing to me. I would be happy meeting with you during my regular office hours. Please click here for to view the days and times I am available.

I am pleased to knowing you have returned to the university with specific goals and much enthusiasm. I welcome you, and I encourage you continue your research. Hopefully, I will be able to provide some guidance. Please stop by soon during my office hours, and we can also discuss the possibility of your being a research assistant next semester. The university will require you submitting a formal application for the position, so it is best starting the process early.

I look forward to meet you in person.

Regards,

Dr. Howard

MyEnglishLab

Sounding Natural

Speaking

A Work with a partner. Look at each <u>color</u> below and try to say the *color* not the word. Say all twelve colors in thirty seconds or less.

red	green	purple
blue	yellow	orange
green	blue	yellow
purple	orange	red

Talk to a partner. Was this activity easy or difficult? Why or why not? Try it again and see if you improve by practicing or if it is still difficult. Which hemispheres of your brain had to do most of the work? Left, right, or both? How could this activity be helpful for people?

This activity was difficult to do because . . .

This was easy to do because . . .

Seeing the word and color at the same time is useful for . . .
. . . left-brain people to be more . . .
. . . right-brain people to become more . . .

B Look back at the reading. Are you left-brained or right-brained? Talk with a partner. Would you like to learn to be more organized or more creative? Why?

- Do you believe it is possible to learn how to use your "whole brain" and think like a genius? Why or why not?
- Do you believe we are born with a certain intelligence level and that learning to improve our intelligence is impossible?

I'd like to be more creative because . . .

I agree because I think that learning is . . .

Listening

A UNDERSTANDING MAIN IDEAS Listen to a program on a science channel. What is the main idea of the program?

____

B CATEGORIZING IDEAS Listen again. Fill in the chart with information. What does the psychologist say are easy or difficult for right-brained people? What does the neurologist say are easy or difficult for left-brained people to do?

	Right-brained	Left-brained
Easy		
Difficult		

C AFTER LISTENING Talk to a partner. Compare your answers from Part B. What things would you like to know more about? What do you think the show is going to explore in the next segment?

____

____

Writing

A When you want to brainstorm an idea, you can create a mind map. Read about mind-mapping.

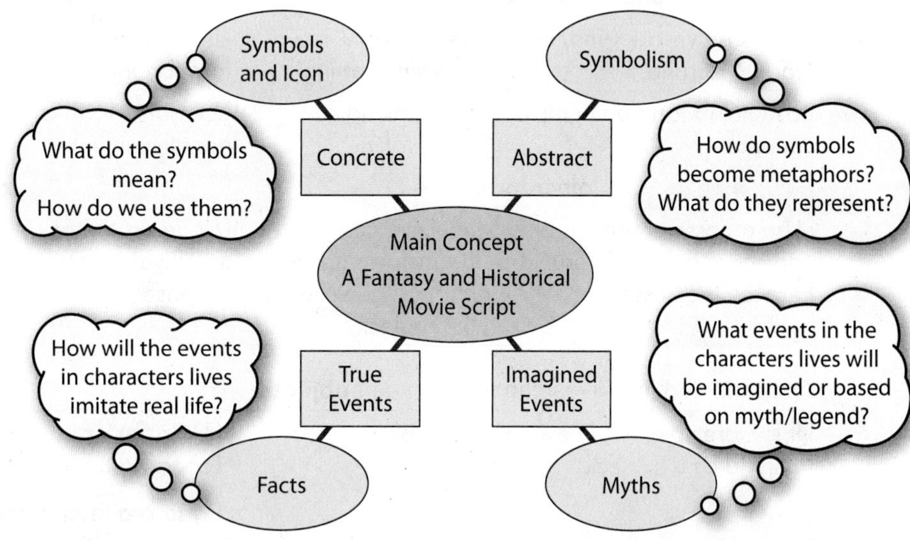

Pop culture psychologist Tony Buzan claims that he created the idea of mind mapping in the early 1970s and has published several books on the subject. The mind map uses pictures, patterns, lines, and colors to make associations between ideas. He believes that you can improve memory as well as unlock the brain's hidden potential by learning how to mind map. By training your brain to process information in more cohesive and comprehensible patterns, you will unlock your brain's potential, which can improve many areas of your life. Some experts even believe that you can discover different powers and skills in the right side of your brain (the creative areas) and begin using the left side of your brain (logical and analytical areas) more effectively.

However, the original concept of putting one's thoughts down on paper—brainstorming—is attributed to the great thinker, Leonardo da Vinci. Leonardo was probably the first to actually create a mind map as a way of organizing information. Both Buzan and Leonardo have used this technique as a form of "visual note-taking," in order to put ideas down on paper and best organize their thoughts. By coordinating both your left (logical, organized, planning) and right (intuitive, imagery-oriented, creative) hemispheres, you can learn to improve your ways of thinking and organizing your ideas. Buzan and Leonardo both followed similar steps to create a mind map.

1. Begin by writing your idea in the center of a blank paper.
2. Draw or find a picture to represent your idea.
3. Use colors to represent different aspects or qualities of your idea.
4. Connect the main branches to the main image.
5. You can create curved and flowing lines.
6. Use a keyword to define each idea on a line, as your map branches out.
7. Use images and numbers to represent associations between your ideas.

B Use your mind-mapping technique to write about skills or activities you have been naturally good at doing since childhood (that is, no one taught you) and things you learned how to do. What are your natural skills? How do you use them? What would you like to learn? How can you improve?

> I have always wanted to be a chef ever since I was a small child because I thought it would be easy for me to do. When I was twelve, my grandmother showed me how to cook. She taught me the basic things, like measuring and how to use the stove and oven.

C Exchange your essay and talk to a partner. What mind-mapping techniques do you have in common? Do you have similar natural skills or abilities? What differences do you see?

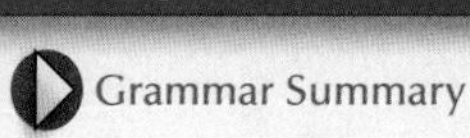

Grammar Summary

Gerunds and infinitives are formed from **base verbs**.

Gerund		Infinitive	
affirmative and negative		**affirmative and negative**	
Use base verb + *(-ing)* to form a gerund.	brainstorm + ing = *brainstorming*	Use *to* + base verb to form an infinitive.	to + improve = *to improve*
Use *not* to form a negative gerund.	not + taking = *not taking*	Use *not* to form a negative infinitive.	not + to improve = *not to improve*
other forms		**other forms**	
Use a possessive noun or adjective before a gerund to express possession.	I believe our **brainstorming** was an important step of the project.	Use *in order not* + infinitive to express purpose.	He uses mind maps **(in order) to** improve his mind.

Gerunds and infinitives can function as **subjects**.

It is more common in everyday English to use a gerund as a subject.	(1) **Brainstorming** is attributed to the great thinker, Leonardo da Vinci. (2) **To brainstorm** means putting one's thoughts down on paper. [*More common: Brainstorming means . . .*]
The subject pronoun *It* often functions as a "place holder" for an infinitive or infinitive phrase.	(3) It is very helpful **to use colors** when you make a mind map. [true subject = "to use colors"]

Gerunds and infinitives can function as **objects**.

Objects of prepositions (indirect objects)	
Only gerunds can be indirect objects.	(1) Who is credited with the idea of **mind mapping**?
Objects of verbs (direct objects)	
Some verbs can only be followed by an infinitive.	(2) You'll manage **to organize** your ideas better if you learn about mind mapping.
Some verbs can only be followed by a gerund. techniques to improve your way of thinking.	(3) Practice **using** Tony Buzan's and Leonardo's techniques to improve your way of thinking.
Some verbs can be followed by either a gerund or an infinitive and there is no difference in meaning.	(4) I like **using** images to represent my ideas. (5) I like **to use** images to represent my ideas.
Some verbs can be followed by either a gerund or an infinitive, but the choice creates a difference in meaning.	(6) I remember **using** a mind map. (= *recall*) (7) Remember **to use** images. (= *do not forget to do*)

Gerunds and infinitives can function as **complements**.

Gerunds and infinitives can function as complements after linking verbs.	(1) The students seem **to enjoy** the challenge. (2) The challenge is **using** both sides of their brains.
Gerunds and infinitives can function as complements after some nouns.	(3) I spent a lot of time **making** branches on my mind map. [verb + noun object + **gerund**] (4) My wish **to become** a better thinker just might come true! [noun + **infinitive**]
Infinitives can be complements after verb + noun object combinations.	(5) I challenge you **to make** your own mind map today!
Infinitives can be complements after participial adjectives and other descriptive adjectives.	(6) I'm determined **to be** a "whole brain" thinker. (7) It's exciting **to know** I can unlock my potential. (8) I'm always happy **to learn** more.

Self-Assessment

A (4 points) Complete the sentences with a gerund subject. Use the verbs in parentheses.

1. ____________________ a mind map is not as easy as showing one. (explain)

2. ____________________ your thoughts with a key idea in the center is the first step. (map)

3. ____________________ branches for related ideas then gives structure to the process. (use)

4. ____________________ visual clues helps engage more of your brain. (provide)

B (4 points) Complete each sentence with an infinitive subject. Use the verbs in parentheses.

1. ____________________ intelligence only to nature robs a person of the chance to develop the mind. (attribute)

2. ____________________ physical exercise is a means to improve one's mental health. (increase)

3. It is rare ____________________ ambidextrous naturally and not through training. (be)

4. It will be fun ____________________ mind mapping to my friends. (demonstrate)

C (4 points) Combine each pair into one sentence. Use the words in bold to make an infinitive of purpose.

1. I ca**n't forget this information**. That's why I'm using a mind map right now.

____

2. Our teacher reminded us **to prepare for the quiz**. That's why I am reviewing my notes.

____

3. Talking with a classmate helps me **to retain information from class**. That's why I joined a study group.

____

4. I wanted our teacher **to answer course-related questions**. That's why he has office hours.

____

D (8 points) Circle the correct words to complete the conversation.

A: Professor Griffin advised me **1. speaking / to speak** with you.
B: Yes, she spoke to me about you. I understand you plan **2. conducting / to conduct** a study.
A: Yes. I'm interested in **3. determining / to determine** how easily ambidexterity is learned.
B: How will you manage **4. doing / to do** that?
A: I need right-handed subjects to train through the exercise of left-handed **5. writing / to write.**
B: You'll need volunteers who can tolerate **6. doing / to do** repetitive tasks.
A: Yes, I will. I also intend **7. asking / to ask** them to brush their hair and teeth with their left hands.
B: You didn't mention **8. having / to have** any way to measure success. Let's talk more about that aspect.

Unit Project: Puzzles and brain power

Think back to the quiz you took at the beginning of Chapter 16. Are you left brained or right brained? Find a partner who is the opposite of you. Try to complete the activity in 20 minutes or less. Then answer the questions.

1. **Numbers Puzzle.** Complete the puzzle with numbers 1–9 in every column and row. Use each number only once in each row and column.

1				9				7
			1		5		4	
		6				1	2	3
3		8		6	1		9	4
		9		8		3		
4	7		9	5		6		2
2	3	5				7		
	9		8		7			
8				3				9

2. **Crossword Puzzle.** Complete the puzzle with the correct words.

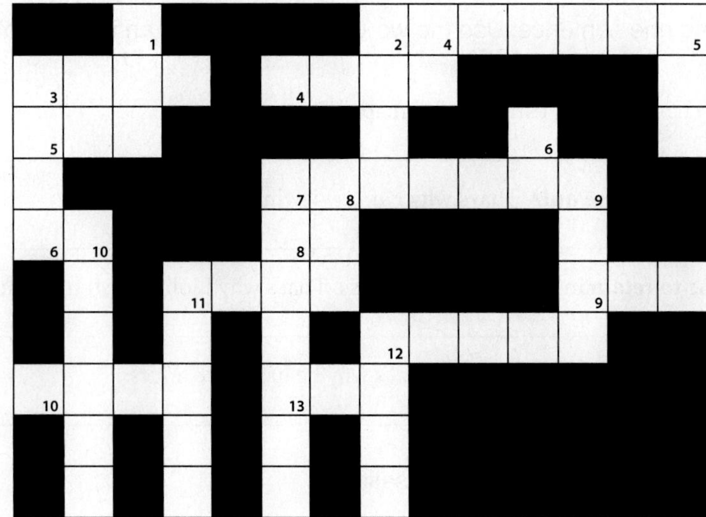

Across

2. Doing this may cool you, but it makes flames burn m
3. Yours, ______, and ours
4. Stay ______, cool, and collected.
5. Salt ______ pepper (same as 1 down)
6. To be, for he or she
7. A dog's specialty especially for food
8. Get ______ the bus!
9. I hope the moving ______ fits all my furniture.
10. Work to ______, don't ______ to work.
11. ______ a text message or a letter.
12. You hear sirens do this.
13. ______ got a secret.

Down

1. The conjunction of connection
2. We wave it on a national holiday.
3. Famous short story: "The Gift of the ______"
4. To be, after "I"
5. The criminals had a "______-away car!
6. He's ______ vacation.
7. People or molecules connecting
8. All good things must come to an ______.
9. ______ and take.
10. "______ is believing."
11. What you do with money or time.
12. Where have you ______ all day?

Complete the puzzles and discuss your results in teams or with your class. How did you analyze your skills? Use the questions below to talk with a partner or in a group.

1. Do you think you are logical or creative? Which skills did you use the most to do these puzzles?
2. Which of the puzzles was easy to do? Which was difficult to do? Why?
3. Which was the most challenging to finish in 20 minutes or less?
4. Which parts of the puzzles were you or your partner able to do more easily?
5. Which puzzle did you enjoy doing?

I enjoyed doing {x} puzzle because . . .

I used . . . skills to solve the puzzle.

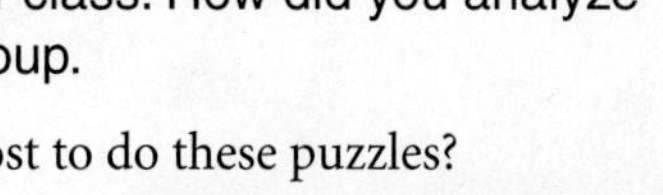

MyEnglishLab

Unit Test

MyEnglishLab

Search it!

UNIT 9

Across the Universe

OUTCOMES

After completing this unit, I will be able to use these grammar points.

CHAPTER 17

Grammar Focus 1
Present and past factual (real) conditionals: Habitual events and facts

Grammar Focus 2
Factual (real) conditionals: Inferences, predictions, and intentions

CHAPTER 18

Grammar Focus 1
Imaginative (unreal) conditionals: Present and future

Grammar Focus 2
Imaginative (unreal) conditionals: Past and mixed time periods

Grammar Focus 3
Omitting information in conditional sentences

MyEnglishLab

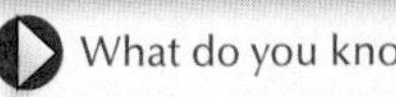

Chapter 17 Out of This World

Getting Started

A What if someone out there is listening? Until 2011, the SETI (Search for Extraterrestrial Intelligence) Institute received funding from the U.S. government to monitor activities on radio frequencies in outer space. When the SETI project was shut down by NASA, private citizens created and volunteered for an organization called *SETI@home* in order to continue the search. Talk to a partner. What do you think will happen if volunteers from *SETI@home* make contact with aliens?

B Read the statements. Write *T* next to the statements that you believe are true.

_____ **1.** If *SETI@home* members receive a message from space, it will take a long time to decode it.
_____ **2.** If NASA observed an unidentified flying object (UFO), they would record its location.
_____ **3.** If astronauts traveled to the Moon, they flew faster than the speed of sound.
_____ **4.** If life forms exist on other planets, there must be water somewhere.
_____ **5.** If NASA cannot deny the existence of UFOs, they also cannot deny life on other planets.
_____ **6.** If SETI receives a signal from outer space, the public will probably not be informed about it.

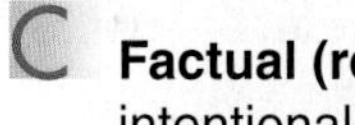

C **Factual (real) conditionals** express events and ideas that are factual. They can be habitual, intentional, predictive, or used to make inferences. Conditional sentences have two clauses: the *if*- [condition] clause and the main [result] clause.

1. The **present** and **past real conditional** express an action that is **general knowledge, factual, or habitual.** The word *if* can be replaced by *when* with no change in meaning.
   If a NASA probe travels through our solar system, it always **sends back** images.
   If a NASA probe traveled through our solar system, it always **sent back** images.
2. The **present real** also expresses factual conditionals that are **inferences.** Look at the two types below. Note the difference in verb forms.
   Type 1 If NASA **can** afford to repair its spacecrafts, it **can** afford to fund the SETI project.
   Type 2 If SETI **detects** a narrow-bandwidth signal, it **must be** from an extraterrestrial.
3. The **future real conditional** states an action that is **predictive, intentional,** or **likely to occur** in the future.
   If the images from space **are** blurry, technicians **will** adjust them.

Look back at Part B. Decide if the sentences are present, past, or future time. Then determine the category of conditional for each sentence. Write the number of the sentence in the correct box in the chart.

Factual (real) conditional categories	Past	Present	Future
General truth			*1*
Habitual			
Inference type 1 (implicit)			
Inference type 2 (explicit)			
Predictive			
Intentional			

MyEnglishLab

Vocabulary Check

Reading

A WARM-UP What is "interstellar communication?" If NASA scientists or *SETI@home* volunteers receive a message from outer space, what do you think they will do? How do you think they will feel about receiving a message from space?

B PREDICTING If we want to make contact with extraterrestrials, what method of communication will we use? If extraterrestrials contact us, what language should we respond in? How will world leaders react if we receive a message from outer space? Read the article and check your answers.

Voyager's Golden Mission:

If someone answers our message, how will we reply?

In 1977, NASA launched twin probes Voyager 1 and 2 in opposite directions to explore space beyond our solar system. The probes are programmed to receive signals or capture images of planets. When they receive signals, the spacecraft immediately send communication back to Earth. As the Voyagers move farther away from Earth, the signals take longer to reach us. Each probe has an identical gold-plated record attached to it, which is a kind of "time capsule." These records contain numerous sounds and 115 images that best represent the diversity of life on planet Earth. The sounds and images are encoded in each disc along with directions that are written in symbols, so if the records are intercepted, they can be played on a standard record player.

Renowned astronomer and cosmologist, Dr. Carl Sagan (1934–1996), led the committee that selected the discs' contents. In addition to recordings of human voices, the discs also included sounds from nature: wind, rain, surf, thunder, and vocalizations of various animals, dolphins and whales, and bird species. The audio also includes spoken greetings and music from all over the world. If extraterrestrials play the record, they will hear greetings in 55 languages. The first language they will hear is Akkadian, a 6,000-year-old language from ancient Sumer. The 90 minutes of music represents a worldwide selection of compositions and songs. Dr. Sagan predicted that the record can be played only if the spacecraft encounters a civilization advanced enough to decode the directions. It may take 40,000 years before the spacecrafts reach a solar system similar to ours.

If NASA launched these probes into space, obviously, they anticipated a response. Our current technology analyzes in-coming signals for the possibility of patterns or characteristics within the signals that are "language-like." If scientists detect signals at a high radio frequency, the signals must be extraterrestrial because our own signals do not operate at high frequencies. Unless scientists can actually decode an alien message, we won't know what to do next.

The problem the scientists face is one of precedent. Many astrophysicists and cosmologists believe that if we reply without having a protocol or plan established by world leaders, we will create a dangerous dilemma. What language should we use to reply? If we can create a spacecraft, can't we also create an interstellar language? Unfortunately, it's not that simple. At the present time, we don't have a Rosetta Stone to use for translating alien languages, even if we were to receive communication from someone in space tomorrow.

C Answer the questions in your notebook. Write full sentences using an *if*-clause. The information in parentheses tells you what kind of conditional the sentence is.

1. If an extraterrestrial intercepts a golden disc, what will they do? [predictive]
2. What language will the extraterrestrials hear first if they play the record? [fact]
3. What does NASA do if it detects a signal from space? [habitual]
4. What does the author imply about the detection of high-frequency signals? [explicit inference]
5. What can we infer about NASA if it has the capability to create advanced spacecraft? [implicit inference]
6. What dilemma will Earth face if we receive an interstellar message? [predictive]
7. If we want to decode a message from space, what will we have to do? [intentional]

MyEnglishLab

Reading Comprehension

Grammar Focus 1 Present and past factual (real) conditionals: Habitual events and facts

Examples	Language notes
(1) **If the record is played at 16-2/3 revolutions per minute** [condition], spoken greetings **are heard** in 55 languages. [result]	**Conditionals** are statements that describe situations with a condition and a result. When the condition is met, an event occurs. Conditionals have **two clauses**. The dependent (subordinate) clause is the ***if*-clause** and contains the condition. The independent (main) clause contains the **result**.
(2) Some argue that **if we send a message without deciding how to reply**, we create a dilemma. (= *Some argue that we create a dilemma* ***if we send a message without deciding how to reply***.) If images are sent from space, **then** scientists carefully study and record their findings.	We can begin conditional sentences with the *if*-clause or the result clause. The meaning is the same. When the *if*-clause comes first, use a comma to separate it from the result clause. When the *if*-clause comes second, we can use *then* to emphasize the sequence of events. In conversation, both patterns are common. In writing, we usually begin sentences with the *if*-clause.
(3) Does NASA have a plan **if they receive an alien signal**? What happens **if scientists receive a signal from space**?	We can use conditionals in *yes / no* and *wh-* questions.
(4) If a space probe **captures** images at any time, it **sends** them back to Earth. [habitual action]	To form **present factual conditionals** that express habitual actions, we use: simple present [*if*-clause] + simple present [result clause]
(5) If a civilization **is** advanced, it **has** a system of communication. [fact]	Present habitual conditionals are more common in everyday conversation than in formal speech. However, we often see this structure in academic writing to state facts.
(6) Scientists record a signal **when they receive one**. (= . . . ***if they receive one***.) [result + condition]	We can also form conditionals that express a fact or habitual action using ***when*** or ***whenever*** instead of *if*.
(7) If astronomers **have** a radio telescope, they **can search** for extraterrestrial signals.	**Modals** and **semi-modals** can be used in the result clause of present factual conditionals to express ability. simple present [*if*-clause] + modal / semi-modal + base verb [result clause]
(8) If you discover a signal from space, . . . **report** it to authorities. [instruction] . . . **don't assume** it's extraterrestrial. [advice] . . . **don't send** a response independently. [warning]	We can use the **imperative** in the result clause to give a general instruction, advice, or warning.
(9) If there **was** a scheduled shuttle launch, NASA **selected** the crew long before the launch date. If NASA **scheduled** a shuttle launch, many people **would travel** to the launch site in order to witness the event.	To form **past factual conditionals** that express **habitual actions**, we use: simple past [*if*-clause] + simple past [result clause] OR simple past [*if*-clause] + *would* + base verb [result clause]
(10) **Whenever astronauts landed on the moon** [condition], they would collect samples of moon rocks. [result] (= ***If astronauts landed on the moon***, . . .)	We can also form past factual conditionals that express a fact or habitual action using ***when*** or ***whenever*** instead of *if*.
(11) If U.S. astronauts met with Russian cosmonauts on the space station Mir, a common language was always needed.	We often use adverbs of frequency in the result clause of past and present factual conditionals.

Grammar Practice

Circle the result clause that correctly completes each condition.

1. If you are an astrobiologist,
   a. you specialize in the study of life in the universe.
   b. you would specialize in the study of life in the universe.
   c. specialize in the study of life in the universe.
2. If large radio telescopes were available in the early 1990s, such as those in New South Wales, Australia,
   a. they were considered as possible instruments for Project Phoenix, which lasted from February 1995 to March 2004.
   b. they are considered as possible instruments for Project Phoenix, which lasted from February 1995 to March 2004.
   c. consider them as possible instruments for Project Phoenix, which lasted from February 1995 to March 2004.
3. If Project Phoenix astronomers needed to determine whether a signal was truly extraterrestrial,
   a. then they use an additional, smaller telescope hundreds of miles from the main instrument.
   b. then they would use an additional, smaller telescope hundreds of miles from the main instrument.
   c. use an additional, smaller telescope hundreds of miles from the main instrument.
4. If astronomers use a large number of small dishes, such as the Allen Telescope Array,
   a. they spent less money in their search for signals than when they use one large antenna.
   b. they spend less money in their search for signals than when they use one large antenna.
   c. spend less money in their search for signals than when they use one large antenna.
5. If you sign-up for *The Signal*, an e-newsletter,
   a. learn more about SETI projects and research.
   b. you learned more about SETI projects and research.
   c. you can learn more about SETI projects and research.

Rewrite the underlined statements as a present or past factual conditional with *if*. Keep the sequence of ideas and use a comma if necessary. The boldfaced words will help you identify the condition or the result.

1. You gain a better understanding of SETI **when** you watch the movie *Contact*, which follows the experiences of a scientist, Dr. Ellie Arroway, as she discovers an extraterrestrial signal.
   You gain a better understanding of SETI if you watch the movie "Contact," which follows the experiences of a scientist, Dr. Ellie Arroway, as she discovers an extraterrestrial signal.
2. Once you read about Dr. Jill Tarter, **then** similarities between Tarter and Arroway become visible. ____________________
3. The story of Dr. Arroway proves that ambitious people achieve results. **But for that to happen**, they must first be given the resources and the opportunity. ____________________
4. She detects a signal from space with headphones, but **after** you check the facts you learn that this piece of fiction doesn't match reality. Computers scan for signals, not people with headphones. ____________________
5. The film raises an important question: One day we may need to communicate with an alien civilization. **When that day comes**, is mathematics the only universal we can use? ____________________

Grammar Focus 2 Factual (real) conditionals: Inferences, predictions, and intentions

Examples	Language notes
(1) If people **support** the idea of sending a space probe with messages from Earth, they obviously **believe** in alien life forms. [parallel structure (Type 1 inference): implicit; the outcome is understood] **If** there **is** alien life, it **must exist** at a great distance because we have yet to make contact. [mixed verb forms (Type 2 inference): explicit; the outcome is stated directly]	To use the conditional to make an **inference** about a **present or past situation**, we use: parallel structure (same verb tense in both clauses) To make an **inference** about a **present situation**, we can also use: present form [*if*-clause] + modal of certainty + base verb [result clause] ***Note:*** We cannot use *when* or *whenever* with conditionals that express an inference.
(2) **If** alien life forms **send** us a message, who **will decipher** it? **If** Voyagers 1 and 2 **continue** their journey, it**'s going to be** 40,000 years before they come close to any other planetary system.	To use the conditional to make a **prediction**, we use: simple present <u>or</u> present progressive [*if*-clause] + future with *will* <u>or</u> *be going to* [result clause]. In future conditionals, we cannot substitute *when* for *if* without a significant change in meaning. The use of *when* shows 100% certainty that the condition will take place. ***Compare:*** *When alien life forms send us a message . . .* = certainty that this event will happen.
(3) **If** the time capsule **continues** its journey through space, [strongest] ↑ . . . it **will** reach an alien civilization. . . . it **should** reach an alien civilization. . . . it **may** reach an alien civilization. . . . it **might** reach an alien civilization.	Different **modals** can be used in the result clause to express **different degrees of certainty**.
(4) If scientists **ever** receive a signal, the global community will need to decide how to respond. If scientists **should** receive a signal, the global community will need to decide how to respond.	We use the adverb ***ever*** in the *if*-clause to suggest a **higher degree of unlikelihood**. The modal ***should*** can be used for the same purpose, but this use is less common.
(5) **If you like**, you can find out more about the composition of an interstellar message on the *SETI@home* website.	When the speaker assumes to know what action(s) will please the listener, we can use the **idiomatic** *if*-clause ***if you like*** or other variations: *If you like (you'd like / you want), +* *will / could / can* [result clause]
(6) If we**'re going to** communicate with an alien civilization, we **have to** agree on how we can do that.	To form a future conditional that expresses **an intention that will require certain action**, we use: *be going to* [*if*-clause] + modal of necessity <u>or</u> imperative [result clause]
(7) <u>**Unless we discuss**</u> **ideas now**, we won't know how to respond to an alien signal when the time comes. (= ***<u>If we don't discuss</u> ideas now . . .***)	***Unless*** has a negative meaning. It expresses that a result will occur if a condition is <u>not</u> met.
(8) **Even if** an alien civilization receives our time capsule, there is no guarantee they can send a message back to us.	The adverb ***even*** sometimes appears in the *if*-clause to clarify that an outcome would be the same regardless of the condition. Note that *even* always comes before *if*.

Grammar Practice

A Choose the correct verb forms to complete the text.

How will contact be made? If Ronald Bracewell **1. is / is going to be** correct, our first contact with aliens **2. isn't / won't be** through large antennas on Earth. In 1960, Bracewell introduced the idea of messenger probes—automated spacecrafts with advanced computer systems. If we **3. send / will send** such probes to biologically interesting star systems, we **4. are able / will be able** to scan for radio transmissions in the habitable zone of each system. If any transmission **5. is detected / will be detected**, the probes will record it and send it back to Earth. Such a probe, in theory, can deliver a signal stronger than anything sent from our distant planet, making initial contact through the probe more likely.

How will we communicate? The uses of math, music, and images have already been discussed by the scientific community. If we **6. are going to consider / will consider** all possible forms of communication, perhaps we should explore the usefulness of a simpler yet meaningful language—that of dolphins. Dolphins have a vocabulary that is limited to squawks, clicks, whistles, and squeaks, but there are clear patterns that scientists have begun to decipher. Perhaps social exchanges with aliens might be easier through "dolphin speak?"

Will there ever be face-to-face contact? Let's not forget the possibility that aliens will find us before we find them. We might gain a few ideas if we **7. look back / are going to look back** at the alien encounters that we have seen in Hollywood movies. Steven Spielberg's 1977 film *Close Encounters of the Third Kind* depicts a friendly meeting between humans and aliens in which the people use a five-note melody, a colorful display of lights, and a short sequence of hand signals to begin a dialogue. Could fiction become reality one day? According to Spielberg, if we **8. are going to see / see** a UFO (*encounter of the first kind*) and then find further evidence of that alien civilization (*encounter of the second kind*), contact with the aliens should soon follow (*encounter of the third kind*).

B Complete each inference with the correct verb form. Some sentences may have more than one correct answer.

- If the SETI Institute **1.** ___has___ (have) a program in interstellar message composition, then it **2.** __________ (be) clear that SETI scientists **3.** __________ (believe) that such communication will be needed one day.
- If in 1974 scientists **4.** __________ (send) a broadcast from the Arecibo Radio Telescope in Puerto Rico to a star cluster 21,000 light-years away, they obviously **5.** __________ (not expect) an immediate response.
- If our earliest TV broadcasts have already reached nearby stars, then any alien viewers **6.** __________ (*modal verb* + be) able to detect the signals with the help of a large and powerful antenna.
- If an alien civilization responds to a signal from us, they **7.** __________ (*modal verb* + have) very advanced technology.
- If an alien civilization has advanced technology, it **8.** __________ (suggest) they **9.** __________ (understand) the need to organize and cooperate in order to survive.

MyEnglishLab

Sounding Natural

Speaking

A Read the information about NASA's transmission of a song into space. Then, work with a partner and answer the questions.

> On February 4, 2008, NASA transmitted the Beatles 1968 song, "Across the Universe" into deep space to mark the anniversary of the song's recording and the 50-year anniversary of the founding of NASA. They aimed the transmission toward the North Star, Polaris, which is 431 light-years away from Earth. NASA chose this song because they believed it represents the concept of universal peace.

If NASA sends a message today, what songs do you think they will transmit based on our society and what is relevant to the world now? Why?

B If we create a "Golden CD or DVD " of music and movies to represent the late 20th and early 21st century, what music will we include that is different from 1977? What games, music, or movies would you choose to put on the CD/DVD?

> *I think that if we create a golden CD we should include the music of Nirvana because . . .*
> *If we put a DVD together we should have games like* World of Warcraft *and movies like* Titanic *because . . .*

Listening

A UNDERSTANDING MAIN IDEAS Listen to a conversation. What are the speakers discussing? Where are the speakers?

B DISTINGUISHING BETWEEN HABITS, INTENTIONS, PREDICTIONS, OR INFERENCES Listen again. Check (✓) whether the speaker states a habit or intention, or makes a prediction, or an inference.

		Habit	Intention	Prediction	Inference
1	If we can't work at the Institute because our funding is cut, we have to continue our work somewhere else.				
2	If I can use spectrometers and telescopes, I can download a simple program.				
3	If they're set up correctly, our computers will become part of the SETI supercomputer.				
4	If you want to use *SETI@home*, you can download the software from their site.				
5	If our computers detect that type of signal, it provides evidence of extraterrestrial technology.				
6	If the computer detects anything on that frequency, it must be an extraterrestrial signal.				
7	. . . if we pick up that particular frequency, we'll know it's an E.T.!				
8	If anyone detects a signal, there is a protocol to follow.				
9	. . . even if we sit here for 20 years, we might not hear a bleep or detect anything.				
10	If only we could be the first. . . .				

C AFTER LISTENING What do you think about *SETI@home*? If you can use it on your home computer, will you try it?

MyEnglishLab

Linking Grammar to Writing

Writing

A Read the information about the discovery of a new planet. Take notes about its distance from Earth, location, size, climate, environmental and geographical characteristics, and what you would like to know.

In 2011, astrophysicists used a high-resolution telescope to detect a planet orbiting the star Gliese 581, which is about 20.3 light-years (194 trillion km) away from Earth. If the Voyager I probe continues to travel beyond our solar system, it will take more than 300,000 years to get there. This planet, Gliese 581d, is a "super Earth." It is seven times heavier than our Earth, and twice as large. It is so large that its gravity would be double Earth's gravity. It is called an "exoplanet" because it is outside our solar system. Scientists believe that Gliese 581d may be a "habitable planet" because its orbit is within a reasonable distance from its Sun, so it's not too hot, not too cold.

If scientists determine that Gliese 581d is truly habitable, they believe it would be a strange place to visit. The air is dense and there are a lot of clouds, which keep the surface of the planet in a foggy twilight state. The skies over Gliese 581d are probably reddish in color. It is probably cooler than most places on Earth. However, one side of the planet seems to permanently face its sun, while the other side remains in constant dark. Its surface appears rocky and mountainous, but it probably has large and deep oceans, rainfall, and it is quite windy.

B In 2009, an organization called *HellofromEarth.net* invited people to post messages to the possible inhabitants of a planet called Gliese 581d. *Hello from Earth* actually collected 26,000 messages, which were transmitted from one of NASA's facilities. The signal will arrive at Gliese 581d in January 2030.

Messages: HellofromEarth

Hello citizens of Gliese 581d.
Please visit us in the future.
—Shakti, Delhi, India

G'day people of Gliese 581d! Come and see our wonderful country and enjoy our friendly citizens.
—Jonah, Sydney, Australia

Greetings to Gliese 581d from Berlin, Germany.
We send you our best wishes.
Auf wiedersehn . . . . Petra.

Dear people of Gliese 581d. Are you there? Can you hear us? If you can hear us, please answer soon. We want to meet you.
—Jane, Albuquerque, New Mexico, USA

Compose a message to someone on Gliese 581d. Describe facts about Earth and its inhabitants. Make predictions about how the citizens of Gliese 581d might experience life on Earth and how they will perceive us. Use the questions to guide your message.

1. If the visitors can breathe our air, what other things can they probably do?
2. If they see Earth's sky and sunrise or sunset, what colors will they see?
3. If they are used to a cold climate, where will you tell them to visit or not visit?
4. If they visit your country, will they be comfortable? If not, what advice will you give them?
5. If they visit certain countries, what languages will they read and hear?

Welcome to Earth! We're the third planet from a large star we call the "Sun." If you come here, you'll see a blue sky, but when our sun sets, you might see red, purple, pink, orange, or other colors.

C Exchange messages with a partner. Did you come up with similar or different answers?

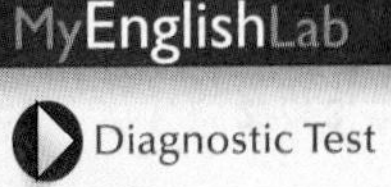

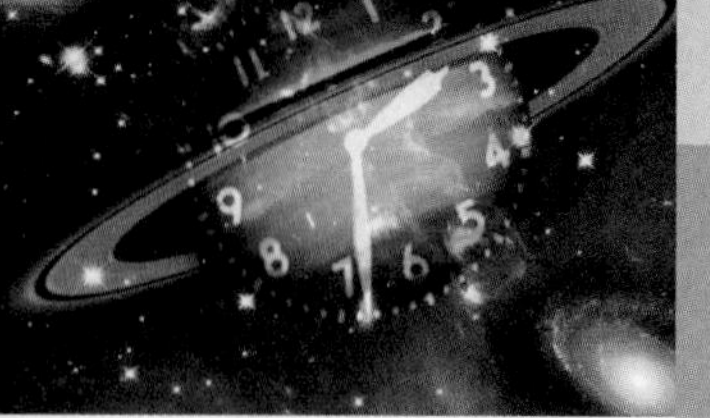

CHAPTER 18 Time and Space

Getting Started

A What do you already know about time travel? Take this quiz. (Answers are at the bottom of the page.)

1. Which of the following do you believe is true?
   a. If you traveled back in time and prevented your grandparents from meeting, you would no longer exist.
   b. If you were to travel to the future, you could possibly become your own grandchild and therefore alter history.
   c. If you had traveled in a time machine, you could not have visited an ancestor from your family's past.
2. If you encountered a wormhole in space, you would have found . . .
   a. an empty space. b. a black hole. c. a pathway through time and space.
3. The *Twin Effect:* Twin brothers live on Earth. If one brother traveled through space at the speed of light, when he returned he would be . . .
   a. the same age as when he left. b. the same age as his twin. c. older than his twin.

Scene from the movie *Timeline.*

B If you want to experience time travel, you need to know some information. Read each statement. Write *RS* for *real science* or *SF* for *science fiction.* Discuss the theories with a partner.

_____ **1.** To use a time machine, you have to travel near the speed of light.
_____ **2.** If you were going to travel to the past, you would have to be careful not to meet yourself.
_____ **3.** If time travel were possible, travelers from the future would already be walking among us.
_____ **4.** If you found a wormhole, you could travel through it and you might come out at exactly the same place you began.
_____ **5.** If scientists had created a faster-than-light (FTL) drive, we could have traveled to the edge of the universe by now.

C **Imaginative (unreal) conditionals** represent **impossible, hypothetical,** or **counterfactual ideas**. In these types of conditionals, use the simple past to refer to present or future time. Use the past perfect to refer to the past.

Present, Impossible: If travel to the past **were** possible, visitors from the future **would be** here now.
Future, Hypothetical: If we **created** a time machine, we **could travel to** the future.
Past, Counterfactual: If we **had met** our grandparents in the past, we **might have changed** our history.

Look back at Part B. Decide if the situation is impossible, hypothetical, or counterfactual and write the number of the sentence in the correct place in the chart.

Impossible	Hypothetical	Counterfactual

Answers: **1.** a, **2.** c, **3.** b

MyEnglishLab

Vocabulary Check

Reading

A WARM-UP Do you believe that it is possible to travel through time? If time travel were possible, would you like to travel to the past, the future, or both? Why?

B SCANNING Before you read, scan the article. Find three scientists who contributed to the theory of time travel. Find two physicists who contributed to film or fiction. Then read the entire article.

What if we could travel through time? What scientists really *think.*

Time travel has captured the human imagination throughout history. But, what do scientists really think about it? Until the discovery of electricity and magnetic fields, most scientists were skeptical about the concept of time travel. However, inventors such as Thomas Edison (1847–1931) and Nikola Tesla (1856–1943) were intrigued by the idea of traveling through time. But while Edison concentrated his efforts on practical experiments, Tesla spent hours researching the effects of magnetic fields on teleportation—travel through time and space. Tesla's experiments were later part of the basis for the 1943 hoax, "the Philadelphia Experiment," in which magnetic fields allegedly caused navy ship, the USS *Eldridge*, to vanish, only to reappear off the coast of Virginia a few hours later. Physicist Albert Einstein supposedly contributed his 1905 "Special Theory of Relativity," to that experiment. Later, his 1915 general theory of relativity explored the notion of wormholes— cosmic pathways between time and space in a "fourth dimension." He also theorized that if we wanted to travel through time, we must create a spacecraft that moved near the speed of light (186,000 mps).

In the 1980s, astrophysicist Carl Sagan hypothesized that even if wormholes existed, time travel to the past would be impossible. Sagan further explored this idea in his novel, *Contact*, which later became a Hollywood blockbuster film.

For years, leading cosmologist Stephen Hawking hesitated to publicly discuss time travel, fearing that if he had done so, his colleagues would have considered him a fraud. In his 2010 documentary, *Stephen Hawking's Universe*, he agreed with Sagan that time travel to the past is not possible but travel to the future could be. Applying Einstein's theory that "as objects accelerate through space, time slows down around them," Hawking claimed that it could be possible to move forward through time. He said that if we built spaceships that could fly faster than the speed of light, one day of space travel would be equal to one year on Earth. Hawking speculated that if time travel to the past were possible, people from the future would already be walking among us. But if a person travels into the future, he would be trapped there, unable to return to the present. Hawking said that if he had a time machine, he might, " . . . travel to the end of the universe to find out how our whole cosmic story ends."

C UNDERSTANDING FACTS AND DETAILS Answer the questions.

1. Match the scientist with his theory about time travel.

_____ **1.** Tesla — **a.** Even if wormholes existed, we could not travel backward through time.

_____ **2.** Einstein — **b.** To travel though time, we would need to fly near the speed of light

_____ **3.** Hawking — **c.** If the teleportation of the USS *Eldridge* had happened, it might have been caused by magnetic fields.

_____ **4.** Sagan — **d.** If travel to the past were possible, visitors from the future would be walking among us.

2. What does Stephen Hawking mean when he says, "If time travel to the past were possible, people from the future would already be walking among us?"

a. Time travel to the past is unrealistic.
b. It is unlikely that scientists will ever create a time machine.
c. It is certain that we will never be able to travel to the past.
d. It is only possible to go forward in time.

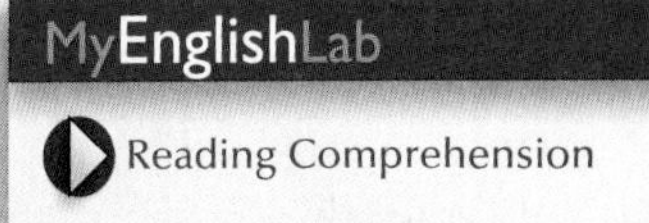

Grammar Focus 1 Imaginative (unreal) conditionals: Present and future

Examples	Language notes
(1) If we **built** spaceships that could fly near or at the speed of light, one day of space travel **would be** equal to one year on Earth. [hypothetical conditional with strong certainty about result]	To form **imaginative conditionals** that express an unlikely or impossible event in the present or future, we use: simple past [*if*-clause] + *would / could / might* + base verb [result clause] Note that the simple past in the *if*-clause refers to the present or future.
If a person **traveled** into the future, he **might be trapped** there. [hypothetical conditional with less certainty about result]	A **hypothetical conditional** suggests that the speaker is imagining a possible situation in the present or future.
If we **had** a more advanced space program and the money to run it, we **could send** a probe into a wormhole and test out the theory of time travel. [counterfactual conditional with imagined result]	A **counterfactual conditional** suggests that the speaker is imagining a completely unreal situation in the present or the future.
(2) If time travel **were** possible, travelers from the future would already be walking among us.	Use ***were*** for all singular and plural subjects when *be* is in the *if*-clause of a hypothetical or present counterfactual conditional.
(3) If people **were traveling** through time already, wouldn't we see proof of this?	We also use ***were*** for **all subjects** with progressive verbs in hypothetical conditionals. Note that the past progressive in the *if*-clause refers to the present or future time.
(4) **If you were to travel** to the past, you could possibly eliminate your grandparent, and therefore alter history. (= ***If you traveled . . .***)	In hypothetical and present counterfactual conditionals, we can use *were* + infinitive in the *if*-clause. The meaning is the same as the simple past, but this pattern is more formal.
(5) **If I were Hawking or another brilliant scientist**, I'd put all my effort into making time travel a reality. What would you do **if you were him**? **If I were you**, I'd focus on science and not science fiction.	In present counterfactual conditionals, we often use *were* + object pronoun / noun object. ***Note:*** *If I were you*, . . . is commonly used to give advice. It means "if I were in the same situation." We usually use this in an informal situation with a close friend or family member.
(6) **Let's imagine for a moment** that we can use wormholes for time travel. If we had use of even one wormhole, who would get to use it? There would be great debates over the rights to use it.	Hypothetical and counterfactual conditionals often help speakers begin a discussion about an imaginary situation. The larger context can contain set phrases which indicate that the ideas that follow are purely imagined: *(Just) imagine . . .* *Hypothetically speaking, . . .* *Imagine for a moment that . . .*
(7) Wouldn't it be amazing **if we could travel through time**? We might travel to the past and see history in the making. Or we could travel to the future and find out all the exciting technology that will be invented one day . . .	Often a single *if*-clause is stated once at the start of a conversation, and then a number of hypothetical outcomes are stated without repeating the condition.

MyEnglishLab

Grammar Plus 1
Activities 1 and 2

Grammar Practice

A Complete the hypothetical and present counterfactual conditionals with the correct verb forms.

Physicist Michio Kaku has already considered the choice of traveling to the past versus to the future. If it **1.** ________________ (be) possible today, Kaku **2.** ________________ (choose) to move forward in time and learn what the distant future holds. But what would likely be the means for such travel?

Kaku recognizes the theories about using wormholes and building spacecrafts to explore them, but he suggests other alternatives for time travel. Hypothetically speaking, if an alien civilization **3.** ________________ (be) advanced enough to visit Earth, they might have the technology for time travel already and be willing to share it with us. A similar transfer of knowledge could take place between generations. Imagine if our great-great-grandchildren **4.** ________________ (come) from the future. Wouldn't it be possible for us to use the same technology to begin our own travels through time?

Kaku has also given thought to the paradoxes that could result from time travel. For example, if someone **5.** ________________ (travel) to the past, **6.** ________________ this person ________________ (have) the power to change history? Kaku argues no. If a time traveler **7.** ________________ (alter) the natural course of events, his or her future **8.** ________________ (stay) the same, but a parallel universe **9.** ________________ (be created). In theory, history can split into different timelines. Your personal timeline **10.** ________________ (not change) even if you somehow **11.** ________________ (alter) past events in your life.

One question we should all consider is this: if we **12.** ________________ (discover) a means to travel through time, **13.** ________________ our society ________________ (be) ready and willing to accept the risks as well as the responsibilities?

B Combine the sentences to form conditionals. Check (✓) the correct box to show whether each conditional is hypothetical or counterfactual.

1. An astronaut could travel close to the speed of light. Then it might take a minute to reach nearby stars.
   If an astronaut traveled close to the speed of light, it might take a minute to reach nearby stars.
   Hypothetical ☑ *Counterfactual* ☐
2. An astronaut could possibly be traveling almost at the speed of light. However, one minute for him would be equal to about four years on Earth.
   ____
   Hypothetical ☐ *Counterfactual* ☐
3. We don't have a spacecraft that can accelerate to the speed of light. Having one would allow us to test many theories about space and time.
   ____
   Hypothetical ☐ *Counterfactual* ☐
4. We don't have pieces of UFOs or pieces of other alien technology. Having these things might allow us to reproduce technology that makes time travel possible.
   ____
   Hypothetical ☐ *Counterfactual* ☐
5. No human spacecraft can zig-zag in midair or hang in the air silently. Having such a spacecraft would explain the many UFO sightings.
   ____
   Hypothetical ☐ *Counterfactual* ☐

Grammar Focus 2 Imaginative (unreal) conditionals: Past and mixed time periods

Examples	Language notes
(1) If scientists **had created** a faster-than-light drive, we **would have traveled** to the edge of the universe by now. If Hawking **had done** so, his colleagues **would have considered** him a fraud.	To form **imaginative conditionals** that express an <u>unreal possibility in the past</u>, we use: past perfect [*if*-clause] + *would have / could have / might have* + past participle [result clause] In this type of conditional, the speaker is imagining an alternative outcome <u>if it were possible to change a past situation</u>. Note that the **past perfect** in the *if*-clause refers to the past.
(2) If the past **had changed** during the course of someone's time travels, we **would** never **know** of this in our present reality.	Imagining **unreal past events** can lead to <u>speculation about alternative outcomes in the present</u>. For this type of conditional, we use: past perfect / past perfect progressive [*if*-clause] + *would / could / might* + base verb [result clause]
(3) If we **were** in contact with aliens, we **might** already **have gained** the knowledge to build a time machine.	Imagining **unreal present events** can lead to <u>speculation about an alternative past</u>. For this type of conditional, we use: simple past / past progressive [*if*-clause] + *would have / could have / might have* + past participle [result clause]

Grammar Practice

A Read the information about the movie *Back to the Future*. Then read the conditionals based on the story, and check (✓) the boxes next to the true statements.

Back to the Future is a popular film trilogy that tells the exciting and humorous tale of Marty McFly, an American teenager in 1985 who finds himself in a time machine being sent to 1955, 2015, and then 1885. The inventor of the machine, Doctor Emmet Brown, is a friend and advisor to Marty.

1. If Doc Brown hadn't stolen a large amount of plutonium, he wouldn't have had enough energy to make his time machine work.
   ☐ Doc Brown stole a large amount of plutonium.
   ☐ Doc Brown didn't have enough energy to make his time machine work.
2. Marty wouldn't understand what the machine is capable of if Doc hadn't explained how it worked.
   ☐ Marty understands what the machine is capable of.
   ☐ Doc never explained how the machine worked.
3. If Marty had prevented his parents from meeting, he would not exist in the present.
   ☐ Marty prevented his parents from meeting.
   ☐ Marty didn't erase his own existence.
4. If in 1955 Marty hadn't told Doc Brown about the future, Doc Brown wouldn't be able to protect himself from danger in 1985.
   ☐ In 1955, Marty didn't tell Doc Brown about the danger in the future.
   ☐ Doc Brown is able to protect himself in 1985.
5. If Marty hadn't known about an upcoming lightning storm in 1955, Doc Brown wouldn't have been able to get the energy needed for the trip to 1985.
   ☐ Marty didn't know about an upcoming lightning storm in 1955.
   ☐ Doc Brown was able to get the energy needed for the trip back to 1985.

6. If Doc hadn't taken a trip to 2015, he wouldn't have been able to warn Marty about future problems in the McFly family.
   ☐ Doc didn't take a trip to 2015.
   ☐ Doc was able to warn Marty about future problems in the McFly family.
7. If Doc and Marty had been more careful, the time machine wouldn't have been stolen by Biff Tannen in 2015.
   ☐ Doc and Marty weren't careful enough with the time machine in 2015.
   ☐ Biff Tannen didn't steal the time machine.
8. If Marty hadn't gone back to 1955 a second time, he wouldn't have prevented Biff Tannen from using future information to become rich.
   ☐ Marty traveled to 1955 only once.
   ☐ Marty prevented Biff Tannen from using future information to become rich.
9. Marty wouldn't have known how to get out of 1955 if Doc Brown hadn't sent a letter from 1885.
   ☐ Marty had no way to get out of 1955.
   ☐ Doc Brown sent a letter to Marty from 1885.
10. Doc Brown would be a lonely man today if he hadn't met his true love back in 1885.
   ☐ Doc Brown remains a lonely man.
   ☐ Doc Brown met his true love back in 1885.

B Complete the conditionals with the correct verb forms.

The Man Who Could Have Been the First Time Traveler

American aeronautical legend Gordon Cooper died in 2004, but if scientists **1.** ________________ (invite) him to be the first time traveler, he **2.** ________________ (agree) without hesitation. Cooper knew scientists who were intrigued by the idea of building a time travel vehicle. For Cooper, who was a test pilot and an astronaut, taking risks was nothing new. If he **3.** ________________ (pilot) a time machine, the ride **4.** ________________ (might be) one way only, but even knowing this, he was still willing. What would make a person feel so adventurous?

Cooper's courage was combined with knowledge that he gained from an unusual experience. In 1951, Cooper was a pilot in the U.S. Air Force. Over Germany, he was certain he saw a large group of UFOs—and not just once, but a few times. If Cooper **5.** ________________ (not see) so many alien spacecrafts, he **6.** ________________ (not believe) that an advanced alien civilization could exist. He noted the way the spacecrafts had moved and was convinced he had not been seeing human technology at work. However, all he had to share after those encounters was his own report—his words, but no evidence. If Cooper or another pilot or astronaut **7.** ________________ (provide) proof of an alien encounter, the world **8.** ________________ (take) the idea of UFOs more seriously. Cooper claimed that evidence was indeed recorded at a later sighting, but the military took the film away.

The connection between UFOs and time machines is important to understand: if aliens **9.** ________________ (already reach) Earth from a distant galaxy they **10.** ________________ (could develop) the technology to travel at the speed of light, the speed needed for time travel. However, without evidence, the existence of UFOs and time travel remain theories rather than facts.

Grammar Focus 3 Omitting information in conditional sentences

Examples	Language notes
(1) Do you like reading about time travel? **If so**, you might like H.G. Wells's novel. (= ***If you like reading about time travel, . . .***) Would you like to travel in a time machine? **If yes**, where to? **If no**, why not?	We can use ***if so, if not, if yes, if no,*** and ***if necessary*** to take the place of a full *if*-clause. These forms are used to imply the condition. They must refer back to information already given to the listener. We often see *if yes* and *if no* together to present two alternatives.
(2) **To use a time machine**, you have to travel near the speed of light. (= ***If you are going to use a time machine****, you have to travel near the speed of light.*)	An **infinitive of purpose** can begin a conditional statement. The full condition is implied and the subject is the same as the subject in the main clause. We use the form: infinitive of purpose + result clause.
(3) **If only we had** the help of a more advanced civilization. (= ***I wish we had the help . . .***) **If only Einstein had discovered** a sure way to travel through time. (= ***I wish Einstein had discovered . . .***)	We can use ***if only*** **+ noun clause** to express a wish to change the past or present. No result clause is needed. To express a wish to change the present, we use: *If only* + (subject + simple past / past progressive). To express a wish to change the past, we use: *If only* + (subject + past perfect / past perfect progressive).
(4) The scientist promised to share her research **only if** we promised to read it with respect and an open mind. (= *Unless we promised to read her research with respect and an open mind, the scientist wouldn't share it.*)	Do not confuse *if only* with *only if*. The first expresses a wish to change reality. The second is used to restrict an action.
(5) Q: **What if someone invited you to use a time machine?** (= *What would you do if someone invited you to use a time machine?*) A: I'd visit the future.	Hypothetical and counterfactual conditionals do not always appear as full questions. We often use ***What if . . .?*** to prompt an answer in the form of a result clause.
(6) Q: For years, Hawking hesitated to discuss time travel publicly, though he had much to say about it. **What would you have done?** A: I'd also have worried that others wouldn't take me seriously as a scientist.	When a hypothetical or counterfactual condition is understood from context, speakers typically form a question based only on the result. This takes the form of ***What would you do?*** or ***What would you have done?*** *If you were (had been) in that situation* is implied.
(7) Q: Would you still be willing to go in a time machine even if you knew you couldn't return? A: **Yes, I would. / No, I wouldn't.** Q: If I lend you the novel, will you read it? A: **Yes, I will. / No, I won't.**	Answers to conditional questions are typically short and limited to only the result clause.

Grammar Practice

A Complete the text with words from the box.

if necessary	if no	if only	if so	if yes	only if

According to Einstein, time slows down with speed. Imagine that a person vanished for 50 years and then reappeared not having aged more than a day. Would time travel explain the paradox of the missing person who never grew older? **1.** ________________, what or who could have caused the person's disappearance from Earth? These questions were key in developing the American TV series *The 4400*, which was broadcast from 2004 to 2007.

The 4400 follows the experiences of 4,400 people who disappeared from Earth over the course of 50 years. Their return is even more intriguing because it occurs on a single day at the same moment in one location. Government agents are sent to investigate. **2.** ________________ answers could be found! Strangely, no one can explain what happened. The other problem is the future of these people. Can the 4,400 people simply go back to their old lives? Yes, but **3.** ________________ their homes and families are still there. Some are able to return home, but when and **4.** ________________, government agents will continue to ask the 4400 questions.

Agents Tom Baldwin and Diana Skouris quickly discover that their investigation of the 4400 will create more questions than answers. At least one person begins to show superhuman strength. Does that mean others among the 4400 have extraordinary abilities? **5.** ________________, why not? Why would only one be given a special power? **6.** ________________, what are they and will such powers endanger or help other people?

Throughout the series, the plot takes surprising turns, even into parallel dimensions. *The 4400* may be fiction, but its storyline uses scientific theories. Not all our theories about time and space could be wrong, could they?

B Choose the correct words to complete the statements about Bob Lazar, a former government scientist.

1. **What if / Even if** you worked on secret projects in a secret location?
2. Would you keep silent about your work or talk about it **if / what if** you believed the public should know?
3. Bob Lazar, a former government scientist, faced this dilemma in 1989, and he decided to talk about his work **even if / only if** it meant facing doubt and anger.
4. Lazar claimed he had worked on extraterrestrial spacecraft at Area 51, a military base in Nevada, but **if only / unless** he had proof, no one was ready to believe him.
5. Lazar explained that the alien UFOs were powered by an element named 115, which didn't exist on Earth in 1989. This means that **only if / if** Lazar was right, then the substance must have come from a solar system other than ours.
6. However, **only if / even if** Lazar is never proven right, he remains certain about what he saw at Area 51.
7. Today Lazar doesn't waste time thinking, "Oh, **if / if only** I had kept silent." He feels the truth is on his side.

MyEnglishLab

Sounding Natural

Speaking

A What do you know about hoaxes and conspiracy theories? A hoax is a type of fraud that is arranged to look like something that really happened. Similarly, a conspiracy theory is the interpretation of incidents or events that people believe were set in motion by secretive but powerful forces (like wealthy people or the government). Read about the "Philadelphia Experiment," an alleged U.S. government hoax.

> What if the "Philadelphia Experiment" were true? There are claims that in 1943, the theories of Nikola Tesla and Albert Einstein were tested in an alleged, secret project called "Project Rainbow." Later known as the "Philadelphia Experiment," it involved the navy ship USS *Eldridge* and its crew. During the experiment, a green fog enveloped the ship and it mysteriously disappeared from the Philadelphia harbor, only to reappear off the coast of Norfolk, Virginia, 24 hours later. Some say that this experiment was part of the U.S. government's mission to use the Earth's magnetic field for inter-dimensional travel (teleportation) and explore time-space compression technology—in which the perception of long distances seems to decrease because it takes less time to travel that distance. But questions remain: Had the ship actually traveled through time and space? Was this a hoax? If this experiment really did take place, what happened? U.S. military reports deny that the experiment ever took place and most official government documents state that the USS *Eldridge* never left the harbor.

B Talk to a partner. Think about the evidence. Do you think the Philadelphia Experiment was a hoax or conspiracy theory? Why? Use some of the expressions below to start your discussion.

I don't know if that is true, but if it were then I think that it is probably top-secret information . . .
I think that if that had happened it was probably a hoax because . . .

Listening

A UNDERSTANDING MAJOR IDEAS Listen to the lecture. Check (✓) which course would most likely include this lecture.

- ☐ Introduction to Astronomy
- ☐ Sci-Fi Filmmaking
- ☐ Writing for Science Fiction
- ☐ The Physics of Science in Science Fiction

B UNDERSTANDING HYPOTHETICAL AND COUNTERFACTUAL INFORMATION Listen again. Check (✓) the facts that you heard.

☐ **1.** Students who have seen *Star Trek* think that the science fiction is unrealistic.
☐ **2.** In the *Stargate* series, people use wormholes as the method of time travel.
☐ **3.** The *Back to the Future* film series was made recently.
☐ **4.** Most filmmakers do not understand basic theories of physics.
☐ **5.** French physicists discovered particles that move faster than the speed of light.
☐ **6.** The car used for time travel in the *Back to the Future* film series really exists.
☐ **7.** The Klingon language from *Star Trek* was created with the help of linguists.
☐ **8.** Researching history was important for the creation of the film *Timeline.*
☐ **9.** Teleportation really works but it can't work on humans.

C AFTER LISTENING Talk to a partner about science-fiction movies. Which ones seem the most realistic? If you could use any form of space-time travel from the movies—like teleporting or beaming from place to place as in *Star Trek;* going through a special gate or wormhole as in *Stargate;* or traveling in a time machine as in *Back to the Future* or *Timeline*—which would you use? Why?

Writing

A Read the biographical information about and the quotes by Leonardo da Vinci, Albert Einstein, and Stephen Hawking. Imagine that you have a time machine. If you could send one of these geniuses to a time in his future or the past and choose one to remain in or visit our present year, who would you choose? Why? Use the chart of important events to guide your choices.

Leonardo da Vinci (1452–1519), inventor, artist, scientist: "If once you have tasted flight, you will forever walk the earth with your eyes turned skyward, for there you have been, and there you will always long to return."
Albert Einstein (1879–1955): theoretical physicist: "If you could send a message faster than the speed of light, you could send a telegram to the past."
Stephen Hawking (1942–): cosmologist, astrophysicist; "Time travel would seem to lead to contradictions, if one were able to go back and change the past."

The past	1905	1969 / 1971	2011	The future
??	Wright Brothers fly first plane at Kitty Hawk. Einstein discovers speed of light and "Special Theory of Relativity."	Man walks on the Moon. Atomic clock invented	French scientists discover "neutrinos" (sub-atomic particles) that travel faster than light.	??

B Describe the reasons why and what would happen if the scientist were transported to a different time. How would life be different now if this had happened?

Use an outline to plan your essay. Write at least one short paragraph for each of your choices.

I. Use the quotes as the "hook" to each paragraph.
II. Introduce your time traveler with biographical and background information.
III. Explain your hypothetical situation and give reasons for your choice. Use counterfactuals to support your decisions *not* to send one of the scientists to a particular time.

Use the example of contemporary scientist Michio Kaku as a model.

Michio Kaku said, ". . . If you could obtain large quantities of negative energy—and that's a big "if"—then you could create a time machine that apparently obeys Einstein's equation and perhaps the laws of quantum theory." I would send Kaku back to 1905 to meet Einstein. If Michio Kaku had been able to work with him when Einstein had first discovered the speed of light, perhaps Kaku could have made an important contribution to the Special Theory of Relativity. I think that if they had worked together, we'd have time machines now!

If Einstein had been alive when the first man walked on the moon, in 1969, he would have been really excited to see that happen . . . If he had been able to work with NASA or any other scientists he probably would have helped them create better and faster spacecraft and other technology.

Lastly, I would bring Leonardo da Vinci to the present, so he could see his famous artwork on display and talk to scientists and historians. I think Leonardo could have fascinating conversations with people like Michio Kaku and Stephen Hawking if he were here.

Grammar Summary

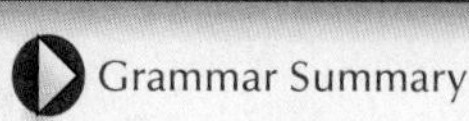

Grammar Summary

Factual (real) conditionals express habitual actions, state facts, and make predictions.

<table>
<tr><th>Past</th><th>Present</th><th>Future</th></tr>
<tr><td>simple past [if-clause] +
simple past [result clause]
<u>or</u>
simple past [if-clause] +
would + base verb [result clause]

If an Area 51 worker was asked about his or her work, the person would give no information.</td><td>simple present [if-clause] +
simple present [result clause]

If the U.S. government receives a UFO report, they always say the object can't be extraterrestrial.</td><td rowspan="2">simple present <u>or</u> present progressive [if-clause]
future with be going to <u>or</u> modal verb (will, should, may, might) [result clause]

If we are already discussing interstellar travel today, then it will likely be possible tomorrow.</td></tr>
<tr><td colspan="2">We can form factual or habitual conditionals with when / whenever.

Time slows down when (if) an object accelerates through space.</td></tr>
<tr><td></td><td>To make an explicit inference, we can also use
present form [if-clause] +
modal of certainty + base verb [result clause]

If more than one astronaut has seen a UFO, aliens must exist.</td><td>To state an intention, we can use
be going to [if-clause] +
modal of necessity <u>or</u> imperative [result clause]

If we are going to have a dialogue with aliens, we should decide on forms of communication now.</td></tr>
<tr><td colspan="2">To make an implicit inference, we use parallel structure (same verb tense in both clauses)

If it's possible for aliens to travel to distant galaxies, it's possible for us.</td><td></td></tr>
<tr><td colspan="3">We can use even if to clarify that an outcome would be the same regardless of the condition.

Even if we don't contact aliens in our lifetime, talk about interstellar messages remains important.</td></tr>
<tr><td colspan="3">We can form many conditionals with unless, which has the meaning of if . . . not.

Unless we master travel near the speed of light, we won't likely visit distant galaxies. = If we don't master . . .</td></tr>
</table>

Imaginative (unreal) conditionals express counterfactual events and imaginary events.

<table>
<tr><th>Past</th><th>Present</th><th>Future</th></tr>
<tr><td rowspan="2">past perfect [if-clause] +
would have / could have / might have + past participle [result clause]
If aliens had tried to make contact with us before now, we would have known about it.</td><td colspan="2">simple past [if-clause] + would / could / might + base verb [result clause]
If I ever met an alien, I would try to photograph it or film it.</td></tr>
<tr><td colspan="2">When be appears in the if-clause of an imaginative conditional, we must use were for all singular and plural subjects.

If time teleportation were possible, we wouldn't need planes anymore.</td></tr>
<tr><td colspan="2">To imagine unreal past events and speculate about alternative outcomes in the present, use:
past perfect / past perfect progressive [if-clause] +
would / could / might + base verb [result clause]

If we had already established contact with a more advanced civilization, they could help us develop our science programs.</td><td rowspan="2"></td></tr>
<tr><td colspan="2">To imagine unreal present and past events, use:
simple past [if-clause] +
would have / could have / might have + past participle [result clause]

If we lived in an intergalactic community, marriages between humans and aliens might have already taken place.</td></tr>
</table>

Self-Assessment

A (4 points) Complete each sentence with the correct form of the verb to complete each factual conditional.

A: If you **1.** ________________ (enter) a black hole, you don't come out somewhere else.
B: Right. Things get pulled in and destroyed when they **2.** ________________ (be) near a black hole.

A: Kip Thorne explained that if you **3.** ________________ (go) down through a black hole, your atoms **4.** ________________ (be) stretched and squeezed along with space and time.
B: Exactly. But the experience of entering a wormhole might be different.

B (5 points) Circle the correct form of the verb.

1. If in the past you studied theories about wormholes, you likely **encountered / had encountered** the works of John Wheeler and Kip Thorne.
2. Whenever I had free time in high school, I **had read / would read** about time travel.
3. If a wormhole **was / is** only open for a short amount of time, we need to determine how to hold the mouth open before trying to travel through it.
4. If **we'll try / we're going to try** to hold a wormhole open, we'll need to create negative energy.
5. Even if we **manage / would manage** to hold a wormhole open, who will volunteer to go through it?

C (4 points) Circle the correct form of the verb.

1. People wouldn't be so curious about the activity at Area 51 if the military **weren't / won't be / couldn't be** so secretive.
2. If the government reported that some UFO sightings were real, the news **caused / could cause / causes** fear and panic throughout the world.
3. If the military had technology that few know about, it **explained / would explain / will explain** many of the UFO sightings.
4. Interstellar travel might be possible for humans today if we **had captured and studied / will capture and study / would have captured and studied** an alien spacecraft to learn its technology.

D (7 points) Correct the seven conditional errors.

In February 1951, Lieutenant Graham Bethune saw a group of UFOs while he was flying a navy plane over the Atlantic Ocean. If Bethune weren't in the military then, he would speak freely about the experience. However, he was told to talk to no one at the time. He only made his story public many years later. He estimates that the UFO was about 300 feet in diameter. If it was smaller, he would fly below it, but the monstrous size made that impossible. He could only watch while it remained in the air in front of him for a minute and then quickly vanished. What if it was a spacecraft full of extraterrestrials? Why then didn't they try to communicate with Bethune and his crew? If only Bethune had the means to send some kind of communication to the UFO. Who knows what would happen!

Unit Project: Time capsule

A time capsule is a way of communicating with people from the future because its contents represent a certain time span in the history of civilization. It is a kind of "time machine."

Work in a small group. You and your team will create a time capsule that will be sent into outer space. Try and use grammar from the unit in your presentation. Follow the steps:

1. Each team will place 11 things into the time capsule. The first thing is the message, in both written and recorded forms, which persuades an alien culture to contact us. The message should describe how we want to exchange ideas, establish peaceful relationships with them, and gain knowledge from the alien culture. What will the message say? (The recorded message can be delivered via audio MP3 or video.)
2. The remaining 10 objects should be cultural and historical symbols from all over the world that best represent Earth's peoples over the past 500 years. These objects should represent our past, present, and our future. Try to choose two objects from each era.
3. Create a chart to plan and structure your presentation:

Number of objects from each era	Object	Reason for inclusion
2 from (1400–1599)	♦ Leonardo da Vinci's Codex Leicester notebook ♦ Chinese and Korean typeset	♦ If we included it, people from the future would be able to read about and see ideas of one of Earth's greatest geniuses. ♦ If we include it, aliens might see how we first created typed or written words.
3–4 from (1600–1899)	♦ First clock ♦ Steam engine ♦ Telephone	♦ If we put the first nautical clock into the capsule, people from the future will know how we marked time.
4–5 from (1900–2010)	♦ Automobile ♦ Airplane ♦ Computer ♦ Atomic clock	♦ If people see our computer they might be able to understand how we communicated in the twenty-first century.

4. Write your presentation. Imagine you are proposing your ideas for this time capsule to a panel of world leaders. Include images of as many objects as possible. Be prepared to defend your choice of objects. Why should you include each object and what would people know about Earth's civilizations if you include it?

B Prepare a presentation for the class. Follow the steps.

1. Explain the message you have included and discuss what might happen if it is received by an alien culture.
2. Explain why you have selected each item. Describe what each item represents and persuade the panel to accept the items you propose.
3. Predict what will happen if an alien culture hears and reads the message and sees the items in the time capsule.

UNIT 10

Signs of the Times

Outcomes

After completing this unit, I will be able to use these grammar points.

Chapter 19

Grammar Focus 1
Direct speech

Grammar Focus 2
Reported speech

Chapter 20

Grammar Focus 1
Embedded questions

Grammar Focus 2
Tag questions and negative questions

MyEnglishLab

 What do you know?

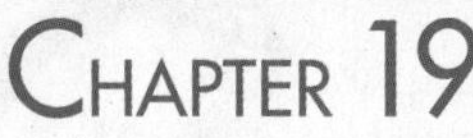

CHAPTER 19 It's a Sign

Getting Started

A Match each gesture or facial expression with the statement that best reflects its meaning. Then review your answers with a partner.

A

B

C

D

E

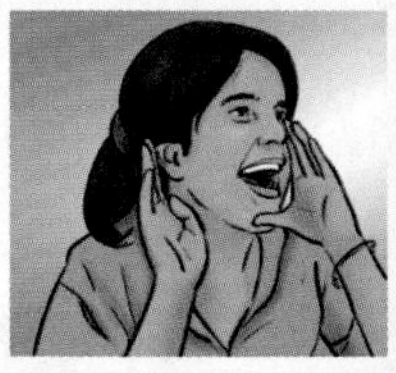
F

_____ **1.** *I said that I couldn't hear you!*
_____ **2.** *Please don't ask me any personal questions.*
_____ **3.** *I don't believe you just said that!*
_____ **4.** *I feel threatened. I sense danger.*
_____ **5.** *I don't mean to brag, but I told you so!*
_____ **6.** *I see food! I'm going to eat!*

B Some gestures or facial expressions can convey meaning without words. To emphasize a point, we often use words with body language or facial expressions at the same time. Write *G* if the statement is easily understood by using only a gesture. Write *S+G* if the statement would be stronger with speech and a gesture. Then work with a partner and decide which gesture you would make for each statement.

_____ **1.** "Shhh! Be quiet!"
_____ **2.** "Stop right there! Don't move!"
_____ **3.** "I'm too tired to go to the party."
_____ **4.** "He went that way, officer!"
_____ **5.** "We've got a deal!"
_____ **6.** "I can't stand horror films."

C Look back at Parts A and B. Complete the tasks.

1. **Direct speech** is spoken directly to another person, for example, "*Come here.*" Circle the examples of direct speech.
2. **Indirect speech** reports something a person said or wrote, for example, *She said to come here.* Underline the examples of indirect speech.
3. Look at the chart. Write the direct speech from Part B next to the reported speech.

Reported (indirect) speech	Direct speech
1. They told the police which direction he went.	
2. We said we both agreed and shook hands on it.	
3. The librarian asked them not to speak.	
4. He told me that he was too exhausted to come.	
5. She said she couldn't stand scary movies.	
6. The crossing guard said we had to wait.	

MyEnglishLab

Vocabulary Check

Reading

A WARM-UP Work in a small group. Do facial expressions and body language mean the same thing all over the world? Can you think of some expressions or gestures that could be misinterpreted by someone from another culture?

B UNDERSTANDING MAIN IDEAS Read the questions. Then read the text and write the number of the paragraph that includes each answer.

_____ **1.** Who uses the FACS tool for animal behavior studies?
_____ **2.** What are the basic expressions of emotion and how many are there?
_____ **3.** What have psychologists said about Paul Ekman's universal facial expressions theory?
_____ **4.** What examples does the author give of how people misinterpret each other's non-verbal cues?

READING BETWEEN THE SIGNS

1. Did you know that it takes about 90 seconds for someone to form a lasting opinion about you? How do you feel when you meet someone who keeps their arms crossed? What if she doesn't have a strong handshake? Anthropologists and psychologists generally agree that people recognize non-verbal signals or "cues" easily. Body language and expressions of emotion—anger, contempt, disgust, fear, joy, sadness, and surprise—are signs of our feelings and self-expression. As a child, you may have heard, "don't make *that* face," or "don't slouch!" Many believe that non-verbal behavior makes a lasting impression. Psychologist Paul Ekman stated that, "The face makes one's behavior more predictable and understandable to others."

2. Dr. Ekman has spent most of his life investigating gestures and facial expressions. In the 1970s, Ekman and W.V. Friesen developed a tool known as FACS—Facial Action Coding System. This system is used by detectives and even became the premise of a TV show. Ekman said that whether we speak the truth or tell a lie, our faces display "micro-expressions" —tiny muscular movements such as raising the eyebrow or curling the upper lip. He claims that these expressions are involuntary and almost impossible to suppress.

Is Body Language Universal?

3. Regardless of cultural background, most people seem to be able to identify facial expressions of emotion. Certain gestures, on the other hand, can vary among cultures. If an American uses the "V" sign in France, or the "OK" sign in Turkey, people might interpret the meaning very negatively. Some psychologists have disputed Ekman's theory of universal facial expressions. They reported that between people from Western and Eastern cultures, misinterpretations of facial expressions often occur.

Monkey See, Monkey Do?

4. When we see a cat's back go up and it hisses, we, and other animals, know it is a warning to "stay away." If we look at images of a chimpanzee, its facial expressions are familiar to us. Anthropologist Seth Robson used the FACS system to analyze videos of zoo animals: chimps, gorillas, and monkeys. In apes, body language—highlighted by facial expressions of joy or calm—seemed to be a way of expressing social harmony. Robson's research suggests that primates use facial expressions to "resolve conflicts peacefully." Whether in humans or apes, a smile seems to be universally understood.

C UNDERSTANDING INFERENCE Answer the questions in full sentences.

1. What body language could be perceived as defensive or negative? _____

_____

2. What did Ekman mean when he stated, "The face makes one's behavior more predictable and understandable to others"? _____

_____

3. What does Robson imply about the facial expressions of primates?

_____

MyEnglishLab

Reading Comprehension

Grammar Focus 1 Direct speech

Examples	Language notes
(1) Ekman stated, **"The face makes one's behavior more predictable and understandable to others."**	**Direct speech** (or **quoted speech**) states the exact words that a speaker used. We must use quotation marks around the original statement. Final punctuation falls within the quotation marks.
(2) **Robson wrote,** "My measure of facial mobility allows for comparisons across species." [**reporting clause** + direct speech]	Direct speech usually includes a **reporting clause**, which must have a noun or pronoun subject and a reporting verb.
(3) **The mother scolded,** "No. Don't make that face." "No," **the mother scolded,** "Don't make that face." "No. Don't make that face," **the mother scolded.**	The reporting clause can appear before, after, or in the middle of the quoted speech. Note the placement of **commas** and **periods** in all three positions.
(4) **"Don't slouch!"** the father reminded his son.	We can use an **exclamation point** for statements that express strong emotion. We don't use a comma to separate the quoted speech from a final reporting clause.
(5) **"How do primates use facial expressions?"** I asked the anthropologist. I asked the anthropologist, **"How do primates use facial expressions?"**	A **direct question** requires use of a **question mark**, which is inside the quotation marks. The reporting clause can appear before, after, or in the middle of the quoted speech.
(6) "Hey!" **I began**. "What did you make that face for?" **He replied,** "What face?" "You know what face I mean!" **I shouted**. "You're getting upset over nothing," **he complained**.	A reporting verb can focus on **time**, **purpose**, or **manner**: Verbs telling the time the statement was made: *add, begin, continue, finish, start* Verbs expressing the purpose: *challenge, complain, concede, inquire, query, request* Verbs expressing the manner: *joke, insist, mumble, shriek, shout, tease, whisper, yell*
(7) "Body language improves communication," **said the scientist. / the scientist said**.	In a middle or final position, the reporting clause can use **normal or inverted word order**.
(8) "Facial expressions help us predict behavior," **she said**. (***Incorrect:*** ~~said she~~) "The truth is always in the eyes," **many investigators have said**. (***Incorrect:*** ~~have said many investigators~~) "The lie detector suggests the suspect is telling the truth," **the investigator told the others**. (***Incorrect:*** ~~told the others the investigator~~)	Do not use inverted word order in these situations: • with a pronoun subject • with a complex verb (one with an auxiliary verb) • with the listener mentioned

See Appendix Y on page A-14 for a list of reporting verbs.

MyEnglishLab
Grammar Plus 1
Activities 1 and 2

Grammar Practice

A Circle the correct reporting verbs to complete the conversation between two comic book readers.

Symbols of Superheroes: Subject to Change?

Magneto and his helmet

A: "I got into another heated talk with Craig yesterday," Rick **1. began / continued**, as he took a seat next to his friend.

B: "I assume it was about comics?" Mike **2. queried / replied** with raised eyebrows.

A: "What else?" **3. laughed / yelled** Rick. "You know we love to argue with each other on this topic. This time Craig actually dared to suggest that some superheroes needed costume updates."

B: "Why is changing a costume so bad?" Mike **4. mentioned / challenged**.

A: "Why?" Rick almost **5. shrieked / whispered** with disbelief as he shot to his feet. He took a breath to calm himself, and then lowered his voice. "Some costumes are iconic. I mean, they're famous! And the parts of some costumes represent important ideas."

B: "You mean like Superman's *S*?"

A: "Exactly!" Rick **6. questioned / spoke** with emotion. "The red and yellow *S* against blue creates a strong contrast. And the design is very bold. Superman's *S* is a symbol of strength. It goes hand in hand with his signature stance—you know, hands on hips with feet apart. Ready for action. No artist should touch the *S*."

B: "I guess not," Mike **7. asked / replied**. "But sometimes there's a need to change a character's appearance."

A: "Like when?" Rick **8. wondered / offered**, as he stopped in his tracks and looked hard at his friend.

B: "What about Magneto?" **9. suggested / informed** Mike calmly. "Didn't his costume change when he joined the X-Men? That represented a move from evil to good. It was weird to see Magneto lose his helmet, but it was also symbolic. It was like he lost his true identity, but in time it was restored. He left the X-Men and fought against them . . . in his old helmet, right?"

A: "True," **10. agreed / complained** Rick, although not very willingly. "But," he **11. added / teased** "there have been other costume changes that had little to do with symbolism and everything to do with marketing to get people to buy more comic books."

B: Mike spread his arms in defeat and **12. threatened / conceded**, "You win on that point."

Now go back and underline the 12 reporting clauses.

B Rewrite the statements with correct punctuation and capitalization.

1. you must separate observation from interpretation the trainer said

"You must separate observation from interpretation," the trainer said.

2. can you base your interpretation of a behavior on multiple observations she asked

3. did you know inquired the trainer that gorillas use nose-to-nose greetings

4. in contrast she went on lions use head rubbing to greet one another

5. to protect their young, female giraffes kick at predators the trainer told the group

6. pandas show anger by staring at the animal that is threatening them explained the trainer

7. if the other animal is close she added then a panda will growl and swipe its paw to scare the other animal

8. the trainer explained young bull elephants push over trees to test their strength

9. you must learn to interpret animal behavior if you want to stay safe and appreciate the animals she concluded

Look again at your sentences. How many reporting clauses use *subject + verb* word order? _____
How many reporting clauses use *verb + subject* word order? _____

Grammar Focus 2 Reported speech

Examples	Language notes
(1) The scientist stated, **"I've spent years doing research on this topic."** [direct speech] The scientist stated **that he had spent years doing research on that topic.** [reported speech]	**Reported speech** (also called **indirect speech**) describes something someone said or wrote without using the exact words. Reported speech does not use quotation marks.
(2) Ekman claims **that these expressions are involuntary**. [subject + verb + **object** (reported speech)]	In reported statements, the **main clause** has a subject and a reporting verb. The reported words form a **noun clause**, which is the **direct object** of the reporting verb.
(3) "**Stay away** from a cat that hisses." ***Compare:*** The mother **advised her little girl to stay away** from a cat that hisses.	To report an imperative, we can use: reporting verb + (object pronoun) + infinitive The choice of reporting verb gives information about the purpose or manner of the original statement.
(4) "My report will be done by tomorrow," she promised her professor. → **She promised her professor that the report would be done by the next day.**	**References** to time and place as well as the choice of pronouns need to keep the speaker's original meaning.
(5) "Crime **is** a problem in all major cities," said the police officer. ***Compare:*** The police officer said that crime **is** a problem in all major cities. [= general truth]	We **do not usually change the verb forms** to report • facts or events that remain true at the time they are stated • general facts that remain true all the time • statements made immediately after they are spoken
(6) "There **is** news of a robbery in our area." → They said that there **was** news of a robbery in their area. "The thieves **have stolen** money." → They reported that the thieves **had stolen** money.	When we **change direct speech to reported speech**, we usually shift all verb forms back: **Direct Speech** → **Reported Speech** simple present → simple past present progressive → past progressive present perfect → past perfect present perfect progressive → past perfect progressive simple past → past perfect past progressive → past perfect progressive past perfect → (no change) past perfect progressive → (no change) future with *will* → *would* future with *be going to* → *was / were going to* In everyday English, some speakers do not change the simple past to the past perfect.
(7) "The thieves **may be hiding** in the city." → The police reported that the thieves **might be hiding** in the city.	Only some modal verbs change in reported statements. **Direct Speech** → **Reported Speech** *may* (possibility) → *might* *may* (permission) → *could* *can* → *could* *must* → *had to*

(8) "If the thieves **are caught**, they **will face** up to 25 years in jail." [real] → Authorities said that if the thieves **were caught**, they **would face** up to 25 years in jail. [real] "If I **were investigating** the crime, I**'d examine** similar robberies in the country." [unreal] → My friend said that if she **were investigating** the crime, she**'d examine** similar robberies in the country." [unreal]	We make **changes in verb tenses** when we report real (factual) conditionals, but not in unreal (imaginary) conditionals.
(9) "Is there a room for us to study?" we asked the librarian. → We asked the librarian **if there was** a room for us to study. *Also:* We asked the librarian **whether (or not) there was** . . .	In **reported questions**, we don't use quotation marks or a question mark. To report a ***yes / no* question**: 1. Use *if* or *whether* in a reported question. *If* is more common. *Whether* can be used with or without *or not* and is more formal. 2. Use statement word order (subject + verb).
(10) "Where can we continue to study as a group?" we wondered. → We wondered **where we could continue** to study as group.	To report a ***wh-* question**, use question word + statement word order (subject + verb).

See Appendix Z on page A-14 for changes to time, place, and pronouns in reported speech.

Grammar Practice

A Use the reporting verbs in parentheses to report the statements of each expert. Make necessary changes to the reference words and verbs.

1. "At one time it went against etiquette for a lady to go out in public without gloves and a hat." (recalled) "Suitable attire communicated a suitable social position." (explained)

Virginia recalled that at one time it had gone against etiquette for any lady to go out in public without gloves and a hat. She explained that suitable attire communicated a suitable social position.

Virginia, fashion historian

2. "Gloves will never disappear from fashion because they have a practical use." (predicted) "Glove designs have changed, but some of the etiquette hasn't." (observed) "One example is the need for men to remove gloves before shaking hands as a way to express openness." (stated)

____

____

____

____

Lee, clothing designer

3. "With a change in women's fashion came a change in etiquette." (argued)
   "Women used to lift their long skirts in a curtsy as an act of acknowledgment." (note)

Marcy, historian

4. "Gentlemen in past centuries used their hats to signal respect for others." (informed us)
   "Males young and old would tip their hats to greet, thank, and apologize." (insisted)
   "If young people who love baseball caps today would take a look at the past, they might understand the gesture of removing their hats indoors." (commented)

Jacob, author of historical fiction

B Find and correct the error in each reported statement.

1. Our professor ~~said~~ told us that body language can also be called kinesics.
2. Psychiatrists agree that "people are not always conscious of signals they're sending with their body."
3. I asked my professor if whether Ekman believed that facial expressions came from nature or nurture.
4. A classmate inquired was intonation a part of kinesics.
5. One student asked why do women seem to be more skilled at sending and interpreting nonverbal signals.
6. The professor said we might use a Darwin text as one of our resources for the term paper.
7. We asked the professor which human emotions are universally recognized through facial expressions?
8. Our professor told to us that one signal can have multiple meanings.
9. He explained that the meaning of hand gestures sometimes changes whether they are used in different cultures.
10. I commented that if Darwin had been alive today, he would be pleased to learn how much his theories are discussed.

MyEnglishLab

Sounding Natural

Speaking

 Work with a partner. Choose one quote and explain the main idea to your partner. Make sure you change the quoted text into reported speech. Use the phrases below to help you.

1. "Body language is a very powerful tool. We had body language before we had speech, and apparently, 80% of what you understand in a conversation is read through the body, not the words."
   —Deborah Bull, dancer
2. "There are four ways, and only four ways, in which we have contact with the world. We are evaluated and classified by these four contacts: what we do, how we look, what we say, and how we say it."
   —Dale Carnegie, author and motivational speaker

When Deborah Bull said that body language was a very powerful tool, she meant that . . .

When Carnegie talked about how we have contact with the world, he meant that . . .

B Idioms are expressions that have a special (not literal) meaning. Many idioms are about facial expressions, gestures, and body language. Match each expression with one of the phrases in the list. Then work in pairs or a team and use the expressions to talk about emotions.

We were left scratching our heads is another way of saying that we didn't understand why something happened. We asked if he was upset.

_____ **1.** Keep your fingers crossed.	**a.** Great!
_____ **2.** Well, keep your chin up!	**b.** Don't get mad!
_____ **3.** Wipe that smile off your face!	**c.** It's not funny!
_____ **4.** He gave it the thumbs up.	**d.** That was shocking!
_____ **5.** That really raised their eyebrows!	**e.** Don't be sad!
_____ **6.** Don't get your back up!	**f.** Hope for the best!

Listening

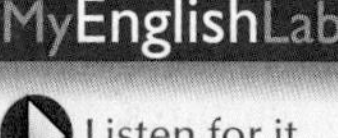

MyEnglishLab

Listen for it.

 UNDERSTANDING MAIN IDEAS Listen to the interview. Check which facial expressions are mentioned. Then talk to a partner about what you think they mean.

☐

☐

☐

☐

B UNDERSTANDING SEQUENCE Listen again. Number the events in the correct order (1–7).

_____ **a.** The interviewer described the muscles of the upper and lower face.
_____ **b.** The interviewer questioned the animator about different animation techniques.
_____ **c.** The animator quoted Paul Ekman.
_____ **d.** The animator mentioned that he had shaken the interviewer's hand.
_____ **e.** The animator described how he used the Facial Action Coding System.
_____ **f.** The animator told the interviewer that there were 44 different facial actions.
_____ **g.** The interviewer introduced the topic and the guest.

C AFTER LISTENING Talk to a partner. Can you tell when someone is lying to you or telling the truth? What facial expressions have you noticed?

Writing

MyEnglishLab
Linking Grammar to Writing

A Imagine you are a reporter for a cultural blog. Interview three or four people from different countries, cities, or cultures. Ask them about each American gesture or custom and what that gesture or custom means to them. What is their impression? Write *P* for *positive* or *N* for *negative* in each column.

Student	Country, city, or culture	American custom or gesture				
		waving with palm outward	smiling when you say "hello"	standing with hands on hips	making OK sign	placing a hand in your lap at dinner

Ask them about their country's, city's, or culture's customs and gestures. What would they want Americans to know before visiting there? Take notes. Use some of the reporting verbs from the box.

agree	believe	indicate	report	tell
ask	disagree	mention	say	think

B Write a short article for the blog. Discuss your findings and whether you agree or disagree with the other students. Use grammar from the unit, including reported speech and direct quotes.

> Students from {X} thought the gesture meant . . . while two students from {Y} believed it meant . . . Two out of four students agreed that the gesture . . . means . . .

C Share your writing with the class. Talk in a group about different gestures in different countries or places. What things can be interpreted negatively? Have you ever had that experience?

Chapter 20 Signs of Life

Getting Started

A Look at the symbols. Do you know what each one means? Then match each symbol with its definition or description.

A B C D

_____ **1.** An **ideogram** depicts exactly what was seen or heard and is similar to ancient hieroglyphics.
_____ **2.** A **rebus** is what is used to stand for a spoken sound.
_____ **3.** Milton Glaser used a **phonogram** when he wanted to represent the sound of "love" in an image.
_____ **4.** If you don't know where the drinking fountain or restroom is, can't you follow a **pictogram**?

B Match the question or description with its symbol.

_____ **1.** When you see or "get this," it usually means the way is safe and clear, doesn't it?
_____ **2.** It is not clear how this came to stand for peace.
_____ **3.** What this represents is the idea of help and medical aid.
_____ **4.** This floral ideogram holds meaning in cultures where it is often both decorative and religious.
_____ **5.** We know how old this staff with birds and reptiles is because Greek physicians used it in ancient times.
_____ **6.** Archaeologists are not sure what this animal symbolized when it was discovered.

a. cave bear
b. green light
c. red cross
d. Caduceus sign (staff with wings and snakes)
e. lotus
f. white dove

C Look back at A and B. Complete the tasks.

1. Circle the parts of any **sentences that end with a question**.
2. Underline the ***wh-* words** in each sentence.

MyEnglishLab

Vocabulary Check

Reading

A WARM-UP Talk to the class. Imagine what it would be like to discover 32,000-year-old cave paintings. What might future societies think if they find 21st century graffiti?

B SCANNING Scan the reading and find the answer. Who created the world's oldest graffiti? Then read the whole text.

Signs of Life: From Paintings in Caves to Men on the Moon

We never know who writes on the walls, do we? Though exactly who painted the prehistoric graffiti of Chauvet Caves is unknown, their unique representation of life is invaluable to our understanding of how early humans lived. The caves are covered with colorful depictions of various animals—bears, bison, lions, and many now-extinct animals—yet, there is no indication that Paleolithic people —early humans— had ever actually resided in the caves. The pristine environment of the Chauvet Caves—their constant temperature and lack of light—are what preserved this ancient graffiti, these symbols of life, as a kind of time capsule from 32,000 years ago.

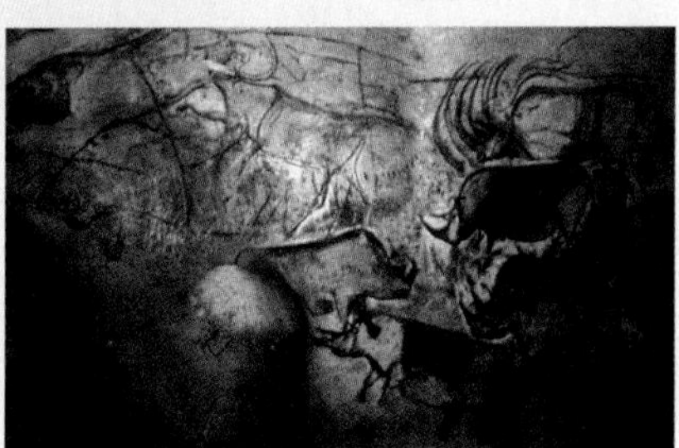

The aesthetic quality of these paintings is unsurpassed. Writer Judith Thurman, one of the few non-scientists allowed to visit the caves before they were closed to the public, noted, "What those first artists invented was a language of signs for which there will never be a Rosetta Stone; perspective, a technique that was not rediscovered until the Athenian Golden Age; and . . . by the flicker of torchlight, the animals seem to surge from the walls, and move across them like figures in a magic lantern show (in that sense, the artists invented animation)."

Signs, Sounds, and Symbols. Artifacts such as a flute allow us to further explore the history of human behavior. Sounds from our past, once believed lost forever, now offer clues to how prehistoric people communicated. Humans have invented innumerable ways to transmit messages. We can see how music or sound developed parallel to the evolution of writing: from ancient hieroglyphs on a pyramid wall to modern graffiti spray-painted on a subway car; from the low tones of the primative flute to a cell phone ringtone. A red traffic light is just another way of communicating, "stop," isn't it? Symbols for money, cultural pictograms, or astrology signs, even our clothing—all are representations of ways to send messages. Symbols and signs—whether visual or aural—are markers of what we stand for. Society should find a way to preserve them for the future. If we don't, they will simply become an enigma to our descendants, as the Chauvet paintings are for us today. What inspired prehistoric man to paint on the walls is a question that remains unanswered. Perhaps it was as simple as when astronaut Buzz Aldrin planted the American flag on the Moon: a desire to say, "We were here."

C UNDERSTANDING FACTS AND DETAILS. Write *T* for the true statements and *F* for the false statements.

_____ **1.** We don't have an exact date for when the Chauvet paintings were created.
_____ **2.** We don't know if the animals depicted on the walls of Chauvet were painted by early humans.
_____ **3.** Scientists don't know what the cave paintings represented.
_____ **4.** It is not clear why the caves were closed to the public.
_____ **5.** We know how the early humans' flute sounds.
_____ **6.** There is a parallel between what ancient hieroglyphs represent and modern graffiti.
_____ **7.** We may not be able to determine why prehistoric people painted on cave walls.
_____ **8.** Why astronauts were inspired to leave a flag on the Moon is a mystery.

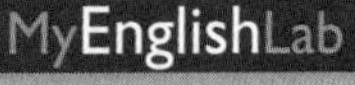

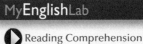

Grammar Focus 1 Embedded questions

Examples	Language notes
(1) We want to know **what possessed early man to paint on the walls**. [embedded question] We asked the professor **what possessed early man to paint on the walls**. [reported speech as embedded question]	**Embedded questions** are **noun clauses** which begin with a question word. They appear inside another statement. The embedded question is part of a larger statement, so a **period** is used, <u>not</u> a question mark. **Reported questions** are a type of embedded question.
(2) The pristine environment of the Chauvet Caves are **what preserved these symbols of life**.	An embedded question uses **statement word order** (subject + verb).
(3) Do you know **where the Chauvet Caves are located?** Would you please tell me **how the symbols were preserved for so long?**	An embedded question can be **inside another question**. In this case, a question mark is needed. Embedded questions are often used to form **indirect questions**, which are considered more polite.
(4) **<u>Whether or not</u> the paintings were done by early humans** is still disputed. *(Based on the question: Were the paintings done by early humans?)* Dr. Clottes recognized the insight that cave paintings offered on **<u>what</u> European Paleolithic people thought**. *(Based on the question: What did European Paleolithic people think?)*	Embedded questions can be based on ***yes / no* questions** or ***wh-* questions**: Word order 1: *if [or whether (or not)]* + subject + verb Word order 2: question word + subject + verb
(5) **What possessed early man to paint on the walls** is a question that remains unanswered. [subject] I'd like to know **what possessed early man to paint on the walls**. [direct object] The discussion focused on **what possessed early man to paint on the walls**. [indirect object] <u>The main question</u> is **what possessed early man to paint on the walls**. [subject complement] <u>The question</u> **what possessed early man to paint on the walls** is much discussed. [noun complement] No one is <u>certain</u> **what possessed early man to paint on the walls**. [adjective complement]	Because embedded questions are noun clauses, they can function as a **subject,** an **object,** or a **complement**.
(6) I wouldn't know **what to preserve** for future generations. (= ***What should I preserve?***)	We can form embedded questions with **question word + infinitive** to express the meaning of *should* or *how to*.

MyEnglishLab

Grammar Plus 1
Activities 1 and 2

Grammar Practice

A Complete the dialogue with embedded questions. Use the direct questions in parentheses. Be sure to use the correct final punctuation. One embedded question will use a short form.

TEACHER: Do you know 1. *how many symbols there are on the U.S. Treasury Seal?* (How many symbols are there on the U.S. Treasury Seal?) Look closely at the bill.

STUDENT: I see three symbols, but I don't think I can explain 2. ______________________ (What does each one mean?)

TEACHER: We'll work together. You must learn 3. ______________________. (How should we interpret symbols?) Can you guess 4. ______________________ (Why are there thirteen stars?)

STUDENT: The stars must represent the thirteen original colonies, but I'm not sure 5. ______________________ (What does the key symbolize?)

TEACHER: The key is a symbol of official authority. Can you tell me 6. ______________________ (How is justice represented?) Look closely!

Look back at the six embedded questions. Write *O* above the ones used as objects. Write *C* above the ones used as complements.

B Correct the errors in the text. There are six more errors.

Chinese astrology dates back so far that no one knows the exact year when *the Chinese zodiac was* ~~was the Chinese zodiac~~ created. To help establish a timeline, a brief study of the Chinese calendar is needed.

Many agree that Emperor Huangdi invented the Chinese lunar calendar in 2637 B.C. The calendar is based on a 60-year cycle. Within a cycle are sets of 12 years, and each year is assigned the name of an animal. How were those animals determined remains unclear? One legend tells how did Buddha invite every creature on Earth to participate in a race. What did the first 12 winners receive was an honored position on the Chinese calendar?

Names of years grew into astrological signs that people began to associate with personality traits, and so the Chinese zodiac was born. The zodiac was officially recognized during the Han Dynasty (206 B.C.–220 A.D.) Over time, other cultures adopted similar astrological signs, and today it is impossible to estimate just how many people around the world follow the Chinese zodiac?

From business forecasts to marriage counseling, the 12 animal signs and corresponding traits are given much significance in modern society. Those who believe in the zodiac look to it for guidance. The zodiac can help people decide what should do and when to do it. Some even proudly display their signs in the form of a tattoo as a constant reminder of who are they and what is their nature. There is no doubt whether the Chinese zodiac remains influential or not so many centuries after its creation?

Grammar Focus 2 Tag questions and negative questions

Examples	Language notes
(1) A red traffic light is just another way of depicting "stop," **isn't it?**	A **tag question** is a question added to the end of a statement. Tag questions always follow a comma and have inverted word order (verb + subject). Tag questions must end in a **question mark**.
(2) They don't allow tourists to view the paintings any more, **do they?** There aren't any humans depicted in those cave paintings, **are there?** Society should find a way to preserve them for the people of our future, **shouldn't it?**	To form tag questions, we use: auxiliary verb + pronoun subject If the verb in the main statement is in the **simple present or past**, use a form of ***be*** or ***do*** to form the tag. If the verb in the main statement has an **auxiliary verb**, use the **same auxiliary** to form the tag.
(3) The paintings were done by early humans, **weren't they?** The paintings weren't done by early humans, **were they?**	If the verb in the main statement is **affirmative**, the verb in the tag question is **negative**. If the verb in the main statement is **negative**, the verb in the tag question is **affirmative**.
(4) The paintings were done by early humans, **were they not?** [less common]	Negative contractions are more common in conversation than full forms.
(5) I'm right, **aren't I?** *(= I am right,* ***am I not?****)*	For the subject pronoun *I*, use the negative verb *aren't* in the tag question. The full form, however, is *am I not.*
(6) [I bet] those cave paintings are really old, **aren't they?** [Well,] they have to be at least 5,000 years old, **don't they?**	Introductory expressions such as *I bet, I'm sure,* and *Well*, can introduce a statement that is followed by a tag question. Make sure the tag question matches the subject and verb in the main statement, not the introductory expression.
(7) You've heard about the Chauvet Caves before, **right?** (= *haven't you?*)	Informal tags such as *okay* and *right* are common in conversation.
(8) You got a new ringtone, **didn't you?**	We use tag questions in everyday English when we want confirmation.
(9) It's convenient to have different ringtones for different people, **isn't it?**	We also use tag questions in everyday English to ask rhetorical questions; that is, to make a comment without expecting an answer.
(10) "Let's turn off all the cell phones, **shall we?**" the professor said politely yet firmly.	It is possible, though not very common, to use the question tag *shall we?* following a statement with *Let's* in order to make a polite invitation with the expectation of acceptance.
(11) **Didn't you get** a new ringtone**?** **Isn't it** convenient to have different ringtones for different people**?**	**Negative questions** are independent clauses, but they have the same functions as tag questions: **to confirm and to comment**.
(12) **Don't you know** your Chinese zodiac sign**?**	Negative questions begin with a **negative verb**, usually a contraction, and end with a **question mark**.

Grammar Practice

A Complete the conversation with the tag questions and negative questions below.

aren't they	did you	don't they	isn't it
couldn't you	do you	haven't you	wouldn't that

Sounds of Nature Repurposed

A: Geese are the only birds that honk, **1.** ____________________?
B: I believe so. Other birds chirp, caw, cluck, or hoot.
A: If you think about it, the way we honk our car horns is like the way geese honk, **2.** ____________________?
B: That's funny. You have a point. We usually honk when we're excited or threatened.
A: Well, there are many man-made sounds that seem to be inspired by sounds in nature.
B: **3.** ____________________ make a good topic for an essay?
A: Yes! And what about foghorns? **4.** ____________________ sound a bit like elephants trumpeting?
B: Yeah. I'd have to agree. I think elephants blow through their trunk like that when they need help or when they're angry, so that's similar to the warning purpose of a foghorn.
A: I got another example.
B: Why am I not surprised? I'm sure you could come up with at least a dozen, **5.** ____________________?
A: Well, I know you could, too, right? How about train whistles or any whistles for that matter? We use whistles to signal one another, just like birds.
B: And dolphins. You don't want to leave them out of the conversation, **6.** ____________________?
A: Oh, yeah. Dolphins whistle, too.
B: Every dolphin, in fact, has its signature whistle for identification. I bet you didn't know that, **7.** ____________________?
A: No, I didn't. That's really amazing. That's like a boatswain's whistle if you think about it. You've seen films with old ships, **8.** ____________________?
B: Yeah. The boatswain was the naval officer who gave all the different signals with a whistle, like one for the captain.

Look back at the eight tag questions and negative questions. Circle questions used for confirmation. Underline the questions used to comment.

B Complete the tag questions and negative questions.

1. Everyone can recognize a *No Cell Phone* sign, ____________________?
2. Some public restrooms are used by men and women, so there wouldn't be separate signs, ____________________?
3. ____________________ all countries use the red circle with a slash to state what's not allowed?
4. You've noticed that signs in airports are often written in more than one language, ____________________?
5. I bet a sign for moose crossing looks funny or surprising to some people, ____________________?
6. It's dangerous to drive if you can't read the traffic signs, ____________________?
7. Why is the maid knocking on our door so early? ____________________ you hang up the *Do Not Disturb* sign last night?
8. We're lost and there are no signs in English, but let's not panic, ____________________? Let's ask for help.
9. ____________________ every driver forget what speed limit is posted along a familiar road every now and then?
10. Oh, no! I'm driving down a one-way street, ____________________? I need to turn around.

MyEnglishLab

Sounding Natural

Speaking

A Work with a partner. Look at the symbols, icons, and ideograms. What does each image represent? Do you know what each symbol means? Discuss where you usually see each symbol.

B Work in a group. Do you have graffiti in your country? What do you think about graffiti? Is it art or is it vandalism?

C In a group, discuss which symbols and signs in your culture have significant meaning. For example, what symbols are on your country's flag? Explain what those symbols mean.

In Egypt, there is graffiti on the old pyramids. That graffiti has been there for hundreds of years.

There are stars and stripes on the American flag. They represent the states.

Listening

A UNDERSTANDING MAJOR IDEAS Listen to the lecture. In which type of class does this discussion probably take place?

a. Biology **b.** Art History **c.** Anthropology **d.** Ancient History

B UNDERSTANDING DETAILS AND INFERENCE Listen again and answer the questions.

1. What did the professor imply when he said, "We wouldn't expect early humans—whoever created those paintings—to be thinking about the animation of those pictures."
a. Primitive people were probably not that intelligent.
b. No one imagined that certain primitive humans could paint.
c. Anthropologists aren't quite sure who created those cave paintings.

2. What did Marisa say about her understanding of pictograms and ideograms?
a. She said they were depictions of a concept.
b. She said that she didn't know how they were different.
c. She described a pictogram as an image based on a physical object.

3. What did the professor say about who first developed pictograms?
a. That they were created by the ancient Egyptians.
b. That they are hieroglyphs.
c. That we created them in the 21st century.

C AFTER LISTENING Talk with a partner about some of the ideas in the discussion. Talk about some signs and symbols and give examples of some of the topics the professor mentioned.

MyEnglishLab

Linking Grammar to Writing

Writing

A Look back at the reading on page 209. As you read, complete the summary chart.

Major points	Details
Significance of cave paintings and graffiti	• •
Reasons for signs and symbols Different types of signs / symbols	• •
Visual symbols vs. aural (sound)	• •

We often use an outline to organize information. Create an outline using information from the chart. Follow this example.

I. Introduction
  A. Hook. Use one of the quotes, statements, or a tag question from the article.
  B. Background information. Include important facts that introduce the topic.
    Topic sentence
      Examples / Details

II. Body paragraphs (1, 2, 3, etc.)
  Topic sentence
    Details (paraphrases from the reading)

    Include information on what you learned about cave paintings.
    Include information on what you learned about signs.

III. Conclusion
  Draw a conclusion based on what you read. A conclusion restates the main idea in a few lines.

B Now use the chart and your outline to write a summary of the reading. You can use these sentence starters and vocabulary from the chapter.

> When the author said {X} he meant that . . . Though it is not clear who . . .
> What {scientists} have found is . . .
> What is clear is that . . . What is evident is that . . .
> We can see the difference between what {X} meant and . . .

C Exchange papers with a partner and discuss your findings. Use the sentence starters in Part B to talk about your summaries.

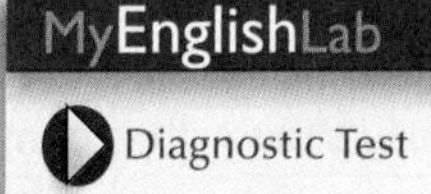

Grammar Summary

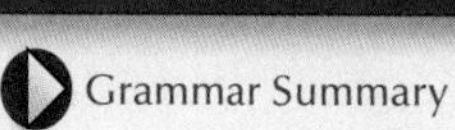

Direct speech and **reported speech** retell someone's words.

Direct speech	Reported speech
Direct speech restates the exact words someone spoke and uses quotation marks. The professor stated, **"The use of hand gestures in greetings has changed over time."**	Reported speech does not use the original words to restate another person's statement and does not use quotation marks. **The professor stated that the use of hand gestures in greetings had changed over time.**

To change direct speech to reported speech, we often need to make changes to **verb forms** and **reference words**.

To report an imperative, use *tell* (someone) + infinitive or choose another reporting verb.	(1) "Look at a soldier's uniform to understand his or her rank," she said. → She **told us to look** at a soldier's uniform to understand his or her rank.
To report a question, use statement word order: 1. *yes/no* questions: *if* or *whether* + subject + verb 2. *wh-* questions: question word + subject + verb	(2) I asked **if the salute changes based on rank.** I inquired **which other professions used uniforms and ranking like the military.**
Pronouns and other reference words need to change to make reported statements logical.	(3) "Off the top of my head, I can think of police officers, pilots, and fire fighters," she replied. → She replied **that off the top of her head, she could think of police officers, pilots, and fire fighters.**
The general practice is to shift verb tenses back in reported speech.	(4) "The uniforms of all these professions include important symbols, from the stripes to the badges," she went on to say. → She went on to say **that the uniforms of all those professions included important symbols, from the stripes to the badges.**

Direct questions are independent clauses that always ask real questions. **Embedded questions** are noun clauses within a larger statement that may or may not ask a real question.

Direct questions	Embedded questions
Direct questions use question word order: verb + subject **Is there any rock art in the U.S.?** **How did scientists find a panel of ancient rock in California?**	Embedded questions use statement word order: subject + verb. I wonder **if there is any ancient rock art in the U.S.** I read **how scientists found a panel of ancient rock art in southern California.**

Tag questions and **negative questions** help us seek confirmation or comment.

Tag questions appear at the end of a statement.	That's the Belgian flag, **isn't it** [confirmation] All nations take pride in their flags, **don't they?** [rhetorical]
Tag questions have inverted word order (auxiliary verb + pronoun subject) and must end in a question mark.	As a flag color, blue usually represents the sky, **doesn't it?**
If the main verb is affirmative, the tag question is negative. If the main verb is negative, the tag question is affirmative.	You recognize the flag, **don't you**? You don't recognize the flag, **do you**?
Negative questions are independent clauses that usually start with a contraction.	**Don't those children know** their own national flag?

Self-Assessment

A (6 points) Circle the correct reporting verbs to complete the conversations.

1. "Americans generally stand at an arm's length from the people they're talking to," **demanded / explained** Josh, who wished to help Henri understand the local culture.
2. "Can I stand closer if it's a close friend?" **inquired / offered** Henri.
3. "A warm smile and a firm handshake is enough of a greeting," **said / told** Josh.
4. Henri **promised / reflected**, "I guess that's why my host family looked surprised when I tried to kiss their cheeks."
5. "Do most Americans use the thumbs-up sign?" Henri **wondered / argued.**
6. "Well, it's one of a few signs that shows approval," **complained / replied** Josh. "It's pretty common."

B (4 points) Change the direct speech to reported speech. Use the reporting verb in bold.

1. "The traditional dress of Vietnam, the Ao Dai, symbolizes feminine beauty," **began** Professor Nguyen.
___
2. "The Ao Dai was influenced by Chinese and French fashion," **said** the professor.
___
3. She **explained**, "The color of the dress can reflect a woman's age and status."
___
4. "If a woman is married, social norms allow for deeper shades," Professor Nguyen **informed** the class.
___

C (5 points) Correct the five errors.

1. I asked the salesperson how many melodies could the doorbell play.
2. Using different ringtones makes it possible to identify who is calling you without looking at caller ID?
3. Alarm clocks allow users to choose whether do they want a buzzer, the radio, or a favorite tune.
4. Sirens on ambulances more than the flashing lights are what do tell people that there is an emergency.
5. Have you ever wondered how did people managed before smartphones with alarms and alert signals?

D (5 points) Complete the tag questions and negative questions.

1. The American flag didn't always have 50 stars, ___?
2. If California ever divided into two states, they'd have to add a fifty-first star to the flag, ___?
3. ___ the three stars on the Filipino flag represent the country's three main geographical regions?
4. ___ Brazil another country with a flag that uses stars to represent regions or states?
5. If I study flags, then I'm a *vexillologist*, ___?

Unit Project: It's a sign!

A Work in a group to create a presentation on a cultural symbol, sound, or sign. Follow the steps.

1. With a partner or a group, research and discuss what a symbol means and its significance. Choose one of these options:
   - a landmark (for example, the pyramids of Giza or Stonehenge in England)
   - a cultural symbol from your country (for example, the color red in China or Japan)
   - an ethnic or national costume (clothing)
   - a pictogram or rebus (sound)
   - a symbol from technology (emoticon or ringtone)
   - your country's currency / money and its symbolism
   - cultural body language or a gesture
   - a national bird or animal from your country and its meaning
2. Create a visual representation using video, PowerPoint, or poster board. Use the storyboard as a guide to organize your ideas. Keep your points between 15 and 30 seconds per slide or poster board for a 3- to 4-minute presentation. Use images when an image of an idea would be eaiser to explain.

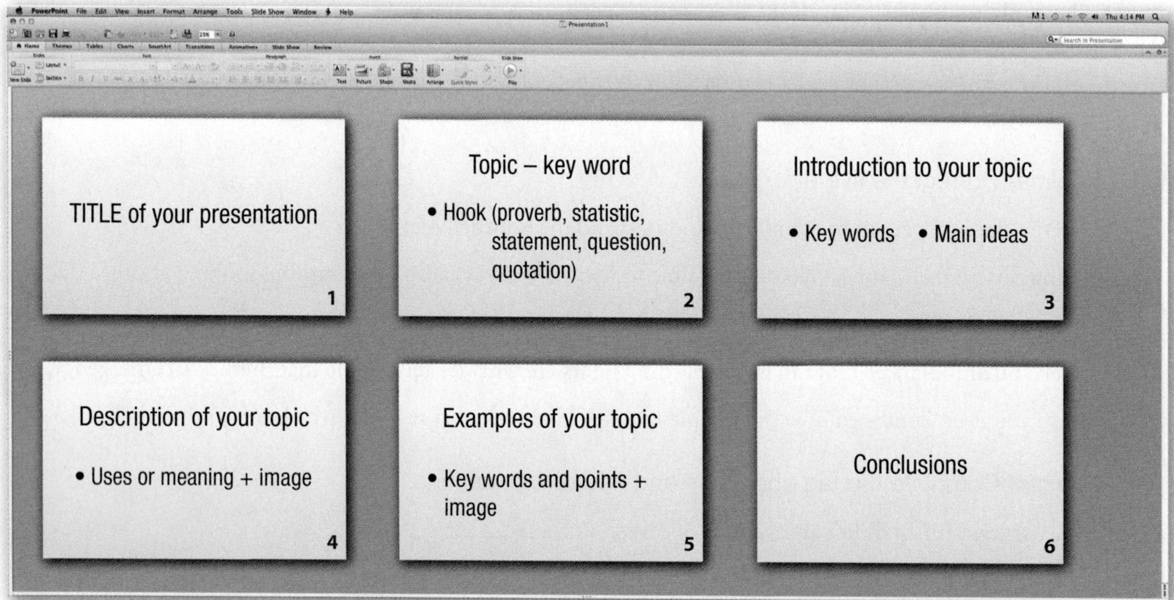

B Make your presentation to the class. Explain why you chose the topic and answer questions from your classmates. If there are classmates who share your culture, ask them what they would have added to the presentation. What other cultural symbols could you have included?

Appendices

A Stative verbs (rarely used in progressive forms)

Categories	Verbs
Verbs for emotions	admire, adore, astonish, desire, despise, detest, dislike, envy, hate, like, love, need, please, prefer, satisfy, surprise, want, wish
Verbs for mental activities	believe, desire, doubt, forget, guess, imagine, know, mean, realize, recognize, remember, suppose, suspect, understand
Verbs for possession	belong, have, include, keep, own, possess
Verbs for senses	feel, hear, know, see, smell, sound, taste
Verbs for states of being	appear, be, consist, contain, deserve, exist, fit, have, impress, involve, lack, last, matter, owe, reach, resemble, satisfy, seem, sound, stop, survive

B Irregular verbs

Base verb	Simple past	Past participle
A		
arise	arose	arisen
awake	awakened / awoke	awakened / awoken
B		
be	was, were	been
beat	beat	beaten / beat
become	became	become
begin	began	begun
bend	bent	bent
bet	bet / betted	bet / betted
bid (offer amount)	bid	bid
bind	bound	bound
bite	bit	bitten
break	broke	broken
breed	bred	bred
bring	brought	brought
broadcast	broadcast / broadcasted	broadcast / broadcasted
build	built	built
burn	burned / burnt	burned / burnt
bust	busted / bust	busted / bust
buy	bought	bought
C		
catch	caught	caught
choose	chose	chosen
clothe	clothed / clad	clothed / clad
come	came	come
cost	cost	cost
cut	cut	cut

Base verb	Simple past	Past participle
D		
deal	dealt	dealt
do	did	done
draw	drew	drawn
dream	dreamed / dreamt	dreamed / dreamt
drink	drank	drunk
drive	drove	driven
dwell	dwelt / dwelled	dwelt / dwelled
E		
eat	ate	eaten
F		
fall	fell	fallen
feed	fed	fed
feel	felt	felt
fight	fought	fought
find	found	found
fit (tailor, change size)	fitted / fit	fitted / fit
fit (be right size)	fit / fitted	fit / fitted
flee	fled	fled
fling	flung	flung
fly	flew	flown
forbid	forbade	forbidden
forecast	forecast	forecast
foresee	foresaw	foreseen
forget	forgot	forgotten / forgot
forgive	forgave	forgiven
freeze	froze	frozen
G		
get	got	gotten / got

Base verb	Simple past	Past participle
give	gave	given
go	went	gone
grow	grew	grown
H		
hand-feed	hand-fed	hand-fed
hang	hung	hung
have	had	had
hear	heard	heard
hide	hid	hidden
hit	hit	hit
hold	held	held
hear	heard	heard
hurt	hurt	hurt
K		
keep	kept	kept
kneel	knelt / kneeled	knelt / kneeled
know	knew	known
L		
lay	laid	laid
lead	led	led
leap	leaped / leapt	leaped / leapt
learn	learned / learnt	learned / learnt
leave	left	left
lend	lent	lent
let	let	let
lie (be positioned)	lay	lain
light	lit / lighted	lit / lighted
lose	lost	lost
M		
make	made	made
mean	meant	meant
meet	met	met
mislead	misled	misled
misspeak	misspoke	misspoken
misspell	misspelled / misspelt	misspelled / misspelt
mistake	mistook	mistaken
misunderstand	misunderstood	misunderstood
O		
outdo	outdid	outdone

Base verb	Simple past	Past participle
outgrow	outgrew	outgrown
outsell	outsold	outsold
overcome	overcame	overcome
overdo	overdid	overdone
overpay	overpaid	overpaid
overrun	overran	overrun
oversee	oversaw	overseen
P		
pay	paid	paid
premake	premade	premade
prepay	prepaid	prepaid
preset	preset	preset
preshrink	preshrank	preshrunk
proofread	proofread	proofread
prove	proved	proven / proved
put	put	put
Q		
quit	quit	quit
R		
read	read (sounds like "red")	read (sounds like "red")
rebind	rebound	rebound
rebroadcast	rebroadcast / rebroadcasted	rebroadcast / rebroadcasted
rebuild	rebuilt	rebuilt
redo	redid	redone
repay	repaid	repaid
reread	reread	reread
rerun	reran	rerun
resell	resold	resold
resend	resent	resent
reset	reset	reset
retell	retold	retold
rewind	rewound	rewound
rewrite	rewrote	rewritten
rid	rid	rid
ride	rode	ridden
ring	rang	rung
rise	rose	risen
run	ran	run

Base verb	Simple past	Past participle
S		
say	said	said
see	saw	seen
seek	sought	sought
sell	sold	sold
send	sent	sent
set	set	set
sew	sewed	sewn / sewed
shake	shook	shaken
shed	shed	shed
shine	shined / shone	shined / shone
shoot	shot	shot
show	showed	shown / showed
shrink	shrank / shrunk	shrunk
shut	shut	shut
sing	sang	sung
sink	sank / sunk	sunk
sit	sat	sat
sleep	slept	slept
slide	slid	slid
smell	smelled / smelt	smelled / smelt
sneak	sneaked / snuck	sneaked / snuck
speak	spoke	spoken
speed	sped / speeded	sped / speeded
spend	spent	spent
spill	spilled / spilt	spilled / spilt
spin	spun	spun
split	split	split
spoil	spoiled / spoilt	spoiled / spoilt
spread	spread	spread
spring	sprang / sprung	sprung
stand	stood	stood
steal	stole	stolen
stick	stuck	stuck
sting	stung	stung
strike (delete)	struck	stricken

Base verb	Simple past	Past participle
strike (hit)	struck	struck / stricken
string	strung	strung
strive	strove / strived	striven / strived
swear	swore	sworn
sweat	sweat / sweated	sweat / sweated
sweep	swept	swept
swell	swelled	swollen / swelled
swim	swam	swum
swing	swung	swung
T		
take	took	taken
teach	taught	taught
tear	tore	torn
telecast	telecast	telecast
think	thought	thought
throw	threw	thrown
typecast	typecast	typecast
typewrite	typewrote	typewritten
U		
undergo	underwent	undergone
understand	understood	understood
undertake	undertook	undertaken
undo	undid	undone
unwind	unwound	unwound
uphold	upheld	upheld
upset	upset	upset
W		
wake	woke / waked	woken / waked
wear	wore	worn
weave	wove / weaved	woven / weaved
wed	wed / wedded	wed / wedded
weep	wept	wept
wet	wet / wetted	wet / wetted
win	won	won

C Spelling rules for plural nouns

Rules	Examples
For most nouns, add **–s**.	photographers, machines, disks
For most nouns that end in consonant + *o*, add **–es**.	heroes, tornadoes. (But: pianos, memos)
For words that end in a vowel + *o*, add **–s**.	studios, videos
For words that end in a vowel + *y*, we add **–s**.	boys, days
For words that end in consonant + *y*, change the ***y*** to an ***i*** and add **–es**.	technology → technologies
For words that end in *-ch*, *-sh*, *-s*, *-ss*, or *-x*, add **–es**.	box → boxes glass → glasses
For words that end in *-f* or *-fe*, change the ***f*** to a ***v*** and add **–es**.	life → lives leaf → leaves

D Irregular plural nouns

Animals

Singular	Plural
buffalo	buffalo
deer	deer
fish	fish
goose	geese
moose	moose
mouse	mice
octopus	octopuses/ octopi
ox	oxen
sheep	sheep

Academics & Concepts

Singular	Plural
analysis	analyses
basis	bases
crisis	crises
criterion	criteria
datum	data
hypothesis	hypotheses
phenomenon	phenomena
thesis	theses

Measurements & Classifications

Singular	Plural
appendix	appendixes/ appendices
foot	feet
index	indexes/ indices
millennium	millennia/ millenniums
series	series
species	species

Inanimate Objects

Singular	Plural
antenna	antennae/antennas
money	monies
tooth	teeth

People

Singular	Plural
businessman	businessmen
businesswoman	businesswomen
child	children
man	men
person	people
woman	women

Note: This is not a complete list of irregular plural nouns.

E Categories of noncount (mass) nouns

Abstract Concepts	Activities	Diseases	Events
adventure* behavior chance* coverage energy * fantasy* fiction hope* information knowledge life* movement* perspective* sound* time* truth* video* vision*	baseball* basketball* biking boxing cards dancing exercise football* gymnastics hockey reading shopping singing soccer study* tennis volleyball* work*	cancer* diabetes flu (influenza) heart disease illness* pneumonia strep throat tuberculosis (TB)	arrival* birth* death* departure* marriage* war*

Gases / Elements	Inanimate Objects	Liquids	Metals / Elements
air air conditioning carbon dioxide oxygen radiation smoke	clothing equipment film* furniture tape	alcohol blood coffee* juice milk oil soda* soup* tea* water	copper gold metal* silver

Occupations	Organic and Man-Made Materials	Qualities	Relations & Communication
advertising banking business* construction education engineering farming law* marketing medicine* sales teaching*	bark chewing gum dirt dust earth fertilizer* glass* ice lava paper* plastic rock* stone* Styrofoam toilet paper wood*	ambition* beauty* bravery confidence* evil* good hesitation importance intrigue invisibility passion* popularity responsibility* strength*	advice communication conversation* discussion* etiquette feedback talking

Solid Foods	States	Subjects	Weather & Nature
beef bread* cake* candy* chicken* corn fast food fish* grain* junk food meat* rice	ambiguity danger* employment extinction freedom* happiness hate hatred love* sleep rage	aeronautics anthropology archeology art* astronomy astrobiology astrophysics biology economics history* linguistics literature mathematics neuroscience physics science* technology* transportation	air pressure atmosphere cold* electricity environment fog heat humidity lightning mist rain* snow thunder weather wind*

*These nouns also have a countable use that is more specific in meaning (specific types, specific instances, etc.)
Note: This is not a complete list of noncount nouns, but all noncount nouns fit into these categories.

F Collective and aggregate nouns

Collective Nouns	Aggregate Nouns
People: audience, class, club, committee, company, crowd, family, faculty, firm, gang, government, majority, minority, party, staff, team	communications congratulations goods information knowledge means media news (the) police* (the) public* thanks works
Animals: flock, herd, pack, school	
Military: army, the Army, fleet, the Navy, the Air Force, troop	
General: bunch, group, set	

Some collective nouns usually follow the definite article.
Note: This is not a complete list of collective and aggregate nouns.

G Nationalities (Generic references)

Afghanistan	the Afghani people	an Afghani
Argentina	Argentinians (also, *Argentines*)	an Argentinian (also, *an Argentine*)
Australia	Australians (informal, *Aussies*)	an Australian (informal, *an Aussie*)
Belarus, Belorussia	Belarussians	Belarus
Belgium	Belgians	a Belgian
Brazil	Brazilians	a Brazilian
Canadian	Canadians	a Canadian
The Czech Republic	the Czech	*
Chile	Chileans	a Chilean
China	the Chinese	*
Croatia	Croatians	a Croatian
The Dominican Republic	Dominicans	a Dominican
England	the English	an Englishman, an Englishwoman
France	the French	a Frenchman, a Frenchwoman
Finland	the Finnish, Finns	a Finn
Germany	Germans	a German
Ghana	Ghanaians	a Ghanaian
Great Britain	the British (informal, *Brits*)	Briton (informal, *a Brit*)
Greenland	Greenlanders	a Greenlander
Honduras	Hondurans	Honduran
Italy	Italians	an Italian
Iraq	the Iraqi people	an Iraqi
Ireland	the Irish	an Irishman, an Irishwoman
Israel	the Israeli people	an Israeli
Ivory Coast	Ivoirians, the people of the Ivory Coast	an Ivoirian/ Ivorian
Japan	the Japanese	*
Kazakhstan	Kazakhs	*
Lebanon	the Lebanese	*
Mexico	Mexicans	a Mexican
Morocco	Moroccans	a Moroccan
Myanmar	the Burmese	a Burmese
Nepal	the Nepali people	a Nepali
The Netherlands	the Dutch	a Dutchman, a Dutchwoman
New Zealand	New Zealanders	a New Zealander
Nigeria	Nigerians	a Nigerian
Norway	Norwegians	a Norwegian
Pakistan	the Pakistani people	a Pakistani
Peru	Peruvians	a Peruvian
The Philippines	Filipinos	a Filipino
Poland	the Polish, Poles	a Pole
Portugal	the Portuguese	*
Puerto Rico	Puerto Ricans	a Puerto Rican
Russia	Russians	a Russian

Saudi Arabia	Saudi Arabians, the Saudi	a Saudi
Scotland	the Scottish, Scots	a Scot
Senegal	the Senegalese	*
Spain	the Spanish, Spaniards	a Spaniard
Sri Lanka	Sri Lankans	a Sri Lankan
Sudan	the Sudanese	*
Sweden	the Swedish, Swedes	a Swede
Switzerland	the Swiss	a Swiss
Taiwan	the Taiwanese	*
Thailand	Thai	a Thai
Tibet	Tibetans	a Tibetan
Turkey	Turks, the Turkish people	a Turk
United Arab Emirates (UAE)	Emirati	an Emirati
United States of American (USA)	Americans	an American
Wales	the Welsh	a Welshman, a Welshwoman

*Those without a singular form require alternative wording, such as *a Chinese citizen or a person from China.*

H Quantifiers for count and noncount nouns

Singular count nouns	*Reference to one:* **each, every, one**
Plural count nouns	*Reference to two:* **both, a couple of** *Reference to a larger number:* **many, a good number of, a number of** *Reference to a smaller number:* **several, a few, few, fewer**
Count and noncount nouns	*Reference to a larger number or amount:* **all, a lot of, lots of, plenty of, more (of), most (of)** *Reference to a smaller number or amount:* **some, any, hardly any, no, none of**
Noncount nouns	*Reference to a larger amount:* much, **a great deal of, a good amount of** *Reference to a smaller amount:* **a bit of, a little, little, less**

I Quantifying collective nouns

an army of . . .	ants, caterpillars
a batch of . . .	tests, cookies
a bunch of . . .	people, files
a chain of . . .	command, stores
a crowd of . . .	students, fans
a flock of . . .	birds, geese
a gaggle of . . .	geese
a gang of . . .	robbers, thieves
a handful of . . .	people, nuts
a herd of . . .	elephants, horses
a host of . . .	problems, possibilities
a mouthful of . . .	air, water
a pack of . . .	wolves, lies
a pod of . . .	dolphins, whales
a pride of . . .	lions
a pile of . . .	papers, books
a school of . . .	fish
a set of . . .	dishes, tires
a swarm of . . .	bees, shoppers
a troop of . . .	soldiers

Note: *If you are not certain about grouping animals, use this guide:*

army, colony	for crawling animals
flock	for birds and sheep
herd	for roaming animals
pack	for predators
pod/ school	for sea creatures
swarm	for flying insects

J Unit nouns (Partitives)

Abstract Concepts		Activities		Behavior		Inanimate Objects	
a bit of . . .	luck, time	**a game of . . .**	cards, chess	**an act of . . .**	kindness	**an article of . . .**	clothing
a chunk of . . .	time	**a round of . . .**	golf	**a moment of . . .**	happiness	**a chip of . . .**	glass, ice
a division of . . .	labor					**an item of . . .**	clothing
a form of . . .	art					**a kind of . . .**	material
a grain of . . .	doubt					**a pair of . . .**	jeans, scissors
a matter of . . .	choice, time					**a piece of . . .**	equipment
a mountain of . . .	work					**a pile of . . .**	trash
a period of . . .	time					**a portion of . . .**	the money
a piece of . . .	advice					**a scrap of . . .**	material
a ray of . . .	hope					**a sheet of . . .**	paper, plastic
a trace of . . .	evidence, guilt					**a speck of . . .**	dust
a way of . . .	life					**a trace of . . .**	smoke
Liquids		**Foods**		**Subjects**		**Weather & Nature**	
a bottle of . . .	sauce	**a can of . . .**	soup	**a branch of . . .**	physics	**a blanket of . . .**	fog
a bowl of . . .	soup	**a chunk of . . .**	cheese, meat	**a type of . . .**	medicine	**a bolt of . . .**	lightning
a cup of . . .	coffee	**a grain of . . .**	corn, sugar			**a clap of . . .**	thunder
a dose of . . .	medicine	**a loaf of . . .**	bread			**a drop of . . .**	rain
a drop of . . .	blood	**a packet of . . .**	sugar			**a field of . . .**	wheat
a glass of . . .	water	**a piece of . . .**	cake, cheese			**a gust of . . .**	wind
a tablespoon of . . .	medicine	**a pinch of . . .**	salt			**a ray of . . .**	sunshine
a teaspoon of . . .	sugar	**a portion of . . .**	food				
		a slice of . . .	bread, meat				

K Linking verbs that come before an adjective

appear*	be	feel	look	prove*	seem*	smell	sound	taste

Notes: Appear, prove, *and* seem *often take* ***to be + adjective***
Feel, look, *and* seem *are often followed by the past participle of a transitive verb*

L Linking verbs that refer to a state of being / change in condition

become	come	fall	get	go	grow	keep	remain	stay	turn

M Separable phrasal verbs

Transitive phrasal verbs (verb + adverb / verb + preposition)			
Must be separated		Separable	
ask *sb* **over**	invite to one's home	**bring** *sth or sb* **back**	make something or somebody return
ask *sb* **out**	invite for a date	**check** *sth* **out**	examine, investigate
keep *sth* **on**	not remove clothing	**give** *sth* away	give for free
		give *sth* **back**	return
		give *sth* **up**	stop doing or using
		keep *sth* **up**	not allow to fall
		pass *sth* **on**	give information to another
		pick *sth* **out**	select
		pick *sth* **up**	lift
		put *sth* **on**	dress in clothing, place on top of
		throw *sth* **on**	put on quickly
		throw *sth* **out**	put in the trash
		try *sth* **on**	see if clothing fits
		try *sth* **out**	see if something works
		turn *sth* **around**	make something face the opposite direction
		turn *sb* **down**	refuse
		turn *sb* **off**	make someone lose interest
		turn *sth* **on**	start operating
		turn *sth* **over**	turn something facedown

N Transitive separable multi-word phrasal verbs

Verb	Particle	Preposition	Meaning
do	**out**	**of**	cheat
frighten	**out**	**of**	scare away
let	**in**	**for**	allow to join
let	**in**	**on**	inform; tell a secret
play	**off**	**against**	cause opposition
put	**down**	**as**	resign to
put	**down**	**to**	assume about
put	**up**	**to**	dare
take	**out**	**on**	treat badly
take	**up**	**on**	agree to
talk	**out**	**of**	dissuade

Intransitive multi-word phrasal verbs

Verb	Particle	Preposition	Meaning
be	**in**	**for**	about to undergo *sth* unpleasant
be	**on**	**to**	suspect, know *sth* about *sb*
break	**out**	**of**	change; escape from
brush	**up**	**on**	practice *sth* to improve
call	**out**	**for**	need
catch	**up**	**on**	recover lost time
clean	**up**	**after**	make neat
come	**across**	**as**	seem to have certain qualities
come	**down**	**on**	punish, reprimand
come	**down**	**to**	resolve to one particular point
come	**out**	**of**	emerge from
come	**up**	**against**	contend with
come	**up**	**with**	get an idea; produce
creep	**up**	**on**	approach quietly or with stealth
cry	**out**	**for**	need urgently
cut	**back**	**on**	reduce in size or amount
date	**back**	**to**	exist since the past
do	**away**	**with**	dispose or get rid of
face	**up**	**to**	admit
fall	**back**	**on**	rely on, use after other plans fail
fall	**in**	**with**	associate with
get	**along**	**with**	be compatible with
get	**away**	**with**	escape with; avoid penalty
get	**down**	**to**	begin
get	**on**	**with**	continue
give	**up**	**on**	lose hope
go	**along**	**with**	agree with; support
go	**back**	**on**	renege on a promise
go	**over**	**to**	transfer; change allegiance
go	**through**	**with**	complete a plan; fulfill a promise
grow	**out**	**of**	increase in size; stop doing *sth*
keep	**in**	**with**	continue to be friendly; remain on good terms
keep	**up**	**with**	remain at pace with; stay at same speed as
lead	**up**	**to**	come before; preceed
look	**down**	**on**	disapprove of, think you're better than
look	**forward**	**to**	be excited about; anticipate eagerly
look	**out**	**for**	observe, care for
look	**up**	**to**	admire; respect
make	**off**	**with**	steal, take
make	**up**	**to**	repair relations
measure	**up**	**to**	reach a particular standard
miss	**out**	**on**	not have a chance
play	**along**	**with**	pretend
play	**around**	**with**	use or spend time without caring
put	**up**	**with**	tolerate
read	**up**	**on**	read to inform (oneself)
run	**away**	**with**	leave quickly with; escape with
run	**up**	**against**	deal with a problem
shy	**away**	**from**	avoid due to lack of confidence
sit	**in**	**on**	join, be included
snap	**out**	**of**	suddenly stop behaving (in a certain way)
stick	**up**	**for**	support, defend
take	**up**	**with**	live with
talk	**down**	**to**	condescend to
tie	**in**	**with**	connect to

Verb	Particle	Preposition	Meaning	Verb	Particle	Preposition	Meaning
walk	**away**	**from**	leave a place, person	**walk**	**out**	**on**	leave a person or an event
walk	**away**	**with**	leave with something	**zero**	**in**	**on**	aim or focus attention on

P Intransitive phrasal verbs

ask around	come in	fall apart	go back	press on	steam up
back away	come to	fall away	go down	rise up	step aside
back off	come up	fall back	go on	run away	step back
balance out	cool off	fall behind	go out	run out	step down
bounce back	crop up	fall out	go under	rush in	step in
branch out	crowd around	fall over	go up	settle down	stick around
break away	curl up	fall through	grow up	settle in	stop by
break out	cut in	fight back	hang around	shop around	stop off
camp out	die away	fool around	hold on	show through	stop over
catch on	die down	gather around	join in	sink in	tune in
chip in	die out	get about	lie back	sit around	wait about
climb down	dine out	get ahead	lie down	sit back	wait up
come about	do without	get along	look ahead	sit down	walk out
come across	doze off	get by	look back	speak up	waste away
come along	drag on	get up	look in	stand back	watch out
come apart	drop by	give in	meet up	stand out	wear off
come away	drop out	go ahead	move over	start out	
come back	end up	go along	pass away	stay in	
come down	fade away	go around	play around	stay on	
come forward	fade out	go away	pass by	stay up	

Q Verbs followed by gerunds

admit	continue*	finish	mention	propose	suggest
advise	delay	forbid	mind	quit	support
appreciate	deny	forgive	miss	recall	tolerate
avoid	discuss	hate*	permit	recommend	understand
begin*	dislike	imagine	postpone	regret	
can't help	enjoy	include	practice	report	
can't stand*	escape	involve	prefer*	require	
celebrate	explain	like*	prevent	risk	
consider	feel like	love*	prohibit	start*	

*These verbs can also be followed by an infinitive with no change in meaning.

R *Go* + gerund for recreational activities

go biking	go (horseback) riding	go sailing	go snowboarding
go bowling	go hunting	go scuba diving	go swimming
go camping	go jogging	go shopping	go surfing
go canoeing	go kayaking	go skateboarding	
go cycling	go rafting	go skating	
go dancing	go rock climbing	go skiing	
go fishing	go rollerblading	go sledding	
go hiking	go running	go snorkeling	

S Verb + preposition + gerund
Adjective + preposition + gerund

verb + (object) + preposition + (gerund)			adjective + preposition + (gerund)	
argue about **care** about **complain** about **dream** about **forget** about **joke** about **talk** about **think** about **wonder** about **worry** about	**escape** from **suffer** from	**warn** *sb* about	**annoyed** about* **concerned** about* **excited** about* **happy** about **nervous** about **worried** about*	**interested** in* **involved** in*
advise against **argue** against	**participate** in **succeed** in	**blame** *sb* for **forgive** *sb* for **praise** *sb* for **punish** *sb* for **recognize** *sb* for **thank** *sb* for	**angry** at **bad** at **good** at	**afraid** of **ashamed** of* **capable** of **fond** of **guilty** of **proud** of **tired** of*
hint at **laugh** at	**approve** of **think** of	**discourage** *sb* from **keep** *sb* from **prevent** *sb* from **prohibit** *sb* from **stop** *sb* from	**famous** for **known** for* **prepared** for* **remembered** for* **responsible** for **sorry** for	**intent** on
apologize for **pay** for	**concentrate** on **insist** on **plan** on	**interest** *sb* in		**committed** to **content** with **dedicated** to* **opposed** to
	argue over	**suspect** *sb* of		**bored** with **fascinated** with
	admit to **confess** to			
	help with			

*These adjectives are the stative passive forms of verbs which describe states.

Note: If you are not certain about using prepositions in these combinations, use this guide:

about = *used to show a relation to a subject*
against = *used to show opposition to*
at = *used to show direction toward*
for = *used to show intention or purpose*
from = *used to state origin or movement away*
in = *used to show inclusion or involvement*
of = *used to show a reason or cause*
on = *used to indicate a focus*
over = *used to show the object of concern*
to = *used to show a position or relation to something*
with = *used to show togetherness or involvement*

T Noun + preposition + gerund

decision about	**transition** from	**advantage** of **cost** of **example** of **habit** of **hope** of **love** of **manner** of **way** of	**authority** on **opinion** on	**alternative** to **reaction** to **thanks** to
desire for **punishment** for **reason** for **reputation** for **reward** for **substitute** for	**belief** in **interest** in **participation** in		**control** over **worry** over	**trouble** with

U Verbs followed by infinitives

afford	begin*	deserve	like*	offer	refuse	wait
agree	can't stand*	expect	love*	plan	seem	wish
aim	care	fail	intend	prefer*	start*	
appear	choose	happen	learn	prepare	strive	
arrange	claim	hate*	manage	pretend	struggle	
ask	continue*	hesitate	mean	proceed	swear	
attempt	decide	hope	need	promise	volunteer	
beg	demand	hurry	neglect	propose	want	

These verbs can also be followed by an infinitive with no change in meaning.

V Verb + noun object + infinitive

Example: The doctor ***advised*** *the patient* *to exercise* *more regularly.*

advise	cause	dare	forbid	invite	persuade	teach
allow	challenge	direct	force	need	prepare	tell
ask	choose	employ	help	order	remind	urge
assist	command	encourage	hire	pay	require	want
beg	convince	expect	instruct	permit	send	warn

W Nouns commonly followed by infinitives

Example: It was a wonderful ***opportunity*** *to learn* *from one of the best in the field.*

ability	chance	hope	invitation	permission	reminder	time
admission	choice	decision	need	plan	right	warning
agreement	claim	desire	opportunity	promise	threat	wish

X Adjectives followed by infinitives

able	careful	due	glad	lucky	ready	stunned*
afraid	certain	eager*	happy	motivated	relieved	surprised*
amazed*	content	easy	hesitant	powerless	reluctant	unable
apt	delighted	fated	inclined	pleased	sad*	upset*
ashamed	disappointed*	fit	liable	prepared	shocked*	unwilling
astonished*	doomed	fortunate	likely	proud	sorry*	willing

*These adjectives are commonly followed by verbs *(discover, find out, hear, learn, see)*

Note: This is not a complete list of adjectives that can be followed by an infinitive.

Y Reporting verbs

Verbs for reporting what someone says (verbally)						
acknowledge	confirm	dispute	maintain	propose	request	swear
add	contend	explain	mention	reassure	respond	teach
admit	continue	forbid	note	recall	reveal	tell
advise	convince	guarantee	notify	recite	rule	threaten
agree	cry	hint	object	recommend	say	urge
announce	declare	imply	observe	record	scream	vow
answer	demand	inform	order	refuse	shout	wail
argue	deny	inquire	persuade	remark	shriek	warn
ask	describe	insist	pray	remind	state	whisper
assert	direct	instruct	predict	repeat	stipulate	write
confess	discuss	invite	promise	reply	suggest	yell

Verbs for reporting what someone thinks			
accept	fear	know	regret
agree	feel	mean	remember
assume	figure	note	resolve
believe	foresee	plan	suppose
consider	forget	ponder	think
decide	guess	pray	understand
determine	hold	prefer	vow
doubt	hope	propose	want
dream	imagine	reason	wish
estimate	intend	recall	wonder
expect	judge	reflect	worry

Verbs for reporting (written) quoted speech				
add	boast	explain	recite	urge
admit	claim	inquire	reflect	vow
advise	command	insist	remark	warn
agree	comment	observe	reply	wonder
announce	complain	order	report	write
answer	conclude	ponder	respond	
argue	confess	pray	say	
ask	continue	proclaim	state	
assert	decide	promise	suggest	
beg	declare	read	tell	
begin	demand	reason	think	

Z Reference words in reported speech

Changes in Time and Place Words

Direct speech	**Reported speech**
now	then, right then, at that moment
today	that day
tomorrow	the next day, the following day
the day after tomorrow	two days later
yesterday	the day before
last week	the week before, one week earlier
last month	the month before, one month earlier
last year	the year before, one year earlier
next week	the following week, one week later
next month	the following month, one month later
next year	the following year, one year later
these days	those days
this week	that week
a week (month, year) ago	one week (month, year) earlier

Direct speech	**Reported speech**
here	there

Example:
"Can you come **here today**?" he asked
He asked me if I could go **there that day**.

Index

A / an, 44, 46, 62
About to, 10
Abstract nouns, 32, 34
Academic writing, passive in, 136
Active sentences, 134, 148
Adjective clauses
  explanation of, 56, 62, 84
  non-restrictive, 56, 62
  as noun modifier, 62
  relative pronouns in, 56, 58
  restrictive, 56, 62
  with *where* and *when,* 72
Adjective complements, 168
Adjectives
  comparative, 50
  descriptive, 50, 62, 154
  participial, 50, 140, 144
  past participles as, 148, 168
  possessive, 156
  present and past participles as, 148
  present participles as, 144, 148, 168
  stative passive, 140
  superlative, 50
  use of, 50
Adverbs
  of frequency, 4, 178
  in phrasal verbs, 104
  of time, 26, 28, 84
A few, 48
Affirmative statements, 28
After, 78
Aggregate nouns, 36, 40
A little, 48
Already, 68, 78, 84
Always, 68
Amplifiers, 115
Any, 48
Are, 20
Articles
  definite, 44, 46, 62
  indefinite, 44, 46, 62
  use of, 46, 62
  zero, 44, 46, 62

Be
  with participial adjectives, 144
  in past perfect, 78
  in simple present, 10
  in tag questions, 212
Be about to, 16, 20, 26, 40
Be allowed to, 112
Be called, 136
Be going to, 10, 12, 14, 20, 115, 180
Be made, 136
Be to, 112
Be used, 136
Before, 68, 78, 84
Binary nouns
  explanation of, 36, 40, 48
  quantifiers with, 62
By, 78, 80, 84, 134
By-phrase, 134, 148
By the time, 78, 80, 84

Can, 112, 115
Can't, 112
Certainty
  degrees of, 116, 124, 180
  modals of, 115, 124, 128
  in past, 124, 128
Collective nouns
  explanation of, 36, 48
  quantifiers as, 62
Collocations, 48
Commas
  in direct speech, 200
  with tag questions, 212
Common nouns, 34, 40
Comparative adjectives, 50
Complements
  gerunds as, 158, 172
  infinitives as, 168, 172
Compound subjects, 36, 40
Concrete nouns, 32, 34
Conditionals
  counterfactual, 184, 186, 190
  explanation of, 178
  factual real, 178, 180, 194
  future real, 176, 180
  hypothetical, 184, 186, 190
  imaginative unreal, 184, 186, 188, 194
  for inferences, 180
  for intentions, 180
  omitting information in sentences in, 190
  past factual, 178
  past real, 176
  for predictions, 180
  present factual, 178
  present real, 176
Contractions
  with *are / aren't*, 12
  in future progressive, 14
  with modals, 112
  negative, 212
  with subject pronouns, 70
  with *will / won't*, 12
Could, 112, 115
Could have, 124
Counterfactual conditionals, 186, 190
Count nouns
  explanation of, 34, 40
  quantifiers with, 62

Definite articles, 44, 46, 62
Definite nouns, 46
Dependent clauses
  adjective clauses as, 56, 72, 84
  in conditionals, 178
Descriptive adjectives
  explanation of, 50
  as gerund modifier, 154
  as noun modifier, 62
Determiners, 34
Direct objects, 164
Direct questions, 200, 216
Direct speech
  changed to reported speech, 203, 216
  explanation of, 198, 200, 216
Do, 212
Dynamic passive, 142

Each / every, 48
-ed, 50, 140
Embedded questions, 210, 216
Even, 180
Ever, 68, 84, 180
Expectation, 115

Factual real conditionals, 180, 194
For, 68, 78, 80, 84
Frequency, adverbs of, 4, 178
Future
  with *be going to*, 10, 12, 20
  with present progressive, 16, 20
  with simple present, 16, 20
  with *will*, 10, 12, 20
  time clauses in, 20
  use of, 10, 12, 14, 20
Future progressive, 14
Future real conditional, 176

Generic nouns, 46
Gerund phrases
  explanation of, 154
  as object of verb, 156

Gerunds
as complements, 158, 172
explanation of, 152
following noun and preposition combinations, 158
following verbs, 164
as objects of verbs, 152, 156
as objects of prepositions, 152, 156, 172
possessive gerunds, 156
as subjects, 154, 164, 172
use of, 152, 158, 172
Get, 144
Go, 156
Great deal of, 48

Habitual actions
conditionals for, 178
present progressive with, 6, 20
used to with, 28
Had been, 80
Has / have yet, 70
Have been, 124, 132
Have got to, 112, 115
Have to, 112, 115
Helping verbs, 108. *See also* Modals
How many, 68
Hypothetical conditional, 186, 190

I, 212
Idiomatic, 90, 98, 100
If-clause, 178, 180, 186, 194
If necessary, 190
If no, 190
If not, 190
If only / only if, 190
If so, 190
If yes, 190
If you like, 180
Imaginative unreal conditionals
explanation of, 184, 186, 194
in past and mixed time periods, 188
in present and future, 186
Imperatives, 178
Indefinite articles, 44, 46, 62
Indefinite nouns, 46
Independent clauses, 178
Indirect objects, 136
Indirect speech. *See* Reported speech
Infinitive phrases, 164, 167

Infinitives
as adjective complements, 168
as complements, 168, 172
in embedded questions, 210
explanation of, 164
following verbs, 164
negative, 167
as objects of prepositions, 172
as objects of verbs, 162, 172
of purpose, 152, 167, 190
as subjects, 152, 154, 164, 172
use of, 164, 168, 172
-ing, 50, 152, 154
Inseparable phrasal verbs, 98, 104
Intransitive verbs
explanation of, 134
phrasal, 90, 100, 104
Inverted word order, 200
Irregular nouns, 40
Irregular verbs, 26
Is, 20
It, passive with, 136

Just, 70, 78

Linking verbs
descriptive adjectives following, 50
gerunds with, 158

Main clause, 203
Many, 48
Mass nouns, 34
May, 112, 115
Might, 112, 115
Modals
amplifiers with, 115
of certainty, 115–116, 128
of certainty in the past, 120, 124, 128
with conditionals, 178, 180
explanation of, 108, 110, 128
of necessity, 112–113, 128
of necessity in the past, 120, 122, 128
of possibility in the past, 120
in reported speech, 203
of speculation in the past, 120
Much, 48
Multi-word phrasal verbs, 88, 92, 104
Must, 112, 115

Necessity
degrees of, 112–113, 122
modals of, 112, 122, 128
in past, 122, 128
Negative questions, 212, 216
Negative statements
in future, 12
in future progressive, 14
in past perfect, 78
in past perfect progressive, 80
in past progressive, 26
in present perfect, 68
in present perfect progressive, 70
in present progressive, 6
in simple present, 4
Never, 68, 78
News reports, 136
Non-action verbs. *See* Stative verbs
Noncount nouns, 34, 62
Non-restrictive adjective clauses, 56, 62
Normal word order, 200
Noun clauses, 203, 210
Noun modifiers, types of, 62
Nouns
abstract, 32, 34
aggregate, 36, 40
binary, 36, 40, 48, 62
collective, 36, 40, 48, 62
common, 34, 40
concrete, 32, 34
count, 34, 40, 62
generic, 46
head, 72
indefinite, 46
irregular, 40
noncount, 34, 62
plural, 40
possessive, 156
proper, 34, 36, 40
regular, 40
singular, 40
unique, 36, 40
unit, 48, 62

Object of prepositions
gerunds as, 152, 156, 172
relative pronouns as, 56
Object pronouns, 48
Object relative pronouns, 58
Objects
direct, 164
gerunds as, 156, 172

indirect, 136
infinitives as, 172
with phrasal verbs, 92, 104
of separable verbs, 90
as subjects, 164
Or / nor, 36
Ought to, 115

Parallel structure, 194
Participial adjectives
explanation of, 50, 140
present participles as, 144
use of, 144, 148
Participles
explanation of, 66, 90, 98
past, 142, 144, 148
present, 10, 144, 158
Passive
dynamic, 142
participial adjectives in, 144
in perfect forms, 136
in simple present and simple past, 134
stative, 142, 148
use of, 132, 136, 148
verbs in, 148
Past. *See* Simple past
Past factual conditionals, 178
Past participles
as adjectives, 148, 168
in passive constructions, 142, 144, 148
Past passive, 132
Past perfect
explanation of, 76, 78
to form imaginative conditional, 188
use of, 78, 84
Past perfect passive, 132, 136, 148
Past perfect progressive
explanation of, 76, 80
use of, 84
Past progressive
negative statements in, 26
simple past used with, 26
use of, 24, 26, 40
wh- questions in, 26
yes / no questions in, 26
Past real conditional, 176
Periods, 200
Phrasal verbs
explanation of, 88, 90, 104
idiomatic, 98
with idiomatic meaning, 90, 98, 100
inseparable, 92, 98, 104
intransitive, 90, 96, 100, 104
multi-word, 88, 92, 104
objects with, 92, 104
particles with, 90, 92, 98, 100, 104
prepositions in, 90
separable, 90, 92, 104
transitive, 90, 96, 100, 104
transitive / intransitive, 100, 104
use of, 90, 104
Plural nouns, 40
Plural verbs, 36
Polite refusals, 112
Possessive adjectives, 156
Possessive nouns, before gerunds, 156
Predictions, 10, 12, 115
Prepositions
following past participial adjectives, 144
object of, 56, 152, 156
in phrasal verbs, 90, 104
with stative passive, 142
Present. *See* Simple present
Present factual conditional, 178
Present participles
as adjectives, 144, 148, 168
be +, 10
use of, 158
Present passive, 132
Present perfect
affirmative statements in, 68
explanation of, 66, 68
just, already, and *yet* in, 68
negative statements in, 68
time expressions in, 68
use of, 68, 84
Present perfect passive, 132, 136, 148
Present perfect progressive
explanation of, 66, 70
use of, 70, 84
Present progressive
with future meaning, 16, 20
for habitual actions, 6, 20
negative statements in, 6
simple present vs., 6
time expressions in, 16, 20
use of, 2, 6, 20
wh- questions in, 6
yes / no questions in, 6
Present real conditional, 176
Progressive. *See* Future progressive; Past progressive; Present progressive
Promises, 10
Pronouns
object, 48
relative, 56, 58
subject, 70
Proper nouns
agreement with, 40
explanation of, 34
singular verbs with, 36

Qualitative adjectives, 50
Quantifiers
explanation of, 48, 62
use of, 48, 62
Question marks, 200, 210, 212
Questions. *See also Wh-* questions; *Yes / no* questions
direct, 200, 216
embedded, 210, 216
in future progressive, 14
indirect, 210
negative, 212, 216
reported, 204, 210
in simple present, 4
tag, 212, 216
Quoted speech. *See* Direct speech

Real conditionals. *See* Factual real conditionals
Refusals, 112
Regular nouns, 40
Regular verbs, 26. *See also* Verbs
Relative pronouns
in adjective clauses, 56, 58, 62, 84
object, 58
subject, 58
zero, 58
Reported speech
direct speech changed to, 203, 216
explanation of, 198, 203, 216
use of, 203–204
Reporting clause, 200
Restrictive adjective clauses, 56, 62

Scientific reports, 136
Semi-modals
of certainty, 115–116, 128

of certainty in past, 124, 128
with conditionals, 178
explanation of, 110, 128
of necessity, 112–113, 128
of necessity in past, 122, 128
use of, 112
Sentences
active, 134, 148
omitting information in conditional, 190
passive, 134, 148
Separable phrasal verbs, 90, 92, 104
-s* / *-es, 34
Should, 112, 115
Simple past
to form imaginative conditionals, 186
irregular verbs in, 26
negative statements in, 26
passive in, 134
past progressive used with, 26
regular verbs in, 26
use of, 24, 26, 40
wh- questions in, 26
yes / no questions in, 26
Simple past passive, 132, 148
Simple present
adverbs of frequency in, 4
be in, 10
for future, 16, 20
passive in, 134
present progressive vs., 6
use of, 2, 4, 6, 20
Simple present passive, 132, 148
Since, 68, 70
Singular nouns, 40
Singular verbs, 36
So far, 68
Some, 48
Speech. *See* Direct speech; Reported speech
Statements. *See* Affirmative statements; Negative statements
Stative passive, 142, 148
Stative passive adjectives, 140
Stative verbs, 6
Still, 68, 84
Subject pronouns, 70
Subject relative pronouns, 58
Subjects
compound, 36, 40
gerunds as, 154, 172
infinitives as, 154, 164, 172
of passive sentence, 134, 136
plural, 36
Subject-verb agreement, 36, 40, 48
Superlative adjectives, 50

Tag questions, 212, 216
That, 58
The, 44, 46, 62
Time expressions
explanation of, 16
with future, 20
with past perfect, 78
with present perfect, 68
with present progressive, 16, 20
Titles, descriptive adjectives with, 50
Transitive / intransitive phrasal verbs, 104
Transitive phrasal verbs, 90, 100, 104
Transitive verbs
explanation of, 134, 148
phrasal, 90, 100, 104

Unit nouns, 48, 62
Unless, 180
Unreal conditionals. *See* Imaginative conditional
Up to now, 68
Used to, 28, 40

Verbs
agreement between subjects and, 36, 40, 48
followed by gerunds or infinitives, 164
gerunds with, 156
helping, 108
intransitive, 90, 100, 104, 134
irregular, 26
linking, 50
in passive, 148
phrasal, 88, 90, 92, 98, 100, 104
plural, 36
regular, 26
separable, 90, 92
singular, 36
stative, 6
in tag questions, 212
transitive, 90, 100, 104, 134
Voice, passive, 132

Was / were going to, 40
Were, 186
What if, 190
When, 72, 84, 178, 194
Whenever, 178, 194
Where, adjective clauses with, 72, 84
Which, 58
While, 26
Who, 58
Whom, 58
Wh- questions. *See also* Questions
conditionals in, 178
embedded questions as, 210
in future, 12
in future progressive, 14
in past perfect, 78
in past perfect progressive, 80
in past progressive, 26
in present progressive, 6
in reported speech, 204
in simple present, 4
with *used to*, 28
Will, 10, 12, 20, 115
Will be, 14
Will / won't, 12
Word order
in direct speech, 200
for embedded questions, 210
Would, 28, 124

Yes / no questions
conditionals in, 178
embedded questions as, 210
in future, 12
in future progressive, 14
in past perfect, 78
in past perfect progressive, 80
in past progressive, 26
in present progressive, 6
in reported speech, 204
in simple present, 4
with *used to*, 28
Yet, 68, 84

Zero article, 34, 46, 62
Zero relative pronoun, 58